D1526143

Contemporary Collecting

Objects, Practices, and the Fate of Things

Edited by
Kevin M. Moist
David Banash

THE SCARECROW PRESS, INC.
Lanham • Toronto • Plymouth, UK
2013

Published by Scarecrow Press, Inc.
A wholly owned subsidary of The Rowman & Littlefield Publishing Group, Inc.
4501 Forbes Boulevard, Suite 200, Lanham, Maryland 20706
www.rowman.com

10 Thornbury Road, Plymouth PL6 7PP, United Kingdom

British Library Cataloguing in Publication Information Available

Library of Congress Cataloging-in-Publication Data

Contemporary collecting : objects, practices, and the fate of things / edited by Kevin M. Moist, David Banash.
    pages cm
  Includes bibliographical references.
  ISBN 978-0-8108-9113-5 (cloth : alkaline paper) — ISBN 978-0-8108-9114-2 (ebook)
  1. Collectors and collecting. 2. Collectors and collecting—Social aspects. 3. Collectors and collecting—Psychological aspects. I. Moist, Kevin M., 1969– II. Banash, David C.
  AM231.C66 2013
  790.1'32—dc23
                                                                    2012050180

ACC LIBRARY SERVICES AUSTIN, TX

This book is dedicated to collectors past, present, and future who show us the many things in our many worlds, and in doing so help keep alive the experience of wonder.

Contents

Acknowledgments

Thanks to the Popular Culture Association (PCA). An initial impetus for this book came from the Collecting and Collectibles division of the PCA; several of the chapters here began as presentations at the annual Popular Culture Association/American Culture Association conference. Thanks to everyone who participated in those panels over the years and to Ron Bishop for passing the baton. Thanks to Chris Nasso and everyone at Scarecrow Press for supporting the project. Special thanks to Stanley Cavell for generously allowing us to republish his essay in this collection. Thanks also to Judi Hardin, Mark and Amy Mossman, Andrea Spain, Bill Reader, and Jennifer Streb for unwavering and generous support throughout the project. Extra special thanks to Kevin McFadin for the cover collage.

Introduction

So let us not be hasty in arriving at very firm conclusions about what our relation to collections is, hence what relation they may propose concerning our bond with the world of things as such.

—Stanley Cavell, "The World as Things"

Practices of collecting have always played a central role in human culture, at the heart of our meaningful relations with objects. Ancient religions collected sacred objects imbued with magical powers to negotiate the hazards of this world and the next. When art became secular, the wealthy collected paintings and sculptures to display their power and taste. The rise of science gave birth to cabinets of curiosity, vast and varied collections of objects that sought to capture and control the scope of the natural world. The advent of the modern museum codified and ordered such anarchic assemblages, even as growing numbers of individual private collectors continued to amass collections of both "high culture"—great art, books, porcelain, bones, shells, and insects—and the odd and ephemeral products of mass manufacture: toys, cereal boxes, and trading cards. Collecting is, moreover, not just a matter of history, institutions, and eccentrics; nearly every child makes collections of anything from stones picked up in a yard to expensive toys bought by parents. So collecting is both deeply enmeshed in the basic processes of cultural meaning and found in the roots of almost every personal history.

Specific forms of collecting develop and decline along with broader shifts in societal institutions, patterns of knowledge, and technologies of production and communication. We are currently living in the midst of one of those extended periods of metamorphosis, as new digital media increasingly virtualize our experiences of the world and at the same time make available seemingly every possible kind of cultural object via the Internet. The accompanying changes in society, culture, and the economy are radically reshaping the meaning of things and our relationships with them. Collecting continues to grow in popularity even as contemporary society becomes increasingly virtual and fragmented. The status of objects may be changing, but people's meaningful attachments to them have only become stronger.

Collecting is a consistent and growing presence in popular culture, as evidenced by television programs such as PBS's *Antiques Roadshow* or "reality shows" like *American Pickers*. In the online world, websites such as eBay simplify and speed up access to items of all kinds, new and old, profound and mundane; at the same time, collecting activities have begun to move into purely digital spaces, with users collecting everything from MP3 music files to "friends" on social networking sites. In tandem with popular collecting passions, institutional collectors are also updating themselves for the new environment, as library catalogs go online and museums use new technologies to help generate record attendance for exhibits of their more traditional collections.

The emergence of collecting as a unique topic of study is relatively recent. Although the importance of collections has been clear in the sciences and humanities for several centuries, serious attention has only gradually been focused on the social and cultural significance of collecting practice. Collecting is an inherently interdisciplinary topic, and important writings have come from a number of perspectives, most often as stand-alone pieces tied to particular writers' backgrounds—for example, philosopher Walter Benjamin's musings on his book collection in the 1930s or anthropologist James Clifford's reflections in the 1980s on the role of collecting in shaping our understanding of art and culture—rather than being integrated into a wider study of collecting itself.

Given its current popularity, it is not at all surprising that quite a few books about collecting have been published in recent years; an Amazon.com search on the subject turns up more than nineteen thousand results. The vast majority are price guides for collectors, or "how to" instructions for collecting particular types of objects (antiques, etc.), rather than scholarly investigations of the topic. There have been a few academic overviews from particular disciplines, such as business scholar Russell Belk's *Collecting in a Consumer Society* (1995), psychologist Werner Muensterberger's *Collecting: An Unruly Passion* (1995), and museum scholar Susan Pearce's work on institutional collecting; as well as several anthologies, including *The Cultures of Collecting* (1994), edited by Jon Elsner and Roger Cardinal, and *Acts of Possession* (2003), edited by Leah Dilworth, which view collecting in a more historical perspective. The goal of this volume is to build on the best aspects of all that work, reassessing the nature of collections and collecting practices in light of ongoing changes in society and culture.

Contemporary Collecting: Objects, Practices, and the Fate of Things assembles twelve new scholarly essays and one key reprint that situate and articulate collectors and collections in our contemporary context, as well as discussions of older collections and collectors that show how our changing world finds new meaning in their legacy. What do the practices of collectors, surviving collections, and new and emerging fields of collecting reveal about our contemporary world and our changing sense of the past? Collectors and their collections force us to consider our relationship to objects, as the collector's obsession, scope, practices, and care cast into dramatic relief the role of objects in our lives. From a cultural perspective, collecting is a barometer of and a window onto the nature of those broader developments. The essays gathered here capture collecting in its many varied forms—and the state of our thinking about them—at a moment of significant transformation.

The book is organized thematically into four broad areas. The first section, "Collecting in a Virtual World," grapples directly with new types of collecting generated by and through new technologies, both changing the objects people collect and creating new kinds of collecting practices. Marcus Boon considers, in the form of his accidentally deleted MP3 music collection, what it might mean to collect "things" that exist not as physical objects but as endlessly replicable patterns of data, including new social and legal control issues that are created along with them. Matthew James Vechinski reexamines the status of book collecting in the social media era, describing how websites such as Goodreads add new layers of online interactivity atop what once seemed a fairly solitary activity (reading), in the process perhaps altering the nature of the activity itself. Phillip J. Hutchison looks at how new media processes of connectivity and digitalization make it possible for private collectors to share ephemeral content from the early days of another medium, television. He explores the significance of fan websites that remediate seemingly lost local entertainment programs from the 1950s to the 1970s for new viewing communities gathered not around the electronic hearth, but a digital one.

At the same time, those new technologies and practices also transform our access to traditional collections and, just as important, what those established collections might mean as we interact with them in new ways. Part II investigates from various viewpoints our "Changing Relationships with Things." David Banash argues that thinking about collecting can help us understand the ways that contemporary consumer culture and new virtual technologies alter the roles of objects in our lives. The very existence of a luxury collectors' market for deluxe reproductions of quotidian objects such as vintage pencils, he says, indicates that the status of "things" has entered some new phase. D. Robert DeChaine writes about another seemingly disposable object—PEZ candy dispensers—that has developed a considerable collector constituency, showing how collectors' relationships with such "trivial" items grow from the same play of memory and desire as those with more respectable and "serious" objects. William Davies King is a recognized connoisseur of the unvalued and thrown away (he calls them his "collections of nothing"); here he reflects on his own collections of secondhand suits and water bottle labels in terms of both consumption and collage, providing an object lesson on the potential for idiosyncratic perspectives to illuminate the ambiguities of our relations with things. The seemingly endless variety and common underlying principles of those relationships are subjects of Stanley Cavell's celebrated essay on collecting and philosophy (first published in 1998), which analyzes the thought of various important philosophers—Emerson,

Wittgenstein, Heidegger—in terms of both their outlooks on the existence of things in the world and the ways their philosophies can be seen as collections of ideas about the world.

In thinking about how collectors relate to the things they collect, several of the essays in part II touch on the main topic of the third section, "Collecting and Identity, Personal and Political." Stephen P. Andon explores the tension between personal and public collecting through the story of a baseball memorabilia collector whose huge private collection becomes part of a professional team's new consumer-oriented "mallpark." Andon describes how the personal and historical meanings the objects held as part of their original collection are stripped away as the items are reworked by the team's corporate marketing and public relations strategies. Mechtild Widrich examines the crossing of personal and political aspects of collecting in the form of cigarette trading cards in Nazi Germany in the 1930s and 1940s. The commercially produced cards were already a popular collectible among young people, and the National Socialists coopted the form with cards that told stories promoting the Führer's great deeds—privatizing propaganda via consumer goods aimed at young collectors. Terri Baker addresses the role of gender in collecting, noting that it is often and incorrectly seen as a male activity. She illustrates the importance of women collectors in Great Britain and the United States during the Victorian era, both on a personal level, asserting their own individual identities through their collecting, and through the contributions their collections made to contemporary narratives of national identity.

The final section, "Collecting Practices and Cultural Hierarchies," approaches collecting both as an expression of the meanings and values we ascribe to objects and as a process through which those meanings are created. This is perhaps most obvious and most commented upon in terms of public museums' role in setting the boundaries of the "official" culture they represent. The essays in this section, however, show that this process also takes place in less official types of collecting and in ways that can at times challenge those very hierarchies. Sophie Thomas looks all the way back to the late eighteenth century, a historical moment when the older "cabinets of curiosity," and their attitude of fascinated wonder about the collected objects displayed, were giving way to the more orderly and rationalized modern museum. Thomas shows how, through their surprising juxtapositions and demand for active participation, these older types of collection and display prefigure in many ways the current collections discussed in part I. Mary Titus tells the tale of Wisconsin tourist attraction House on the Rock and its creation by founder Alex Jordan Jr. as a mockery of famous architect Frank Lloyd Wright's nearby Taliesin. Titus argues that Jordan's house, a disorienting, rambling structure containing an overwhelming array of illogically arranged collections of varying authenticity, works as a carnivalesque, postmodern parody of Wright's high modernist aesthetic and has a number of parallels with today's popular culture. Kevin M. Moist concludes the volume with some thoughts on record collecting and its role in both defining and undermining the canons of popular music. Moist focuses on four collector-run, independent record labels that specialize in reissuing recordings from times and places well outside established musical centers, discussing the ways their releases have been redrawing the maps of consensus music history.

It may be noticed that no specific definition of collecting is included here. This is not an oversight, but rather a recognition of the caution expressed in the epigraph from Stanley Cavell that opens the introduction; especially in light of the diversity of collecting examples discussed herein, any simple definition is bound to be partial and limited. Similarly, we have resisted providing too much interpretation of the individual chapters, beyond the thematic arrangement and shared conceptual concerns described previously. Attentive readers will undoubtedly discover a wide range of connections among the essays on their own, an experience that should be part of the enjoyment of any collection, and one we would not wish to preempt.

I

COLLECTING IN
A VIRTUAL WORLD

1

Meditations in an Emergency: On the Apparent Destruction of My MP3 Collection

Marcus Boon

For it is an irretrievable image of the past which threatens to disappear in any present that does not recognize itself as intimated in that image.

—Walter Benjamin, "Edouard Fuchs: Collector"

THE ANGEL OF HISTORY AS A COLLECTOR

Walter Benjamin ironically celebrated the figure of the collector, noting that such figures only become intelligible at the moment of their extinction. He didn't exactly say why the collector should have been on the verge of extinction in the early 1930s, but given the emphasis on ownership in the essay, it's not difficult to connect it to Benjamin's thoughts on mechanical reproduction, because if private ownership sustains the object as a set of historical traces that travel, in commodity form, from bookstore to bookshelf to auction block and back to bookshelf, mass reproduction destroys the aura of the object, an aura that is not entirely separate from the "set of historical traces" that Benjamin described. If the collector is nourished not by generic books but by particular "copies of books," the very technology of mass reproduction that makes these copies also inundates and finally dissolves the aura that makes them collectible. Benjamin's texts on collecting were written during a period (1931–1937) when the lingering possibility of socialist revolution radicalized this split within the collectible object: Benjamin would reluctantly give up the pleasures of private ownership of his collection for the liberation of the masses.[1]

Benjamin's meditations on book collecting, and his study of collector/archivist Edouard Fuchs are well known. But the figure of the collector has significance in his work beyond these specific texts. The *Passagenwerke* is itself a collection the purpose of which, through its particular mode of arrangement, was to intervene in the understanding of history and reconfigure it through a set of juxtapositions that illuminated the present. Beyond this, the much-celebrated figure of the angel of history in "On the Concept of History" can be understood as a collector also. If in "Unpacking My Library" Benjamin already wrote about the end of the epoch of the collector, the angel of history is a figure of the apocalypse of the collector—one who is no longer able to collect the objects or signs of history, who watches the debris of history pile up before him or her, who would like to gather and save all that debris, but who is driven back in the very attempt to save things. Benjamin argued that things take on their deepest significance at the moment that they disappear. I consider this statement, and some of Benjamin's other remarks about collecting, in the light of digital collections, unknown twenty years ago, but now pretty much ubiquitous. In particular, I want to discuss what it means to lose a digital collection.

LAST SATURDAY

The topic is on my mind because last Saturday I accidentally deleted most of my iTunes library, while trying to remove duplicate tags for more than 20,000 sound files that somehow appeared when I migrated all my data to a new computer. I thought I was just removing the extra tags, but inadvertently also removed the actual sound files and sent them to the trash, where they sat for weeks, until one day, in a moment of bored New Year's resolution, I absentmindedly emptied the trash and its surprisingly vast contents. Consider these meditations in an emergency, written as I try to deal with the situation.

The first, frankly instrumental question that you are likely to ask, in an attempt to dismiss the validity of what follows, is: Why didn't I make a backup? Well, I did make one last summer, but that back up is on an old external hard drive locked in my office five hundred miles away. Couldn't I just rip the files off of my iPod? Good idea, but my iPod is relatively old and contains only a relatively small but significant subset of the files that I own. The contingency of my collection, its uniqueness, is situated somewhere beyond these other two collections. This chapter is very much concerned with contingency.

My MP3 collection is probably the single thing that I own that I care the most about—which should be enough to establish my credentials as a collector. I too have my memories: of a summer weekend in upstate New York when K shared his hard drive with me. Of the moment when I discovered that there were La Monte Young recordings on Napster. And so on. But the event of erasing my collection left me oddly unmoved, in a way that, say, a fire that destroyed the 3,000 plus vinyl LPs that I own would not. Why? For a couple of reasons, at least. First is the issue of the materiality of the collection. As has been established in recent years, computer files do have their materiality, rendered as a series of electrical charges on microchips. But my MP3 collection did not occupy visible space in the same way that my vinyl collection does, and it does not have the same quality of finitude that the vinyl does. Although I could conceivably replace the entirety of my vinyl collection (though who can actually remember everything he owns!), it would be an enormous work of reconstruction, perhaps impossible. In all likelihood, I would have to face the fact of my loss, especially if confronted with the burnt remains of the collection, which would likely be rendered not as total disappearance but as an extreme form of defacement, as some of the photographs of destroyed collections or libraries that can be found on the Internet suggest. Anyone whose house has caught fire knows the feeling of surveying the remains afterward: objects still recognizable yet deformed, a book cover burnt at the edges, saturated with water; a broken record; a photograph whose paper has bubbled and warped. The disappearance of an MP3 collection leaves no smell, no charred remains. What it does leave is something more ambiguous.

I am in the process of getting a data recovery person to recover the files. When I tried to do it myself using an app called Desk Drill, I managed to recover a third of the collection, in a folder of anonymous numerically sequenced files that hopefully can be read by iTunes and relabeled. As I await the news from the file recovery team, the memory of the files on the hard drive, even after deletion, may amount to a real and almost painless possibility of the total resuscitation of those files. The object here is almost identical to its memory; in fact, it "is" memory.

What I discover from my error is that despite the rhetoric or promise of total recall that surrounds digital collections, my collection is truly an existential one, marked by finitude and contingency at every level. Heidegger devoted some paragraphs of *Being and Time* to retrieval as an essential part of true historiography.[2] Although retrieval is conventionally thought of as an objective matter, Heidegger pointed out that retrieval always only occurs as a possibility in a particular moment. I, and my collection, have been thrown, and we find or lose each other within the possible modes of enframing that exist in this moment.

TUESDAY

Update, three days later. I got my hard drive back this morning from the file recovery service. I stood in the office while the process took place. It took nearly four days to do, partly because the video card on the computer that was scanning my drive fried during the first scan and the scan had to be aborted. The first surprise was that the computer was able to locate more than 400 gigabytes of deleted files on a hard drive that is only 300 GB, of which I had deleted approximately 160 GB of files. This adds a further twist to the notion of the collection as a form of memory, because even when I consciously delete or erase part of my collection, it can still often be recovered. This complicates the notion of the materiality of the digital file, though, as I discovered when I got the drive home. The portion of recovered files that were audio files was roughly equivalent to what I had deleted, so I put the folder of audio files back into my iTunes library and then ran "Add to library." Most of the files appear as duplicates, but suddenly duplicates don't seem so bad.

How can it be that by deleting my MP3 library, I actually recovered a quantitatively much larger batch of data than I originally lost? The most obvious response is that the MP3 collection is really a virtual one rather than an actual one, and that when seeking the Real of whatever marks of my collection still exist on my external hard drive, what I encounter is not just the barecode itself, corresponding to the deleted files, but a much larger, chaotic, and ghostlike set of traces that constitute the sum of my activity in using that hard drive. It is a collection of files that is more or less unfamiliar to me, especially since it consists mostly of generically numbered files. As such it's not a collection that I feel I own. *Collection* usually presupposes ownership, as Walter Benjamin reminded us while unpacking his book collection, but what is at issue here is not that I have not read or listened to every MP3 file in my collection, but that I actually don't recognize or remember most of the restored files at all.

One of the curious things about Stanley Cavell's celebrated essay "The World as Things" (included in this volume) is that although he discusses the problem of description as being foundational for twentieth-century philosophy, whether Heidegger, Wittgenstein, or for that matter Husserl, he doesn't mention set theory, which is a formal way of describing things as a collection of other things. It is Alain Badiou who pointed out, in *Being and Event*, that set theory addresses a problem of ontology.[3] Furthermore, as Badiou's work suggests, the problem of what is collectible in a set is a political one. What Badiou's work does not address directly is the issue of digitization, and the development of the computer, which can be tracked to issues in set theory, and the problem of a formal logic of description, which Alan Turing for example addressed in his papers on computation.[4] Would digitization stand on the side of Badiou's truth procedures exposed to the event, or on the side of the situation or spectacle, part of the ideological infrastructure that maintains power in our society without any reference to eventality and its truth? At first the answer seems obvious: digitization as the process of translation into code must stand on the side of the situation, of a "mathematical ontology" that stands opposed to the singularity of the event. However, recent events suggest that matters are more complicated.

We live increasingly in a world of sets, of collections, in which we either have access or do not, in which something is either part of the set or not. Netflix for example, is a collection of files that we can choose from. If we search for a movie and it is not in Netflix's database, that's pretty much the end of it. If it is part of the set of films in the Netflix database, then we can watch it. Contrast this with a visit to a video store. Although it's true that you could ask the video clerk whether the store has such and such a movie, access to movies tends to be partial, based more on browsing the racks, and if a movie I want has already been taken out by someone else, then I can't watch it. In other words, the question of whether a particular movie is in or out of the set or collection of movies that is available to me is highly contingent, and the sense of there being a collection there is much weaker.

The recent emergence of WikiLeaks' distribution of government archives, quasi-legal cultural archives such as AAAAARG.ORG or UbuWeb, and file-sharing communities such as The Pirate Bay, points to the way that formal mathematical arguments about belonging form the core of a new kind of explicit politics of collection online. In a recent issue of *Radical Philosophy*, Finn Brunton points out that in his writings, Julian Assange emphasizes that the goal of WikiLeaks isn't breaking into archives, but making it easier for someone in a closed community that keeps secrets (he calls this a conspiracy) to leak something.[5] His goal then is to undermine the stability of the group that keeps secrets, and in a formal, almost mathematical way, shift the balance from groups that keep secrets to a public or commons where there are no secrets, as well as to shift from injustice to justice based on the notion that the secrets of unjust groups are more likely to be revealed than those that are based on a just and public practice of engagement. In Assange's formulation, the question of community comes down to making robust routing decisions. The other side of this situation would be what Cory Doctorow recently called "the coming civil war against general purpose computing."[6] This is, in other words, the struggle among legal, political, and technical attempts to protect certain definitions of intellectual property and therefore also collections as private, with restricted access, and the acts of hackers, ordinary citizens and some businesses to make use of the basic principles of computation to copy and share things and allow the flourishing of diverse kinds of collections.

All of this suggests that events, in Badiou's sense, also occur in the coded world of mathematical ontology. Russell's paradox ("Is there a set of all the sets that don't contain themselves as elements?"[7]) cannot itself be coded; it can only be presented and decided upon, negatively, affirmatively, or as undecidable. The fact that there is no foundation of mathematics in set theory, that the problem of belonging in set theory has no definitive answer, haunts all phenomena of collecting. It haunts collecting in the form of an inevitable disruption of the collector's plans for completing a collection.

WEDNESDAY

Next morning. At first it looks as though my library has been restored. This is because the iTunes library directory itself is identical to the way it was before I deleted the files. It is only when I click on a track that an exclamation mark appears, indicating that there is no audio file linked to the track. There are duplicates of almost all the tracks. Some of the duplicates connect to a file; some don't. Sometimes I can locate the lost file, sometimes I can't. Nearly everything is there. But sometimes a track is missing from a particular record. Or sometimes a five-minute track now appears to be forty-six seconds long and cuts off short. My Dam Funk record is gone! I know it exists just a click or two away in the iTunes store, but finally, I experience a feeling of loss and grief.

The feeling doesn't last. Part of me feels relief, like a burden has been removed. I understand the burden of carrying an amassed horde of physical objects around from apartment to apartment: those sixteen boxes of vinyl that now sit in my basement waiting for the day when I live somewhere big enough that I can display them. Benjamin doesn't say much about the labor of transporting or even coexisting with a collection, but there's a sense he knows the work of "unpacking." In his lovely early rumination on his MP3s, Julian Dibbell writes:

> I AM UNPACKING my CD collection. Yes, I am. Not the way Benjamin famously unpacked his book collection, seven decades ago, amid "the disorder of crates that have been wrenched open, the air saturated with the dust of wood, the floor covered with torn paper." Not hardly. I'm unpacking my music the way we generally unpack information these days: by setting it free entirely from dust and paper and crates of any kind. By making it immaterial.[8]

But this only points to how puzzling it is that I still experience my collection as a burden. Perhaps the physical labor that Benjamin wrote about, complete with crates that need to be wrenched open, the dust of the wood, has now been replaced by immaterial labor. Didn't I get into this mess by seeking to "tidy" my collection up? By seeking to remove all the extra copies, inaccurate copies, unnamed copies or inexisting copies that obstructed my easy access to the original copies that I believe my collection should consist of? The plug-in "Super Remove Dead Tracks" and the iTunes tool "Find Duplicates" both promise to alleviate this work. But instead the work has redoubled itself. I finally understand the defiant attitude of Laroche, the orchid collector in the movie *Adaptation*, who obsessively collects some category of things, only to rigorously and repeatedly abandon them to invent a kind of historical closure for himself that allows him to move on, interminably.[9]

I imagine that my collection could be replaced with another one that is equally interesting. It's not hard to find collections today. In fact, it's often easier to get access to a collection than to an individual object. BitTorrent seems to encourage the sharing of vast collections. If I want to replace my copy of *Toeachizown* by Dam Funk, it's actually easier to download Dam Funk's entire discography today. Such collections have the status of a gift, but in a strange way, because we get much more than we asked for, much more than we want. I cannot store all the collections that I have access to. I do not want all the collections that I have. Nor am I even aware of a large part of the collection. At any rate, the resurrection of my collection stands in a curious legal limbo.

Benjamin saw the potential of a mass art, as well as that of a publicly held collection such as that of a museum or library, but it's unclear that he recognized the possibility of a political class, that is, a mass of collectors, and the struggle between publicly and privately held collections for the attention of the masses. Thus today there's a modification of capitalism in the direction of the cloud, of services like Spotify, wherein I never own the music; it is always available as a vast privately held collection that I pay for access to. Thinking dialectically, it is impossible that such a service could really be the final word on collections. The idea feels as absurd as Fukuyama proclaiming the Hegelian end of history at the end of the Cold War. But: why? What is it that lies beyond the accumulation of objects, either as private or state property, sold or given to us on loan?

SATURDAY AGAIN

The truth of the matter is that my collection is a mess. Though not fastidiously or obsessive-compulsively clean, I am far from being a stereotypical nerd or geek, every surface covered in stacks of books, moldy paper cups, and dead pieces of computer equipment. But suddenly I do feel like Benjamin's angel of history, his hands thrown up in horror as the mislabeled, broken MP3 files pile up in front of him. Partly I am kidding. Partly I know that my experience is utterly banal, shared by many many people, although no doubt in different media, as they look at their computer screens at this very moment. But that should also be cause for thought: What if every person at his or her computer screen today was an instance or iteration of the angel of history, the very picture of the crisis of the collector, no longer just a member of a small elite, but the very picture of the modern subject, 2013, a subject who still seeks to define himself or herself in terms of the set of his or her properties or possessions, even in the moment when, as Marx and Engels wrote, "All that is solid melts into air."[10]

So what is that enormous pile of debris piling up in front of us? Perhaps it's a commons. And what the angel of history experiences is the collapse of property structures such that the private ownership of collections or histories is no longer possible. This means that password-protected services, with their reasonable monthly fees and intellectual property rights, will also disappear, leaving us with an ever-expanding pile of rubble or garbage that isn't yet formally available as an organized commons in which lines of access to potential subjects who would organize a society around it would emerge. The reasons for this lack of formal availability are, broadly, legal, sociotechnical, and political. There are laws that prevent unlimited sharing, and they are enacted in the software of my iPod, in legal restrictions on file-sharing, and so forth.

This vision is in line with other aspects of Benjamin's thought on history. For example, regarding the dialectical image, "Articulating the past historically means recognizing those elements of the past which come together in the constellation of a single moment."[11] So the collection is a kind of constellation, but the full power of constellation can only appear when collections are liberated from the grip of ownership. They can only appear when they become truly public, or more tragically, when they become the image of a possible public, one that flashes before us in the moment that it disappears, as the quote with which I began this chapter indicates. This would explain why it is so difficult to see the new digital archives as actual things that exist within a solid property regime, and why, conversely, my own digital collection neither feels like mine nor like a substantial object. It's only when I lose the collection that an image of a genuine public sphere momentarily appears, a sphere out of which my collection emerged and from which it may in fact be restored. In a radical sense, a constellation as a set of individual inherently existing objects does not exist. It "exists" only insofar as processes of reification pull us into structures in which we performatively enact a belief in ownable, existing objects that form a collection. Liberated from ownership, the full power of constellation is revealed as a kind of actor network in which individual entities appear.

Significantly, such a thought of a new commons after ownership speaks to a significant body of recent post-Benjaminian scholarship, which runs from Agamben's *The Coming Community* through Hardt and Negri's discussions of "the common," to Esposito's work on depropriation and communitas.[12] What all these theorists share is a vision of a community that is not identitarian, that is not built around a full coming to presence of any particular universalizable subject or object, but rather is built around the shared recognition of contingency, finitude, and incompleteness. This community is "depropriated" because it is not based on an identification of common properties that would provide the basis of a unification, and recognizes that ultimately property, both in the sense of intellectual property and in the broader philosophical sense of a quality that intrinsically belongs to something, is an unsustainable illusion.

What I find problematic in this tradition is the lack of a clear articulation of what it means to live collectively with incompleteness, beyond a passivity that is often in danger of collapsing into nihilism. Here I find Buddhist tradition more specific in its examination of the ultimate absence of intrinsic essences or properties. The recognition of the ultimate impossibility of property regimes need not be a nihilistic one. Nor does it imply a chaotic free-for-all—as Esposito shows in his brilliant reading of Hobbes's state of nature. It simply implies other kinds of relationship than that of ownership. This is precisely what we see happening today in debates about a digital commons, and in the practices of online and offline constellation formerly known as collecting. It is not a question of seeking a utopia of total availability, but of recognizing, via the actual shocks that new technologies deliver to the realm of the possible as delineated by law and custom in the age of global capitalism, that the failures of ownership, in which the figure of the collector also is implicated, open up other, hitherto obscured possibilities for a shared world.

SIX MONTHS LATER

I am back home. Time Machine is telling me that it cannot complete the backup of my computer. I have bought new backup drives. I have mapped out a plan. I found the old Firewire drive on which I backed up my MP3 collection in the basement in a stack of boxes. This surprises me because I thought that I had treated the drive with great care, but obviously I was quite indifferent to it, until I needed it. The next surprise is that the backup dates to February 2010, rather than summer 2011, as I had imagined. This means that there is a year and a half of collecting activity that is basically irretrievable. It is possible that the actual files exist, either on my iPod or in the attempt to restore the hard drive.

I end up deleting the files of my entire iTunes library up to the date that I deleted the duplicates, and I also delete the entire block of files that were retrieved from my external hard drive. Then I clear the entire file listing in iTunes. I build up the collection again from the February 2010 back up and then I click "Add to Library." My collection is, to some degree, restored, with a year and a half gap. It is free of duplicates for the first time in many years. The price that I pay for being rid, at least for now, of the simulacra of my collection, all those irritating and redundant doubles, is a gap, a hole in time. Some of it may be retrievable from my iPod. Some is gone for good. I feel OK about that, except for those moments when I search for a track that I imagined I own, only to find it missing.

I am left wondering whether it is actually possible to collect things today in the sense that Benjamin, Cavell, even Baudrillard have understood collections. My objection to contemporary collection might begin with the problem of ownership. On the one hand, the existential fact of the presence or absence of digital files or code on my computer or drives continues to define what is "mine." The virtualization of this presence through backups, copies and other iterations still comes down to whether or not those copies can come to hand or not when required. And the retrievability or not of these copies is marked by a specific history in which I did or did not make backups or copies, which did or did not contain certain files. My more or less unconscious activities in moving files around is a history that determines what my collection is. On the other hand, this unconsciousness, my casual indifference to my actions in securing or not securing files, again marks off my situation from that of Benjamin unpacking his book collection. I remember very little about what I got when and how when it comes to MP3s. Only at the moment of its disappearance, to paraphrase Benjamin, does its historicity start to exist for me.

Yet this unconsciousness is not simple carelessness or stupidity (whatever those things are). It may actually be a sign of my confidence in the worldly existence of those things that I care about, the possibility that I do not have to secure them to enjoy them or care for them. This confidence also has its own historicity, related to changing notions of publicness, commons, and so forth. The accessibility of certain rare and therefore desirable music files was different in the age of Napster (1999–2002), the age of Rapidshare and Megaupload and music blogs (2004–2009), and that of BitTorrent (2008–?). Today, I find myself being forced back into the historical situation of the collector by the aggressive shutdown of various new technosocial forms of publicness through the expansion and enforcement of IP laws. But I do not want to be a collector. I have tasted a better life. The problem remains: How do I create the conditions in which it can flourish?

NOTES

1. "Unpacking My Library: A Talk About Collecting" (1931), trans. Harry Zohn in Walter Benjamin, *Selected Writings*, Vol. 2, Part 2, ed. Michael W. Jennings, Howard Eiland, and Gary Smith (Cambridge, MA: Harvard University Press, 1999), 486–493; "The Work of Art in the Age of Its Technological Reproducibility" (1935–1936), trans. Edmund Jephcott and Harry Zohn, in Walter Benjamin, *Selected Writings*, Vol. 3, ed. Howard Eiland and Michael W. Jennings (Cambridge, MA: Harvard University Press, 2002), 101–122; "Edouard Fuchs: Collector" (1937), trans. and ed. Howard Eiland and Michael W. Jennings, in Walter Benjamin, *Selected Writings*, Vol. 3 (Cambridge, MA: Harvard University Press, 2002), 260–285; "On the Concept of History" (1940), trans. Harry Zohn, in Walter Benjamin, *Selected Writings*, Vol. 4, ed. Howard Eiland and Michael W. Jennings (Cambridge, MA: Harvard University Press, 1999), 389–397.

2. See section 74, "The Essential Constitution of Historicity," particularly comments on 352–353, in Martin Heidegger, *Being and Time*, trans. Joan Stambaugh (Albany: State University of New York Press, 1996).

3. See Alain Badiou, *Being and Event*, trans. Oliver Feltham (London: Continuum, 2005), 81–111, particularly the chapter "The State of the Historical-Social Situation," 104–111.

4. Alan Turing, "Computing Machinery and Intelligence," *Mind* 59, no. 236 (October 1950): 433–460.

5. Finn Brunton, "Keyspace: WikiLeaks and the Assange Papers," *Radical Philosophy* 166 (2011): 8–20.

6. Cory Doctorow, "The Coming Civil War over General Purpose Computing," http://boingboing.net/2012/08/23/civilwar.html (accessed 31 October 2012).

7. Bertrand Russell, "Letter to Frege" (1902), reprinted in *From Frege to Gödel: A Source Book in Mathematical Logic, 1879–1931*, ed. Jean van Heijenoort (Cambridge, MA: Harvard University Press, 1967), 124–125. Russell writes in that letter: "[T]here is no class (as a totality) of those classes which, each taken as a totality, do not belong to themselves. From this I conclude that under certain circumstances a definable collection does not form a totality" (125).

8. Julian Dibbell, "Unpacking My Record Collection," http://www.juliandibbell.com/texts/feed_records.html (accessed 17 January 2011).

9. *Adaptation*, directed by Spike Jonze (2002; Los Angeles: Image Entertainment, 2010), DVD.

10. Karl Marx and Friedrich Engels, *Manifesto of the Communist Party* in *The Marx-Engels Reader*, ed. Robert C. Tucker, 2nd ed. (New York: Norton, 1972), 476.

11. Benjamin, "On the Concept of History," 403.

12. Giorgio Agamben, *The Coming Community*, trans. Michael Hardt (Minneapolis: Minnesota University Press, 1993); Michael Hardt and Antonio Negri, *Multitude: War and Democracy in the Age of Empire* (New York: Penguin, 2004); Roberto Esposito, *Communitas: The Origin and Destiny of Community*, trans. Timothy Campbell (Stanford, CA: Stanford University Press, 2010).

2

Collecting, Curating, and the Magic Circle of Ownership in a Postmaterial Culture

Matthew James Vechinski

Collections have long been studied as reflections of the individuals who assemble them. Professor of business Russell W. Belk, paraphrasing the art and literature scholar Susan Stewart, notes that "the collection is especially implicated in the extended self because it often visibly and undeniably represents the collector's judgments and taste."[1] Asking why a particular item belongs in a collection prompts the collector to explain his or her choices, inevitably touching on questions of value that extend outside the collection and reflect the individual's judgments and taste more generally. A collection usually consists of an arrangement of objects, even if they are not on display for others. In *The Meaning of Things: Domestic Symbols and the Self* (1981), Mihaly Csikszentmihalyi and Eugene Rochberg-Halton considered the home one such space where individuals "achieve some unique expression by careful selection and combination of items."[2] This chapter focuses on the virtual space of social networking websites and explores how the personal profile functions as a collection. It approaches the profile as the representation of identity that issues from the sum of the information an individual shares while using these sites. The profile is an arrangement of data rather than a set of objects owned, with much more fluid boundaries than the home in Csikszentmihalyi and Rochberg-Halton's book. Whereas their study demonstrated that significant household items such as televisions and appliances are both useful and symbolically meaningful to families, this chapter examines how the practical and the representational collide in the sharing of information. "Updating" an online profile serves an immediate purpose by providing the most current information, and it also leaves a trace so that the total display of information reflects an individual's overall tendencies in judgment and taste.

This chapter analyzes the social networking site Goodreads (www.goodreads. com), at which the aggregation of information about reading activities creates for users a virtual book collection. Users assemble an online library of book titles they are reading, have read, or want to read, and classify their selections with customized tags. The site provides readers with a means of keeping track of their reading habits independently of the ownership of books. A profile on Goodreads is a glorified reader's diary, albeit shared with the public, shaped by the site's means of organizing information. This chapter considers how the interface design of Goodreads influences the display of the virtual collection, simultaneously separate (a set of book titles listed in a profile) and connected (the list linking to other areas of the site). Goodreads relies on the book title to represent any copy its users might encounter. It does not privilege rarity, format, or even the material condition of the book, unlike many collectors of physical books. Although the interface of Goodreads collapses the distinction between book title and unique copy on which book collecting depended in the past, the site allows users to envision the expansion of their online library over time and to classify titles as they wish. These forms of custodianship bring virtual collecting in line with the collection of material objects.

Book collecting then and now is an especially relevant subject, because it exhibits the complex overlap of the virtual and the material at the heart of this inquiry. Walter Benjamin, writing about book collecting in the 1930s, described it as the "locking of individual items within a magic circle" that fixes the collector's associations in physical objects.[3] Accounts of the benefits of reading often portray books serving as subjects for reflection and discussion, as well as the building blocks of self-fashioning. A book's title has always been a convenient referent for what it contains and represents. Goodreads capitalizes on the fact that readers today are less concerned with the format or edition of books, especially because there are alternatives to the physical book (e-books, audiobooks) and resources that make it easier to obtain scarce titles (Google Books, online consortiums of bookstores such as Abebooks.com, print-on-demand). Even today, the experience of reading opens onto a discussion that surpasses the text, in whatever object form, that motivated it. The book is an example of a representation that blurs object and experience, and this chapter considers how the same phenomenon occurs on social networking sites when users share information that refers to persons, places, and things. This condition—not the virtual replacing the material, but their coexistence and overlap—is here termed *postmaterial culture* and regarded as a consequence of social networking and the dissemination of information on the Internet in general.

The goal of this chapter is to examine how collecting practices that originally involved material objects exclusively are still compatible with postmaterial culture. Because information may reside in social networking profiles, but remains connected to its sources and open to recirculation, the profile demonstrates how collecting need not imply ownership and control of physical objects. Collecting in today's postmaterial culture exemplifies the "systematic collection," defined by museum studies scholar Susan M. Pearce as a set that "depends upon principles of organization which are perceived to have external reality beyond the specific material under consideration."[4] This chapter seeks to explain how the social networking profile as a collection would be perceived as substantial, figuratively speaking, when a display of information substitutes for the possession of objects. The principles of organization in question are in part a function of how social networking sites promote the sharing and managing of information, making it also necessary to consider the design and features of sites such as Goodreads.

CURATING AND COLLECTING:
THE TRANSACTION AND THE TRACES LEFT

This chapter insists that systematic collections are readily compatible with postmaterial culture, but for some the very idea of collecting may evoke what Pearce terms the fetishistic collection, "an attempt to create a satisfactory private universe . . . by trying to lift objects away from the web of social relationships, to deny process and to freeze time."[5] Recently, *curating* has become a buzzword, and its usage acknowledges the conditions of postmaterial culture, especially circumstances in which acts of judgment call attention to individuals. Although the term accurately describes the addition of information to social networking profiles, curating privileges the transaction, the moment of conscious choice, while theories of collecting more fully address the dynamics of arranging sets of items over time.

An article in the "Sunday Styles" section of the *New York Times*, "The Word 'Curate' No Longer Belongs to the Museum Crowd" noted, "The word 'curate,' lofty and once rarely spoken outside exhibition corridors or British parishes, has become a fashionable code word among the aesthetically minded, who seem to paste it onto any activity that involves culling and selecting."[6] It is telling that the author of the article, Alex Williams, never mentions collecting, which could very easily be described as "culling and selecting." The "aesthetically minded" tastemakers Williams discusses appear to emphasize selectivity as if it were separate from accumulation. This compares the objects set aside by these curators to information in constant circulation, passed through key individuals. But with respect to museum exhibitions, the term *curate* signifies selections made from a larger aggregate, and in that sense there can be no curating without first a collection. The culling remains outside of the transfer, in other words.

Williams's article acknowledges that the current curating trend creates desirable niche markets and implies that the overabundance of product choices inspires consumers to seek out the amateur curators to find for them the diamonds in the rough. Williams quotes a thrift-store owner who is careful not to suggest to her customers that her store is "selling stuff that was gross and old and had been crammed in trunks for years. It would have very specific pieces, selected purposefully."[7] These pieces are not necessarily rare in the most literal sense and may only appear uncommon or striking relative to the usual kinds of used items found in a thrift store. Visitors to her store would perceive the items as collectible because she sets them apart as individual pieces. That is to say, the goods for sale have already met the approval of one discriminating purveyor, the owner. One might presume that the store visitors desire the owner's validation along with the products themselves. Therefore, the transaction involves the buyer echoing or extending the experience of discrimination initiated by the curator through selecting an object already singled out in its discovery and promotion to the sales floor.

The interdependence of object and experience characteristic of postmaterial culture goes further than that, in Williams's estimation. His curators do not just rescue stuff from trunks; they organize events, like a club promoter "curating an evening of music."[8] The live music in question is available to whoever pays the cover price and gains entry. It is not passed from one exclusive owner to another, meaning participants may readily insert themselves into the narrative of the experience offered. Yet just as before, the fact that the musicians have been selected and slotted to perform on the same evening makes the listeners perceive that the event is exclusive, indeed singular. The combination or juxtaposition of elements, here musicians or bands, matters just as much as their discovery and selection. The success of the combination reflects not on the bands, but on the acumen of the club promoter. The curator is also individualized. Williams writes, "Among designers, disc jockeys, club promoters, bloggers and thrift-store owners, curate is code for 'I have a discerning eye and great taste.'"[9] To garner attention, the thrift-store inventory or concert must make selections that resonate with others, hence the notion of a *cohesive* evening of music or *purposefully* selected thrift-store items representing more than one curator's fancy.

Despite the fact that curators usually offer up their selections for public evaluation, whereas collectors may not, scholars such as Belk and Pearce stress that collectors' preferences are not entirely idiosyncratic. They arrange their sets at least in part by using socially informed categories, even if they seem to develop and follow their own principles of organization. Cultural studies scholar Rey Chow argues that

> however pure and secluded an object may be in its owner's fantasy, it is virtually impossible to avoid its coming into contact with a system of evaluation that is external to and other than itself (such as money, social recognition, or the professional approval of the connoisseur); the intrinsic or use-value of an object, that is, comes inevitably to be validated by what is foreign or extrinsic to it. By implication, the collector who only collects for the sake of the object (for the love of art) is at best a fantasy.[10]

Her point is that collecting can never be disinterested, yet the semblance of it being so may be important to the collector. Curating involves a similar fantasy, that the acumen of the curator transfers to the consumer through the object or experience the curator makes available. These two illusions have something in common: the semblance of unclouded, decisive exercise of judgment. In collecting, there is an inevitable disconnect between the distinct moments when principled choices are made and the set that results, due to the passage of time, which creates a complex sum of decisions about acquisition and organization.

With its emphasis on the point of transaction, curating does not consider the evolution of the set, which is necessary in any investigation of collecting practices. For this reason, this essay links social networking to collecting, even though Williams's examples of curating may at first glance seem more appropriate. The nature of continual updates to social networking profiles means that the self-representation afforded by social networking appears to emerge effortlessly. Pieces of information added by the user or recorded there to mark activities performed by the user gradually build a set. The set is the profile, essentially. Social networking creates community through promoting the drive to stay current, and yet each action that serves to update the profile also leaves traces that accumulate. Although users may regard their contributions to social networking sites as curators would, at the moments that they share information, their growing profiles are indeed collections.

The social networking site operates on continual expansion, more like the collection's expandable set than the discrete transactions involving the curator. However, the collector of objects faces material limitations that would not seem to apply to the circulation of information facilitated by the Internet, also a condition of postmaterial culture. Collectors must reconcile their aspirations, the collection they would like to have, with the reality of what they can and do own. In "No Two Alike: Play and Aesthetics in Collecting," Brenda Danet and Tamar Katriel describe this as the way that collectors "intentionally create an agenda for the production of, and reduction of, manageable tension."[11] The tension implied in social networking is the desire to remain current, despite the constantly expanding virtual space of the site. Updating allows the endless reconfiguration of the profile through the sharing of new information over time. There are also features to manage the display of profiles' contents, such as tagging. Users add and organize information to represent themselves as they feel fit and also to represent themselves to others, demonstrating the overlap between the intrinsic and the extrinsic that Chow describes in the extract on the previous page. The openness of the profile corresponds to the unfolding of the individual's life. Susan Stewart, in her classic study *On Longing: Narratives of the Miniature, the Gigantic, the Souvenir, the Collection* (1984), asserts that "the collection offers example rather than sample, metaphor rather than metonymy."[12] The number of examples may be multiplied as collectors see fit to actualize their selection and organizational principles via the set, and the frequency of profile additions and alterations is at the discretion of users.

It is perhaps a fantasy that users regard the profile as an original expression, because it is part of a network of links and references that prevent it from ever being self-contained. Yet Stewart believes that "the collection is not constructed by its elements; rather, it comes to exist by means of its principle of organization."[13] The virtual space of the Internet, separated from the traditionally material concerns implied in collecting, intensifies the focus on the principle of organization. Its vast aggregation of content, without any definitive arrangement, requires that users filter out extraneous information to find content with value. Though search engines have typically fulfilled this role, social networking sites also provide content filtering: the profile brings together information a user values. A *New Yorker* profile on Mark Zuckerberg, founder of Facebook, describes how the site intends to rival Google: "Eventually, the company hopes that users will read articles, visit restaurants, and watch movies based on what their Facebook friends have recommended, not, say, based on a page that

Google's algorithm sends them to."[14] Facebook is already inspiring its users to look to the preferences of others rather than the impersonal logic of the search engine, just as some consumers look to Williams's curators rather than rely on advertising and marketing, doubtless because social networking facilitates unexpected discoveries while allowing recommenders to become acknowledged tastemakers.

The quotation above attests to the predominance of information added to profiles that serves as an explicit or tacit recommendation of objects or experiences available to others offline. These references to persons, places, or things further exhibit how "the making of a collection"—here the set of information in a profile—"is one way in which we organize our relationship with the external physical world,"[15] to use Pearce's words. She means that this relationship is an often unintended consequence of all the collector's judgments, identical to the gradual accumulation of information in the profile, which in turn reflects the user's personality.

The next section considers why books as a subject of discussion readily inspire the sharing of information from which a profile may emerge. It examines how the virtual library of books assembled by users of the social networking site Goodreads might share many of the qualities found in a collection of physical books. As mentioned previously, books have always implied both an object (the text) and an experience (reading), and this condition has constantly influenced the activities of book collectors and readers alike. Moreover, reading and one's relationship with books are commonly regarded as an expression of personality, which is what the social networking profile attempts to reflect.

THE "SUBSTANCE" OF BOOKS AND HOW TO "ACQUIRE" IT

Walter Benjamin's 1931 lecture "Unpacking My Library" provides a useful starting point for comparing the virtual library to the physical collection. His notion of the "magic circle" in particular suggests how the social networking profile might achieve a collection of information that resembles a set of owned objects. For Benjamin, "ownership is the most intimate relationship that one can have to objects. Not that they come alive in him; it is he who lives in them."[16] Arguably, Benjamin celebrates the act of possession because it introduces the single object into the owner's set:

> The most profound enchantment for the collector is the locking of individual items within a magic circle in which they are fixed as the final thrill, the thrill of acquisition, passes over them. Everything remembered and thought, everything conscious, becomes the pedestal, the frame, the base, the lock of his property. The period, the region, the craftsmanship, the ownership—for a true collector the whole background of an item adds up to a magic encyclopedia whose quintessence is the fate of his object.[17]

The phenomenon of ownership parallels how the historical materialist encounters a monad described in Benjamin's 1940 essay "Theses on the Philosophy of History."[18] The book as object serves as the monad, the magic circle of the collection a kind of historical constellation. In "Unpacking My Library," Benjamin maintains that "the most important fate of a copy is its encounter with [the collector], with his own collection."[19] So although the magic encyclopedia is essentially a suite of associations, it results from the individual book gaining a position within the larger context of the personal collection. Acquisition serves to anchor these associations. The magic circle of the social networking profile likewise furnishes a frame for information. Every addition carries with it a web of references, and although this information comes from without or is open to further sharing, the profile draws a circle with the hope of containing it. Property for Benjamin represents simply the consolidation and management of value within the magic circle, possible even in the collection of information. The "thrill of acquisition" resembles the moment of transaction privileged in curating, though Benjamin is interested in what retains the associations that exceed the object that inspires them. Ownership is one means to preserve an item's whole background; the profile, in postmaterial culture, is another.

Benjamin's discussion of property in relation to collecting also affirms that the collector gains "a relationship to objects which does not emphasize their functional, utilitarian value—that is, their usefulness."[20] In the case of books, this means the collector is more concerned with the book as a physical object than with the experience of reading it, which could be said to be its functional value. Likewise, a salt and pepper shaker, for example, has an obvious function but antique collectors see in it other qualities (craftsmanship, rarity, age, etc.) that motivate their desire to possess it. Benjamin maintains that book collectors do not necessarily need to read what they collect, especially when rarity motivates their activities.[21] In other words, book collectors readily separate the object from the experience it gives rise to, deeming the latter an insufficient measure of a book's value. For readers, the contents of the book and the experience of reading it would probably matter most. Yet whenever collectors or readers purchase and retain a book they have read or want to read, their perception of value conflates the appreciation of the book as object with an evaluation of its content. Further, nonreading is not exclusive to collectors, because readers can familiarize themselves with a book's contents and what those contents may be worth, without having to experience them. This is the subject of Pierre Bayard's *How to Talk About Books You Haven't Read* (2007), in which he considers culture as one vast library wherein the respective place a single book title occupies usually is more important than actually reading that book. "Being cultivated is a matter not of having read any book in particular," Bayard argues, "but of being able to find your bearings within books as a system, which requires you to know that they form a system and to be able to locate each element in relation to the others."[22] This system is a magic circle as well, but one that contains information: a set of book titles and the cultural value they hold.

Bayard's study stresses the importance of one's "inner library," the "set of books—a subset of the library of culture—around which every personality is constructed and which then shapes each person's individual relationship to books and to other people."[23] The inner library and the library of culture are themselves virtual networks of associations, anchored by a set of book titles, wherein ownership plays no part. For Bayard, the personality constructed from books is what Pearce calls a "relationship with the external physical world," and thus extends beyond the set itself. Bayard's argument regards the inner library as the result of curating and collecting, because what matters is the selection and combination of examples from the library of culture, and that subset matters more than the individual books of which it consists. Yet the construction of an inner library parallels the evolution of a personality rather than corresponding to a fully formed sense of self:

> Books—whether read or unread—form a kind of second language to which we can turn to talk about ourselves, to communicate with others, and to defend ourselves in conflict. Like language, books serve to express us, but also to complete us, furnishing, through a variety of excerpted and reworked fragments, the missing elements of our personality.
>
> Like words, books, in representing us, also deform what we are. We cannot coincide completely with the image the totality of our readings presents; whether the image makes us look better or worse than we should, behind it all our particularities vanish.[24]

We talk about books to talk about ourselves, Bayard thinks, to "shore up our coherence" when our self-image fails us.[25] Because personalities and inner libraries do not simply mirror each other, Bayard suggests, at times books revise one's self-concept as much as they provide a means of describing it. Nonetheless, Belk's claim that collections are *extensions* of the self suggests how they may provide reassurance and direction. "The notion that collections represent one's extended self," he writes, "accounts for many of the self-enhancing motives given for collecting, such as seeking power, knowledge, reminders of one's childhood, prestige, mastery and control."[26] Bayard's advice about using a subset of books to orient oneself in a culture advocates careful accounting, instead of immersive experience with individual titles, as a form of empowerment.

The management of the collection, or how collectors feel they achieve "mastery and control," is important to consider alongside the "culling and selecting" that Williams describes in curating. Benjamin notes, "For what else is [a] collection but a disorder to which habit has accommodated itself to such an extent that it can appear as order?"[27] Perhaps "mastery and control" are simply means of accommodation, principles of selection and organization that emerge as a result of the collector's efforts to make sense of a large array of elements. Collectors respond to what is available as much as they seek out the particular. Benjamin claims that "inheritance is the best way of acquiring a collection," because it forces the collector to work from a set that was not assembled through the collector's own choices.[28] Similarly, Belk argues that "many collections are discovered by their creators long after the materials have been gathered."[29] Benjamin and Belk show the difficulty of locating the origin of a collection, which may be nothing more than the moment when a set becomes regarded as such; more important, they suggest that principles of selection and organization are often retrospective justifications of what collections have become. Books, already having a place in a cultural system, especially underline the need for continual reorientation with every encounter. Ownership accommodates the disorder, but other anchors, such as the social networking profile, might function the same way, as long as it includes management options. The next section analyzes how the design of the Goodreads site provides tools to achieve control, or at least the perception of control, over the set of books users encounter over the course of their lives.

THE ANATOMY OF GOODREADS

The design of any online interface enables certain practices to occur and, in the case of social networking sites, shapes how users perceive each other's activities. The ability of a virtual library on Goodreads to resemble a physical collection of books and serve as a consolidation of a personality and extension of the self depends on the features of the site. Goodreads comprises three different types of web pages: personal profiles that display an individual's virtual library and log his or her reading and re-viewing; pages that represent a particular book title and list reviews and popular user classifications (hereafter called "book title web pages"); and groups pages or message boards for communities of users. By emphasizing the personal profile as a record of all the activities performed by a user, Goodreads highlights curating as well as collect-ing. Each action is a choice, and the sum of the choices represents the user and his or her collection of books. Other users regard the profile as a document of taste, and they form relationships with users whose judgment they admire. This focus on the profile establishes a resemblance to the self-fashioning and networking capabilities of sites such as Facebook. Like Facebook, Goodreads provides a free service and does not sell products to its users, although it does direct users to booksellers' websites and features advertising for books and authors.

Goodreads even distances itself from other online retailers that encourage users to review products. Amazon.com and other major commercial websites make it possible for visitors to see what products others have bought and in what combina-tion. Goodreads, by eliminating the associations of purchasing, attempts to keep the focus on the experience of reading. Users do not have to review every book they have read—they can simply rate books or add titles to their virtual shelves—nor do they need to comment on only the books they own. Some of the most popular books on the site are those that are frequently assigned in high schools. The second most popular book of all time on the site is *To Kill a Mockingbird*, and the sixth is *Catcher in the Rye*; these titles earned their status through the sheer number of high ratings they received.[30] After rating a book, Goodreads automatically adds that title to a user's virtual library, making it easy to start building an online collection. New users to the site often decide to add these formative books to their virtual shelves soon after joining, rather than begin with an empty profile. The impulse to go back and designate the significant reads sets the tone for their use of the site and inspires users to see their shelves as a reflection of themselves. Though a site like Amazon. com may allow customers to specify which items they already own to refine the system-generated recommendations, one must review a product to have it be linked to the user profile. Users of Goodreads also build their profiles by designating the books they want to read, which indicates their intentions to expand their virtual collections. Wish lists on online shopping sites may be broadcast to other users, but they often are not framed as sets unless they are organized around product type, and even then they cannot easily show how new items would extend existing collections.

The reviewing and wish list functions of most online shopping sites do not represent time in ways that social networking sites can. Lists alone can easily tally the past (items bought) and future (items to buy), but have trouble illustrating the present. Goodreads allows users to log a wealth of information about the books they are currently reading. Users' updates leave traces that make their profiles resemble reading diaries. The users may assign books a "started date" and "read date," which records their present reads becoming part of their collection, and maps out a rough timeline of the books they have already read. If Goodreads knows the length of the book, it can generate a bar indicating a user's progress to completion if he or she wants to provide the page number reached. So not only does the site attempt to provide the absolutely current; all activity is also framed with direction: finishing a book, marking that book as read, and moving it from one context to another in the virtual library. This entices users to visit the site regularly and update, to bring the profile in line with their current preoccupations.

The bookshelf is an essential metaphor for virtual libraries on Goodreads. It may seem inappropriate, suggesting that books' arrangements do not change. The intangibility of the online bookshelf and the titles on it make for easy rearrangement—there are no physical objects to shift around. By default, each profile comes with three shelf options—to-read, currently-reading, and read—and every book on one's profile must be designated with one of these shelves. Thus the default shelves promote thinking about the total set of books as having an underlying narrative sequence, channeling the use of the site across three stages (future to present to past), which are then repeated with the subsequent book title the user encounters. This powerful conceptual precedent does promote the expansion of the set and encourage users to anticipate and set goals for the direction of their reading. At the same time, the "to-read" shelf is not simply a queue, because it can represent a user's aspirations.

Goodreads allows micromanagement through the use of user-defined shelves that function as secondary tags. The labeling of books serves each user's personal sense of organization, which necessarily draws on common classifications and designations of value that others may also appreciate. There is an impetus to label and organize for the user's own reference while keeping the tags meaningful to other users, even in light of the three default shelves with which any tag will combine. A user-defined shelf like "beach books" could be used to set aside titles from the "to-read" shelf appropriate for vacation reading. "Beach books" already finished would associate these books with a time and place in the user's collection, just as if while such a book was in progress others might assume the user is currently on vacation, or in the mood to read something breezy. Note that as soon as user-defined shelves are employed, virtual books then exist on more than one shelf at the same time. Strictly speaking, the shelves are a mixed metaphor on Goodreads, but they are organizational concepts, not visualizations, of the virtual library. Shelves reinforce the book collection as a series of examples, because a tag has no value if it only belongs to one book title. Moreover, the tags themselves are examples; adding further tags amends the net classification of the book title.

Yet this system for creating shelves does not provide a means of promoting a consistent set of tags to be used across Goodreads, unless readers should incidentally happen to use similar keywords. For example, one person could have a shelf titled "could-not-read," another "did-not-finish" or even "gave-up." These essentially mean the same thing, with slight nuances that matter only to the user who employs them. So while users may be inspired by the tags they see others assigning, they have the option of adopting the same one or a variation on it. Each book title web page lists the top-ten shelves users have assigned to the book. This is designed to highlight the most prevalent classifications, which in many cases may be too generic to be of much significance ("novel," "literature," etc.). When there is too much variance among shelf names, even general information may be lost. For example, *Life of Pi*, winner of the Man Booker Prize in 2002, was put on shelves like "award-winners" and "man-booker-prize," but there were so many slight variations of the same idea that this piece of information did not figure in its top-ten shelves.[31] There is no site-wide standardization of tags to eliminate even the most blatant redundancy. Some users have a shelf called "nonfiction," others "non-fiction." In other cases, user-created shelves duplicate information already collected by the site, yet make the titles' connection to the life-space of users more apparent to themselves and to others. For example, users have named shelves "after-the-move" or "new-york-period" to refer to when they read the books on them, even though the site keeps track of the date on which they indicate they finished reading a book. Some shelves, like "i-own-it" or "audiobooks," serve as references to the user only. They allow users to separate their virtual collections from their material ones or to distinguish which edition of a book they have "read."

Goodreads does not police the bookshelf tags that users devise, but it does take pains to aggregate all editions of a book rather than allow for distinctions among them. The goal is to have one web page per book title, regardless of format, media, or even language, so that all user activities refer to a common title and not a specific edition or copy. Too much emphasis on the exemplar would disperse rather than concentrate users' references, but simultaneously the aggregation directs the attention from the rarity of a copy, which would have been an essential consideration of book collecting in Benjamin's time, to the generality of a title. At first glance, the obvious implication is that the aggregation of editions helps readers find the in-print version for retail purchase. However, Goodreads also links to used bookstores and specifies which edition is available for purchase, or one can do a WorldCat search for the title as a library book, with or without specifying an edition. Although there are many inessential differences among editions, Goodreads goes so far as to aggregate revised editions and translations, and it marks no difference in media (print volumes, e-books, audiobooks). Though in many respects Goodreads is a self-regulating community, the aggregation of editions requires manual labor. The site designates certain volunteer users as "librarians: a new status that we bestow on those [users] interested in helping keep things nice and tidy."[32] The librarians might think of themselves as curators, in that they have a special role that helps the site function as intended, but for the most part they follow procedure and rarely have an opportunity to exercise judgment. The title "librarian" is apt because it is more of a technical function that attends to cataloging details behind the scenes, as it were, without influencing the activity of adding books to shelves on users' profiles. Through its librarians, Goodreads cares about the accuracy of the aggregation to draw attention away from the existence of different editions. Instead, the book title signifies a topic for discussion, independent of the object that contains the text.

Though Goodreads does not prevent readers from commenting on individual copies of books, the format of the site certainly does not encourage it. Reviews centered on specific editions would introduce distinctions among readers' access to books. Hence the label "community reviews" is on the book title web pages, coupled with the presumption that the content and reading experience of each book is presumably the same regardless of the format of a title. The achieved equivalence of book title and discussion topic would not surprise Pierre Bayard. In his argument for nonreading, he says that one ought to be concerned with the idea of the work from afar, rather than "risk getting lost in its details. To take this theory to its extreme," Bayard writes, "what is interesting about a text—which is not the work itself, but the qualities it shares with others—might be best perceived by a critic who closes his eyes in the presence of the work and thinks, instead, about what it may be."[33] Not surprisingly, many of the reviews on Goodreads lament what a book title is not and do not include close readings of passages, only vague references to events or ideas. It is also the case that on a site that wants to persuade other readers to pick up books, the reviews steer clear of "spoilers" that reveal too much about what happens or what the book is about (writers of revealing reviews can opt to make their reviews hidden unless users opt to see them). Scrolling down a screen of reviews, the frequent use of the first person is obvious. The reviews resemble notes about readers' general impressions after having finished the book, perhaps recently or maybe years previously, but in any case they have already moved on to consider other titles.

The community reviews remain free of fine critiques or detailed appraisals, in part because a third area of the Goodreads site, Groups, allow an outlet for the discussion of books that might otherwise intrude on blanket accessibility of the book title web pages. In these forums, users extract the narratives embedded in their history documented in their profiles, as it were, and recast them as exchanges on message boards. The site touts the Group pages as virtual book clubs, freed from requirements of time and place, but this does not accurately describe the typical interactions on many of these forums. Although groups may select a book for members to read at the same time, this is not a requirement, and many groups spring up around genres, theories, and general topics (e.g., "Zombies!," "Historical Fictionistas," "Atheists and Skeptics," "Readers Who Blog"). It appears that the groups may be most useful for helping users find like-minded readers whose activities on the site they might follow. Many groups ask new users to post a message about their favorite books or their investment in the kind of book discussed in the group, for instance. This information could be gleaned from users' profiles, but by writing messages the users discuss a much smaller set of favorites and provide at a glance a condensed justification of their selection and organization principles.

As message boards, the Groups pages do not necessarily foster an exchange of ideas among members. Many posts are essentially book reviews aimed at a more limited audience, not nearly as general as the users who would happen upon the book reviews featured on book title web pages. (The Groups pages are kept separate from the pages for each book title; the latter provide a way to access the former, as long as the group is open to all users, but no content from groups is prominently aggregated into the book title web pages. If the title happens to be referenced on posts on Groups forums, the subject lines of those messages will appear under the heading "Discuss This Book" at the very bottom of the book title web page.) The messages on the Groups pages tend to be more allusive and comparative than the book reviews, implying how others with similar reading preferences might contextualize the titles. One user, Kirsten, discussed the book *The World Is Blue* by Sylvia Earle differently in the message board of the "Green Group" (which selected that book to read together) than in her "community review." In the latter, recommending the title "for anyone interested in the ocean, or who eats fish/seafood," she wrote that Earle "really stresses the importance of helping the oceans before it's too late, giving lots of distressing facts and figures, but I think she also has a good balance of solutions and encouragement, saying we really can turn things around before it's too late." She also mentions she "has a strong background in the topic" yet finds the book's style accessible.[34] On an exchange on the Green Group, Kirsten remarks that Earle's book does contain a warning and that "gloom and doom definitely has its place, though. Obviously the oceans are being trashed and if the author were rosy about it, then people would be like 'oh look, everything's fine.' That being said, I think sometimes environmental types could use to be a little less dramatic. (I have an ES degree, I can say that from personal experience.)"[35] Here Kirsten invokes her specialization more explicitly and actually criticizes her colleagues who are too adamant about environmental dangers and alienate the general public. She cites personal experience in the forum of the Green Group to make a point about the issue and not primarily to evaluate the book. Kirsten's two reviews of *The World Is Blue* shows that the message board format of Groups uses the book title to discuss a topic that bears on an issue of concern to a select audience, here the efficacy of inspiring fear to motivate environmental consciousness among those not yet interested in activism.

CONCLUSION: THE ETHIC OF COLLECTING

The separation of Groups from "community" reviews suggests a duplication of effort, perhaps proliferating the kind of redundant content that could be mined by advertisers and search engines. Jaron Lanier, author of *You Are Not a Gadget* (2010), distrusts social networking sites because they generate information that drives on-site advertising, turning online communities into marketing opportunities.[36] Allowing groups a more exclusive space (which may be designated members-only), however, creates a barrier to the aggregation of data across the three areas of the site. These criticisms are common to any social networking site, and critics of Internet technologies and online culture have been quick to point out the unfortunate consequences of providing free services that dovetail with marketing and scatter user activity to increase the amount of information the site collects. Yet the design of Goodreads, though it may fragment the discussion in certain ways, makes the profile a record of each user's activities, making it possible to follow the circulation of information through the traces accumulated there. Goodreads provides a structure for users to orient themselves in the ongoing discussion of books that is not present when searching the entire web and following links across various sites.

Whether the overarching structure of Goodreads results in increased and enriched user engagement is debatable. Critics of new Internet technologies argue that dispersed information promotes passive browsing of websites. In *The Shallows: What the Internet Is Doing to Our Brains* (2010), Nicholas Carr claims, "The Net is, by design, an interruption system, a machine geared for dividing attention."[37] Throughout *The Shallows*, Carr compares Internet use to the reading of books; the latter for him represents deep, sustained intellectual engagement not possible in the navigation of the World Wide Web. He underlines his point by insisting that making books available on the Internet alters the way that they are read and valued: "To make a book discoverable and searchable online is also to dismember it. The cohesion of its text, the linearity of its argument or narrative as it flows through scores of pages, is sacrificed."[38] Virginia Heffernan, in her column on new media in the *New York Times Magazine*, contested Carr's assumption that "certain cultural objects [are] more compelling than others" and the very "idea that a big attention span is humankind's best moral and aesthetic asset."[39] Bayard's challenge to the privilege accorded to immersive reading by advocating knowing the gist of books and their cultural standing follows Heffernan's line of thinking. Although Carr may have a point, he unfortunately does not distinguish among types of sites on the Internet. It may not be accurate to compare a social networking site to a book, because its strengths, especially how it represents personality, rely on the nonlinear circulation of information. Also, Goodreads provides a forum to discuss books, but does not provide users with the reading material under review. It is notable that the site refers to complete books via their titles while providing a virtual platform to discuss them. That is, Goodreads promotes books as independent wholes, distinct titles on users' virtual bookshelves.

Goodreads puts into practice Bayard's theory that readers use books to talk about themselves or as a springboard for discussing related topics. His belief that "books serve to express us, but also to complete us" is compatible with a regard for the integrity and independence of book titles. The referential function of the book title serves to embrace its entire content as well as the many associations readers might make from the text, so dismemberment is not the issue. Carr seems aware of this fact when he argues that the reading of printed books gave rise to the self-conscious construction of personal identity: "The development of knowledge became an increasingly private act, with each reader creating, in his own mind, a personal synthesis of the ideas and information passed down through the writings of other thinkers. The sense of individualism is strengthened."[40] He seems to agree with Bayard about an individual's "totality of readings," only Carr envisions a more deliberate aggregation of information. A personal synthesis achieved through the encounter with discrete, whole books, he believes, makes reading a "means of personal instruction and improvement."[41] However, this "ethic of the book,"[42] which Carr finds absent on the Internet, appears tied to the presumed linearity and unity of a single title: linearity may have value in concert with the magic circle of the book collection. That is, perhaps the combination of the self-contained item (book) and the ever-expanding set (the "inner library" or the physical collection) creates the conditions and a place for personal synthesis to occur.

Because the "ethic of the book" implicates collecting practices and the overlap of object with experience, the book is not the victim of postmaterial culture, pushed out by other forms of media. Further, this suggests social networking sites can actually foster an "ethic of the book" through their collection of references to objects and experiences in the world. Perhaps Heffernan is right to question the privilege accorded to cultural forms such as the book or modes of engagement like immersive reading, because the "sense of individualism" Carr describes is possible outside the mind, represented in physical and virtual collections of all sorts, including in the set of information that comprises the social networking profile.

NOTES

1. Russell W. Belk, "Collectors and Collecting," in *Interpreting Objects and Collections*, ed. Susan M. Pearce (London: Routledge, 1994), 321.

2. Mihaly Csikszentmihalyi and Eugene Rochberg-Halton, *The Meaning of Things: Domestic Symbols and the Self* (Cambridge, UK: Cambridge University Press, 1981), 94.

3. Walter Benjamin, "Unpacking My Library," in *Illuminations*, ed. Hannah Arendt, trans. Harry Zohn (New York: Schocken, 1968), 67.

4. Susan M. Pearce, "Collecting Reconsidered," in *Interpreting Objects and Collections*, ed. Susan M. Pearce (London: Routledge, 1994), 201.

5. Pearce, "Collecting Reconsidered," 201.

6. Alex Williams, "The Word 'Curate' No Longer Belongs to the Museum Crowd," *New York Times*, 2 October 2009, http://www.nytimes.com/2009/10/04/fashion/04curate.html (accessed 21 September 2010).

7. Williams, "The Word 'Curate.'"

8. Williams, "The Word 'Curate.'"

9. Williams, "The Word 'Curate.'"

10. Rey Chow, "Fateful Attachments: On Collecting, Fidelity, and Lao She," in *Things*, ed. Bill Brown (Chicago: University of Chicago Press, 2004), 374.

11. Brenda Danet and Tamar Katriel, "No Two Alike: Play and Aesthetics in Collecting," in *Interpreting Objects and Collections*, ed. Susan M. Pearce (London: Routledge, 1994), 229.

12. Susan Stewart, *On Longing: Narratives of the Miniature, the Gigantic, the Souvenir, the Collection* (Baltimore, MD: Johns Hopkins University Press, 1984), 151.

13. Stewart, *On Longing*, 155.

14. Jose Antonio Vargas, "The Face of Facebook: Mark Zuckerberg Opens Up," *New Yorker*, 20 September 2010, 63.

15. Susan M. Pearce, *Museums, Objects, and Collections* (Washington, DC: Smithsonian Institution Press, 1992), 37.

16. Benjamin, "Unpacking My Library," 67.

17. Benjamin, "Unpacking My Library," 60.

18. Walter Benjamin, "Theses on the Philosophy of History," in *Illuminations*, ed. Hannah Arendt, trans. Harry Zohn (New York: Schocken, 1968), 253–264.

19. Benjamin, "Unpacking My Library," 61.

20. Benjamin, "Unpacking My Library," 60.

21. Benjamin, "Unpacking My Library," 62.

22. Pierre Bayard, *How to Talk About Books You Haven't Read*, trans. Jeffrey Mehlman (New York: Bloomsbury, 2007), 10–11.

23. Bayard, *How to Talk About Books*, 72–73.

24. Bayard, *How to Talk About Books*, 128.

25. Bayard, *How to Talk About Books*, 128.

26. Belk, "Collectors and Collecting," 322.

27. Benjamin, "Unpacking My Library," 60.

28. Benjamin, "Unpacking My Library," 66.

29. Belk, "Collectors and Collecting," 318.

30. "Popular Books," Goodreads, http://www.goodreads.com/book/popular?category=all &country=all&duration=m (accessed 27 October 2010). The most popular book of all time is the first book of the Harry Potter series, *Harry Potter and the Sorcerer's Stone*.

31. "*Life of Pi* by Yann Martel," Goodreads, http://www.goodreads.com/book/show/4214 .Life_of_Pi (accessed 27 October 2010). It does not appear that the "read" default shelf figures in the top-ten shelves. Interestingly, nearly 300 users tagged *Life of Pi* with "book-club," suggesting that many users read or want to discuss the title in groups.

32. "Librarian Manual," Goodreads, http://www.goodreads.com/help/librarian (accessed 22 September 2012).

33. Bayard, *How to Talk About Books*, 29.

34. "Kirsten's Review of *The World Is Blue*," http://www.goodreads.com/review/ show/124947115 (accessed 21 October 2010).

35. "*The World Is Blue* by Sylvia Earle," Green Group, Goodreads, http://www.goodreads .com/topic/show/404759-the-world-is-blue-by-sylvia-earle (accessed 11 October 2010).

36. "The hope of a thousand Silicon Valley start-ups is that firms like Facebook are capturing extremely valuable information called the 'social graph.' Using this information, an advertiser might hypothetically be able to target all members of a peer group just as they are forming their opinions about brands, habits, and so on." Jaron Lanier, *You Are Not a Gadget* (New York: Knopf, 2010), 54.

37. Nicholas Carr, *The Shallows: What the Internet Is Doing to Our Brains* (New York: W. W. Norton, 2010), 131.

38. Carr, *The Shallows*, 165.

39. Virginia Heffernan, "The Attention-Span Myth," *New York Times*, 19 November 2010, http://www.nytimes.com/2010/11/21/magazine/21FOB-medium-t.html (accessed 21 September 2012).

40. Carr, *The Shallows*, 67.

41. Carr, *The Shallows*, 62.

42. Carr, *The Shallows*, 67.

3

Searching for Cap'n Ernie's Treasure Chest: Collecting and Sharing the Lost History of Live Local Television Genres

Phillip J. Hutchison

Beginning in the early 1980s, the following scenario played out countless times in local television stations across America. The station would receive a letter or a phone call from an enthusiastic former viewer who was seeking artifacts—particularly recordings—of memorable local programming that the station featured during America's postwar years. In response, station employees almost invariably would explain that because such programs aired live, the station did not record them. If inquirers pursued the issue further, they found out that local stations did not maintain much of anything else, either. To the chagrin of both former viewers and broadcast historians, the experience of early local television was distressingly ethereal; very little of the "here today, gone today" era of live television was documented, much less archived. Thus, other than memories, almost nothing remained of the countless local entertainment programs that filled the broadcast spectrum from the late 1940s through the mid-1970s. Or so it appeared.

This situation began to change in the late 1990s, when numerous television nostalgia websites started appearing on the nascent World Wide Web. These websites not only highlighted network programming; many paid tribute to now-extinct locally hosted television genres, which included children's cartoon shows, late-night creature features, midday home fairs, and various local dance parties. Initially, because of the paucity of artifacts, early tribute websites emphasized textual accounts of these programs. Over time, however, a notable phenomenon began occurring with great consistency. As audiences engaged these virtual tributes, website visitors began sharing artifacts of this programming, most of which the fans had maintained for decades in drawers, closets, basements, and attics throughout the nation. These artifacts included thought-to-be lost photographs, an array of promotional items, and in rare cases, homemade recordings.

By sharing this personally collected material in these virtual forums, the former viewers and website hosts transformed these websites into virtual broadcast museums. As of this writing, dozens of local television tribute sites have become mainstays on the World Wide Web. Each site is a virtual gathering place that often attracts thousands of visitors annually. Even though these web-based collections are not defined by prescribed generic standards, and the website hosts rarely interact with one another, the websites reflect notable similarity in content, structure, and appearance. In addition, each website emphasizes the sort of archival material noted previously, much of which came from informal private collections. These contributors consistently describe their artifacts as very personal keepsakes, relics that sat dormant in their homes for decades, invariably surviving countless spring cleanings, and in some cases, geographic moves.

COLLECTING AND MEDIATED RITUALS

To students of collecting, this phenomenon is revealing at multiple levels. From the broadest perspective, it provides a historically situated example of how interactive media technologies can shape the nature of both what is being collected and how it is collected. In this instance, we see how electronic media technologies transformed collecting practices from private, object-oriented activities into a more social experience, one that promotes both personal identity formation and social memory. In some respects, the motivations for these collections remain consistent with those Jean Baudrillard ascribes to all collections: they displace real time and offer a fixed repository of temporal references that can be portrayed at will.[1] Yet in contrast to traditional collecting practices, these collectors were motivated by a desire to collect what in many ways is uncollectable: the ephemeral experience of early broadcast television.

Thus, we encounter a situation in which former viewers are collecting experiences more so than material objects, and the value of these experiences is constructed and maintained in a virtual world that is eminently social. To better account for social value in this context, it is useful to acknowledge that this situation represents the confluence of two phenomena: former local television viewers across the nation who, for decades, maintained informal private collections of early local television artifacts, and the collectors cum broadcast historians who create and maintain local television tribute websites as repositories for social memory. Ultimately, as website visitors supplemented their recollections by sharing long-dormant collections, they transformed the websites into repositories for collectable artifacts as well. This symbiotic relationship raises questions about the nature and motivations of each side of the equation. Most significant, how does the desire to collect the experience of these extinct television programs (both now and when they originally aired) relate to the form and experience of the contemporary tribute websites?

To effectively address these multifaceted issues, I contend that it is first necessary to better understand the ritual nature of these historical local television genres. In this regard, as broadcast historians Michael Murray and Donald Godfrey point out, "These programs produced interaction between the community and the local station long before the word 'interactive' was popular."[2] This chapter explores both how this interactivity defined these genres when they originally aired, and how it continues to motivate and shape web-based local television tribute collections. I argue that the acts of collecting local television artifacts decades ago and sharing this material via computer-mediated social sites today reflect the interplay of two key facets of ritual: incorporating and inscribing practices. These practices, as Paul Connerton explains, are vital to preserving versions of the past not only in words and images, but also through shared bodily performances in time and over time.[3] In this example, by conceptualizing these forms of collecting as ritual performance, we gain a better sense of how collecting can act as a catalyst that extends interactive rituals across time and media forms.

FROM VIRTUAL RITUALS TO VIRTUAL COLLECTIONS

As I have explained in previous research, hosted local-television genres grew out of practical realities that defined early television across America. During television's first two decades, the moment a local station activated its signal, its programmers encountered a voracious medium for which little prepackaged programming existed. Stand-alone syndication packages for television did not fully develop until the mid-1960s, and network programming covered only a small portion of the broadcast day. Thus, to fill airtime, satisfy viewers, and accommodate advertisers, early local stations modified existing radio formats and programming genres to accommodate the visual aspects of television. Eventually, what worked in one local market was adapted in others, and by the mid-1950s, hosted programming became pervasive across the nation.[4]

Although this programming was extremely popular with viewers, it generally was—and often still is—held in low regard by many broadcasters, media critics, and some scholars.[5] These pundits assail this programming for its prefabricated nature and interchangeable parts; consequently, they tend to dismiss it as trivial, overcommercialized, and generally meaningless junk-food television of the past. In addition to this institutional indifference, such historical programming, whether a hosted children's show, a creature feature, a dance party, or a home fair, shared a common technological reality. It was the ephemeral product of an electronic spectrum that in the 1950s and 1960s resisted documentation and archiving. Once these live programs left the airwaves, in many ways they vanished forever.

Many former viewers and some broadcast historians actively lament this situation. In addition to Godfrey and Murray's observations on this programming's overlooked forms of interactivity, Douglas Gomery lays out a compelling case outlining why local programming was socially significant.[6] In these respects, James W. Carey's portrayal of communication as ritual offers an instrumental framework for addressing the relationship between communication technology and culture over time. Carey argues that in contrast to merely transmitting information from a source to a receiver, a ritual involves the maintenance of society in time: "[It] is the sacred ceremony which draws persons together in fellowship and commonality." When communication is viewed as ritual, Carey contends that it no longer is viewed as a means to an end; instead, it becomes "a presentation of reality that gives to life an overall form, order, and tone."[7]

The relationship between Carey's theories and the act of collecting media artifacts becomes clearer when viewed through the prism of Connerton's theories of ritual and social memory. Connerton portrays memory and identifies formation—both of which are basic motivations for any collection—as cultural rather than individual processes. Social experience, he contends, reflects "a structure of exemplary recurrences" that is actualized through structured bodily performances of value-laden rituals. As such, he explains, social experience is realized through a rhetoric of ritual reenactment that comprises three modes of performance: calendrical (acknowledging temporal markers within a cyclical conception of time), verbal (uttering or acknowledging utterances that are special to the ritual), and gestural (embodied practices that are identifiable with the ritual). He argues that these performative modes can reflect very different forms, but that variations animate all ritual performance.[8]

Equally significant, Connerton explains that rituals can be extended in time and space through two types of prescribed social practices: incorporation and inscription. Incorporating practices extend ritual performance outside of ceremonial venues by prescribing behaviors that are associated with a ritual (e.g., handshakes or special greetings), whereas inscription "traps and holds information long after the human organism stops informing."[9] From this perspective, classic conceptions of object collecting would largely be classified as acts of inscription. Connerton acknowledges that incorporating and inscribing practices often overlap, but he seeks to fundamentally differentiate them. He does so by distinguishing the performative nature of incorporating practices with the often-mechanistic modes of inscription (e.g., recordings, photographs, written record).

Any such distinctions, however, become problematic when we examine mediated rituals, in which the nature of the physical body itself is problematic. In this regard, N. Katherine Hayles, Allucquère Rosanne Stone, and Sherry Turkle each explain how interactive communication technology acts as an electronic prosthesis of sorts; as such, it radically transforms both social interaction and the way we construct personal identity.[10] These factors blur the boundaries among ritual performance, social actors, ceremonial sites, inscription, and incorporation. Therefore, to build upon Murray and Godfrey's observation, it is important to acknowledge that television rituals—both the original broadcast iterations and their resurrected forms on the Internet—emphasized mediated interactivity in largely virtual settings. Thus, collecting and sharing artifacts of these rituals are performative acts that simultaneously serve to incorporate and inscribe the rituals. In a virtual setting, these activities help stabilize the relationship among mediated performance, material artifacts, and social experience over time.

The Programs

In this context, Connerton's assertion that everyday life represents a structure of exemplary recurrences oddly—but naturally—parallels a second-person autobiographical remark that film star Tom Hanks made in a nationally televised speech in 2008: "Time (during the 1950s and 1960s) is not told by watches or clocks, but by whatever is on TV. After Marshal J and the cartoons, you go to school."[11] Both Connerton and Hanks reference the cyclical nature of social life, but Hanks advances the concept a step further. He, in effect, alludes to the calendrical rhetorics implicit in the ritual act of watching a particular San Francisco area children's show in the 1960s. Local television tribute websites across the nation include many similar accounts from site visitors. These personal narratives consistently reflect the extent to which, in the eyes of former viewers, the programming epitomized the exemplary recurrences that defined daily life in mid-twentieth-century America. Furthermore, this programming did not merely delineate temporal experience; it engaged viewers through the full range of performative modes that Connerton describes.

Indeed, as Hanks suggests, this programming structured time, not only in the form of daily, clock-based rituals such as children's shows and home fairs, but also in weekly programming such as creature features and some music programs. In addition to viewer recollections of this factor, which I address later, the nature and form of the programs capitalized on the cyclical nature of the clock and calendar. Children's programs were tied to school schedules; they typically aired before children left for school or immediately after they returned home. Many dance parties drew older children and teenagers to the television in the late afternoon, occasionally creating conflict with younger siblings over which ritual would prevail on the family's single television receiver. Home fairs typically punctuated the late-morning or early-afternoon routines for homemakers in postwar America; the programming's mediated activities complemented—in both content and schedule—the era's domestic routine. Beginning in the mid-1950s, locally hosted creature features defined weekend late-night television rituals across the nation. Most series appeared after 10:30 PM on Friday or Saturday nights, a time when viewers (school-aged children and many adults) could stay up late, and networks offered little alternative viewing fare.

The few surviving recordings of these programs indicate that hosts routinely emphasized the cyclical, continuous nature of their respective programs. The recordings indicate that hosts of daily programs routinely acknowledged the day of the week (e.g., "Have a great weekend; I'll see you again on Monday") and often developed programs around cyclical events such as national holidays and locally significant anniversaries. Such temporal references served nicely as a bridge to the verbal and gestural performances that shaped all of these genres. As an example, Hanks's boyhood hero Marshal J always ended his programs (in both San Francisco and an earlier version in Iowa) with his thematic farewell, "Hasta Luego Vaqueros."[12] Similarly, like many children's show hosts, "Sheriff John" Rovick of KTLA in Los Angeles sang a unique theme song, "Laugh and Be Happy."[13] Creature feature hosts were known for their macabre taglines, but one sponsor-host of a memorable Midwest creature

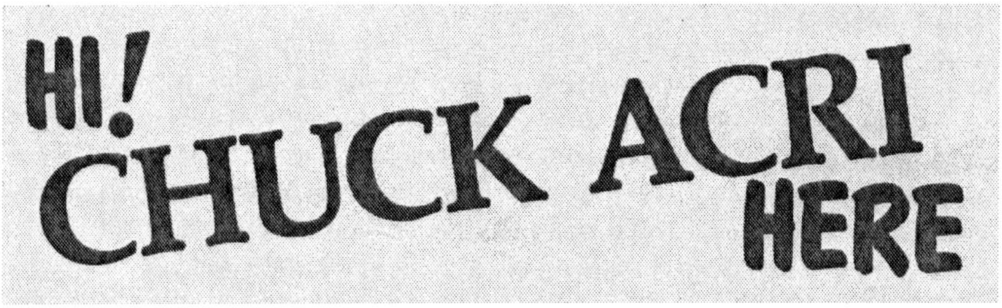

Figure 3.1. Local television hosts often developed distinctive taglines to fortify the verbal rhetorics associated with each program. This circa 1971 promotional bumper sticker not only inscribed such a tagline, it also allowed fans to incorporate program rituals by displaying—and, in this case, archiving and sharing—the ritual artifact. Image courtesy of Phillip J. Hutchison.

feature simply entered the set by calling out, "Hi, Chuck Acri Here!" (see figure 3.1). Many local programs used participative call and response rituals similar to network television's *Howdy Doody*: "What time is it kids? It's Howdy Doody time!" In addition to recognizable content, verbal rituals also reflected the affected vocal patterns that distinguished each genre: the cheery home fair host, the ghoulish or spooky creature feature host, the hyperenthusiastic children's show host, and the more-subdued, but still enthusiastic, dance party host.[14]

In many instances, verbal rituals served as segues to gestural rituals. Any viewer of the nationally franchised, but locally produced, *Bozo's Circus* series instantly recognized the performative ritual that followed the ringmaster's call, "It's time for Bozo's Grand Prize March!" Most dance parties across the nation featured some variant of special line dances or spotlight dances. Across genres, acknowledging viewer mail was perhaps the most common performative ritual. In this regard, because the programming was eminently local, it allowed for distinctly personal interaction between the host and audience members. Consequently, many viewers wrote letters to program hosts; in response, hosts structured program rituals around viewer mail. Children's show hosts often read or displayed select letters on a special board or wall; others featured write-in contests or drawings for prizes (see figure 3.2). Home fair viewers shared recipes and other domestic tips; dance parties featured assorted write-in popularity contests. Creature features, as Elena Watson documents, emphasized mail rituals perhaps more so than any other genre. These letters were often elaborate literary and artistic efforts, all of which were thematically consistent with the tone of each local program.[15]

In the context of our present focus on virtual rituals and collecting, viewer mail rituals exemplify the extent to which television itself is an early example of virtual social community and interaction. Viewer mail acted as an important bridge between material and virtual experience; it was the central venue for fostering the interactivity that defined these genres. Each time a host acknowledged a letter on air, it fortified

Figure 3.2. Mail rituals were central to the performative structure of early local television. Here Jay "Marshal J" Alexander proudly displays the thousands of viewer letters he received in response to an on-air promotion in 1963. Image courtesy of Kate Yoemans.

a bond between viewers at home and the action in the television studio. To viewers, this experience emphasized the material reality of the virtual action they were engaging through a phosphorescent window in their homes.

Yet for all the emphasis on rituals, it should be understood that broadcasters created these programs as transient vehicles for local advertising. Thus, even as a

rhetoric of reenactment shaped the experience of this programming, efforts to incorporate television rituals outside of the ceremonial site (i.e., the television studio)
were unfocused at best. Tom Hanks, for example, may have adhered to Marshal J's
deputy's code, which included prescriptions such as "a deputy is free of racial and
religious prejudices" (see figure 3.3). Or, like many Marshal J fans in both Iowa and
San Francisco, he may have ritualistically donned cowboy gear while watching the
marshal.[16] Such practices, however, stand in contrast to the sorts of incorporation
practices typically associated with face-to-face interaction. Most notably, to the extent that former viewers incorporated local television rituals, they generally did so
in a virtual setting: at home in front of a television screen. Moreover, if incorporation practices were unfocused and inchoate, inscription practices proved to be even
more neglected. Very few stations recorded or documented this programming, and
although promotional materials may have inscribed some of its rituals, no formal
mechanisms maintained this material. Ultimately, it was up to audience members to
incorporate and inscribe these television rituals, and many did just that.

The Curators

In 2004, when Rich Birley of Moline, Illinois, created captainernieshowboat.
com as a tribute to a memorable Mississippi Valley–area children's show, he shared
a common goal with the hosts of nearly all other similar websites: to reconstruct
lost popular-culture experiences that defined his childhood. Birley, like his peers,
quickly discovered that very little of the history of local television programs still
existed. He perceived the situation as a major gap in the historical record, and he
created his website to help track down sources and reconstruct as much history as
possible before sources died off—a reality that all the hosts have dealt with repeatedly
over the years. Thus, searching for Cap'n Ernie's treasure chest has both literal and
metaphorical meaning to Birley. Literally, it involves finding and preserving material artifacts from local television mainstays such as *Cap'n Ernie's Cartoon Showboat*,
a well-remembered children's show that featured several showboat "Cap'n" hosts
on Davenport, Iowa's WOC-TV (now KWQC-TV) from 1958 to 1974. In this
case, the treasure chest was a studio prop that facilitated a key interactive ritual: a
daily viewer mail drawing. Metaphorically, the treasure chest represents the treasure
of lost history associated with dozens of extinct television-based rituals. Birley in-
stinctively understood that these programs were very important to former viewers;
consequently, he sought to create a virtual gathering place that would reanimate
these hosted-program genres. Equally important, he hoped the website would help
uncover more program artifacts, particularly recordings:

> A lot of people assume that these stations had a library where they stored recordings and
> other material from these programs. They did: the dumpster. You start to realize that this
> history actually means something and are you just going to let it die? I ask myself "Am
> I the only one saving this, and if I don't who will?"[17]

This certifies that

_____

having helped the children of this community
by assisting on the "Parade of Stars Tele-
thon", is a
DEPUTY MARSHAL

Marshal "J"

MARSHAL'S CODE

1. A deputy never takes unfair advantage even of an enemy.
2. A deputy never betrays a trust.
3. A deputy always tells the truth.
4. A deputy is kind to small children, to older folks and to animals.
5. A deputy is free from racial and religious prejudice.
6. A deputy is helpful and when anyone's in trouble lends a hand.
7. A deputy is a good worker.
8. A deputy is clean about his person and in thoughts, words and deeds.
9. A deputy respects womanhood, his parents, and the laws of his country.
10. A deputy is a patriot.

Figure 3.3.   This circa 1962 promotional deputy's card outlines the incorporative practices associated with the *Marshal J Show* as it appeared on KPIX-TV in San Francisco from 1961–1964. Image courtesy of Kate Yoemans.

Across the nation, dozens of website hosts have asked themselves similar questions. Mike Ransom of Tulsa, Oklahoma, addressed such issues in 1998 when his lingering interest in *Fantastic Theater*, a 1960s Tulsa science fiction television program,
intersected with his interest in creating websites. He combined these passions to create tulsatvmemories.com, one of the largest local television tribute sites in America.[18]
Manny Interiano was a "regular" on a popular San Francisco–based program, *KPIX
Dance Party*, which aired on KPIX-TV from 1959 to 1963. In contrast to some tribute websites, Interiano'skpixdanceparty.org focuses on reconstructing the history of
a single program at a level of detail that appeals to both former regulars and viewers.
His efforts, in addition to resurrecting an array of program artifacts, have expanded
beyond the virtual world and resulted in several formal and informal *KPIXDance
Party* reunions.[19] Southern California resident John Whisler portrays himself as mad
scientist "Dr. Jitters" on his website houseofjitters.com, a tribute site that commemo-
rates local television programs Whisler watched as a youth in Illinois.[20] Russell Wells
of Birmingham, Alabama, engaged the process in reverse. He originally created his
website to feature extinct Birmingham retail enterprises, but eventually expanded the
site to emphasize Birmingham television programs.[21] In addition to these websites,
dozens of comparable, but less robust, tribute sites reflect similar objectives, content,
and presentational forms.[22]

Although the scope and tone of these websites vary, each site serves as a digital
repository for historical artifacts and social memory. In each case, the website's host
acts as a virtual museum curator who solicits, compiles, classifies, and presents
artifacts. As part of this process, each host identifies a clear hierarchy of artifacts: recordings, which preserve the experience of this programming more completely than
the other artifacts; documents (including photographs); and personal testimonies
from former viewers and program participants. Hosts actively search for artifacts,
primarily by seeking out program principals (or their surviving relatives) and re-
questing copies of any surviving career memorabilia. Birley, for example, established
a personal relationship with "Cap'n" Ernie Mims, who eventually found his original
treasure chest buried among debris in a studio basement. Occasionally, hosts find
artifacts on eBay, most of which can be purchased for less than $12.

As I have argued in previous research, it is helpful to consider these observations
in the context of Maurice Rheims's oft-cited view that "museums are the churches
of collectors."[23] Rheims's characterization seems particularly appropriate in this case,
because in many ways local television hosts presided over their television rituals with
levels of precision and enthusiasm that paralleled liturgical celebrations. Website
visitor testimonies confirm this observation. Accordingly, contemporary websites,
in addition to serving as digital archives, extend these ritual celebrations across time
and into different media forms. Thus, Russell Belk's depiction of collectors applies
to these tribute site hosts: "They participate in the process of reconstructing shared
meanings for the objects they collect."[24] In this role, the hosts act as lay ministers
of sorts; they create a space for ritual celebration and position themselves as arbiters
of sacred knowledge. They become, in effect, acolytes who preserve the respective
canons of Cap'n Ernie, Engineer Bill, Peter Hardt, or Ghoulardi.

When tribute-site hosts interact with their congregation of website visitors, they seek to preserve the essence of the original television ritual.[25] They gain some of this effect through the structure and tone of their sites, which typically emphasize the performative aspects of the historical programming. Accordingly, hosts employ thematic website graphics and navigational tools that simulate the original program ritual. Whisler, for example, highlights his Dr. Jitters persona to evoke the macabre, but tongue-in-cheek, nature of creature features (see figure 3.4). Birley greets website visitors with thematic graphics that denote a children's show, and he augments this with a .wav file blast of the original cartoon showboat *Dixie Belle*'s horn. Tulsatvmemories.com employs a simulated video interface that organizes material into "channels" that facilitate navigational graphics. Interiano serves as a virtual museum guide who, in this role, highlights his status as a program regular to take visitors behind the scenes of the program. In this capacity, he provides biographical vignettes of other regulars, insights about *KPIX Dance Party* politics, and a visit to the Arizona home of retired program host Dick Stewart.[26]

These activities synthesize incorporating and inscribing practices, and each employs web-based rituals to link contemporary collections with past rituals. At the heart of this phenomenon, websites emphasize collectible artifacts—particularly photographs—that viewers can engage for the first time in decades. "Engagement" becomes a vital principle in this context; each website emphasizes audience participation, which is realized through acts of seeing, hearing, and sharing in a virtual forum. Tribute-site hosts solicit and display audience participation through either guest books or e-mail, both of which typically feature web-based interfaces that

Figure 3.4. As part of the performative structure of tribute websites, site hosts often employ thematic graphics, personas, and navigational tools to recreate the tone of the original television rituals. Tribute site host John Whisler developed his Dr. Jitters persona to achieve this effect. Screen shot courtesy of www.houseofjitters.com.

associate visitor participation with each program's erstwhile viewer-mail rituals (e.g., Cap'n Ernie's seabag). In either case, two notable patterns stand out. Responses are thematically consistent with the nature of each program genre, and they illustrate how website collections become a catalyst for resurrecting the experience of extinct television rituals.

The Contributors

In her influential writings on collecting, Susan Stewart observes, "The collection marks the space of nexus for all narratives, the place where history is transformed into space, into property."[27] Accordingly, each of the artifacts associated with these websites, whether it sat dormant in a basement for decades or emerged as part of a tribute-website host's research, has a story behind it. For this reason, the relationship among artifacts and narratives is central to constructing meaning within all these websites, a factor that is particularly apparent when reading posted audience testimonies. These accounts vary in scope and quality, but each provides a sense of how viewers valued the original programming. Furthermore, regardless of the source or quality of the response, the accounts reflect consistent patterns of themes and content. In effect, this programming was not merely something the respondents watched during their youth; in many respects their narratives portray the programs as part of who they *were* during this distinctive era.

As a common thread, most narratives convey the great pleasure each viewer associated with the programs. For example, a website visitor expressed the emotions he felt upon finding captainernieshowboat.com: "It literally brought tears of joy to my eyes and took my breath away. The last time that happened was 24 and 26 years ago when my children were born."[28] Several kpixdanceparty.org visitors describe similar emotional reactions: "Manny, I was futzing around and googled, "KPIX Dance Party Dick Stewart," and up popped your wonderful site. I cried—I was shaking when I went through all the pictures. This site means so much to me."[29] It is common for respondents to associate both the program and the tribute websites with very personal memories:

> I remember watching the *Acri Creature Feature* with my folks. My dad would wake us up to watch it on weekends with the smell of his special frozen pizzas cooking as a treat. The nice thing was that it was family time: just the pizza, the root beer, brothers and sisters, Mom and Dad, the old zenith TV, the lights all turned off, and the shag carpet.[30]

Reflecting the virtual nature of their experiences, respondents consistently situate the television rituals in their homes. These circumstances, as many viewers explain, transformed the program into a virtual respite or a safe place where, as a respondent explains, "Captain Ernie was the one bright spot that I could always count on in my day. No matter how things went at the school I knew Ernie was there for me when I got home."[31] Moreover, viewers were keenly aware that they could interact with such local programs in their personal lives, unlike network or syndicated programming. For example, many letters emphasize the ways in which viewers personally interacted with the on-air principals in both formal promotions and chance encounters in public. In addition, viewers who lived in outlying areas still could—and often did—travel manageable distances to participate in program promotions. Even if some viewers did not meet the host in a face-to-face venue, many respondents describe their mediated interaction with the host: "I'm proud to say that one of my drawings I sent in not only made it on the show, but Captain Ernie even held it up and told the audience what a good drawing it was! I think that led to my career in photography and art."[32]

As with the Tom Hanks anecdote, viewers commonly associate these programs with the personal calendrical and clock-based rituals that structured their daily routine for years. Hundreds of children's show fans across the nation recount "running home from school" to meet with the host via television. As a rural variant, a viewer from an Illinois farm remembers arriving home from school and "hurriedly watching the *Cartoon Showboat* before doing the farm chores."[33] Similarly, distant viewers also recall the need to adjust antennas as part of their daily participation with the programming: "Many times my brother and I would take turns turning the antenna (with a set-top rotor) while the other one watched the black and white TV in an attempt to receive the best picture possible."[34] In many cases, viewers convey rituals involving food and the programs: "The *Acri Creature Feature* and a $3 pizza were a regular weekend date for me with my boyfriend when I was in high school."[35] Some of Interiano's visitors exemplify other ways that such programs index life experiences, both then and now: "It was the Summer of '59—and I was in James Denman Jr. High. I spent almost every day taking the long bus rides (1 transfer) to the Van Ness studios, in the hope—sometimes realized, and often not—of being allowed into the Inner Sanctum."[36]

To further underscore Stewart's observation, if each artifact has a story attached to it, some website visitors also attach artifacts to their stories. Such items include personal photographs of appearances on the programs (see figure 3.5) or historically revealing promotional material. The latter includes various thought-to-be-lost photo composites and 45-rpm recordings that date to the mid-1950s (see figure 3.6).[37] Also significant, although the stations and principals rarely recorded these programs prior to the late 1970s, fans occasionally made makeshift recordings by either filming their television screens or holding an audiotape recorder up to the receiver's speakers.[38] In 2006, Whisler received a response from a former *Acri Creature Feature* fan who had preserved nearly eight hours of homemade (circa 1971) audiotapes of the program:

> I taped it because it was important to me and I wanted to save it. So I kept the tapes with all the other things that were important to me a that time in my life—like yearbooks and my swimming awards. . . . Until I saw John's [Whisler's] site, I had not thought about the *Acri Creature Feature* for a long time. It brought back a lot of good memories and I thought he would like to hear the recordings too.[39]

Figure 3.5. **When former fans discover tribute websites, they occasionally share re-vealing program artifacts from their personal collections. This circa 1966 image depicts peanut gallery members interacting with "Cap'n Ernie" Mims, who is standing next to his treasure chest. Image courtesy of Richard Birley.**

Even more so than oral histories, these personal collections, all of which were as-sembled as individual acts separate from any social network or monetary concerns, attest to very personal perceptions of value. The affective content of accompanying respondent narratives often testifies to the close relationship between the artifacts and personal identity. For example, a former *KPIX Dance Party* fan forwarded photo-graphs her father had taken on the set: "I thought you might get a kick out of these pictures, circa 1960 or so. My dad was a cameraman at KPIX, so we got to sit on the sidelines of the shows" (see figure 3.7).[40] Similarly, a Marshal J fan sent me a ruler that he had signed at a promotional appearance fifty years ago (see figure 3.8). She offered a poignant account of how she waited patiently behind hundreds of children

Figure 3.6. This promotional brochure is the only known artifact to survive from *The Captain Jet Show*, which aired in the mid-1960s on KWWL-TV in Waterloo, Iowa. It emerged in response to a call for artifacts on a tribute website. Image courtesy of Richard Birley.

Figure 3.7. Internet-based tribute sites often evoke very personal memories for site visitors. In this case, a former fan enthusiastically shared a photograph of *The KPIX Dance Party* host Dick Stewart that her late father created in the early 1960s. John Shurtleff Stevens photograph courtesy of Anne Stevens.

Figure 3.8. **This composite image depicts an autographed promotional ruler that a Marshal J fan saved for five decades. Image courtesy of Phillip Hutchison.**

for the chance to meet her television hero, how she prized the ruler throughout her grade-school years, and how she kept it for five decades.[41] Even more poignant, an octogenarian mother forwarded circa-1958 photographs of Marshal J providing a special show for her terminally ill four-year-old son, who soon afterward died of leukemia: "That was one of the best days our David could have had. He so enjoyed the things Marshal J did for him, and the ride on the horse. I will never forget the kindness shown to a little boy who did not have too long to live."[42]

As a reflection of social memory that for decades had little formal outlet, the act of individually saving—and later sharing—local television artifacts provides us with a better sense of how viewers experienced local television rituals and how they valued those experiences over time. In this regard, a fifty-year-old promotional ruler can measure more than just inches and feet. It can also help us gauge the relationship among rituals, collections, and media forms that otherwise might have escaped the net of inquiry.[43]

RITUALS, NOSTALGIA, AND FATE

By design, I have tried to avoid using the word "nostalgia" to characterize these phenomena. Although nostalgic impulses clearly motivate much of what I have described, I contend that conceptualizing it primarily as nostalgia tends to paint the situation with too broad a brush. Theories of nostalgia do not adequately address the performative aspects of these collections, particularly as these factors are manifest across time and media forms. In addition, and perhaps more significant, nostalgia clearly did not motivate the original act of saving artifacts decades ago. At the time, these acts were not oriented toward the past; rather, they sought to preserve a sense of the moment so that it could endure over time. In this respect, the manner in which this material sat dormant also becomes relevant to this discussion. Dormancy, as with its biological equivalent, implies more than inactivity; it also suggests a basic vitality that can remain latent until the right conditions prevail. In this instance, these artifacts' vitality relates to their ritual (versus commercial) significance; ultimately, the combination of web-based technology and enterprising website hosts provided the conditions necessary to revitalize these long-dormant relics.

We can better conceptualize these issues, therefore, by focusing less on nostalgic motivations and more on the ritual performance implicit in acts of incorporation and inscription. This perspective gives us a clearer sense of how these collections exemplify what Paul Grainge describes as a new kind of relationship between contemporary American life and the past. This association, as Grainge contends, is manifest in "the proliferation of nostalgic modes, markets, genres, and styles that reflect a new kind of engagement with the past, a relationship based fundamentally on its cultural mediation and textual reconfiguration in the present."[44] Local television tribute websites demonstrate how computer-mediated technologies can revitalize latent media rituals and "reconfigure the textual traces of the past in new and dynamic ways."[45]

As this chapter demonstrates, these collections appeal to large audiences across the country. Yet even as these artifacts reflect great symbolic value to many people, specific artifacts reflect little commercial value. Vendors on eBay regularly feature such collectibles, but very little sells for more than $12.[46] This reality is consistent with the nature of these collections and the discussion to this point. Across the nation and across genres, audiences value these artifacts as reflectors of local rituals. In this respect, former viewers make it clear that viewers engaged these programs—and remember them now—as distinctly local experiences. They portray these experiences as every bit as local, for example, as patronizing locally owned restaurants or businesses.

The fact that almost all of these artifacts lack broad commercial appeal underscores the social value of these collections, and it foreshadows their future. Beginning from day one, when fans tucked away then-contemporary local television artifacts in closets and drawers, the value of this material has related to its ritual impact—most notably its ability to collect social experience and foster identity and social memory among baby boomers. Ultimately these collections are of little significance to those who did not engage in the original television rituals, which largely transpired between 1950 and 1975. Thus, as former viewers die off, so will the symbolic value of these collections. In fact, unless professional archivists show more interest in these amateur collections than they have to date, this material—like the television programming it seeks to commemorate—may also disappear.

Assuming, however, that professional archivists step up to the challenge and better account for these collections, this material will remain historically valuable into perpetuity. Yet because its ritual value will be gone, its appeal will be limited; these collections primarily will be of interest to professional historians of future generations. This highly specialized audience will be defined not by the rituals associated with these programs, but by a far different shared interest: a desire to better understand the exemplary recurrences that defined American life during the first generations of both television and the World Wide Web.

NOTES

1. Jean Baudrillard, "The System of Collecting," in *The Cultures of Collecting*, ed. John Elsner and Roger Cardinal (Cambridge, MA: Harvard University Press, 1994), 16–17.

2. Michael D. Murray and Donald G. Godfrey, eds., *Television in America: Local Station History from Across the Nation* (Ames: Iowa State University Press, 1997), xxiv.

3. Paul Connerton, *How Societies Remember* (New York: Cambridge University Press, 1989), 72–73.

4. Phillip J. Hutchison, "Transmitters, Antennas, and Rituals: Constructing Television Communities in Illinois, 1949–1975," *The Journal of Illinois History* 14, no. 2 (Spring 2011): 21.

5. Douglas Gomery, "Rethinking Television History," in *Television Histories: Shaping Collective Memory in the Media Age*, ed. Gary Edgerton and Peter Rollins (Lexington: University Press of Kentucky, 2001), 282–308; Neil Hickey, "Skipper Chuck and Buckskin Bill are not Feeling Very Jolly," *TV Guide*, 2 June 1973, 9–15.

6. Gomery, "Rethinking Television History."

7. James W. Carey, "A Cultural Approach to Communication," *Communication* 2, no. 2 (December 1975): 8.

8. Connerton, *How Societies Remember*, 64–65.

9. Connerton, *How Societies Remember*, 72–73.

10. N. Katherine Hayles, *How We Became Posthuman: Virtual Bodies in Cybernetics, Literature, and Informatics* (Chicago: University of Chicago Press, 1999); Allucquère Rosanne Stone, *The War of Desire and Technology at the Close of the Mechanical Age* (Cambridge, MA: MIT Press, 1995); Sherry Turkle, *Life on the Screen: Identity in the Age of the Internet* (New York: Simon & Schuster, 1995).

11. Connerton, *How Societies Remember*, 61–65; Tom Hanks, "Rock and Roll Hall of Fame Induction Remarks: The Dave Clark Five" (speech presented at the Twenty-third Annual Rock and Roll Hall of Fame Induction Ceremony, Waldorf Astoria Hotel, New York, 10 March 2008).

12. Phillip J. Hutchison, "The Lost World of Marshal J: History, Memory, and Iowa's Forgotten Broadcast Legend," *Annals of Iowa* 68 (Spring 2009): 143.

13. Tim Hollis, *Hi There, Boys and Girls! America's Local Children's TV Programs* (Jackson: University Press of Mississippi, 2001), 50–51.

14. The author formulated these observations after reviewing more than fifty commercially available kinescopes of such programming across the nation.

15. Elena M. Watson, *Television Horror Movie Hosts—68 Vampires, Mad Scientists and Other Denizens of the Late-Night Airwaves Examined and Interviewed* (Jefferson, NC: McFarland, 2000), 62. Watson points out that macabre hosts typically received macabre letters and items (some were quite vulgar), and glib, campy hosts typically received similarly themed mail.

16. Hutchison, "The Lost World," 138.

17. Richard Birley, e-mail message to author, 10 June 2007.

18. Mike Ransom, "On the Web: 'Memories' of Mazeppa," *Tulsa TV Memories*, http://tulsatvmemories.com/mazmem.html (accessed 1 September 2012).

19. Manny Interiano, e-mail message to author, 9 August 2005.

20. John Whisler, e-mail message to author, 13 April 2004.

21. Russell Wells, "Birmingham Rewound," http://www.birminghamrewound.com/about.htm (accessed 1 September 2012).

22. Good examples of other "robust" tribute sites are Ed Golick, Detroitkidsshow.com, http://www.detroitkidshow.com; and Brent Nebeker, Wallace and Ladmo, http://www.wallaceandladmo.com. Examples of smaller sites that adhere to similar principles are Christopher Gross, Sandy Becker's Page, http://www.christophergross.com/becker/becker.html; and Julian West, Axel's Treehouse, http://mnkidvid.com/twincities/wcco/axel/treehouse.html (all accessed 1 September 2012).

23. Maurice Rheims, *Art on the Market* (London: Weidenfeld and Nicolson, 1961), 26, as cited in Phillip J. Hutchison, "Magic Windows and the Serious Life: Rituals and Community in Early American Local Television," *The Journal of Broadcasting and Electronic Media* 56, no. 1 (March 2012): 29.

24. Russell W. Belk, *Collecting in a Consumer Society*, The Collecting Cultures Series (London; New York: Routledge, 1995), 55.

25. As a point of contrast, sites such as *Broadcast Pioneers of Philadelphia*, http://www.broadcastpioneers.com (accessed 1 September 2012) are formal web-based archival sites that emphasize formal historical standards more so than rituals. These types of sites, for example, do not include postings from former viewers—a staple of tribute sites.

26. Manny Interiano, *KPIX Dance Party: The Dick Stewart Show*, http://www.kpixdanceparty.org (accessed 1 September 2012).

27. Susan Stewart, *On Longing: Narratives of the Miniature, the Gigantic, the Souvenir, the Collection*, 1st paperback ed. (Durham, NC: Duke University Press, 1993), xii.

28. Gerry Marr, e-mail message to Richard Birley, 19 October, 2005. http://www.captainerniesshowboat.com/seabag.html (accessed 1 September 2012).

29. Lydia Labine, e-mail message to Manny Interiano, 1 December, 2005. http://www.kpixdanceparty.org/Memories.html (accessed 1 September 2012).

30. Todd Fosdick, e-mail message to John Whisler, 11 April, 2005. http://www.houseofjitters.com/drjittersguestbook.htm (accessed 1 September 2012).

31. Brenda Jackson, e-mail message to Richard Birley, 1 April, 2007. http://www.captainerniesshowboat.com/seabag.html (accessed 1 September 2012).

32. Steven Smith, e-mail message to Richard Birley, 22 April 2008. http://www.captainerniesshowboat.com/seabag.html (accessed 1 September, 2012).

33. Michael Homrighausen, e-mail message to Richard Birley, 16 August 2006. http://www.captainerniesshowboat.com/seabag.html (accessed 1 September, 2012).

34. Michael Starnes, e-mail message to Richard Birley, 19 September 2007. http://www.captainerniesshowboat.com/seabag.html (accessed 1 September, 2012).

35. Jean A. Greene, e-mail message to John Whisler, 23 July 2004. http://www.houseofjitters.com/drjittersguestbook.htm (accessed 1 September, 2012).

36. Sandra Sweeney, e-mail message to Manny Interiano, 9 June 2008. http://www.kpixdanceparty.org/Memories.html (accessed 1 September, 2012).

37. Both Ransom's and Birley's collections contain several examples of such promotional 45-rpm recordings.

38. Interiano, e-mail message to author. Interiano explains that the only known kinescope of the *KPIX Dance Party* is a homemade 16mm film shot of a viewer's home television screen.

39. David Epland, telephone interview with author, 4 June 2006.

40. Anne Stevens, e-mail message to Manny Interiano, 28 October 2007. http://www.kpixdanceparty.org/Memories.html (accessed 1 September, 2012).

41. Kathy Warden, correspondence to author, 12 May 2005. Letter.

42. Patricia Nievas, correspondence to author, 13 October 2005. Letter.

43. Hutchison, "The Lost World," 167.

44. Paul Grainge, "Nostalgia and Style in Retro America: Moods, Modes, and Media Recycling," *Journal of American and Comparative Cultures* 23, no. 1 (Spring 2000): 33.

45. Grainge, "Nostalgia and Style in Retro America."

46. Website hosts, who obtain a good deal of their collections from eBay, confirm this observation.

II

CHANGING RELATIONSHIPS
WITH THINGS

4

Virtual Life and the Value of Objects: Nostalgia, Distinction, and Collecting in the Twenty-First Century

David Banash

Most theories of collecting tend to emphasize one aspect of the practice and thus to focus on certain kinds of collectors and collections. For example, Susan Stewart thinks about collecting almost solely as the pursuit of a complete series. She writes, "[T]o have a representative collection is to have both the minimum and the complete number of elements for an autonomous world—a world which is both full and singular."[1] From this perspective, collecting is about trying to overcome some fundamental lack, but the only collections that really matter then are those that include a complete set—be it a unique object like an original work of art or a complete series, old master prints or the first year of *Star Wars* action figures. For some, collecting is about classification, and for these critics (John Elsner and Richard Cardinal come to mind), collecting is not so much about having the whole impossible series but about making groups of things. Elsner and Cardinal write, "and if classification is the mirror of collective humanity's thoughts and possessions, then collecting is its material embodiment."[2] Another school of thought distinguishes collecting from consumption, as Walter Benjamin does. Benjamin jokes about how extreme this imperative against use was for his own book collection for a time: "This was its militant age, when no book was allowed to enter it without the certification that I had not read it."[3] Although most theorists of collecting consider how collecting is caught up in many aspects of human life, their emphasis tends toward one or another rather fixed notions of collecting. I am no exception to this, except insofar as I am more interested in how figures of collecting and collections help us understand other practices and facts about everyday life in a world of consumerism and virtual technologies.

In this chapter, I want to concentrate on the continuum between collecting and consumerism and on the difference between practices of collecting that remove things from use and practices of consumption that destroy through use. In the most obvious example, to collect a pencil is to preserve it, whereas to use a pencil is to destroy it. However, given the rise of the virtual world, in which use is no longer tied to destruction (one's virtual music never wears out; one's word processor never needs additional ink), contemporary changes in consumption need the image of the collector to rethink the meaning of everyday objects in our lives. As I argue in the following, collecting can illuminate the figure of the contemporary consumer and our relationships to both virtual and physical objects, but to do so, it is necessary to see collecting from multiple positions, to think of it as both practice and metaphor.

THE STRUCTURE OF
COLLECTING AND CONSUMER CULTURE

To think through the relations between the practices of collecting, I begin with a semiotic square that diagrams the relationships between the contradictory pair collecting-consuming (see figure 4.1).

The left-hand point denotes pure practices of collection that exclude consumption. Noah would be the mythical figure of such a collector, seeking a complete series through total classification—two of each—and keeping them not to use but to preserve. Though Noah voyages into the future, his practice is fully about the past, as what he seeks to do is preserve from that past. The right-hand point joins together

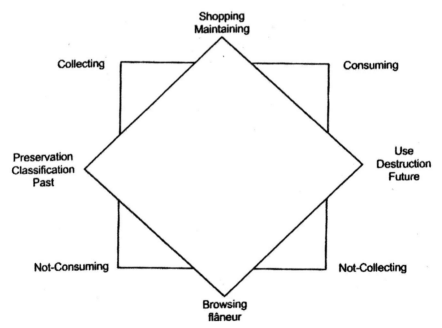

Figure 4.1. A semiotic square diagramming the collecting-consuming binary opposition. Image courtesy of David Banash.

pure consumption without collecting, that is, absolute destroying use, and here we might think of both the figure of craftsman and the glutton, taking and using what has been gathered. Neither leaves the materials behind, but each uses them up in some way. There is no imperative for preservation, although there might be some kind of transformation. Consumption is oriented toward a future, because in liquidating its objects, it must always seek more, and of course in capitalism the purchase itself is always the promise of magical, total fulfillment to come. The bottom of the square offers the figure of the flâneur, browsing through the market, seeing what is on offer, but not buying, using, or preserving those things. This practice of noncollecting/not-consuming is perhaps the most philosophical position one can adopt in consumer culture, though more likely it is the position imposed on one by poverty. Last is the figure that most interests me in this chapter, the synthesis of the collector and the consumer, and this I take to be the shopper or the consumer who attempts to maintain rather than destroy things. Shopping is not yet pure consumption, because it is the moment of moving through the store, putting things in the cart, choosing but not yet using. The shopper engages in a collecting practice by gathering together and classifying, but does so with only an eye toward use. After the point of purchase, the consumer who tries to maintain objects moves against the imperatives of consumption, acting in many ways like the collector, fetishizing and trying to hold the object. In a way, the consumer who wants to maintain seeks an impossible position, as if she or he were trying to return to that moment of selection before the inevitable, corrupting touch of use. To maintain is also to turn away from the promise of the new and hold onto a present that, in the objects of consumer culture, can only mean trying to hold onto the past, because the economy always demands a new desire for the next purchase. Recent developments in both luxury replicas of ordinary things and the appearance of virtual objects try, in different ways, to occupy the position of this impossible synthesis.

USE, PRESERVATION, AND THE QUALITY OF THINGS

There is a great paradox in our contemporary moment, for although there is ever more depth, quality, and scope available for free in the virtual world of the Internet, many everyday objects available to ordinary people at reasonable prices have become noticeably less well-made. Somehow it almost seems as if our newly found virtual abundance were being paid for by a marked impoverishment of everyday physical objects, particularly the most ordinary kinds of objects. Global mass production has undergone vast changes that have created new and unprecedented forms of consumption, particularly in the last thirty years. Not only do we use more in the economies of the global North, to use things completely and dispose of them seems more complete somehow, as if we were all being put in the position of becoming wasteful gluttons. One can still remember a world in which every city had specialty stores that existed to maintain mass-produced goods. Both mechanical and quartz movement watches could be taken to a local jeweler, who could repair any damage or malfunction. Even the smallest town had a shoemaker, ready to repair and maintain not only dress shoes but also work boots. Most towns had one or more tailors or seamstresses who could repair clothes, not just one's best items, but also quite everyday clothing. Indeed, a generation ago, women and men frequently spent time mending their own clothes, and both married and single people usually had at least one sewing kit among their possessions. Not only clothing, but also the appliances of modern life used to be repaired on a regular basis. One can see the repair of televisions in a relatively recent film like Hal Hartley's *Trust* (1990) or nostalgically evoked in the film *Pleasantville* (1998), in which Don Knotts plays a television repairman driving around with a van full of tools and tubes to tune and maintain the expensive, wood-cabineted devices of the 1950s. Today cable television companies will come and hook up a new television, but no one will come to repair one.

A watch, a television, a pair of shoes, a pair of jeans, a computer, a typewriter, and even a blender or a toaster were once expected to last through maintenance. They were made out of materials that were themselves not meant to be easily cast off. For example, a good typewriter was made out of iron and steel, and properly maintained it could last one a lifetime. There are legendary stories about the typewriters of Woody Allen and John Updike, unchanged for years despite new technologies. Novelist Cormac McCarthy's typewriter recently sold at auction for $254,500, and it is estimated that he probably banged out something like five million words in fifty years on it.[4] Meanwhile, few people could even power up a ten-year-old computer, and more and more writers, like myself, take advantage of things like Google Docs, writing and drafting in a completely virtual world mediated through any number of more cheaply made, disposable machines. Mass production has changed, particularly with the introduction of newer, lightweight, and less-expensive plastics. A typical personal printer has a life of only a few years and contains almost no metal, and the consumer is fully expected to throw it away. Maintenance is not even a question; one simply replaces it. This is true also of shoes, watches, clothes, and most appliances in everyday life. Shockingly, even buildings are conceived of as short term, and a typical fast-food franchise will often remodel not by moving to a new, more ornate building on a new site, but by destroying its current building and constructing a new building on the same site. The only thing that lasts now is the land itself. It as if a culture that used to be centered somewhere between the poles of the preserving collector and the destroying consumer has been technologically pushed closer and closer to an ideal of destruction and endless, serial consumption, described by Vance Packard in *The Waste Makers*. Packard observed how cheap manufacturing costs and the need to stimulate more sales to keep the economy humming turns into an imperative for destruction. Packard took a 1960 advertising chant for deodorant pads as the mantra and lesson of all advertising, manufacturing, and consumer culture in general: "You use it once and throw it away . . . you use it once and throw it away."[5]

While imperatives for recycling try to deal with the volume of waste and destruction in consumer culture, there are yet other emerging modes of consumption that demand the figure of the collector to understand a shift in contemporary practice. In *Zero History*, William Gibson reflects on the fate of disposable objects, particularly clothes, in everyday life. The novel follows the adventures of Hollis Henry, an ex-rock star hired by a mysterious cultural entrepreneur, Hubertus Bigend, to track down the designer of Gabriel Hounds, an obscure brand name found on some odd denim jackets, jeans, and a few other items. These clothes are difficult to find and worn only by the most cutting-edge hipsters. The jeans and jackets of Gabriel Hounds are, of course, unusual. Rather than the contemporary styles of bleached, sanded, and otherwise textured and treated denims that attempt to manufacture the simulacrum of a patina, Hollis is presented with something altogether different. The first piece of Gabriel Hounds she sees is a denim jacket, so deeply died with indigo that it borders on black and smells of the dye.[6] The brand is labeled at great expense as well, with a thick leather label that carries its unique logo.[7] Hollis takes the jacket to a specialist, who tells her that the weight of the denim is "twenty ounce" and also points out to her that its details of style and function are copied from a jacket produced in the early 1950s.[8] This last detail is the most telling, because it points out that in an age of cheap mass production, the cutting edge is no longer the future but the past. The materials, their weight, quality, and design, all look back to an era valuing higher quality in manufacturing. The jacket does not aspire to some stylish cut or designer name, as jeans have since the early 1980s; rather, its magic is that it captures the quality of the quotidian, anonymous, mass-produced, but extraordinarily high-quality work wear of the mid-twentieth century.

In addition to the nostalgia for a lost, quotidian quality, what most interests Gibson is the way that quality now becomes a marker of cultural capital by its sheer unavailability. Gabriel Hounds is a "secret brand," which distributes its wares clandestinely, at very dear prices, to select groups of customers. One cannot simply buy Gabriel Hounds, or the several actual secret brands that mostly originate in Japan. One must be chosen in some way, brought into the very cutting edge of hip by a friend or chosen by the designers. The detective plot thus fuels the suspense in Gibson's novel, but Gibson uses this suspense to say something more substantial about what global, multinational capital has done to the most ordinary of objects.

In Hollis's search for the designer of Gabriel Hounds she meets people who pick and then resell vintage, quotidian items to collectors. For instance, she finds that her jacket has come from a man who picks and sells the anonymous work wear of the twentieth century.[9] The demand for such things is itself remarkable. When Hollis does finally meet the designer and maker of Gabriel Hounds, the woman describes part of her motivation as the realization that beautiful things had been made for pennies' in the past, but to re-create them now would mean production in places like Japan. Moreover, such reproductions would have to sell for hundreds of dollars.[10]

Paradoxically, the future no longer lies before us exactly, but at least in part in a past that in some crucial ways was far more well-made then our virtual, disposable present, though the quality of that mass-produced past is now only available to an elite who possess money, information, and a desire for it, or to pickers and collectors who unearth what is left of it. The focus of Gibson's work is fashion, but I look at the same phenomena happening with another, even less remarkable quotidian object: the pencil.

DISTINCTION, NOSTALGIA, AND THE BLACKWING 602: FROM CONSUMPTION TO COLLECTING

Although pencils are still produced by the millions and are used in many contexts, both the virtual world and inexpensive plastics have altered pencil manufacture and marketing, and today the disposable plastic pen is the writing instrument of choice for most people when they are not typing on a keyboard. Thirty years ago, one could walk into a drugstore and find literally dozens of pencil brands and makes for every conceivable purpose, and at a large office supply or art store, one could find hundreds. Over the last thirty years, however, the quality of pencils one might buy at a local drugstore or office supply store has been drastically reduced as large corporations like Sanford, a subsidiary of Newell Rubbermaid, have bought up companies like Berol and Eberhard Faber. Over the years, cost-cutting measures have eliminated dozens of brands or models and significantly diminished the quality of those that remain on the market, particularly in America. Sanford's acquisition of Eberhard Faber in 1994 and Berol in 1995 brought about the demise of two storied writing instruments in American culture—the end of production for the Eberbard Faber Blackwing 602 and significantly diminished quality for the Mirado Black Warrior.[11] The sudden unavailability of the Blackwing 602 in 1998 caused many complaints from writers, artists, and designers, and it ultimately revealed both a whole professional culture dedicated to this unique instrument and a culture of collectors devoted to the history and preservation of the 602. In 1998, a single Blackwing sold at retail for 50¢, but shortly after the turn of the millennium, a single unsharpened Blackwing could bring more than $30 on eBay, and complete boxes easily fetched hundreds of dollars.

Although any pencil one buys today, even the most poorly made, will write, and usually better than most of the early pencils produced in the eighteenth and nineteenth centuries, the Blackwing provided something much more at a very affordable price. What most distinguished the Blackwing was its lead: a proprietary formulation of graphite, clay, and wax. The lead in the 602 made a strong, black line, but did so with little pressure, seeming to float over the page while nonetheless holding a point. The slogan "half the pressure, twice the speed" was foil stamped on its barrel. It was made of high-quality incense cedar that could be sharpened without splintering, and leads rarely separated from the wood. The finish on the barrel was a lustrous grey, and the quality of the lacquer gave it a luxurious texture. Most distinctively, the brass assembly that holds the eraser was shaped more like the ferrule and heel of a fine paintbrush, giving the pencil a unique profile that suggested not mere writing but the artists' brushstroke. The large, rectangular eraser could be replaced, as it was held inside the ferrule by a metal clip. Although the lead in a 602 was the basis for its success, no doubt its appearance had a tremendous charisma that appealed, particularly to writers and collectors.

The Blackwing 602 is mentioned in almost every serious scholarly work on the pencil. For example, Henry Petroski's magnificent book *The Pencil: A History of Design and Circumstance* points out that the Blackwing was the favored writing instrument of John Steinbeck and Vladamir Nabokov, and it is often considered as perhaps the best pencil ever made.[12] The definitive history of the Blackwing has been written by collector Sean Malone, who maintains a website called *The Blackwing Pages*. Malone's heavily illustrated, 6,000-word essay, "No Ordinary Pencil: A Portrait of the Eberhard Faber Blackwing 602," details the history of the 602's manufacturing, provides a catalog of writers and artists who used the pencil, and is the most complete account available of the 602's appearances in fiction and film, including *The Glenn Miller Story*, *Lord Love a Duck*, *Soylent Green*, and *Jaws*. Malone writes: "Who would have thought that something as unremarkable as a pencil could have become the object of such remarkable devotion? But the 64-year history of the Blackwing is only a footnote to a larger, more important story—one about culture, tradition, and America herself—that is sadly and rapidly becoming lost to history."[13] That sense that the culture that created the Blackwing has passed is pervasive in discussions of the pencil, and it echoes the title of Gibson's meditation on the lost quality of clothes in *Zero History*.

The Blackwing disappeared in 1998, just as the networked world came fully online, and it seemed the future was clearly digital. Initially, almost no one knew the pencil had disappeared, as the culture had largely forgotten about such a humble creation. The same thing, of course, could have been said at the time about vinyl records, which had all but ceased to have a presence in record stores by the end of the 1990s. In our contemporary moment, the ubiquitous CD and DVD will soon be gone, and vinyl, always prized by collectors, is again being produced and distributed at inflated prices for a niche market. However, although there were always collectors of CD, DVD, and any other music format one could mention, pencils are one of those objects that are almost beyond or below notice, like the work wear of the 1950s, so ordinary no one could anticipate there would be a need to collect them.

Henry Petroski observes that in his research, really early pencils were almost impossible to find. He notes that the pencil is so ubiquitous and cheap that it seems to be almost without value. Indeed, one of the virtues of a pencil is that it is destined to be used up. To use a pencil is also to destroy it, and unlike a plastic "disposable" pen, a used pencil has little more than a bit of metal, wood, rubber, and glue left, all biodegradable. When cleaning out an old desk or a trunk, the first instinct of most people is simply to discard the seemingly worthless pencils. Petroski went on a search for old pencils and found that almost no one had them. Hoping that a shop in London specializing in antique carpenter's tools might have kept the pencils that are part of the trade, he found they had not: "When asked where he keeps the pencils, the shopkeeper replies he does not think there are any about. Pencils, he admits, are often found in the toolboxes acquired by the shop, but they are thrown out with the sawdust."[14] For Petroski, this absence reveals something more:

> These stories of absence are interesting not so much because of what they say about the lowly status of the wood-cased pencil as an artifact as because of what they say about our awareness of and our attitudes toward common things, processes, events, or even ideas that appear to have little intrinsic, permanent, or special value. An object like the pencil is generally considered unremarkable, and it is taken for granted. It is taken for granted because it is abundant, inexpensive, and as familiar as speech.[15]

Like Gibson's fictional brand of jeans, Gabriel Hounds, the Blackwing, a lost object of the ordinary, is now reincarnated in an expensive, luxury version of what was once cheap and ordinary. After all the massive consolidation in the industry, Charles Berolzheimer II, descended from the family that once owned the Eagle Pencil Corporation and the American Berol pencil company, was left with California Cedar Products, primarily supplying wood to bigger manufacturers, but also producing a small line of pencils primarily for the art market under the Palomino brand name. Finding that there was such a demand for the original Blackwing, the company discovered the trademarks to the Blackwing name and slogan had lapsed, so Palomino produced two new versions of the iconic pencil: an artist version called the Palomino Blackwing, with the distinctive ferrule, fine wood, and soft graphite, and a slightly harder version in gray lacquer called the Palomino Blackwing 602, stamped with the original slogan, "half the pressure, twice the speed." In 1998 a box of twelve Eberhard Faber Blackwing 602 pencils sold for $6.00; in 2012 a box of Palomino Blackwing 602 pencils sold for $19.95. Not only has the price increased to reflect the Blackwing's status as a luxury, but it is also in part a reflection of globalization. To create the Blackwing, California Cedar sends its wood to Japan, where Japanese technicians and machines create the lead and assemble the casing, then send these back to be finished with the stamping and ferrule in the United States.[16]

NOSTALGIA AND DISTINCTION

In his chapter for this volume, Marcus Boon writes about how the meaning of a collection only becomes apparent at a moment of loss. It was not until his MP3 collection disappeared that many of its meanings became apparent. In part, what Boon has in mind here is the way we do not seem to experience our collections as the kind of hermetically sealed, fetishized, funeral monuments that the image of the collector often conjures up. Instead, as subjects of modernity, collecting objects is how much of our life practice is often organized. Boon writes, "We live increasingly in a world of sets, of collections, in which we either have access or do not, in which something is either part of the set or not."[17] Although he has in mind digital collection here—like Netflix or YouTube—this is just as true of the mass-produced objects we surround ourselves with and which we expect to be continually available as we consume them. Boon follows Walter Benjamin's insight, in part articulated in one of the most important essays on collecting ever written, "Unpacking My Library." Benjamin wrote: "But, as Hegel put it, only when it is dark does the owl of Minerva begin its flight. Only in extinction is the collector comprehended."[18] Hegel of course suggested that knowledge of the world can come only after the experience of it, that we cannot reflect on what the events of the past mean until they are in fact past, lost to us. Benjamin, writing at a moment when it seemed that private collections might all become public through a global communist revolution, argued that the meaning of the collector could only be known at this moment of transformation. However, in the English translation, the phrase "only in extinction is the collector comprehended" suggests a very different reading—that what creates collectors is extinction itself, and perhaps the extinction of the objects they use or seek. Think of it this way. People collect all sorts of objects, surrounding themselves with them, a vast gathering together of things. As they are consumed, they are replaced. Use is one way to distinguish the consumer from the collector. Yet to the extent that consumers become devoted to a particular kind of object—be it a car, a make of jeans, even a humble pencil—their consumption is also a kind of collecting, but one that unfolds serially with use. Only when the object is unavailable do consumers recognize themselves in the figure of the collector. This sudden unavailability can also drive some to not only recognize themselves in the figure of the collector but also consciously approach consumption as a collector.

To become a collector, or at least to see oneself in the image of the collector, is to engage profoundly with the past and the energies of nostalgia. The Japanese brand Buzz Rickson, another favorite of William Gibson, produces replicas of military and work wear from the mid-twentieth century at extraordinarily high prices. A single MA-1 jacket can cost more than $500. The company is fueled by a particular kind of nostalgia. On the English version of its website, it states: "We are devoted historians, dedicated to marketing a variety of historically related products and services that represent the epitome in their class worldwide." The site goes on to observe that "the goods and services we market are intended to embody and pay homage to these lost qualities of that era, consequently powerful and instantly identifiable images of WWII are synonymous with our focus."[19] The company's meticulous, historically correct reproductions are not just about the quality of the object, but about a profound relationship to the past. This is not just true of Buzz Rickson, but of the resurgence of companies offering reprints of classic and contemporary albums on 120 gram vinyl records, Blackwing pencils, and remakes of vintage clothes, particularly denim. The high-quality reproductions made by boutique companies at inflated prices are also inflated by a new relationship to the past. The analog warmth of vinyl records is a metaphor for the warmth of a lost era, just as the Palomino version of the Blackwing can be "not just a pencil" but an "experience."[20]

In *On Longing: Narratives of the Miniature, the Gigantic, the Souvenir, the Collection*, Susan Stewart distinguishes the souvenir from the collection: "The collection does not displace attention to the past; rather, the past is at the service of the collection, for whereas the souvenir lends authenticity to the past, the past lends authenticity to the collection."[21] This distinction makes clear how collectors and consumers of contemporary vintage facsimiles regard the past. For some kinds of collectors, their objects serve the role of a holy relic—something to fetishize because of an auratic connection to a particular moment in time; thus a signed first edition of a famous book, for example, is a souvenir of the author and a particular moment in the past, the very point of origin for the impact of the work. The souvenir, be it a book, a battlefield relic, or a program from a famous ballet, always signifies first and foremost that the past actually did happen, that there is a proof of it, and just as the relic of the saint was in part the confirmation that he or she had indeed lived, the souvenir is the connection to that past. Although certainly collections sometimes do function this way, for Stewart the practice of collecting is different because it creates a very different relationship to time: "In the collection, time is not something to be restored to an origin; rather, all time is made simultaneous or synchronous within the collection's world."[22] The object in the collection is validated by the past, but rather than taking us into a lost past and proving it happened, the collection makes the past available to us as "reverie."[23] Her argument is tied to the often byzantine ways that individual collectors organize and narrativize their objects. Her point, however, rings with insight into consumers of vintage facsimiles. These consumers cannot see in them proofs of the past, but only the loss of that past. In a profound way, these objects take the past and try to make a reverie, a feeling, an experience or practice from that past available to the present. In this way, the consumer acts very much like a collector, seeking the same emotional and tactile satisfactions of the collector, but insisting that things still be available to use. Of course, this reverie does not come cheap.

That pencils, vinyl records, and ubiquitous jeans—all the most quotidian of objects—become costly boutique fetishes at the very moment the virtual world offers so much for free, and that virtual technologies have significantly contributed to the use of cheaper materials and production methods, should be seen as a fully dialectical phenomenon. The virtual world of streaming music or writing on a screen approaches the paradoxical synthesis of the collector/consumer, existing in a world in which nothing need be actually consumed. One can indulge in endless use without anything wearing out. While the virtual offers seemingly eternal plenitude, more and more everyday manufactured objects become temporary, designed to last for only a brief instant. It is as if many ordinary physical objects of everyday life anticipate their own demise, seek almost to become disembodied as soon as they feel the physical touch of use. They are thrown away so quickly, and with such ease, they seem somehow less substantial, almost less real than much of the object world of the past. Paradoxically, of course, the plastic corpses of our easily disposable consumer culture are all but literally eternal, maddeningly embodied in plastic molecules that return to haunt the sea in particular, while the objects of the past were almost all biodegradable, truly temporary. Yet because we throw away so much, so thoughtlessly, there is a pervading sense that what we surround ourselves with is both cheap and temporary—in a sense, meaningless—and as such, it is sometimes difficult to invest emotionally in these objects. Does one feel about a disposable plastic printer the way Cormac McCarthy felt about his typewriter, or even the way Nabokov felt about his pencils? With the recent death of Steve Jobs, there has been a great deal of comment on the emotional appeal of Apple's design of physical objects, and yet most Apple computers and phones that are more than ten years old (or even five years old) are not functioning, not used by their owners, and certainly not proudly displayed in their homes after their usefulness is at an end. Given the rise of virtual environments and the cheapening of material everyday life objects, some consumers are turning to reproductions of a lost ordinary that supports a profoundly emotional and embodied experience, though that experience now is really the commodity being sold, and the object is, in some sense, a kind of self-conscious prop that enables it. Understanding these desires and consumer choices becomes clearer when we see their practices in the image of the collector.

NOTES

1. Susan Stewart, *On Longing: Narratives of the Miniature, the Gigantic, and Souvenir, the Collection* (Durham, NC: Duke University Press, 1993), 152.

2. John Elsner and Richard Cardinal, eds., *The Cultures of Collecting* (London: Reaktion, 1994), 2.

3. Walter Benjamin, "Unpacking My Library," in *Illuminations: Essays and Reflections*, ed. Hannah Arendt (New York: Shocken, 1968), 62.

4. Randy Kennedy, "Cormac McCarthy's Typewriter Brings $254,500 at Auction," *The Arts Beat* (blog), *New York Times*, 13 December 2009, http://artsbeat.blogs.nytimes.com/2009/12/04/cormac-mccarthys-typewriter-brings-254500-at-auction/ (accessed 31 October 2012).

5. Vance Packard, *The Waste Makers* (New York: David McKay, 1960), 54.

6. William Gibson, *Zero History* (New York: Berkley, 2010), 31.

7. Gibson, *Zero History*, 31.

8. Gibson, *Zero History*, 32.

9. Gibson, *Zero History*, 46.

10. Gibson, *Zero History*, 336.

11. Alex Taylor, "The Great Blackwing Pencil Brouhaha," *CNN Money*, 18 May 2011, http://money.cnn.com/2011/05/18/smallbusiness/blackwing_pencil_controversy.fortune/index.htm (accessed 13 October 2012).

12. Henry Petroski, *The Pencil: A History of Design and Circumstance* (New York: Knopf, 2000), 354.

13. Sean Malone, "No Ordinary Pencil: A Portrait of the Eberhard Faber Blackwing 602," *The Blackwing Pages*, http://blackwingpages.com/no-ordinary-pencil/ (accessed 13 October 2012).

14. Petroski, *The Pencil*, 4.

15. Petroski, *The Pencil*, 6.

16. Grant Christensen (California Cedar Executive), interview with author, 13 September 2012.

17. See chapter 1 in this volume, page 6.

18. Benjamin, "Unpacking My Library," 67.

19. "About Us," *History Preservation Associates*, http://www.historypreservation.com/hpassociates/aboutus.php (accessed 13 October 2012).

20. "Palomino Blackwing," Pencils.com, http://www.pencils.com/blackwing (accessed 12 October 2012).

21. Stewart, *On Longing*, 15. Stewart wants to strongly separate the souvenir and the collection, and she writes: "This difference in purpose is the reason why the scrapbook and the memory quilt must properly be seen as souvenirs rather than as collections. In apprehending such objects, we find that the whole dissolves into parts, each of which refers metonymically to a context of origin or acquisition" (152). Stewart draws her distinction too broadly here, ignoring, for example, how Walter Benjamin sees book collecting in just such metonymic terms in "Unpacking My Library." However, Stewart's insight that the collection also creates a much different kind of relationship to time is tremendously valuable.

22. Stewart, *On Longing*, 151.

23. Stewart, *On Longing*, 150.

5

Memory, Desire, and the "Good Collector" in PEZhead Culture

D. Robert DeChaine

O bliss of the collector, bliss of the man of leisure!

—Walter Benjamin, "Unpacking My Library"

"It's Mine! All Mine!" Daffy Duck chortles diabolically from my living room television, as he jealously guards a cave full of treasure from imagined claim jumpers. I chuckle at the odd familiarity of the feeling Daffy evokes in me. Suddenly, I'm swept back to my childhood and the joy of assembling my first marble collection. For me, each small glass sphere represented a kind of conquest: this one from the money earned mowing a lawn; that one acquired in a heated marble match. I vividly remember the strange anxiety, the mixture of accomplishment and pride but also the unsettling *hunger* for the yellow "aggie" my friend had but was unwilling to trade. Later, my joyful anxiety gave way to obsession as a teenager building a record collection, an obsession accompanied by the anguished realization that, barring a lottery jackpot, my collection could never be complete. And so it goes: child to teenager, teenager to adult. My Daffy-inspired play of memories leads me to marvel at the deep meaningfulness of human experience evident in our impulsive bliss and in our blissful impulse to collect.

I have often wondered what it is we are really doing when we say that we're "collecting." What kind of meaning does the practice of collecting hold for us? What's the nature of our urge to collect and of the magical life we share with our collected objects—objects often deemed trivial, childish, or even meaningless by others? In an essay titled "Unpacking My Library" in his collected volume *Illuminations*, philosopher Walter Benjamin offers us a fascinating glimpse into the world of the book collector. For him, it's a passionate world that entangles the collector and the collection together in a chaotic play of memories and desire. Sitting alone in his library for hours on end, Benjamin poetically describes a scene rife with desire and "the thrill of acquisition," a swirling ecstasy of accumulation and power.[1] He states that "for a collector—and I mean a *real collector*, a collector as he ought to be—ownership is the most intimate relationship that one can have to objects."[2] For Benjamin, power, memory, and desire intertwine in the collector's play, giving life and force to the collected objects. The passionate world of the "real collector" that Benjamin describes gives us clues about how our collecting habits are linked to our sense of self. In his view, when we are collecting, we are actually channeling memory, obsession, and desire in such a way that it contributes to our identity. In doing so, we maintain a largely private, even antipublic relation to things. In effect, we collect inwardly, by ourselves and for ourselves, reveling in our own experiences and accomplishments. I certainly remember feeling this way about my various collections from my youth—hoarding, classifying, and reclassifying the objects in the privacy of my bedroom. In my adult years, I still find myself shut away in the den ("the collection room") with my objects, most recently reveling in my latest passion: a collection of antique fountain pens.

But is collecting simply an individual pursuit, done merely for private happiness and personal gain? Are our collecting habits just a manifestation of unbridled narcissism, edification, and self-affirmation? I suggest that there is more at stake in our peculiar passion for collecting, and importantly, what our collecting practices can tell us about ourselves as social creatures. Against Benjamin's "real collector," I assert that our collecting habits also include an attention to matters of culture, social values, and self-presentation. Anthropologist James Clifford aptly draws attention to these matters in his conception of "the good collector." In his essay "On Collecting Art and Culture," Clifford argues that a good collector must be concerned not only with self-satisfaction, but also with making "good" collections—of balancing individual desire with social considerations of taste and appropriateness.[3] Moreover, appropriate social conduct calls for a pedagogical ethics of collecting, a sharing of knowledge that says something about both the collected objects and the collector. In this way, miserly passion should give way in the good collector to a passion motivated by public, not private, ends. In other words, Clifford's "good collector" has to keep Benjamin's "real collector" in check, as a matter of social propriety. I further argue that there is a fascinating and meaningful kind of play, or precarious negotiation, that brings private and public motives together. A kind of "impression management," in sociologist Erving Goffman's terms, needs to take place in the transformation of the collector from the realm of the formally private to that of the formally public.[4]

An apt illustration of the passionate play of modern collecting is seen in the culture of the "PEZhead." PEZ candy dispensers, a children's toy originating in Austria in the 1920s, became popular in the United States in 1952.[5] Though originally marketed for children as a disposable toy, PEZ has since become a rabidly collected commodity among both youths and adults in the United States and other countries, spurring a global network of collectors.[6] Self-identified as PEZheads, these collectors have fashioned a community supported by annual conventions, monthly PEZhead newsletters, and highly publicized auctions. The cult of celebrity has also brought PEZ collecting to the fore in American popular culture, with such personalities as Roseanne Barr, Jerry Seinfeld, and even the animated Marge Simpson publicly touting their PEZ dispensers. In recent years, PEZ collecting reached an unprecedented level of popularity in the United States, and the activity continues to thrive. My interviews with PEZheads reveal how they view themselves as collectors and how PEZ culture contributes to the shaping of individual and collective identities. As such, the culture of the PEZhead highlights a significant and underexplored facet of the process of identity formation.

An additional aspect regarding my motivations bears mention. Products of popular culture are routinely dismissed by scholars and critics as ephemeral and inconsequential—fleeting objects of mere entertainment to be eschewed in favor of more substantial, "serious" objects of study. Even within the purview of popular culture studies, there is often a tacit understanding that certain objects, such as books, records, films, and politicized forms of artistic production, are inherently more worthy of analysis than others. This is perhaps owing to an assumption that such objects function as archives for the transmission of cultural knowledge in a way that other objects, often disparagingly consigned to the category of "kitsch," do not. In this chapter, I take issue with such an assumption. Cultural objects, like other elements of culture, need to be considered in terms of their circulation within complex relations of production and exchange. Within such relations, no particular commodified objects are inherently or naturally privileged; their meanings and status are defined entirely on cultural terrain according to ever-shifting, affect-charged scales of valuation, which are themselves moving targets: high-low, serious-trivial, authentic-fake, and so forth. As a throwaway commodity originally designed to sell candy, PEZ dispensers evidence their implication in these shifting valuative scales to the extent that they are now taken seriously—very seriously—by their collectors. Students of collecting and collections stand to gain much by examining such "trivial" cultural objects for what they reveal about relations between people and things in advanced capitalist society.

THE PLAY OF THE GOOD COLLECTOR

What kinds of activities are involved in collecting? What operations do collectors perform upon themselves and others as they collect, and what external factors are guiding collectors' practices? In order to get at such questions, I begin by considering an enigmatic suggestion from Benjamin: "Every passion borders on the chaotic, but the collector's passion borders on the chaos of memories."[7] What does he mean by this? In part, he is trying to describe a feeling, a feeling perhaps beyond mere language, that many a collector will recognize: the passionate play of memory and desire that collected objects can incite. In his view, books become repositories for memory, each one summoning forth the specific details of its acquisition as well as the history of its former life. Within the playful "chaos of memories," collected objects can help us to remember things, to relive experiences and emotions, possibly to recapture a kind of wholeness and purity.[8] Through our collections, Benjamin suggests, we gain opportunities to unearth sedimented deposits of experience, deeply meaningful truths about ourselves.

The activity of collecting is intimately connected with the activity of remembering and the profound, "magical" desire that collecting brings into play.[9] In her introduction to Benjamin's *Illuminations*, philosopher Hannah Arendt notes that "collecting was Benjamin's central passion."[10] She suggests that the "chaos" of which Benjamin speaks is due largely to what the collected object becomes for the collector. According to Arendt, the object can't be classified in any systematic way by the collector, because once it has been collected, it takes on a new status, a powerful, new kind of authenticity or genuineness that overshadows its former use-value. Benjamin speaks of this transformation of the object as motivated by the collector's desire for completeness, which he describes as "a grand attempt to overcome the wholly irrational character of the object's mere presence at hand through its integration into a new, expressly devised historical system: the collection."[11] In and through this impulse for completeness and wholeness, the collector "levels all differences" that were formerly bestowed on the collected object; it becomes, in effect, an entirely new object, cleansed "of everything that is typical about it."[12]

Accordingly, there is something important at work in the collector's passionate chaos: a strangely empowering process of destruction and renewal. There is a point at which collectors are able to fix their objects between what they used to be and what they are about to become. Benjamin speaks of the collector's "most profound enchantment" as the ability to freeze objects within "the magic circle" of their fate as collectibles, while the ultimate "thrill of acquisition" washes over them.[13] He insists, "It is the deepest enchantment of the collector to enclose the particular item within a magic circle, where, as a last shudder runs through it (the shudder of being acquired), it turns to stone. Everything remembered, everything thought, everything conscious becomes socle, frame, pedestal, seal of his possession."[14] The collection for Benjamin represents "a new, expressly devised historical system," every object of which "for the true collector . . . becomes an encyclopedia of all knowledge of the epoch, the landscape, the industry, and the owner from which it comes."[15]

Moreover, the thrill and enchantment of collecting results from more than just a power over objects. It is also a kind of operation performed on the self. Assuming the role of devoted collector allows an individual an important avenue for gaining identity through self-definition. Through their collecting rituals, collectors are afforded a small but meaningful feeling of control over both things *and* themselves.[16] Part of this control comes about through the collector's attempt to render the collected object as near, as *present* as possible. And, as Benjamin suggests, "The true method of making things present is to represent them in our space (not to represent ourselves in their space)."[17] An important part of the passion of collecting thus takes shape as a kind of power: power to define oneself as a devoted, passionate, "real" collector, and power over the life and death of an object and its fixing in its final resting place, as a piece in a collection.

There is also, however, a less-than-cheery dimension of this power that complicates any simple formulation of a collector's identity. In an earlier essay on collecting children's books, Benjamin notes that "arrogance, loneliness [and] bitterness" constitute "the dark sides of many a highly educated and contented collector."[18] Here, he seems to suggest that there is much more to the passion at work in the "real" collector" than meets the (public) eye. Certainly, there is a tension involved in the chaos of leveling and reordering objects and in claiming one's identity. But what about these darker impulses? Undoubtedly, the real collector prides himself or herself on expertise. However, as Benjamin insists, there is more to a collector's attributes than just money or expert knowledge. Real collecting also requires "flair" and craftiness: "Property and possession belong to the tactical sphere. . . . Collectors are people with tactical instinct."[19] These qualities have also traditionally characterized the swindler, the miser, and the egotist—the individual in pursuit of selfish, material advantage.

The sum total of these impulses—the thrill of acquisition; the tactical maneuvers by which one acquires objects and the empowering ability to recontextualize them; the precarious tightrope walk between order and disorder, passion and obsession; the play of memory and desire; the arrogance, anxiety, and chaos—all of these come together in the identity of "the real collector," the term I have borrowed from Benjamin. The real collector represents the unabashed, private self—the swirl of egoism and obsession that, if allowed a public exhibition, would elicit disdain or worse. Benjamin reflects upon his private bliss as, alone, sitting among his cartons "way past midnight," he confesses his conceit for the collector, "the man of leisure":

> Of no one has less been expected, and no one has a greater sense of well-being than the man who has been able to carry on his disreputable existence in the mask of Spitzweg's "bookworm." For inside him there are spirits, or at least little genii, which have seen to it that for a collector—and I mean a *real collector*, a collector as he ought to be—ownership is the most intimate relationship that one can have to objects. Not that they come alive in him; it is he who lives in them.[20]

In this remarkable passage, Benjamin vividly describes a blissful, magical kind of power, a power realized in ownership. Indeed, for him it is this mystical, "most intimate relationship" to objects that enables the making and remaking of the self-as-collector.

By itself, however, this peculiar, magical relationship to ownership that marks the real collector must consign itself to midnight confession; it reveals too much in broad daylight. It has to be tempered, constrained, brought into balance with rules of proper social conduct, with the admirable qualities of the teacher, the curator, and the cultural historian. The real collector's motivations ultimately have to don a public face—to borrow Clifford's term, there can only be "the good collector" in culture. As Clifford argues, "The *good collector* (as opposed to the obsessive, the miser) is tasteful and reflective. . . . Accumulation unfolds in a pedagogical, edifying manner."[21] Here, Clifford brings the private face of the real collector to its limit. His view of the good collector as "reflective" speaks directly to Benjamin. He states, "Collecting appears as an art of living intimately allied with memory, with obsession, with the salvaging of order from disorder."[22] Insofar as we, the benefactors of the collector's art, are concerned, the real collector will always be—*must* always be—subsumed by the good collector. Clifford's view of the collector can be seen to combine with that of Benjamin. Together, they elaborate the precarious, contradictory forces that the collector confronts.

Clifford does more than just highlight the friction among passion, greed, and social conduct in the good collector's reflective stance. He also lays out the terms of that reflectivity: the good collector has to have "taste." But what is the nature of this taste? In his discussion of the collecting habits of children, he states that "in these small rituals we observe the channelings of obsession, an exercise in how to make the world one's own, to gather things around oneself tastefully, appropriately."[23] In other words, Clifford views part of the taste as a reflection on the individual, much in the same sense that Benjamin's real collector is able to "live" in his or her objects.

But there is another aspect of taste that Clifford also makes plain: one's culture. He adds that along with individuals' character traits, collected objects also bear the stamp of wider cultural norms, such as methods of classification, aesthetic sensibilities, moral values, and gender hierarchies.[24] In this way, the individual's taste as a collector is a reflection of the taste of the individual's culture.[25] It is here that the *play*—the precarious movement between desire and cultural appropriateness—is brought to bear on the collector. Collectors have to constantly choreograph a dance between individual desires and cultural expectations. Moreover, this play is not without rules and real stakes. As Clifford notes, "An excessive, sometimes even rapacious need to *have* is transformed into rule-governed, meaningful desire. . . . Thus the self that must possess but cannot have it all learns to select, order, classify in hierarchies—to make 'good' collections."[26] The good collector thus has to be highly skilled in the artful play, and the playful art, of negotiating cultural identity.

The overtaking of the privately motivated real collector by the publicly motivated good collector is fraught with tension. This, I assert, is largely because for the operation to be successful, it requires an intense and sustained attention to self-presentation on the part of the collector. Goffman and his dramaturgical paradigm of cultural interaction can help us to understand how this works. In his view, all of us are social actors. Our life experiences are like scenes, and our acting takes place in both "front" and "back" regions of the "stage of life," so to speak. In our particular frontstage and backstage behaviors, Goffman says, we try to maintain an appropriate orientation between ourselves and our fellow actors. Whether publicly or privately, we are constantly performing our social identities.

This "impression management," as Goffman terms it, carries with it important ethical implications. As he states, "The cultural values of an establishment will determine in detail how the participants are to feel about many matters and at the same time establish a *framework of appearances* that must be maintained, *whether or not there is feeling behind the appearances*."[27] In other words, impression management doesn't necessarily concern the "real" feelings of the performer. Rather, our morality is largely determined by how well, in our public performances, we attend to "the ethos that is to be maintained by rules of politeness and decorum."[28] As an ethical activity, impression management is concerned with a desired response, a culturally appropriate impression of the performer. With Goffman's help, we can thus see that the good collector's main goal is to publicly "act out" an appropriate view of the self. This self, if performed convincingly, will seem both knowledgeable and informative, passionate and restrained, individual and cultured, while avoiding any taint of egoism or vanity. Such a performance involves quite a complex negotiation of identity, a maneuver that implicates not just the collector but those with whom the collector interacts. Whether performed in a bedroom or in a museum, the play of the good collector is always rife with self-conscious tension.

Thus far, I have offered a rather theoretical account of the relationship between collecting and identity formation. In outlining the figure of the good collector, my aim has been to highlight some of the complexity, tension, and artful play that the collector negotiates in the movement between private and public selves. In the interviews with PEZheads that follow, I turn explicitly to the voices and behaviors of collectors themselves to more fully explore the significance of the connections between identity and collecting that I have meant to suggest.

"LET ME SHOW YOU MY FULL BODY SANTA": THE PEZHEAD AS GOOD COLLECTOR

In the collecting practices of U.S. popular culture, the PEZhead embodies many important aspects of the good collector that I have outlined. In what follows, I examine the culture of the PEZhead as I experienced it in two separate interview meetings with each of two PEZheads. My initial contact with them took place over a glass display case full of PEZ in an antique store near my residence. Both graciously agreed to separate interviews and to share their collections with me. The interviews were conducted in the individuals' homes, wherein each of their primary collections were housed.[29] Although I have attempted to remain faithful to the words and behaviors of the interviewees as I recorded and perceived them, I also think it is important to acknowledge my status as an outsider to PEZ culture. My analysis is thus necessarily subjective, colored by my particular culturally conditioned perceptions and expectations.

Barbara, age thirty-one, a librarian in Southern California's Inland Empire, greets me at her front door. "I hope I don't let you down," she laughs nervously. "Come on in and I'll show you my collection." She leads me to a den toward the back of her house. In the room, circling around each wall, are two levels of wooden shelves. Along the length of each shelf are hundreds, maybe thousands of brightly colored PEZ dispensers and PEZ-related memorabilia. I am evidently overwhelmed by the sight. "Yep, I'm a PEZhead," she smiles. Her description of a PEZhead, I learn, is "anyone who really, *really* cares about PEZ." I begin by asking her if she considers herself a hobbyist or a "serious" collector. "I'd say it's important . . . a *very* important part of my life." She notices that my eyes are wandering around the room. "Let me show you my Full Body Santa," she says, leading me to an area of a shelf containing a neat row of six or seven different variations on Santa Claus—one with a small, white head, another with more lifelike features, yet another with seemingly removable hair. "This is my favorite piece," she gleams, pointing to what appears to be a small, plastic Santa ornament. "I only paid a hundred [dollars] for him. He's one of the rarest PEZ figures, made in the fifties. See, he has a full body, not just a head. Besides the Full Body Robot, which I'll *never* find, he's the only one like it." Suddenly, she stops herself. "I'm probably boring you, eh?" she asks. I look at her, puzzled. She continues, "I used to have three of 'em, but I sold one and gave the other to my cousin. She's going to start with an awesome collection."

I ask her why she collects PEZ. Her answer seems almost rehearsed: "Because originally they're cheap, they're cute, they're small . . . . They won't break during California earthquakes. And because—how do I put this—when you collect something like *frog* figures, it's endless, but with PEZ, you always know you could have everything. Some of the different designs change from year to year or from country to country, so you'd have to be rich. But you *could* have everything—at least, just about everything. You can always complete a series." I ask her how she goes about her collecting process. "They [PEZ] always start out cheap, if you can find them. I try supermarkets first—then swap meets, yard sales. . . . The best [situation] is where you find something you never expected to find. I love going to antique stores where they [the shop owners] don't know what they have"—she stops herself—"but that doesn't happen too often these days." She states that price is a consideration for her. "I'm not one of those that will pay anything for a PEZ. There are lots [of PEZheads] like that. I won't pay more than a hundred for anything." She laughs, then adds, "At least, not at this point." When I ask her about her collection's location (in her den), she states, "I've thought about seeing if the library [where she works] would display them in a glass case, but then I think, it's not really *that* amazing a collection, you know?" I tell her I think it is. She answers, "Well, maybe the average person thinks it is." She pauses and looks down at the carpet, smiling. "I guess most people would think it's pretty amazing," she finally adds. "But you should see some other PEZ-heads' collections."

As this conversation demonstrates, the play of the "good collector" was clearly in evidence in Barbara's words and behaviors. Her demeanor was at once energetic and reflective, and she took care to catch herself, it seemed, whenever she sensed too much of the "real collector" taking over the performance. She was deliberate about demonstrating her level of expertise, but she also remained cognizant of my interests. Whenever she sensed that my eyes were drifting toward a particular part of her collection, she would walk me over to the area and either explain the dispensers' significance or make some type of qualifying remark, such as, "Oh, I got these *real* cheap," or "Some PEZheads have *way* more variations on this series." In these instances, she seemed wary of the real collector's vanity overwhelming the good collector's temperance. By qualifying herself, she thus avoided the possibility of any such appearance in her performance. Moreover, her studied, instructive tone made clear her ethical motivations: to aid the uninitiated in understanding the history and significance of PEZ as objects worthy of collection and public interest. She was not just collecting for her personal edification, but for our benefit as well.

An interesting facet of Barbara's commentary was her admission of the impossibility of acquiring a particular piece (the Full Body Robot) and her explanation of the strategy of completing series of PEZ. In these examples, she revealed another aspect of the collector's motivations: a need to have induced by a lack of completion. I have already alluded to Benjamin's discussion of the collector's passionate power over the fate of the object. Philosopher Jean Baudrillard elaborates on this point in his view that an object is generally guided by one of two functions: "[I]t can be utilized, or it can be possessed."[30] In the case of a collected object, Baudrillard asserts (following Benjamin) that the act of possession involves a collector's "abstract mastery" of the object by divesting it of its original use-value.[31] Such an emptying of use-value was evident in Barbara's answer to my question about whether she ever "used" her PEZ. Looking puzzled, she replied, "Oh, these aren't something you use—they're just to look at." Whether or not she recognized the fact that her "abstract mastery" over her PEZ is a kind of use in itself, her answer revealed something of the passionate power of the collector to reorder her objects.

Furthermore, Barbara's comment about the PEZ items she didn't have pointed toward the collector's powerful impulse toward completion. Baudrillard suggests that there is more to a collection than simply its existence as a conglomeration of accumulated objects. This "more," he says, is due to "the fact of its incompleteness, the fact that it *lacks* something."[32] Describing this lack somewhat differently, Benjamin points to the "most deeply hidden motive" for collecting, which he describes as the collector's "struggle against dispersion."[33] Driven by the desire for wholeness and completeness, in reordering and remembering the collected objects, the collector "brings together what belongs together," an operation both dogged and spurred by the knowledge of the impossibility of the complete collection: "[F]or let [the collector] discover just a single piece missing, and everything he's collected remains a patchwork."[34] Much of Barbara's wistful allusion to elusive PEZ seemed to me to indicate that she was partly motivated by a kind of longing—the anxiety and excitement of an offhanded chance discovery or a sudden PEZ windfall. Yet she seemed perfectly comfortable with the fact that her dream as a PEZhead of "having everything" should remain a dream—a perpetual "what if" to spur her on in her future PEZ adventures.[35]

I also noticed the "flair" and "craftiness" of Barbara's "real collector" peeking through at times, especially in her explanation of attempting to outwit unwary antique dealers. This was evident, for example, in her statement about shop owners who "don't know what they have," and other subsequent references to some of her amazing garage sale finds. In such instances, she was usually quick to emphasize that she wasn't out to take advantage of unsuspecting non-PEZheads, thereby demonstrating to me her "good collector" as her moral guide. Finally, Barbara's simultaneous desire and apprehension about eventually displaying her collection publicly reveals something of the good collector's anxiety about cultural performance. Barbara recognizes that the majority of viewers would consider her collection "amazing," yet she is nagged by the possibility of being unmasked by those more knowledgeable— namely, other PEZheads with bigger and better collections. She may feel that her expertise could be called into question, or that her "good" motivations—her desire to instruct the uninitiated about PEZ—may give way to an appearance of vanity. Either way, she is clearly uneasy about the prospect, even as she is driven toward the desire for her collection to become the object of public presentation.

Armed with a bit more knowledge of PEZ culture, I met with R. G., a retired businessman, originally from New York and currently a Southern California resident. When asked about his motivations for choosing to collect PEZ, he blurted out, "Because they're such lovely little creatures," pausing to look up at my expression. He continued: "It's a fun hobby, that's all. They bring back memories, you know? Jeez, if I'd kept all those [PEZ dispensers] from when I was a kid, I'd be a millionaire." He leads me to a glass cabinet in a hallway between the kitchen and living room of his home. "Here's some of my collection," he says. "I've got more in the bedroom, in cartons under the bed. Do you remember Daniel Boone?" He extracts the small, green dispenser from the glass case. "I got this one for forty bucks. He's a *floppy head* [a PEZhead term, I learn, for a PEZ dispenser which, due to wear, has lost its taut spring action], but do you know what he's worth? Two and a half, *easy*." He beams. "And this is *nothing*."

R. G. spends nearly two hours showing me his extended collection—more than eight hundred PEZ dispensers in all. He slowly and meticulously informs me about many of his pieces during the tour, including the details of their acquisition, and he occasionally stops to show me pictures of his rarer PEZ in the various illustrated price guides he owns. He prides himself on the rarity of many of his items; several, he states, are worth over $300. "You can get 'em cheap if you're willing to hustle," he states. "Each one has a unique personality and history, you know?" I ask him what he means. "Take Daniel Boone. This guy had him sitting in a box for, I don't know, twenty, thirty years. Probably owned him when he was a kid. The guy had it at a swap meet and I almost—I knew he didn't realize what he had. I felt bad, you know? So I told him, 'You know this is worth a lot.' He says, 'What'll you pay for it?' I says, 'Oh, I don't know, maybe forty.' He says, 'Sold!' Can you believe it?" He stops to check my expression. His excitement in telling me this story is obvious. I ask him if he would ever consider selling his collection. "Everything's for sale at the right price, you know what I mean?" He pauses, looking up at me: "Ahh . . . the only pieces I sell are doubles and such," he adds. "But you know, some of these are worth an *awful* lot [of money]."

I ask R. G. if he has ever displayed his collection publicly. "I would, if it was the right place. I'd be afraid that something might happen to 'em, but otherwise, I'd consider it." He gets up from his chair and asks me if I have contacted any of the PEZ listservs on the Internet. I shake my head. Suddenly, I'm whisked into another room and introduced to a (literal) world network of online PEZheads. R. G. has more than one hundred new e-mail messages from PEZheads on this day. He tells me that the majority of his buying, selling, and trading is now done on the computer. "But you know," he lowers his voice and confides solemnly, "I'd never try to take advantage of another PEZhead. We just don't do that. It gets around quick, believe me."

Besides sharing many similarities with Barbara's view of PEZ culture, this excerpt from my first interview with R. G. demonstrates something that wasn't as apparent in the former: his musings include the memories and histories of his collected objects. In relating the details of each of his PEZ, he relives the experiences of his childhood and of his artful acquisition techniques. Like Barbara, R. G. measures rarity in monetary terms for many of his PEZ. However, with R. G. another kind of value is also expressed: the value of memories and half-memories, collapsed into plastic, each candy dispenser now fixed in its black rubber display feet. R. G. has birthed something "new" here for himself—in this row of Mickey Mouse PEZ, the variations of which span forty years, but which now signify a frozen history, a "passionate abstraction," a new order.[36] On these shelves, he seems to have found a way to capture memories as they flash up and reconstitute themselves in passionate, empowering, chaotic play.

Moreover, R. G. acknowledges PEZ culture as a *community* of PEZheads. His notion of the good collector includes an ethical responsibility to fellow PEZheads, both local and global, and a shared sense of cultural propriety. His passion for collecting lives in his performance, demonstrated in his self-conscious displays of knowledge and tactical prowess, but balanced consistently by his pedagogical orientation and bolstered by his stated moral code. Similar to Barbara, R. G. was ever-cognizant of the real collector bubbling under in his discourse. Each time I would ask him a question about the size or value of his collection, he would unfailingly move the discussion toward an explanation of a particular object's historical significance or some other such diversion. The good collector is thus clearly ingrained in R. G.'s collecting practices.

CONCLUSION

In this discussion, I have argued for the significance of the activity of collecting and tried to describe something of the complex and precarious operations at play in the identity of the collector. Along the way, I have left certain questions incomplete or unaddressed, questions that warrant further study. For example, in light of my study's admittedly limited scope, to what extent can the play between the real collector and the good collector that I have identified in PEZ culture be seen to operate within or across other collecting cultures? How might issues of gender and socioeconomic class bear upon collectors' identity constructions and identity performances, and how might the good collector translate across such registers? Also, how does the globalization of PEZ culture shape the online discourse of the PEZhead, and what aspects of public presentation remain important in such mediated exchanges?

Answers to these and other questions could clarify and extend the points I have
raised, and with more development, they might lead to the construction of an analytical framework that could be applied to a variety of collecting cultures.

I hope I have succeeded in illuminating the culture of collecting and its relationship to individual and collective cultural identity. I have also meant, in a not-so-
direct way, to suggest the value in considering the idea of play as an important way
of understanding human symbolic activity. The concept of play is rarely treated as
an object of critical inquiry, in large part because it is usually regarded as concerning
things "not serious in nature."[37] However, play is involved in some of the most fundamental, and fundamentally human, aspects of our lives. In the culture of collecting, identity comes about through a play of memory and desire and a play between
identity and self-presentation. Indeed, it is by way of the vitality, art, and seriousness
of play that the social dimensions of the self converge.

Above all, it is the passion of the collector that remains with me as I revisit my
PEZ adventures. I witnessed in the culture of the PEZhead a sense of the bliss to
which Benjamin's own passion gave poetic voice. In his "Theses on the Philosophy
of History," he provocatively states, "The awareness that they are about to make the
continuum of history explode is characteristic of the revolutionary classes at the moment of their action."[38] Perhaps it's not too far-fetched to suggest that the collector
represents something of this revolutionary figure: poised at the brink of the past and
the future, the maker of a new order, undoubtedly awake into the wee hours, and
resplendent in the chaos of memories.

NOTES

1. Walter Benjamin, *Illuminations*, trans. Harry Zohn, ed. Hannah Arendt (New York:
Schocken Books, 1968), 60.

2. Benjamin, *Illuminations*, 67 (emphasis added).

3. James Clifford, *The Predicament of Culture* (Cambridge, MA: Harvard University Press,
1988), 215–251.

4. See, for example, Erving Goffman, *The Presentation of Self in Everyday Life* (Garden
City, NY: Doubleday Anchor Books, 1959); and Susan M. Pearce, *Museums, Objects, and
Collections: A Cultural Study* (Washington, DC: Smithsonian Institution Press, 1992). For
Goffman, the arts of impression management include "defensive attributes and practices,"
"dramaturgical discipline," and "dramaturgical circumspection" (208–237). Pearce argues that
the transformation from the private to the public is an important dimension of collection
making, and that "provided that a collection remains stable and reaches a relatively substantial
size (itself a highly subjective judgment), it is likely to find itself eventually in some sort of a
museum context" (37). I take this "museum context" to generally signify a public exhibition
of some kind.

5. David Welch, *Collecting PEZ* (Murphysboro, IL: Bubba Scrubba, 1994); Richard Geary,
PEZ Collectibles (Atglen, PA: Schiffer, 1994).

6. David Streitfeld, "Dispenser of Instant Treasures," *Los Angeles Times*, 22 November 2001, A1.

7. Benjamin, *Illuminations*, 60.

8. Naomi Schor, "Collecting Paris," in *The Cultures of Collecting*, ed. John Elsner and Roger Cardinal (Cambridge, MA: Harvard University Press, 1994). Schor suggests that books for Benjamin function as "a form of psychotherapy . . . a means of re-membering his fragmented past, of re-collecting a lost maternal presence, the plenitude of childhood" (253).

9. Walter Benjamin, *The Arcades Project*, trans. Howard Eiland and Kevin McLaughlin (Cambridge, MA: Harvard University Press, 1999), 205; Schor, "Collecting Paris," 254.

10. Hannah Arendt, quoted in Benjamin, *Illuminations*, 39.

11. Benjamin, *The Arcades Project*, 205.

12. Benjamin, *Illuminations*, 45.

13. Benjamin, *Illuminations*, 60.

14. Benjamin, *The Arcades Project*, 205.

15. Benjamin, *The Arcades Project*, 205.

16. Pearce, *Museums, Objects, and Collections*, 56.

17. Benjamin, *The Arcades Project*, 206.

18. Benjamin, *The Arcades Project*, 406.

19. Benjamin, *Illuminations*, 63.

20. Benjamin, *Illuminations*, 67 (emphasis added).

21. Clifford, *The Predicament of Culture*, 219 (emphasis added).

22. Clifford, *The Predicament of Culture*, 219f.

23. Clifford, *The Predicament of Culture*, 218.

24. Clifford, *The Predicament of Culture*, 218.

25. Clifford, *The Predicament of Culture*, 218.

26. Clifford, *The Predicament of Culture*, 218 (emphasis in original).

27. Goffman, *The Presentation of Self in Everyday Life*, 241–242, (emphasis added).

28. Goffman, *The Presentations of Self in Everyday Life*, 238.

29. Each interviewee had additional pieces of his or her collection stored elsewhere; in some instances, the pieces were duplicates or "trades"; in other cases, the items were too delicate or awkward to display.

30. Jean Baudrillard, "The System of Collecting," in *The Cultures of Collecting*, ed. John Elsner and Roger Cardinal (Cambridge, MA: Harvard University Press, 1994), 8.

31. Baudrillard, "The System of Collecting," 8.

32. Baudrillard, "The System of Collecting," 23 (emphasis in original).

33. Benjamin, *The Arcades Project*, 211.

34. Benjamin, *The Arcades Project*, 211.

35. It should be noted that the reality of contemporary PEZ collecting makes it virtually impossible to "have everything." Streitfeld states that as a result of cross-promotions and licensing agreements for PEZ-related merchandise, the actual number of PEZ item variations is now unknown. Adding to the confusion, Streitfeld notes that PEZ Candy Inc. "is now selling its own 'instant collectibles,'" and whereas PEZheads "used to eagerly search for one-of-a-kind factory freaks [such] as a snowman with a yellow face, PEZ Candy now intentionally makes misfits" (A1).

36. Baudrillard, "The System of Collecting."

37. Notable exceptions include Johan Huizinga, *Homo Ludens: A Study of the Play Element in Culture* (Boston: Beacon Press, 1950); Roger Caillois, *Man, Play, and Games*, trans. Meyer Barash (New York: Free Press, 1961); Victor Turner, *From Ritual to Theatre: The Human Seriousness of Play* (New York: PAJ, 1982); and Mihai I. Spariosu, *Dionysus Reborn: Play and the Aesthetic Dimension in Modern Philosophical and Scientific Discourse* (Ithaca, NY: Cornell University Press, 1989).

38. Benjamin, *Illuminations*, 261.

6

Suited for Nothing: Collecting Secondhand

William Davies King

Part of any collecting is learning—about the things of the world, those profligate things, and about oneself as an acquirer, that prodigal self.[1] The vast amount eventually known by the self-taught collector sits oddly within the triviality of the category (e.g., advertisements for Coca-Cola, Smith and Wesson pistols, Indian head nickels). No one else knows as much about bankrupted manufacturers or perforations or memorable typos, and practically no one else would want to. The collector's knowing also often conceals a neurotic blindness, because collectors will not see the silliness of their enterprise, or its ill effect upon others, or the sheer wastefulness of the effort to explain that this growing pile is not some hoard or folly, when it is. Knowing sits amid not-worth-knowing, erudition amid self-delusion, paradoxes piled. Still, the knowing grows along with the collection, and so most narratives of collecting take the form of *Bildungsroman*, with lessons along the way and enlightenment always horizontal, somewhere out there, a day's sail off.

This chapter traces several episodes of my pilgrimage toward the place where I might enter collecting as a proper field of study. It seems that ought to matter for an academic who collects something, if only those things I call nothing. I begin with my life.

Sunday morning, 2002, and it's exceptionally clear for springtime, at 11:37 AM. I am driving on Modoc Road in Santa Barbara, heading home, when I spy the usual sort of hand-lettered, cardboard sign: "ESTATE SALE / Hope Ranch / Saturday 8 to 5 / Sunday 8 to 12." Estate sales are something other—and better—than yard, garage, rummage, tag, or moving sales, because you know that death will be there, browsing by your side. Estates might be grand or tiny, but in estatehood possession comes to an end, and every object makes a sad memorial, even at Hope Ranch, which is a seaside neighborhood where the local lords and ladies reside.

I recollect the precise time I saw the sign, because I had to make a keen calculation whether I would be able to find the house and make any sort of practical survey before the sale closed in twenty-two minutes. Time was flying, the sale itself was dying, and I was not getting any younger, so I made an unforeseen turn.

At the closing bell of such a sale, when the cash box snaps shut, the collectors, the curious, the needy, the traders, and the odd crook have all moved on, and a crew of thirdhand merchandisers might appear to perform the final sift. Some will name a figure, lowball, to clean up the remainder, lock, stock, and barrel, whereas others might brazenly offer to seize the lingering mess for a fee. Either option might seem like a bargain to the holder of an estate's remains, who would otherwise need to carry out the disposal. A last-minute broker will use his or her wits to turn the minimally valuable into the minimally profitable. At the end of the day, the house stands stripped of all remaining goods, and soon it will go on the market, looking spiffed and spanned, with a fresh coat of interior latex to cover the marginal fades where the souvenirs and diplomas used to hang, and with a brand new doormat laid on the stoop by the hopeful realtor: "Welcome to your new and capacious, second-hand home."

What remains in the last nineteen minutes of an estate sale, just before that final flush, is impossible to predict, yet when you see the stuff, it looks like "of course": Christmas crap and dried-up craft supplies and jigsaw puzzles that seem to want one piece; chipped dish, bent fork, recipe book for yesterday's crockpot; K-Tel albums, *You've Got Mail*, the Readers Indigestible effluent slowly circling over a clogged-up drain. As I entered this house, I saw the standard dank et cetera. But that's okay. I can easily be a catfish, finding nutrients in the murk. Even so, this sale did not look promising, though the living room commanded a Pacific view. The books had been culled, leaving just the Clive Cussler paperbacks and Time-Life volumes on a world minus time or life. All that was left of the household art were empty Aaron Brothers frames and dusty prints of the man of La Mancha. The kitchen offered unrelated tableware and bakeware and Tupperware and chippers and choppers from late-night UHF.

Still, some hunch had led me here, and therefore I pressed my hunt into what I deem the least bountiful quarter of any house turned inside out, the bedroom. Hanging in the window was the full dress uniform of a decorated officer of the Army Corps of Engineers, which is quite a sight, full of angles and brass, an unsold point of pride, but it held no power over me. Why was I here? I felt like one of those dogs trained to sniff out corpses in the ruins, yet I was smelling nothing but—nothing but corpses or nothing but nothing, I could not tell.

Then, as the noon hour struck, I glanced into the closet and saw a rack of neatly pressed suits. Opening the jackets, I noticed from the labels that many had been hand-tailored for Colonel Charles H. Unger, whose name had been sewn into the lining. Dark blue pinstripe, brown worsted, gray seersucker, baby blue linen, heavyweight charcoal wool: a small universe of haberdashery clung to wooden hangers in midday shadow.

I have to tell you that I have only rarely worn a suit, but the closer I looked at these suits, the more I felt some strange call, to the degree that I had to take one into the bathroom and try it on.

It fit.

Perfectly.

The pants, the vest, the jacket enfolded me as if some Hong Kong tailor had jotted down my measurements by mistake.

But the sale was just then closing down, and I hate to make a purchase in haste. I don't like to make a purchase at all. So, without even inquiring, after replacing the suit on its hanger, the hanger in the closet, I returned to my Civic and drove home, with nothing. Perhaps it was the hint of sweatshop in the labels of those Chinese tailors. Something put me off. If only Colonel Unger had been not in the Army Corps of Engineers but in the Arty Corps of Bricoleurs, then perhaps I might have seen that an exact fit was destined for me. After all, the root of the word "art" is the same as the root of the words "army" and "armor," a Greek verb meaning "to fit." The first artist might have been the armorer. Art is always on some level about something that fits so rightly that it makes you superhuman, shielding you from the dangers of war, while also enabling you to attack when necessary. Art suits dominance.

Through that Sunday afternoon and evening, my thoughts kept returning to the suits and the possibility of my *putting on the colonel*, because he fit so well. Had I ever worn *any* article of clothing that truly fit? Would it be possible, in some deep sense, for me to become a civil engineer?

So, that evening I drove back to the house, which was now entirely dark and emptier than it had been in decades. I taped a note to the door to declare an interest in the suits. The next morning I received a call from the dead man's daughter, who was touched by my story of finding the fit, or perhaps she was just relieved that she need not consign her father's suits to oblivion. She sold them to me for two dollars apiece, and I took twelve. Since then, I have had a colonel in my closet, and I bring him out on certain occasions when I want to believe what I am building is strong. He is the latent engineer in me, and now on me. I got remarried in him. Ten years later, I'm still wearing the colonel, though it has been a challenge to keep what fit me perfectly then, fitting me perfectly still.

For many collectors, the long-term experience of collecting feels like a growing into, and growing out of, objects. It is a developmental process, and the goal is a fully realized self, except the self can be cataloged and counted and looked up in a price guide. The ethical principles of collecting are clear up to a point: "More is better" until the county health inspector comes to call, and "only the best" works fine until PayPal cancels your account. Most collectors can tell cautionary stories of collectors gone wild, while offering advice on how they have managed to keep collecting sustainable. First-person narratives of collecting are filled with that sort of wary moralizing. A good example of this is Kim Hertzinger's 1996 memoir-essay on collecting in the *Mississippi Review*, in which he shows how a collection is often an example of wisdom once removed from normality but trained to material limits.

Ownership is always tangential to the shape of life, but we learn a lot by those rays. My day at the estate sale had enabled me to slip into a new relation to ownership, one that suited me oddly well.

We all, even the least fashion-conscious, have the problem of what to wear—how to suit ourselves. The word "suit" comes from a Latin verb meaning "to follow." The primary connotation of the word is that the various pieces of a suit all follow, or match, each other. But there is a secondary connotation. Those who followed a commander or a lord or lady—the retinue—would wear clothing selected by the one up front, maybe even clothing handed down. This is the basic sense of the servant's livery, the allowed or "liberated" garment, now worn by the subordinate to complement the new suit worn by the master, who himself is dressing to follow some leader or leading idea. A suit, or suite, expresses an ensemble with a master, a union of different elements, like a set of dances all set in the same key, or like the thirteen hierarchical elements in a deck of cards, all disciples who follow the ace, which both follows and is followed.

When the modern business suit began its rise, in nineteenth-century Western Europe, it obscured rather than clarified the wearer's association with any particular occupation. Wearing a suit still signified you were in retinue, but the master you followed, in basic black or flannel grey, was depersonalized, not a lord but the corporate or professional exponent of capitalist enterprise. A suit was anonymous, discrete, a shield for privacy, but complicit. Groucho Marx once defined the closet as the place "where men are empty overcoats," but the modern suit is itself a closet, where men are empty men, especially so when the man is six feet under, or the man is less than six feet tall. A man might finger the seams of his two-buck Chuck as if his life depended on it. What follows a suit into its afterlife? Does the suit miss Colonel Charles H. Unger, whom it fit, when it finds itself fitting me, whom it misses by a mile?

Hand-me-down clothes usually do not fit well, or else why would secondhand Rose lament? Secondhand does not suit, but every suit implies a follower, whether it be Armani or Salvation Army. Someone puts it on and walks the walk. But a suit might seem like a wrong choice, and there is little freedom in comme il faut. If you don't have the knack to make yourself new, then the world is one large estate sale, and the closets hold nothing but suits.

The zoot suit, as I have heard, is a style based on a way of wearing used clothing. The jacket hangs low and loose, the pants billow except where they are rehemmed at the ankle, because these garments were scooped from the floor and refitted to new and smaller owners. As the Roaring Twenties ended with depression, extravagant clothing flooded the secondhand market or the trash. A domestic servant swept Gatsby's cast-off gabardine back to Harlem, pinned the cuffs, and on his day off styled it at the jazz club. August Wilson's 1990 play, *The Piano Lesson*, set in 1930s Pittsburgh, has a scene showing an aging zoot suiter selling his used suit down the line to a young man just up from the share-cropping South, but the price seems right to the young man, who has just helped sell a truckload of watermelons. It's two dollars. How does it feel to wear a suit worth two dollars? I ought to know.

Eugene O'Neill's *The Iceman Cometh*, set in 1912, brings us a desperately unhappy Willie Oban who has pawned his last suit for just two dollars, and now he wears rags. His father was a phony stockbroker who came to disgrace, and now the son bears his family's guilt to the bottom of a bottle. In all sorts of ways, two dollars seems like a rock-bottom world, but it's the foundation on which a collector of nothing might stand.

In all sorts of ways, shunning my image in the mirror, I have attempted to elude the peril of dressing right, and I have also attempted to elude the peril of dressing left, as in left over. Being "vintage" seems just as fraught with mixed messages as being Brooks Brother. When I wake in the morning, I am naked and need covering, but then I wish I could cover the clothing, which is also naked and so revealing of my choice. I would' like to cover my clothing with other clothing, over and over, until there would be nothing to see, nothing at all. I'd be a ball of self-containment. That's theory. In practice, I do not haunt thrift stores or jumble sales to find my clothing. I typically buy those utilitarian things new that will most quickly look used, my own hand-me-downs, so that I follow only me.

Lately, however, I have taken to bringing things out of my drawers and closets, much more than clothing and much less, a glut of things I choose to call nothing, my nadaism. My collections of nothing have filled a book, from the inside out, with some kind of desperate void in me, an awful aching gulf, in the form of tens of thousands of product labels and envelope linings and Place Stamp Here squares—all confessed, if not absolved. It might be obvious that I am more a case study of the second handler than a principal investigator. I second handle because I collect. But I am insistently a collector of nothing, by which I mean things of no value, hence not collectible, except that I do collect things in profusion and attribute some value, if only in the negative. In this way, I often operate below the level of the secondhand. The notion of resale rarely arises in the accumulation of my things. It is unlikely ever to arise in their future dispersal. What I know, though, is the dirty flux of the recycle, which is an important aspect of secondhand culture: how you need to wash your hands frequently, pinch your nose, spread some newspaper on the floor.

What I can offer is a perspective on soil, stain, wear, degradation, and other phenomena of the lower realm, in contrast to the mint, the pristine, what most people associate with the collectible. The dirt to be encountered also includes the messiness of obsession, dust bunnies of neurosis, stinking pits of maladjustment. The psychotherapist, carrying a mop and a bucket, descends to the lower decks, in search of bilge water. It turns out that there is a lot of art down there, too, albeit in less-than-sanitary frames. Maybe that primitive anxiety about being well-armed for combat is where we need to go to understand collecting.

My collectibles are not of general interest, but my hope in writing the book *Collections of Nothing* was that a common ground with readers could be found in a feeling about living in the modern world, a world where feelings of anxiety, loss, and uncertainty might be allayed, if only temporarily, by the experience of ownership—times one hundred or one thousand or ten thousand.[2] I figured that collectors, at any rate, should get the gist of what I was struggling with. Collecting performs a partially irrational, overdetermined response to the experience of emptiness, and my particular pattern of response fixes on what I call nothingness as a useful term for that emptiness. In the process and in the product, I have found that even noncollectors, who might nevertheless have a sense of that emptiness, recognize something familiar in the book and in the phenomenon of compulsive ownership. At any rate, many people seem to find in my story an analogue for having some strange way of life prove suitable. When collecting fits, you put it on, whether it costs two dollars or two hundred or two million for each item. The irrational largely prevails and envelops, providing uncertain warmth but a little concealment and protection.

There are better and worse narratives one can spin out about one's collecting, about any collecting, about any life holding. Having three eyes seems monstrous, and yet having two seems far preferable to having one. What is the natural logic of having? In a way, "to have" is a reflexive verb. Having should fit the haver. I have (myself) a suit. You have (yourself) an author of an essay about collecting. Having expresses a suitability, and so your author is suited, albeit secondhand, but we are all secondhand at our best, even when we think we're new, especially in academia. The whole concept of "the new" begs for deconstruction. Isn't the new always already the secondhand? Aren't we, as humanists, constantly zoot suiting the discourse?

With a little bit of art, the discarded garments of power can be taken up or refitted as a revolution in the humanities, but the garb we take up is always the same old empty suit, the emptiness of suitability. "Secondhand culture" is a redundancy, because culture always was and always is derived. The notion of primacy—the firsthand, so to speak—is what comes late, and then only as an illusion or delusion, a fiction to be bought and sold. Someone noble, someone in power, someone famous, sets the fashion. How? By acquiring a suit of clothes, which have been designed to look new or even novel. The clothes have been afforded and commissioned and produced, and the wearer sets a trend for others to follow, which helps to solidify a structure of power in the society. However, the clothing goes back to the age-old task of clothing, which is to warm and conceal this needy human being whose power to define the firsthand is largely secondhand—reused and becoming worn. The truly shocking story is not that the emperor has no clothes, but that the emperor consists of nothing more than clothes, all used. This is exactly the point made by Eugene O'Neill's *The Emperor Jones*, in which Brutus Jones strips down to the very essence of nobody. The royal crown is a hand-me-down. For eons, surely, the furs, the headdresses, the ceremonial robes and leggings and boots were passed down—the best to the most worthy or the most powerful, until an era of advanced manufacturing led to the exaltation of the new, and the new was always even then on some level a disguised copy of the inherited robe of authority or distinction. The "new" is as potent an illusion as the "supreme." What is basic is that the human body is unsuited to its nakedness; clothing is required to shield its shameful inadequacy. Fanciness is a strenuous attempt to distract from that lack.

But then there is the corollary effect: the body is a producer of dirtiness and degradation, and the clothing—whether first- or secondhand—will inevitably become stained and soiled and threadbare by use. Cleaning and mending will cope with this condition up to a point, but at last all clothing will disclose the fact of human degradation. Evolution seems to have made human beings less, not more, fit for survival in this regard. As infants, we depend on someone else wrapping us in a fur or blanket and then coping with the fact that we will predictably soil and stain those garments. Shame will always stem from certain parts, and so it is efficacious to mask those parts just until it is mandatory to uncover and clean them. Stink will always seep from certain regions, and we wear clothing in part to contain that vile body. The human needs to be scoured out of us—or it will reek.

Several years ago, I acquired a red sweatshirt, which was left behind in my office by some soon-forgotten student, who also forgot where the sweatshirt had been left. A month or so later I deemed it a windfall and brought it home. It seemed clean, or perhaps I washed it, I can't recall, but I began wearing it now and then. It was acceptable to me. I wore it one winter morning when my wife and I went jogging with our dog at a local park. We make four circuits around this dog-friendly park, and often, after the first or second lap, by the time the dog has done his business, I feel warm enough to leave my sweatshirt on a sign post, expecting to retrieve it later. One day, at the end of the run, I found the shirt was gone, and all I could do was return home without it.

Now, I know my own smell—exercise draws it out, and it's made of toxins and bacteria and various exudations—and I know for certain that the sweatshirt bore a strong trace of my sweating out, which is what "exudation" literally means. This someone had considered the sweatshirt loose property and carried it away, much as I had done. Perhaps he put it on, being cold, or perhaps he planned to wash it first, but for some period of time, wearing it or transporting it home in his truck, then his car, this man had to endure my exudations, heavy and ripe. I could not help but mark the garment with my odor, and he could not help but nose it—me.

Two weeks later, jogging in the same park, I noticed a park employee, a man who picks up the plastic bags of dog poop that someone has forgotten to retrieve, and he's wearing "my" red sweatshirt. I know this for a fact, though it would never stand up in court. Twice, as I circled the park, exuding into different sweatshirt fibers, navy blue, I saw my bright red sweatshirt absorbing the sweat of his exertions. Then he was gone, and I went home to shower. I could not have demanded that he give it back, because it really wasn't mine, except for the sweat, and it really wasn't his, except for the sweat, and it really wasn't the student's, except for the sweatshop, but the student lost track, while this man was on the job, and I was only jogging, so I let it be. His ability to overcome some squeamishness about my sweat and about the possibility that his appropriation might be a form of stealing resulted in his seizure of a secondhand good—actually thirdhand, since I myself had overcome the same squeamishness when I took the sweatshirt in the first place. However, even the purchaser of a new sweatshirt has to overcome a certain squeamishness about sweat, the work that will be necessary to earn the money for the purchase and also the child labor already pumped into the shirt.

In Isla Vista, the student community abutting UCSB, there is an open bin where people deposit used clothing and other people retrieve it. In effect, the bin is a kind of inverted sifter. The clothing that retains some trace of the illusion of the new passes into the hands of a new owner, who will try to sustain that illusion. Doubtful garments will remain near the surface, churned repeatedly by the picking hands, while down below the truly questionable clothing settles, hardening like leaves on the forest floor. My red sweatshirt rode that sort of secondhand surf for a while before settling into silt. Finally, the human drags everything down to death, despite the collector's valiant effort to give a used object new life. Eventually, though, the rookie card, the first folio, even the 1944-S steel cent will decompose, just like the successive collectors who possessed them. From one collector, fallen, grows a new one, like a zombie, and the message is not that of Lazarus ("There is no death"). There is only death, and the collectible is a sandstone monument.

Cultural forms grow around these ironies: rummage sales, thrift stores, pawn shops, dumpster-diving. So, it seems, "used" is the new "new," as certain used car dealers have long been declaring. Where there is use there is the used, so only in the useless do we find the new. This is the perverse corollary I set out to explore in my collections of nothing—both the book and the objects themselves.

Being something to somebody. Being somebody to something. Those are expressions of existence—being—in a material world, when being is always already derived from a material relation. Being *some*thing to *some*body. Being some*body* to some*thing*. You can hear in these terms, especially in the "some," the secondhand. I'm not saying "being *it* to me" or "being *I* to it." There is a deferral of being in the secondhand. What once fit one might later fit another. A garment gathers owners as a word gathers connotations, always comparing sameness and difference. An expanding waist might lead to the waste of a perfectly good suit, just as an expanding collection might lead to the waste of a perfectly good life. Having found Colonel Unger in his being to the suit, I might have assumed the role of engineer and built a bridge to the person I would want to be, suited for success. There were no crates of cereal boxes in his closet, as there are in mine. Instead, I persisted as the person I am, disclosing an ever-widening gap or discrepancy between the something I own and the somebody I have become. Yesterday's perfect fit becomes the sign reused or refitted in a new "mythology," to use Roland Barthes's term, and that refit becomes a sign to be reused and refitted. Only the act of resignifying tends to pick up noise, which is the sound of discontentment, outbursts of despair and anger, the stink of being human. Every successive reuse holds more of human anguish, as well as more of human hopefulness.

I described that secondhand somebody, junk me, in *Collections of Nothing*, thinking it a bit of a freak show, yet readers, not just collectors, found that it fit. Perhaps we are drawn to the secondhand because it bleeds for us—or eats the self-pitying heart out. Memoir is all secondhand, discounted and laid on the lawn for the neighborhood to pick through. Eight years have passed since the book was "finished," and then, in the final pages, I was preparing to marry Wendy. She was the happy ending of a saga that someone called "searing." Now, our seventh anniversary lies behind, and I still amass product labels and "Place Stamp Here" squares, and such, but I'm also trying to take the collecting in a new direction, toward collage.

Collage is the quintessential secondhand art, cut and inserted into a hypertextual world, hence perfectly mimetic of the postmodern condition. In this world, we *ironically* fit our roles as us, and thus we require juxtapositions to suit our self-representations. A book, especially a book of a life, insistently represents the self as a unity, a whole story with a beginning, middle, and end, even if the story is disrupted and chaotic. I tried to figure the disunified state of my collecting self, but the book lured readers, and even me, into believing in a transcendent self who could define it all. Many who read my book regretted that I could not be more celebratory of my collections, as most books on collecting are, and others regretted that I had not taken my journey into the heart of darkness still deeper. To sear or celebrate, that is the question. The book tried to effect a synthesis. It tried to be one book, which is all it could be, at best, because many inconsistent books, fused in this one manuscript, would surely be no book at all, which is an outcome easily imagined by many unpublished writers. The dialogue between book and collection is an uneasy one in any case, but in my case the parties never could agree on the shape of the negotiating table. Perhaps collecting is a little North Korean, on uneasy terms with all.

Since I wrote the book, I have been making book collages, in which I take a book and then I collage into it, in some cases intersecting a new book. I have taken to calling them bibliolages, which gives occasion to enjoy the red squiggly error line of my spell checker. You might call them Merz-books, using Kurt Schwitters's prefix Merz-. It's a syllable perfectly positioned between *Commerz* (commerce) and *Schmerz* (excrement). Merz is the shit that sells, or perhaps it is the sale that turns out to be shit. A Merz-book both contains and excretes its waste.

Here is an example: David Foster Wallace's *This Is Water*, his posthumously printed graduation speech, in which, avoiding all platitudes, he encourages the graduating seniors to be fully aware of life as a mixed-up, painful, and hilarious thing. The gravity of Wallace's death drop paradoxically highlights what an uplifting book this is. I Merz-ed this book by splicing in images from yoga manuals, so that the centered bodies of the yoga masters, no longer bound by gravity, float free on the white page, gracing the single sentences of Wallace's book. All the tension of a difficult world I try to channel through these compositions. Conceptual asinas, you could call them (figure 6.1).

Consider the contrast with this other book, which could also be called *This Is Water*, or, more specifically, water labels. About fifteen years ago, I began housing this portion of my product label collection in an old ledger, because I thought it would be nice to have a book of water housed in a device of commerce (figures 6.2 and 6.3). Unlike, say, my cheese label collection, which holds significantly different cheeses, the product here was basically H-two-O, but crucially different on that label. Dasani

Figure 6.1. *This Is Water* **bibliolage, 2009. Image courtesy of William Davies King.**

is no Déja Blue and Evian no Food Club. A perfect brand name for bottled water might be Différance, because it is mainly on the differentiating surface, the filmic plastic sleeve around the plastic cylinder, that we identify plain water in this era. A collected label wraps flat onto the leaf of my book. Labels take the tangent into the abstract, which is where imagination goes, but they also curve and adhere to the object, which is a cylinder wrapped around a thirst. Even in a muddy puddle, stained with oil, reeking of pesticide, peed out or vomited up, water is still water until it's vapor, until it's dew or rain or sleet, until it flows and is redirected by Arrowhead to another thirst. How *could* it be collectible? By all accounts, water is becoming increasingly scarce in its potable form, but that's on a mass level, which collectors hardly mind. Rarity per se comes only among the relatively rare, so water would seem to be the least fruitful area for collecting. That's like an open door to me.

For the first fifteen or so years of my collecting product labels, covering a wide range, from onion bag tags to Celestial Seasonings to the Reggie Bar, I might have accumulated no more than half a dozen labels of water bottles, the odd bottle of Perrier or Pellegrino from those occasions when I felt frivolous or made a lucky find in the trash. My thirst for collectible labels rarely led me to water, perhaps because water of the labeled sort seemed rare, and my drive for something/nothing steered me away from the rare and exquisite. I wanted to have only what I *could* have, and I had no therapist to ask me why. I was living in Colorado Springs in the early 1980s, and many thought it strange that our neighboring city, Manitou Springs, was putting its mountain spring water in bottles for sale. If you had a free moment, you could take a bottle, any old bottle, and take it directly to the spring to fill all by yourself, right by the side of the road.

Then, roughly a decade later, the water market exploded, with Sparkletts and hundreds of other brands suddenly making us feel that tap water was hardly better than

Figure 6.2. *This Is Water* label collection, ca. 1990 to the present. Image courtesy of William Davies King.

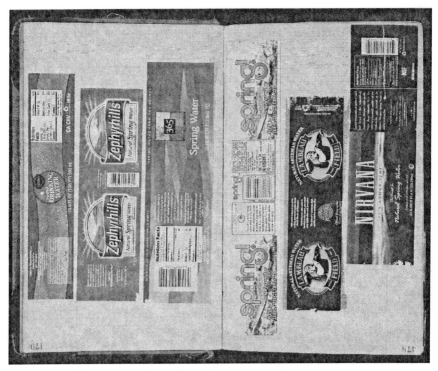

Figure 6.3. *This Is Water* **label collection, ca. 1990 to the present. Image courtesy of William Davies King.**

an open sewer. "Studies" came out to alert us to contaminants and heavy metals in city pipes, while the bottlers beckoned us to return to the mountain, to the rushing spring, to the rippling sky-blue waters. Ever since, it has been difficult to imagine the rivers of blue blue ink that have swirled around clear plastic bottles, the clarity of which announces the nothingness of pure water, except that it isn't so pure. The average quality of water in a bottle, we are now told, does not differ significantly from the average quality of water from the tap.

Clarity has become its own obscurity, and blue is the new red, because plastic water bottles, discarded, not recycled, now number more than a billion per year, and about 17 million barrels of oil go into the production of those bottles, and we bury or cast into the sea or step on or drive over these bottles every day. Some 80 to 90 percent are never recycled. Millions of them mimic purgatory at that place, out in the Pacific, where flotsam accumulates and goes nowhere. Bottles bob endlessly, empty in the water, like the name of a dead man suddenly coming to mind. The message in each bottle is a simple plea for rescue from humankind.

When I was a kid, we had bubblers—Crane, Halsey-Taylor, Delta—and they were our free, public taps, reasonably sanitary. Look up "bubbler" now, and you'll find nothing but bongs. Back to the bottle we went, and the initial nipples were Perrier, but soon we had Fiji, glacier lakes, the burbling forth of crystal peaks, to help us pee away our toxins in the blissful state of not-New Jersey. I remember seeing a photo of a Poland Springs warehouse, with cases of bottled water piled twelve feet high across an acre and a half of floor, a suspended lake, held in place by petrocarbons. For a label collector, this photograph showed just as arid a landscape as the moon, with no variety or rarity or beauty to drink.

For preference, I'll take the side of the road or any old culvert. From a distance, I can spot the dull glint of PET, and next I focus on the label, paper or plastic, to discern an everyday Shurfine or American Falls from an unusual Glacier Clear or Deep Riverrock, Iceland Pure, Oregon Rain, Wissahickon, Ice Mountain, or Déluge. If I have spotted an unusual specimen, I can usually grab it and, without breaking my walking pace, release the label from its grip with my fingernails alone or with a pen knife. I make a point of delivering the naked bottle to the nearest receptacle, ideally a recycling bin, but the label I recycle in my own way, in a book.

And it winds up here, in the least tidy corner of my collection of nothing, five or six hundred water bottle labels. It's grubby. Most of my other labels are packed neatly, whole, inside cartons, or they are mounted on pieces of white paper, singly or in groups. But I had this old ledger book, which I wanted to fill, and then along came the moment when water labels began to pour forth. Recently, the flood has ebbed, as certain large producers have Aquafinalized the outburst, and now it is rare that I Refreshe my collection with anything unusual.

It's embarrassing, in a way, or grotesque, this log of labels (figure 6.4)—water returned to the tree, but far too late because the acid rain is falling through the paper. The plastic labels help preserve the brittle leaves, but in a decade or two the pages will all crack and crumble, turn to dust, and all that will remain is another sort of landfill, relatively portable. The book is a collage of sorts, but it's rooted in collecting in its least savory aspect, which is the drive to stuff life full of something that stands in for life. It's a kind of taxidermy really, pounding one's life into air-mail stamps, Depression glass, bobble-head dolls, or what have you. The rack of vintage golf clubs or the closet full of quilts all simulate the abundant life that might have been lived, but the eyes are made of glass, and the creatures never breathe. In collecting, the skin of life—or you could call it the suit, which is what we can afford to be or grow into—becomes crammed with death.

On the other hand, the water book is also a willful act of conservation, in which the overwhelming waste of a wasteful society is at least momentarily redeemed. I pick up the trash. I sort and preserve and honor it. I mount it for display and study. I give it that life, even though few would have a problem with its return to the trash. There is a little bit of thaumaturgy in this, in which the inanimate skins of an overindulgent society are made to breathe again, to live on in the form of art (latter-day Fluxus), which defies decay by the power of an idea, if nothing else. Water labels are among the scraps of what it was to have been alive in this frightening era of history. Our society sold water, at a premium, and people actually bought it. I have heard it said

Figure 6.4. "It's embarrassing, in a way, or grotesque, this log of labels." Image courtesy of William Davies King.

that water, not petroleum, will be the most contested natural resource in the twenty-first century, and we are living through the first battles in the war of water—the rain of terrorism, if you'll pardon the pun—and bottles are the IEDs. Oil and water, they do not mix, and my gushy grief and parched joy over my collecting do not mix in this hideous and rich oxymoron, my Merzbauhaus monstrosity.

Labels are, at least, the silly necessity of capitalism in a regulated and competitive marketplace. Someone has to sign the contract, vouch for the goods. A water label is another sort of seal, also a filter. The label provides the comforting declaration that the calories equal zero, the total fat and carbohydrates equal zero, protein and sodium equal zero. How comforting to know that this product is, as they say, "not a significant source of calories from fat, saturated fat, cholesterol, dietary fiber, sugars, vitamin A, vitamin C, calcium and iron." We work long and hard enough for those nutrients at other times; it's somehow comforting to know that we can twist open a plastic cap from a water bottle, breaking that magical seal, and find virtually nothing inside, no stain, no swirl, no sediment, nothing to burn and nothing to the naked eye. By means of water, we sheerly live, but there is no body behind this negligée, no development through this unexposed film. Ninety-six percent of us is what we piss away, and so we pay for being so insubstantial.

I feel that deep ambivalence has been my not entirely happy role in the discussion, to map out the conflicted aspects of collecting. Most books by collectors purely celebrate the rich profusion of a world they have been crazy enough to collect. Marilynn Karp's *In Flagrante Collecto*[3] is an especially gorgeous example of such a book. There is a lot of near-nothing in that book, but with a great eye and some clever dealing, she has made her chosen objects magnify each other to the point that the whole array dazzles and delights like the crown jewels, the Bactrian hoard, Tutankhamen's tomb. Her title coyly promises guilt, but the book itself is blissful and unashamed. A good word for the book is glorious, because it shows the splendor of heaven, albeit on a trivial scale. It's the magnificence of the minor she revels in. By comparison, my books—*Nothing, This Is Water*, and (water)—are like compound fractures. The bones of a disturbance, both psychological and cultural, poke through, and the result is painful to look at. Both *In Flagrante Collecto* and my book of water labels are montages of modern life, but mine is the more brutal, grumpy, tormented. That seems to be my lot, my malaise, which of course is not unique to me. Others take a yoga class. I use Elmer's glue.

Several years ago, I spent the month of August in Scotland, doing historical research in the archives of the National Library of Scotland. I was tracking down an obscure anecdote in the history of hypnotism, and by some predicted fortune this month in the stacks coincided with the Edinburgh Festival and its many fringes. So I would emerge at 5 o'clock from the library and head to the high street in search of what might be the most interesting show to see. This short walk was always prolonged by the massed presence of discarded trash, everywhere, including the water bottles of the international theater and music and comedy and film communities.

Edinburgh is a city that has been used and reused and finally transmuted into national heritage. In the nineteenth century, the Royal Mile, now the central tourist attraction, was a horrible, vertical slum, with layer upon layer of crowded warrens and closes just waiting a cessation of the endless rain to burst into flame. Now the central city is a great theater in which the performing arts world flaunts its cutting edge, and prosperous tourists feed their appetites for high culture and jacket potatoes. The slums have gone to the outskirts with the Buckfast Tonic and Trainspotted dick. At least for August, the anger of the displaced meshes with the carelessness of the emplaced. The result of this exchange is a landscape of refuse, upon which I fed. I have rarely seen such a littered city, and it is not just the tourists who think nothing of dumping a cigarette package into the gutter or hurling a glass bottle down the embankment. Residents, too, freely spew trash, along with other noxious emissions. Public trash bins are few and scattered and usually overflowing. This furious degradation of the city became my treasure chest. Empty EU products yielded multilingual labels, such as the Fanta phantasmagoria and many versions of Irn-Bru, which is some sort of Cumbernauld energy drink, a beverage I neither bought nor tasted because the labels were available for free, if I could ignore a certain stickiness. For preference, I'll pick up a water bottle, where the empty turns out even emptier, nothing to rinse. Scotland brought me much new water, such as Aberfoyle, Waiwera, and Harrogate Spa—in the muck.

So I found myself asking, do I degrade myself when I stoop to pick up a water bottle someone has just thrown into the cobblestoned alley? Is it beneath me to reach into a dustbin for a candy wrapper? Can I meet the eye of someone who sees me pocket a beer bottle cap I will later need to soak? In order to have what I want, it seems, I must throw my self-worth into question, which seems . . . crazy. In a chapter of *On Longing: Narratives of the Miniature, the Gigantic, the Souvenir, the Collection*, Susan Stewart explores the linkage between the "proper" and the insane collection:

> Although it is clear that there is a correspondence between the productions of art and the productions of insanity in these cases, it is equally clear that the miser's collection depends upon a refusal of differentiation while the hobbyist's collection depends upon an acceptance of differentiation as its very basis for existence. Thus the "proper" collection will always take part in an anticipation of redemption: for example, the eventual coining-in of objects or the eventual acquisition of object status by coins themselves. But the insane collection is a collection for its own sake and for its own movement. It refuses the very *system* of objects and thus metonymically refuses the entire political economy that serves as the foundation for that system and the only domain within which the system acquires meaning.[4]

Clearly I resist this acquisition by coins and also the "coining-in," but I do not refuse "the entire political economy" that gives my collection meaning. I might be critical of the signs of global economy (Starbuck's and McDonald's trash scattered among the Scottish treasures), and I was often confronted with the homelessness and poverty of a depressed British ex-colony, but that did not stop me from exercising my privilege to stretch my dollars as far as they would go. My collecting was "for its own sake and for its own movement," but surely sort of crazy.

What is a package but a sign, and like all signs empty of meaning, except within a system? My cream cheese boxes, toothpaste cartons, and cat food can labels all once contained a fullness. The label typically tells us the avoirdupois weight contained within, and we depend upon that substantiality; otherwise our cat starves and our bagel goes dry. We die of thirst if the bottle is only a bottle. But once we deplete the measured ounces, the sign becomes empty indeed. If we operate within one cultural system, we crush that emptiness in a bin and a landfill and conceal it from the view of society forever, or perhaps we contain it within a system of recycling and regenerate its potential, but only as an ingredient for another sign. If we operate within still another social system, we do not contain the package but inscribe it on the city, casting it down, so that the mess becomes an eyesore and eventually the mess of someone else, the whole community's problem. Some people litter, which is a mobile form of graffiti, a way of saying that the wrapper should rap on. It's a form of rage. However, it's not my form of rage. Instead, I am the anti-litterer. I reap the benefits of society's contempt for what is useless. The emptiness of the bottle, label, box, or can travesties "the entire political economy" as a sort of street theater. Picking it up, I contain it within my own romantic longing, as if I were Mr. Thoreau living in a trashed and traded world—Walden pawned.

A portion of my collection—and most of what I retrieved from Scotland—comes from litter. Scotland's anger and alienation is written in refuse, and it goes into my book. By my choice, I'm the bookie on a crazy bet. I seize those rejected containers, those empty signs, and they become the vessels of my bitterness and grief. The collection is a stinking graveyard of my bad feelings awaiting resurrection. The collection is also a park, filled with carefully engraved monuments, beautifully covering up the death and the fear of death that lies within us all, which we cannot escape. I am, within myself, Scotland abject and the last king of Scotland.

In that classic neurotic way, I cannot wash my hands of the mess, the "damned spot," much as I try. I collect the absence of the very thing that might make me clean, and I reach into the filth of it over and over. I have to rely on you to picture the vileness I sometimes touch to seize my coveted object, all the rudeness that offends my fingers and nose. It is the pit of my own abasement from which I extract the good, and the slime down there is not just my own self-loathing, it is also the deep shit of our society. I reach and reach, because I know it works for me. Here is the trash heap of my neurosis; here is the Metropolitan Museum of my discernment. Here is the chapel of capitalism's bounty; here is the Riker's Island of its excess. It's not the one without the other. Possession puts us into an exactly ambiguous relation to the world—pathetic and proud, abject and dominant, everything and nothing. The collected world is both fulfilling and emptemptying.

These days, I see a lot of articles in newspapers and magazines about the simple bliss of throwing things away—decluttering, they call it—achieving that faintly Buddhist detachment from the material world by cleaning out the front hall closet and the whatnot, especially the whatnot. Though I insist that excessive possession is not the same as hoarding, the articles instruct that a cluttered house basically signifies a moral weakness or aesthetic imbecility. These articles are the furniture equivalent of weight-loss journalism. Dump Aunt Shirley's ugly old china and the unused barbells in the basement, donate your old videos of *It's a Wonderful Life* and *Platoon*, because you'll feel so much happier with an empty closet shelf and a basement with an echo. But this tsk-tsk attitude toward possession—use it or lose it—fails to grasp how much meaning and value and feeling are invested in objects. The articles urge us to hold onto the memory, not the souvenir, and the friendship, not the gift. To this I say, fine, if your memory, your heart, works so well, then live in your purified experience, but I respect the stubborn persistence of the object, which is empty, but never so empty as the signifier. It suits me fine.

NOTES

1. An earlier version of this chapter was presented as the keynote address at the "Secondhand Culture: Waste, Value, and Materiality" conference at Bard Graduate Center in April 2010. Several of my bibliolages—or "ruined books," as I now call them—can be seen at williamdaviesking.com.

2. William Davies King, *Collections of Nothing* (Chicago: University of Chicago Press, 2008).

3. Marilynn Gelfman Karp, *In Flagrante Collecto (Caught in the Act of Collecting)* (New York: Harry N. Abrahams, 2006).

4. Susan Stweart, *On Longing: Narratives of the Miniature, the Gigantic, the Souvenir, the Collection* (Durham, NC: Duke University Press, 1993), 154.

7

The World as Things:
Collecting Thoughts on Collecting

Stanley Cavell

> *[Fleda] took the measure of the poor lady's strange, almost maniacal disposition to thrust in everywhere the question of "things," to read all behavior in the light of some fancied relation to them. "Things" were of course the sum of the world; only, for Mrs. Gereth, the sum of the world was rare French furniture and oriental china. She could at a stretch imagine people's not "having," but she couldn't imagine their not wanting and not missing.*
>
> —Henry James, *The Spoils of Poynton* (1897)

> *The world is the totality of facts, not of things.*
>
> —Wittgenstein, *Tractatus Logico-Philosophicus* (1921)

I

Not this or that collection is my assignment here, but collecting as such; or, as it was also specified to me, the philosophy of collecting. And presumably not collecting as what dust does on shelves; or rain does in pails; or as what is called a "collector" does on certain roofs, gathering particulates to monitor air pollution—but as someone collects medals, coins, stamps, books, skeletons, jewels, jewel boxes, locks, clocks, armor, vases, sarcophagi, inscriptions, paintings, curiosities of unpredictable kinds. Krzysztof Pomian, in his remarkable study *Collectors and Curiosities*, declares that every human culture has collected and that every movable thing has been collected. As if collecting for possession and display is as primitive as gathering food for survival.

But though we may sensibly ask why certain people collect stamps, jewels, skeletons, and so forth, and why different things seem favored for collection by different classes or ranks of society, or different genders or ages, in different historical periods,

99

does it makes sense to ask why people collect as such—any more than it makes obvious sense to ask what my relation to things is as such, or my relation to language, or what the point of thinking is?

Yet writers about collecting are characteristically moved precisely to advance some idea of what the point of collecting is as such, as a form of human life. For example, Jean Baudrillard articulates collecting as an objectifying of oneself in a simulation of death that one symbolically survives within one's life. Pomian begins with the fact of collecting as removing objects from economic circulation and putting them on display and speaks of a consequent establishment of connection between the visible and the invisible, the realm of religion, made possible (and inevitable?) by the advent of language. Susan Stewart combines the withdrawal of objects from use with the establishment of a commerce between death and life (as if creating a realm of mock exchange [mock religion?]). Robert Opie is one of many who see in collecting an attempt to reproduce and hence preserve or recapture the world. Philip Fisher, concentrating on art museums since the Enlightenment and identifying stages of a history in which an object is removed from its original setting (of use, say, in battle or in prayer), becomes a thing of memory (a souvenir or a relic), and ends up as an object for aesthetic appreciation, arrives at a definition of the museum as a place of the making of art, an institution of practices within which the function of art is operable. Foucault, in the paradigmatic onslaught of his *The Order of Things*, speaks of shifts in our ways of "taming the wild profusion of things." I shall not refrain from certain similar speculations in what follows.

I should note at the outset that an important issue about collections, one that makes news, plays almost no role here, that concerning the right to exhibit or to own objects improperly taken from, or identified with, another culture. My excuse for silence is that such a conflict is apt to be poorly discussed apart from a patient account and interpretation of the forces at play in a concrete historical context, which is not how I have conceived the form of my contribution. James Clifford, in his deservedly admired *The Predicament of Culture*, provides such context for several cases, guided by the principle that living cultures worldwide are inherently appropriating the strange, the evidently predatory cultures together with the obviously victimized.

II

Speculation about the role of collections in human life has been explicit since at least the problem of the One and the Many, made philosophically inescapable in Plato's Theory of Forms, or Ideas, according to which the individual things present to our senses are knowable, are indeed what they are, by virtue of their "participation" in, or "imitation" of, the realm of Forms, which provides us with our armature of classification, to put it mildly. The Platonic hierarchy disparages the things, the life, of ordinary sensuous experience, this realm of the transient and the inexact, in contrast with the perfect, permanent realm of the Ideas. To know a thing in the lower realm is to know which Ideas it imitates in common with other things of its kind: there are many chairs, but just one Idea of (the perfect, hence perfectly knowable) chair; the Form of a chair is what is common to, the common aspiration of, the collection of the things that are, and are known as, chairs. Just how the relation between the many and the one (or as it came to be called in later philosophy, the universal and the particular) is to be conceived became at once a matter of controversy in the work of Aristotle, and the problem of the status of universals has not abandoned philosophy to this day.

But a perplexity other than the relation of universal and particular, or a more specialized version of the relation of a general term to a singular object, is more pressing for us when we attempt to bring the issue of the collection into view. We have, in effect, said that every collection requires an idea (or universal, or concept). (This seems to presage the fact, testified to by many writers on collecting, that collections carry narratives with them, which presumably tell the point of the gathering, the source and adventure of it.) But can we say the reverse, that every idea requires (posits, names) a collection? This is a form of the question: How can signs refer to what is nonexistent? What do expressions such as "Pegasus," "a round square," "the present King of France," refer to, and if to nothing, what do they mean, how can they mean anything, how can anything true or false be said of them? Bertrand Russell and Edmund Husserl were both caught by the importance of such a question; it was, I suppose, the last moment at which what has come to be called analytical philosophy and what (consequently?) came to be called continental philosophy so clearly coincided in concern. It was Russell's solution to the question of the reference of such terms, by means of his theory of descriptions (evaluating the terms by means of modern logic to demonstrate that they do not bear the brunt of referring to something), which can be said to have established a preoccupation and determined the style of analytical philosophy, and the style appears to have outlasted that preoccupation.

The preoccupation also outlasts the style. The first section of Wittgenstein's *Philosophical Investigations* announces its first interpretation of the passage from Augustine with which it opens, in which Augustine recalls his learning of language: "[Augustine's] words give us a particular picture of the essence of human language. It is this: the individual words in language name objects—sentences are combinations of such names.—In this picture of language we find the roots of the following idea: Every word has a meaning. The meaning is correlated with the word. It is the object for which the word stands."[1] It is a picture of language from which philosophers of both the Anglo-American analytical tradition and the German-French tradition continue to perform, in their different ways, hairbreadth escapes.

Of interest here is that the first example (the first "language game" of a sort) that Wittgenstein develops in response to this picture materializes not around a single, absent object, but around a collection: "I send someone shopping. I give him a slip on which stands the signs 'five red apples'; he takes the slip to the shopkeeper, who opens the drawer on which stands the sign 'apples'; then he looks up the word 'red' in a table and finds a color sample opposite it; then he says the series of cardinal numbers."[2]

Reference—if this means linking a sign to an object—is hardly the chief of the problems revealed in this curious, yet apparently comprehensible, scene. How did the shopper know to whom to present the slip? Does the sign "apple" on his slip refer to the sign "apple" on the shopkeeper's drawer? They may not at all look alike. Would it have secured the linkage to have provided the shopper with a photograph or sketch of the drawer and its sign? How does the shopkeeper know what the point of the photograph or sign is supposed to be? (Perhaps he will hang it on his wall.) Does the sign on the slip rather refer (directly, as it were) to the items inside the closed drawer? But we are free to imagine that when the shopkeeper opens the drawer, it is empty. Do the signs on the slip and on the drawer then become meaningless? And if there were only four apples, then would just the word "five" have become meaningless? Do we want an explanation of how it happens that signs retain their meaning under untoward circumstances? Shouldn't we also want an explanation of the fact that the drawer was marked "apples" rather than, say, "red," whereupon the shopkeeper would be expected to look up the word "apple" on a chart of fruits and vegetables? (We won't ask how he knows which of his charts to consult.)

Do we know why we classify as we do? In order to know, would we have to memorize what Foucault says about changing conditions of possibility? Wittgenstein's primitive, and studiedly strange, opening example can be taken as stirring such wisps of anxiety among the threads of our common lives that we may wonder, from the outset of thinking, how it is that philosophy, in its craving for explanation, seeks to explain so little; that is to say, how it conceives that so little is mysterious among the untold threads between us that become tangled or broken. Perhaps Wittgenstein may be taken as redressing philosophy's disparagement of the things of sense, when late in the *Tractatus* he finds: "It is not *how* things are in the world that is mystical, but *that* it exists."[3]

III

Baudrillard declares in "The System of Collecting":

> While the appropriation of a "rare" or "unique" object is obviously the perfect culmination of the impulse to possess, it has to be recognized that one can never find absolute proof in the real world that a given object is indeed unique. . . . The singular object never impedes the process of narcissistic projection, which ranges over an indefinite number of objects: on the contrary, it encourages such multiplication whereby the image of the self is extended to the very limits of the collection. Here, indeed, lies the whole miracle of collecting. For it is invariably *oneself* that one collects.[4]

How well do we understand this final claim? Let us consider that one of the most celebrated plays of the middle of the twentieth century, Tennessee Williams's *The Glass Menagerie* (1944), depends on its audience's capacity for a rapt understanding of the daughter Laura's identification with her collection of fragile glass figures.

And this understanding is not broken, but is deepened, when her Gentleman Caller accidentally steps on her favorite piece, a tiny unicorn, breaking off its horn, and Laura reveals an unexpected independence of spirit, refusing the suggestion of a clumsy castration and instead observing something like, "Now it is just like all the other horses. . . . The horn was removed to make him feel less—freakish," a state she also has reason to desire. Another famous work of that period, Orson Welles's *Citizen Kane* (1941), equally depends on some identification of a person by his collection, but here some final interpretation of its meaning appears to be dictated to us by the closing revelation of the childhood sled, Rosebud. I like to think that when Jay Gatsby is in the course of realizing his fantasy of showing Daisy his house, his showplace, and unfurls his fabulous collection of shirts before her, it is clear that the value he attaches to them, or to anything, is a function of their value to her. No other object contains him; he is great.

So let us not be hasty in arriving at very firm conclusions about what our relation to collections is, hence what relation they may propose concerning our relation to the world of things as such. It may be worth remembering further here that two of a series of films that broke attendance records in the 1980s, Steven Spielberg's *Raiders of the Lost Ark* (1981) and *Indiana Jones and the Last Crusade* (1989), are about the fatality of a quest for a unique object, and that the closing shot of the former, the camera floating over an unclassifiably colossal collection of crated objects among which, some unpredictable where, the unique lost object of the quest is anonymously contained, seems some kind of homage to the closing roving shot of *Citizen Kane*, in which now the integrity of civilization, not merely of a single unsatisfied millionaire, is at stake.

IV

Both Wittgenstein and Heidegger, in something like opposite directions, break with the ancient picture of the things of the world as intersections of universals and particulars. Wittgenstein's way, characteristically, is almost comically plain and casual:

> Instead of producing something common to all that we call language, I am saying that these phenomena have no one thing in common which makes us use the same word for all. . . . Consider for example the proceedings that we call "games." I mean board-games, card-games, Olympic games, and so on. What is common to them all? Don't say: "There must be something common, or they would not be called 'games'"—but look and see whether there is anything common to all. . . . [Y]ou will . . . see . . . similarities, relationships, and a whole series of them at that. . . . I can think of no better expression to characterize these similarities than "family resemblances."[5]

This idea has had the power of conversion for some of its readers—too precipitously to my way of thinking, because it does not account for Wittgenstein's signature play of casualness with profundity. He still wants to be able to articulate the essences of things.

Heidegger's way of breaking with universals is, characteristically, almost comically obscure and portentous. In a seminal essay, "The Thing," he opens with the
assertion, "All distances in time and space are shrinking," surely a banality we might
expect to see in any newspaper. Then he undertakes to show us that, as it were, we
do not know the meaning of the banalities of our lives:

> Yet the frantic abolition of all distances brings no nearness; for nearness does not consist
> in shortness of distance. . . . How can we come to know [the nature of] nearness? . . .
> Near to us are what we usually call things. But what is a thing? Man has so far given no
> more thought to the thing as a thing than he has to nearness.[6]

Is Heidegger here constructing a parable of the museum, perhaps a rebuke to those
who think art brings things near in the empirical manner of museums? He takes as
his most elaborated example that of the jug, which holds water or wine, and he spells
out a vision in which the water, retaining its source in the running spring, marries
earth and sky, and in which the wine, which may be the gift of a libation, connects
mortals and gods. Heidegger concentrates these and other properties of the jug in
such words as these: "The thing things. Thinging gathers. Appropriating the fourfold
[earth, sky, mortals, gods], it gathers the fourfold's stay, its while, into something that
stays for a while: into this thing, that thing."[7] Without giving the German, which has
caused a diligent translator recourse to this near-English, I trust one can see the point
of my saying that Heidegger, in this text (and it variously relates to many others), is
a philosopher of collecting.

What I meant by speaking of the opposite directions taken in Heidegger's and
Wittgenstein's perspectives I might express by saying that whereas Heidegger identifies things as emptying the setting of the world in which they are and do what they
surprisingly are and do, Wittgenstein identifies things as differing in their positions
within the system of concepts in which their possibilities are what they surprisingly
are. We cannot simply say that Heidegger is concerned with essence ("What, then, is
the thing as thing, that its essential nature has never yet been able to appear?"[8]) and
that Wittgenstein is not so concerned (he in fact announces in §371 of the *Investigations* that grammar, which provides the medium of his philosophizing, expresses essence[9]). Nor can we say that Wittgenstein is concerned with language and Heidegger
not, for while Wittgenstein states, "Grammar tells what kind of object anything is"[10]
(or more literally, "It is essence that is articulated in grammar"), Heidegger writes,
"It is language that tells us about the nature of a thing, provided that we respect
language's own nature."[11]

If Heidegger is a philosopher of collecting, Wittgenstein composes his *Investigations* in such a way as to suggest that philosophy is, or has become for him, a procedure of collecting. Only the first, and longest, of its two parts was prepared by him
for publication, and its 172 pages consist of 693 sections; in his preface he calls the
book "really only an album." For some, me among them, this feature of Wittgenstein's presentation of his thoughts is essential to them and is part of their attraction.
For others it is at best a distraction. Ralph Waldo Emerson's writing has also had a

liberating effect on my hopes for philosophical writing, and I have taken the familiar experience of Emerson's writing as leaving the individual sentences to shuffle for themselves to suggest that each sentence of a paragraph of his can be taken to be its topic sentence. I welcome the consequent suggestion that his essays are collections of equals rather than hierarchies of dependents.

V

I do not make the world that the thing gathers. I do not systematize the language in which the thing differs from all other things of the world. I testify to both, acknowledge my need of both.

The idea of a series, so essential to the late phase of modernist painting (epitomized, in one major form, in Michael Fried's *Three American Painters* catalog of 1965, on the work of Kenneth Noland, Jules Olitzki, and Frank Stella), captures this equipollence in the relation between individual and genus or genre. These manifestations of participation in an idea may seem excessively specialized, but the implication of their success (granted one is convinced by their success as art) seems some late justification for the existence of collections and for places in which to exhibit their items in association with one another, as if the conditions of the makeup of the world and of the knowing of the world are there put on display and find reassurance.

This is an odd point of arrival, this emphasis on knowledge as marking our relation to the world, after a bit of byplay between Heidegger and Wittgenstein, whose importance to some of us is tied to their throwing into question, in their radically different ways, philosophy's obeisance to epistemology, its development of the question of knowledge as the assessment of claims along the axis of certainty, certainty taken as its preferred relation to objects (as opposed, for example, to recognition, or intimacy, or mastery). It is in modern philosophical skepticism, in Descartes and Hume, that our relation to the things of the world came to be felt to hang by a thread of sensuous immediacy, hence to be snapped by a doubt. The wish to defeat skepticism, or to disparage it, has been close to philosophy's heart ever since. To defeat skepticism need not be a declared grounding motive of a philosophical edifice, as it is in Kant; it may simply be declared a bad dream, or bad intellectual manners, as in W. V. Quine, who finds skepticism vitiated by science, whose comprehensibility needs from experience only what Quine (in *Pursuit of Truth*) calls certain measured "checkpoints." Philosophers such as William James and John Dewey are forever appalled by what their fellow empiricists have been willing to settle for in the name of experience, steadfastly refusing to give our birthright in return for, it may seem, so specialized a world. (Foucault calls it the world of black and white.)

When Walter Benjamin tracks the impoverishment of our (Western, late capitalist) experience and relates it to a distance from objects that have become commodified, hence mystified in their measurement not for use but for the signs of exchange, he does not, so far as I know, relate this experience to philosophy's preoccupation with skepticism, to an enforced distance from the things of the world and others in it by the very means of closing that distance, by the work of my senses. But then Benjamin seems to harbor a fantasy of a future that promises a path—through collecting—to new life, a reformed practicality with, or use for, objects. He writes in *Charles Baudelaire*:

> The interior was the place of refuge of Art. The collector was the true inhabitant of the interior. He made the glorification of things his concern. To him fell the task of Sisyphus which consisted of stripping things of their commodity character by means of his possession of them. But he conferred on them only a fancier's value, rather than a use-value. The collector dreamed that he was in a world which was not only far-off in distance and time, but which was also a better one, in which to be sure people were just as poorly provided with what they needed as in the world of everyday, but in which things were freed from the bondage of being useful. The interior was not only the private citizen's universe, it was also his casing. Living means leaving traces. In the interior, these were stressed. . . . The detective story appeared, which investigated these traces.[12]

The collector knows that our relation to things should be better, but he does not see this materialized through their more equitable redistribution, or, say, through recollection. That the interior place of Art, and the collector as its true inhabitant, is registered as past may suggest that the place of Art is altered, or that the time of Art and its private collecting is over, or that interiority is closed, or that these proprieties of experience have vanished together.

Take the formulation, "Living means leaving traces." In conjunction with the figure of the detective, the implication is that human life, as the privileged life of the interior and its "coverings and antimacassars, boxes and casings," is a crime scene, that (presumably in this period of exclusive comfort) human plans are contracted by the guilty. So presumably Benjamin's writing is at the same time confessing, in its existence as traces, the guilt of its privilege and declaring that its obscurity is necessary if it is not to subserve the conditions that ensure our guilt toward one another. But the direct allusion to Marx ("[the collector] conferred on [things] only a fancier's value, rather than a use-value"), and hence to Marx's derogation of exchange value as a realm of mystery, suggests a mystery in the living of the life of traces that cannot be solved by what are called detectives.

The idea that the evidence of life produced by each of us is of the order of traces conveys a picture according to which no concatenation of these impressions ever reaches to the origin of these signs of life, call it a self. Then the thrill of the detective story is a function of its warding off the knowledge that we do not know the origins of human plans, why things are made to happen as they do. Traces relate the human body's dinting of the world back to this particular body, but how do we relate this body to what has dinted it? If it was something inside, how do we correlate the events (how compare the sorrow with its manifestation)? If it was something outside, why is *this* the effect (why sorrow instead of contempt or rage)? The discovery of the identity of the criminal is bound to be anticlimactic, something less than we wanted to know.

It does seem brilliant of Edgar Allan Poe, in "The Murders in the Rue Morgue" (1841), to have presented the traces of a crime early in the history of the genre, so that the solution depends upon realizing that they are not effects of a human action, but of those of an ape, as though we no longer have a reliable, instinctive grasp of what the human being is capable of. Was the hand of man therefore not traced in this crime? What brings murderousness into the world? What detective responds to this evolutionary crossroads?

Beyond this, let's call it skepticism of traces, I take Benjamin's portrait, or function, of the collector as the true inhabitant of the interior to suggest that the collector himself is without effective or distinctive interiority, without that individuality of the sort he prides himself on. So that when Benjamin goes on to identify the *flâneur's* search for novelty as engendered by "the collective unconscious" and its craving for fashion,[13] this can be taken to mean that what is interpreted by an individual as his uniqueness is merely an item of impulse in an unobserved collection of such impulses, hence anything but original; call it, after Emerson, the source of conformity, part of the crowd after all.

VI

How did it become fashionable for disparagers of skepticism to tell the story of Dr. Johnson, receiving Bishop Berkeley's "denial" of matter, kicking a stone and replying, "Thus I refute you"? People who know nothing of the motives of skepticism know a version of this story. How strange a scene it offers. Why, to begin with, is kicking a hard object more a "refutation" of immateriality than, say, sipping wine, or putting your hand on the arm of a friend, or just walking away on solid ground, or muddy, for that matter? Why is a sensation in the toe taken to be closer to the things of the world than one in the throat or in the hand or on the sole of the foot? Does Samuel Johnson take himself to be closer to his foot than to his throat or his hand? Or is it the gesture that is important—the contempt in kicking? Emerson assigns to Johnson the saying, "You remember who last kicked you." Is Johnson's refutation accordingly to be understood as reminding the things of earth who is master, as an allegory of his contempt for philosophy left to its arrogance? Or is it—despite himself—a way of causing himself pain by the things of the world, implying that he knows they exist because he suffers from them? Then had he forgotten when he last kicked them, or brushed them by?

VII

Some I know, otherwise than Benjamin offended by claims to individuality, profess to understand the self—presumably of any period and locality—as some kind of collection of things, as though such a collection is less metaphysically driven on the face

of it than the simple and continued self that Hume famously denies or would deny
to all save harmless metaphysicians. Leaving these self-isolating ones aside, Hume,
in his *Treatise of Human Nature,* "[ventures] to affirm of the rest of mankind, that
they are nothing but a bundle or collection of different perceptions."[14] This alternative picture, however, retains relations among the collection such as resemblance,
causation, memory, and the incurable capacity of the whole to torment itself with
"philosophical melancholy and delirium."[15] Then when Hume confesses here, "I
find myself absolutely and necessarily determined to live, and talk, and act like other
people, in the common affairs of life,"[16] how are we to take this assertion against his
earlier, famous assurance in the section "Of personal identity," that "for my part,
when I enter most intimately into what I call *myself,* I always stumble on some
particular perception or other, of heat or cold, light or shade, love or hatred, pain
or pleasure. I never can catch *myself* at any time without a perception."[17] What idea
(held or deplored) must we understand Hume to have of "entering most intimately
into what I call myself"—what perception announces to him this entering? And
what would count as a pertinent perception he has stumbled on when he declares
his "absolute and necessary determination" to live like other people in the common
affairs of life—what perception of absoluteness or determination? And is this determination meant to assure himself that he is like other people? Do other people have
such a determination to live . . . like themselves? If they do, he is not like them (does
not live like them); if they do not, he is not like them (does not think like them).

Hume goes on to say, fascinatingly, that "the mind is a kind of theater," gloss-
ing this as emphasizing that "perceptions successively make their appearance, pass,
re-pass, glide away, and mingle in an infinite variety of ways. There is properly no
simplicity in it at one time, nor *identity* in different."[18] But what isn't there? What is
the metaphysical proposal that must be denied? Setting aside whatever importance
there is to be attached to our "natural propension" to seek some such simplicity or
identity, the question Hume poses is: "From what impression could [our] idea [of
the self] be deriv'd?"[19] For my part, I am prepared to say that, if we derive from the
idea of the mind as a theater the idea that what we witness there are scenes and characters—impressions of a scene in which characters are in light and dark, expressing
love or hatred, manifesting pain or pleasure—these provide precisely impressions
or perceptions of myself, revelations of myself, of what I live and die for, wherein I
catch myself. They are not—I am happy to report—simple and identical the way
impressions of simple, stable things are. They are ones I might miss, as I might miss
any other chance at self-discernment. I must discover a narrative for the scene and
an identity for the characters and see how to decipher my role in the events. No
impression of a thing that failed to relate that thing to itself as a witness or party to
its own concerns (or to understand how it fails in a given case in this role) would be
an impression of a self, of a thing to which to attribute personhood. Whether what I
find is unity or division, simplicity or complicity, depends on the individual case—
both of the one under narration, the collection, and the one doing the narration, call
him or her the collector, or adaptor, or ego.

VIII

In his Introduction to the *Treatise*, Hume remarks, "'Tis no astonishing reflection to consider, that the application of experimental philosophy to moral subjects should come after that to natural at the distance of above a whole century,"[20] constructing his application of Newtonianism to human encounter in the century after Newton's consolidation of the new (corpuscular) science, and considering how long it took Copernicus and the others to arrive at the new science against the reign of Aristotelianism. It took another century and a half after Hume for the Freudian event to arrive, with its methodical discoveries of what the "impressions" or "perceptions" are in conjunction with which we catch ourselves. Call the discoveries new laws, or new ideas of laws, of attraction and repulsion and of the distance over which they act. Whether this span is astonishingly long or short depends on where you start counting from—Sophocles, Shakespeare, Schopenhauer. More urgent than determining the time of the achievement is recognizing its fragility. This new knowledge of the self, as Freud explained, perpetually calls down repression upon itself. Since it is currently again under relatively heavy cultural attack (sometimes in conjunction with philosophy, sometimes in the name of philosophy), it is worth asking what would be lost if this knowledge is lost, what aspiration of reason would be abdicated.

That aside, the idea of a self as a collection requiring a narrative locates the idea that what holds a collection together, specifically perhaps in the aspect of its exhibition, is a narrative of some kind. We might think of this as the issue of the catalog, where this refers not simply to the indispensable list of objects and provenances, but to the modern catalog produced by curators, who are as responsible for circulating ideas as for acquiring and preserving objects. Mieke Bal is explicit in positing a narrative among the objects of an exhibition; Stewart more implicitly invokes narrative interaction in her perception of what she calls the animation of a collection; and Fisher presents his idea of the effacing and the making of art as a sort of counternarrative, even effecting a certain counteranimation of objects. The issue of the catalog is, I think, a pertinent emphasis for Norton Batkin's proposal that an exhibition be informed by its objects' own preoccupations with their fatedness to the condition of display, for example, by their relation to the theatrical, or to the pervasiveness of the photographic, or, perhaps later, to what remains of the experience of collage or of assemblage.

IX

Batkin's concern, evidently, is that the current emphasis on the concept of collecting, on establishing a holding, should not come to swamp the concept and the practices of exhibiting the holding. A shadow of my concern here has been that the concept of a collection should not swamp the concept and perception of the particulars of which it is composed. Both are concerns, I think, that the worth of certain values in the concept of art will not be misplaced, that is, lost—for example, that the demand to be seen, call it the demand of experience to be satisfied, however thwarted or deferred, will not be settled apart from the responsiveness to the claims of individual objects upon experience.

This says very little, but that little is incompatible with, for example, the recently fashionable tendency among aestheticians in the philosophically analytical mode to let the question of conferring or withholding the status of art upon an object be settled by whether or not someone or some place or other puts it on display (with no Duchampian taste for naughtiness and scenes). If it comes to this, I should prefer to let the status be settled by the persuasiveness of the catalog. But artists who work in series can be taken to declare that only art can determine which singularities can sustain, and be identified by, a collection of works of art.

The problem here is already there in Kant's founding of the modern philosophy of art, in his *Critique of Judgment*. His characterization of the aesthetic judgment as placing a universal demand for agreement on the basis of one's own subjectivity in assessing pleasure and purposiveness perhaps draws its extraordinary convincingness from its transferring to the act of judgment what should be understood as the work of the work of art (of, as it were, the thing itself), namely, lodging the demand to watch. It is not news that we moderns cannot do or suffer without intellectualizing our experience. Then we should at least make sure that our intellectualizing is after our own hearts. Criticism, which (drawing out the implication of Kant's findings) articulates the grounds in a thing upon which agreement is demanded, after the fact of pleasure, bears a new responsibility for the resuscitation of the world, of our aliveness to it.

It remains tricky. When Thoreau one day at Walden moved all the furniture in his cabin outside in order to clean both the cabin and the furniture, he noticed that his possessions looked much better to him outdoors than they ever had when in their proper place. This is an enviable experience, and valuable to hear. But it did not make his possessions works of art. Recently I read about some new legislation proposed against schemes of price-fixing at certain prominent auction houses, about which a lawyer remarked that the movement of works of art is now being treated to legal constraints designed for deals in milk and cement. I reported this to Bernard Blistène, my host at the Centre Georges Pompidou, as we were about to enter a splendid exhibition there devoted to structures in cement and iron. He replied that he knew a German artist who works with milk.

But in what continues here I remain indiscriminant in collecting thoughts about collections in the world of things, leaving the differences in the realm of art mostly to shift for themselves, and perhaps, at times, toward us.

X

Chantal Akerman's breakthrough film *Jeanne Dielman/28 rue de Commerce/30729 Bruxelles* (1975)—known for the originality of its vision of film and of what film can be about, for its length (three and a half hours), for its director's age (she was twenty-four when she made it), and for the performance of Delphine Seyrig—can be taken as a study, or materialization, of the self as a collection, in the particular form in which the one who is the subject of the collection is not free (or not moved?) to supply its narrative. I sketch from memory certain events, mostly of its first hour, already knowing that though little happens that in customary terms would be called interesting, the way it is presented, in its very uneventfulness, makes it almost unthinkable to describe what happens in sufficient detail to recount everything shown to us.

It opens with a woman standing before a stove, putting on a large pot under which she lights a flame with a match. The camera is unmoving; it will prove never to move, but to be given different posts, always frontal and always taking in most of a person's figure and enough of the environment to locate that person, once we are given the complete cycle of her or his possible locations. It is difficult to know whether everything, or whether nothing, is being judged. The camera holds long enough in its opening position that we recognize we are in a realm of time perhaps unlike any other we have experienced on film. A doorbell sounds, the woman takes off her apron, walks into the hallway to a door, which she opens to a man whose face we do not see but whose hat and coat the woman takes and with whom she exchanges one-word greetings and then disappears into a room. The camera observes the closed door to the room, a change of light indicates the passage of an indefinite span of time, the door opens, the woman returns the coat and hat to the man, who now appears in full length. The man takes money out of a wallet and hands it to the woman, says something like, "Until next week," and departs. She deposits the money in a decorative vase on what proves to be the dining table, bathes herself, an evident ritual in which each part of her body is as if taken on separately, and then returns to the preparation at the stove. When she is again signaled by the doorbell, she opens it to a young man, or schoolboy. Admitting him, she returns to the kitchen, dishes out the contents of the simmering pot into two bowls, one potato at a time, four potatoes into each bowl, and takes them to the dining room table, where the boy has already taken a seat, and we watch the two of them eat through each of their respective rations of potatoes. Near the beginning of the meal the woman says, "Don't read while you eat"; nothing more is said until the close of the meal, when she reports that she has received a letter from her sister in Canada, which she reads, or rather recites, aloud. It is an invitation to visit the sister, saying she has sent a present to her and containing the suggestion that the sister wants to introduce her to a man, since it has been six years since the death of the woman's husband. She asks the boy—by now we suppose he is her son—whether they should accept the invitation. After dinner she takes out knitting. It is a sweater for the young man; she puts it away after making a few additional stitches. Her son meanwhile has been reading, she listens to him recite a poem from Baudelaire, evidently in preparation for school, remarks that his accent is deteriorating, that he doesn't sound like her, and they move to the stuffed seat on which the son had been reading and unfold it into a bed. As the woman stands at the door, the boy, now in bed, recites that a friend has told him about erections, orgasm, and conception, which he declares to be disgusting, and asks how she can have brought herself to go through it in having him. She replies that that part is not important.

The first day, the screen announces, is over. In the remaining two and a half hours the same activities are repeated, with different economies. The second day, for instance, we see the preparation of the potatoes for the soup, watching, of course, each potato being peeled. Kant says that every object that enters our world is given along with all the conditions of its appearance to us. I should like to say: Every action that we enter into our world must satisfy all the conditions of its completion, or its disruption. (Every human action is, Kant says, handled, performed by the creature with hands, the same action in different hands as different, and alike, as different hands.) With this knife with this blade, sitting in this garment at this table, with this heap of potatoes from this bowl, within these walls under this light at this instant, the woman knots herself into the world. Thoreau says the present is the meeting of two eternities, the past and the future. How does a blessing become a curse?

On this second day, certain things, or conditions, are not in order—a button is missing from the son's jacket, a wisp of her hair is out of place after finishing with that day's client, she lets the potatoes burn, she cannot get her coffee to taste right, even after going through the process of beginning again, throwing out the old coffee grounds, grinding new beans, and so on. The film feels as if it is nearing its end when on the third day we are not kept outside but accompany her with that day's client into her bedroom. After an abstract scene of intercourse in which she is apparently brought to orgasm despite her air of indifference, she rises, moves about her room to her dressing table to freshen herself, picks up the pair of scissors that we had earlier seen her find and take into the room in order to cut the wrapping of the present just arrived from her sister, walks with the scissors over to the man lying on her bed, stabs him fatally in the throat, and slides the scissors back onto the dressing table as she walks out of the room. In the dining room, without turning on a light, she sits on a chair, still, eyes open; we do not know for how long.

I wish to convey in this selected table of events the sense of how little stands out until the concluding violence, and at the same time that there are so many events taking place that a wholly true account of them could never be completed, and if not in this case, in no case. As for a narrative that amounts to an explanation of the stabbing, it would make sense to say that it was caused by any of the differences between one day and the following—by burning the potatoes or failing to get the coffee to taste right or being unable to decide whether to go to Canada or receiving the gift of a nightgown from her sister or slipping against her will into orgasm. To this equalization of her occupations a narrative feature is brought that is as pervasive and difficult to notice as the camera that never moves of itself but is from time to time displaced. Each time the woman moves from one room to another room of the apartment (kitchen, bathroom, her bedroom, the dining-sitting-sewing-reading-sleeping room, all connected by a corridor), she opens a door and turns out a light and closes the door and opens another door and turns on another light and closes that door (except after the stabbing). The spaces are to be as separate as those in a cabinet of curiosities. (What would happen if they touched? A thought would be ignited.)

But if Akerman's film may be brought together with the cabinet of curiosities—an inevitable topic in any discussion of the history of collecting since the Renaissance—it suggests that from the beginning, this phenomenon signified both an interest in the variances of the world and at the same time a fear of the loss of interest in the world, a fear of boredom, as though the world might run out of difference, might exhaust its possibilities. A space I am trying to designate and leave here is for a consideration of Walter Benjamin's perception of the era of the baroque as characterized by melancholy, marked by acedia, or depletion of spirit. As the era arguably of Shakespearean tragedy (*Hamlet* is the implicit centerpiece or touchstone of Benjamin's work on the twin of tragedy that, in *The Origin of German Tragic Drama*, he calls "the mourning play"), it is marked principally for me as the advent of skepticism. This is no time to try to make this clear; I mention it to go additionally with, for example, Pomian's suggestion that funerary display is at the origin of the idea of collecting, and with Nietzsche's suggestion that it is not God's death that causes churches to turn into mausoleums, but the other way around, that our behavior in these habitations unsuits them for divinity—precisely Emerson's point when he speaks, half a century earlier, of preachers speaking as if God is dead.

The pivotal role claimed for Akerman's films as events in the unfolding of contemporary feminism would mean, in this account, that she has found women to bear undistractably, however attractively, the marks of supposedly interesting social partitions or dissociations. Her pivotal role in the unfolding of filmmaking is that she has constructed new means of presenting the world in which these marks perpetuate themselves and has thereby made them newly visible and discussable. Call this a new discovery of the violence of the ordinary. In this she joins the likes of Beckett and Chekhov, but also Rousseau (in his revelation of mankind so far as free and chained—the easiest thing in the world not to notice), as well as Emerson and Nietzsche (in what the former called conformity and the latter philistinism). That Akerman's camera can discover suspense in what is not happening, as if we no longer know what is worth saying or showing, shows a faith in the sheer existence of film, the camera's unadorned capacity for absorption, that approaches the prophetic.

XI

That the occasion of the present reflections is the interaction of two great cities, Paris and New York, enacts the fact that major museums and their collections require the concentration of wealth that is to be found in the modern world in centers of population and power. In thinking of the connection between what he calls the metropolis and mental life (*die Grosstadt und das Geistesleben*) Georg Simmel observes:

> There is perhaps no psychic phenomenon which is so unconditionally reserved to the city as the blasé outlook. . . . The essence of the blasé attitude is an indifference toward

the distinctions between things. Not in the sense that they are not perceived, as in the case of mental dullness, but rather that the meaning and the value of the distinction between things, and therewith the things themselves, are experienced as meaningless. . . . This psychic mood is the correct subjective reflection of a complete money economy to the extent that money takes the place of all the manifoldness of things and expresses all qualitative distinctions between them in the distinction of "how much." . . . The metropolis is the seat of commerce and it is in it that the purchasability of things [this altered relation to objects; "this coloring, or rather this de-coloring of things"] appears in quite a different aspect than in simpler economies. . . . We see that the self-preservation of certain types of personalities is obtained at the cost of devaluing the entire objective world, ending inevitably in dragging the personality downward into a feeling of its own valuelessness.[21]

Simmel announces the topic of his essay by saying that "the deepest problems of modern life flow from the attempt of the individual to maintain the independence and individuality of his existence against the sovereign powers of the society, against the weight of the historical heritage and the external culture and techniques of life."[22] Call the individual's antagonist here the collective and its heritage and techniques its collections, gathered, it may be, as much like pollutants as like potsherds. Might there be some philosophical cunning that permits us to learn from collections how to oppose their conforming weight?

Walter Benjamin evidently thinks not. From his "Eduard Fuchs, Collector and Historian": "[Culture and history] may well increase the burden of the treasures that are piled up on humanity's back. But it does not give mankind the strength to shake them off, so as to get its hands on them."[23] For whom is this said? It was such a perception that set the early Nietzsche writing against a certain form of history, monumental history he called it; Emerson's first essay in his first Series of Essays is "History," written against what he takes us to imagine history to be: "I am ashamed to see what a shallow village tale our so-called History is. How *many* times must we say Rome, and Paris, and Constantinople! What does Rome know of rat and lizard? What are Olympiads and Consulates to these neighboring systems of being? Nay, what food or experience or succor have they for the Esquimaux seal-hunter, for the Kanaka in his canoe, for the fisherman, the stevedore, the porter?"[24] It is part of the concept of my telling another about an event, that I (take myself to) know something about the event that that other does not know, and might be glad to know, or that I am interested in it in a way that other has not seen and might be interested to see. Emerson opposes a history of events that trades upon their having already received significance, so he demands a recounting of what has hitherto been taken to count.

When Freud, in *Civilization and Its Discontents*, introduces the issue of ethics—"the relations of human beings to one another"—into the problem he is bringing before us, "namely, the constitutional inclination of human beings to be aggressive toward one another," he goes on to say:

The commandment, "Love thy neighbor as thyself," is the strongest defense against human aggressiveness and an excellent example of the unpsychological proceedings of the cultural superego. The commandment is impossible to fulfil[l]. . . . What a potent obstacle to civilization aggressiveness must be, if the defense against it [the unslakable superego] can cause as much unhappiness as aggressiveness itself! . . . [S]o long as virtue is not rewarded here on earth, ethics will, I fancy, preach in vain. I too think it quite certain that a real change in the relations of human beings to possessions would be of more help in this direction than any ethical commands; but the recognition of this fact among socialists has been obscured and made useless for practical purposes by a fresh idealistic conception of human nature [namely, that the abolition of private property will eliminate difference, which causes aggressiveness].[25]

Grant that one needn't be a socialist to recognize the necessity of a real change in our relation to things. (Lacan in effect develops this thought of Freud's, in the concluding chapters of Seminar 7, *The Ethics of Psychoanalysis*, in, for example, his assertion that the experience and goals of psychoanalysis demand a break with what he calls "the service of goods.") What change in relation to objects might Freud have had in mind? The most prominent model of his own relation to possessions is figured in his well-known collection of some two thousand ancient Greek, Roman, and Asian objects, mainly statuettes. Putting aside psychoanalytically dependent explanations of Freud's tastes (that the statuettes of gods and heroes are father substitutes, that archaeological finds are emblematic of the finds excavated through the methods of psychoanalysis itself), we might consider certain facts about his reported behavior toward these possessions. Baudrillard, among the prominent theorists of collecting, uses Freudian concepts most explicitly, invoking relations to objects he characterizes in connection with oral introjection and anal retention; yet although he concludes "The System of Collecting" by observing that "he who . . . collect[s] can never entirely shake off an air of impoverishment and depleted humanity,"[26] he does not, so far as I am aware, express interest in Freud's own collecting. John Forrester's essay "Collector, Naturalist, Surrealist" is indispensable on this topic, relating Freud's psychoanalytic practices throughout as modes of collecting (dreams, slips, symptoms) and emphasizing how Freud maintained the life in his collections by adding to them and making gifts from them. It is not easy, in the staid atmosphere of the so-called Freud Museum, his former residence in London, to imagine what it could be like alone with Freud in his apartment of study and treatment rooms, guarded or regarded by these figures. It is known that new figures, before taking their places in the collection, were initially introduced into the family setting, placed on the table at the communal meal. The suggestion has been that Freud used the collection to mark the separation of his working from his family life, but it seems more pointedly true (but then this should amount only to a redescription of the same fact) to say that it served to mark the separation of his patients' work with him from *their* everyday lives.

What could be more pertinent for a holding environment (to use an idea of the British psychoanalyst D. W. Winnicott)—in which the claims of ordinary assertions are to be put in suspension (not to stop us, as in philosophical exercises, from saying more than we know, but to free us from stopping saying what we wish, expressing our desire)—than uncounted gods, who have seen and survived the worst and whose medium is revelation through concealment?

To imagine Freud's collecting anything else is like trying to imagine his having a different face (with apologies to Wittgenstein and his example, in the *Investigations* §183, of the ridiculous and embarrassing results in trying to imagine what Goethe would have looked like writing the Ninth Symphony). Neither a series of objects that in themselves are more or less worthless (e.g., the series of matchboxes mounted in a curved line along a wall that Lacan cites as representing sheer thingness), nor a collection each piece of which may suggest pricelessness (perhaps like the objects in the Frick Museum, New York) fits our idea of Freud. The random voracity of Charles Foster Kane's acquisitiveness, or (somewhat less?) of William Randolph Hearst's at San Simeon, California, on which Orson Welles's *Citizen Kane* was based, seems to fit (indeed to have helped construct) the personas of their acquirers, and to manifest, with touching vulgarity, the proposition—established clinically and theoretically by Melanie Klein, and alluded to in such romantic narratives as Coleridge's *Ancient Mariner*—that the loss of our first object is never fully compensated for.

XII

Is, then, the value we attach to things ineradicably compromised in its assumption of objectivity? The issue takes on various emphases in moral philosophy. It is essential to John Rawls's *A Theory of Justice* that "as citizens we are to reject the standard of perfection as a political principle, and for the purposes of justice avoid any assessment of the relative value of one another's way of life. . . . This democracy in judging each other's aims is the foundation of self-respect in a well-ordered society."[27] How sure are we that we know what constitutes the aims of the ways of life depicted in *Jeanne Dielman* or *The Glass Menagerie* or *The Great Gatsby*? A fundamental implication of the avoidance of relative judgment—call it the rejection of snobbery, that sibling of envy—is that one cannot measure the bearing of another's life (beyond the requirements upon it of justice) without seeing it from that other's perspective. This is emphasized in Christine Korsgaard's Rawlsian/Kantian treatment of the question of the objectivity of value, when she takes as an example of questionable value one in which a collection figures essentially. In considering the question whether value is subjective or objective, a Kantian is bound to measure the question by the formulation of the aesthetic judgment in Kant's *Critique of Judgment*, in which the claim to beauty is both subjective and yet necessarily makes a comprehensibly universal claim—necessity and universality being the Kantian marks of the objective. So one can say that the issue of conflict between the objective and the subjective (in aesthetic matters, as differently in moral) becomes a matter of how, as rational beings, we are to confront one another.

Korsgaard takes the case of someone who collects pieces of barbed wire—presumably a rarified taste—and asks in effect where the claim, if any, upon my respect for this activity is supposed to lie: in the sincerity of the passion for the wire, or in a property of the wire itself? No one else should be counted on to share the taste, and why be interested in someone who has it? A crucial point of moral order is involved for Korsgaard: our respect for other persons must not await our respect for their ends, but on the contrary, respecting their ends must be a function of respecting them as fellow persons. This must be right. But what does "respecting their ends" come to? Given that it cannot require sharing their ends, as the case of the barbed wire is designed to show, it evidently means something like finding the alien end comprehensible, seeing *how* it may be valued. A good society cannot depend on our approval of each other's desires, but it does depend on a certain capacity and willingness to make ourselves comprehensible to one another. Here is where the idea of a collection plays an essential role. An interest in this piece of barbed wire is communicable in association with other, competing pieces, to which a given piece may be taken to allude, comparing it with these others, perhaps, in its effectiveness, economy, simplicity, handling, or producibility. This may not succeed. It does seem that some imagination of the alien desire, of acting upon it, is required for reason to prevail. But then respect, or tolerance, should have a way to prevail in the absence of offerable reasons. It seems hard to imagine the members of a society flourishing when their commitments to one another are based on sheer indifference toward their differences.

It is to show that a commitment to democracy will have to imagine the alien, and to show the room there is for responsiveness to it, if not quite for offering reasons in it, that I can understand, and be grateful for, Dave Hickey's instruction, in his overture to *Air Guitar*, in our "need [for] so many love songs"[28]—there are so many things to learn, well within the range of justice, about satisfying desire. One needn't share Hickey's taste for Las Vegas, but just a fragment of his love song to it flying back from some respectable art panel—"coming home to the only indigenous visual culture on the North American continent, a town bereft of dead white walls, gray wool carpets, ficus plants, and Barcelona chairs—where there is everything to see and not a single pretentious object demanding to be scrutinized"[29]—to rejoice that Las Vegas is, for him, part of the union.

Collecting may serve to allay an anxiety, not exactly that the world can lose its interest, that we may all just disinvest in its differences—but that my interests may make me incomprehensible to others, that safety lies alone in masquerading a conformity with those of others. Early in my reading of Wittgenstein's *Investigations*, in an essay entitled "The Availability of Wittgenstein's Later Philosophy," I summarized my sense of what I will call his vision of language, and what I might now call the stake of our mutual comprehensibility, in these words:

> We learn and teach words in certain contexts, and then we are expected, and expect others, to be able to project them into further contexts. Nothing insures that this projection will take place (in particular, not the grasping of universals or of books of rules), just as nothing insures that we will make, and understand, the same projections. That on the whole we do is a matter of our sharing routes of interest and feeling, modes of response,

senses of humor and of significance and of fulfillment, of what is outrageous, of what is similar to what else, what a rebuke, what forgiveness, of when an utterance is an assertion, when an appeal, when an explanation—all the whirl of organism Wittgenstein calls "forms of life." Human speech and activity, sanity and community, rest upon nothing more, but nothing less, than this. It is a vision as simple as it is difficult, and as difficult as it is (and because it is) terrifying.[30]

Terrifying, because this seems to allow that my meaning anything, making sense, depends on others' finding me worth understanding, as if they might just *decide* that I am without sense. Childhood is lived under this threat. It is no wonder Melanie Klein describes the child's world as hedged with madness, negotiating melancholy for paranoia, reparation for destructiveness.

XIII

In *Art and Money*, Marc Shell recounts through a thousand instances the millennia-long controversies in the West over the relationship between the status of the representation of value by art and by money, and relates the controversies to life-and-death issues of the materialization and dematerialization of God (e.g., over the status of the graven image, the significance of reproducibility, the definition of truth [as "adequacy" between conception and thing]), noting the issue to be alive in minimalist and conceptual art. (Here Michael Fried's "Art and Objecthood" and Clement Greenberg's "Modernist Painting" and "After Abstract Expressionism" are pivotal texts.) But the dematerialization of art and of reality is also at work from Andy Warhol's painted shoes to Heidegger's creepy casualness, in "The Thing," about our relation to the atom bomb, or as he puts it, "Man's staring at what the explosion of the bomb could bring with it. He does not see that the atom bomb and its explosion are the mere final emission of what has long since taken place, has already happened."[31]

What has already happened to us is the loss of distance and ignorance of nearness—our thoughtlessness concerning the nature of the thing—which I glanced at in section IV. Even if, as I am, one is willing to go a considerable way with such signature Heideggerean soundings as "the thing things," there are junctures at the surface around which suspicion should form. What may be dismissed as, let us say, the poor taste of comparing the effects of the atom bomb with a metaphysical process, barely conceals a political claim marked by the careful distinction between the bomb and its explosion. Only one nation has exploded the atom bomb in war, showing "what [it] could bring with it." And the implication is that there is a metaphysical condition that makes the use of the bomb possible, or thinkable, and that Heidegger's thought has been alone in its efforts to outline and counter this condition on behalf of the globe.

Then there is that matter of Heidegger's exemplary jug, in "The Thing," which is suspiciously folkish—pretechnological, precapitalist, predemocratic—in its extravagant aura.[32] I do not wish here to counter a healthy impulse toward disgust with philosophy. One finds oneself recovering the good of philosophy in one's own time, or not. Yet I will say that to miss Heidegger's narration—in which the jug marries earth and sky and its contents form a gift of mortals to gods—and miss the unfolding—in which a ring of celebration (alluding surely to Nietzsche's wedding ring of eternal recurrence) among the fourfold (earth, mortals, etc.) is the work of the thing thinging, a work accessible to us only in stepping back from our millennia of constructions and representations within a heritage of philosophical concepts and leaping free to a form of thinking that is "called by the thing as the thing,"[33] and hence understand ourselves as "be-thinged" ("in the strict sense of the German word *bedingt*"), the conditioned ones (dictionary definitions of *bedingt* are "conditionally," "limited," "subject to"), a condition in which "we have left behind us the presumption of all unconditionedness" (unconditionedness for ourselves, as if we were the gods of creation)—to miss this narration of a new relation to things as such is to miss one of the most remarkable in the history of responses to Kant's derivation and puzzle of the thing-in-itself, and accordingly to risk slighting the distinct contribution Heidegger proposes for an understanding of gathering or collecting, namely one that affirms our finitude (the renunciation of our unconditionedness, of an identification with pure spirituality). This forms a counterweight to the impression, variously given in writing about collections, that collecting is a narcissistic, not to say imperialist, effort to incorporate the world. But would Heidegger consider an empirical collection to provide occasion for the event of entering on his new path toward a different gathering of the world? He himself evidently suggests no exercises for this change of heart.

In the sequence of proposals I have made, leading to Heidegger's, meant to account for our valuing of collecting—that we have an interest in learning nearness, in the stability of materiality, in achieving comprehensibility to others, as well as an interest in the endurance of interest itself—I am continuing a line of thought from earlier moments of my writing that I ask leave to name here. In "Finding as Founding," a reading of Emerson's "Experience," I cite Emerson's search for nearness in terms of his apparent distance from the consciousness of grief over the death of his young son Waldo, standing for all there is to be near to ("I cannot get it nearer to me"), and I observe his discovery that he must thereupon accept the world's nearing itself to him ("indirect" is his word for this direction), an acceptance of a certain revised form of life (philosophy may poorly call it animism) outside himself, outside any human power. This reading goes back to my *World Viewed*, in which I relate the automatism of Jackson Pollock, and of post-Pollock abstraction (somewhat modifying the concept of automatism as introduced by William Rubin into the discussion of Pollock's work), to the achieving of a candidness, or candor, or uncanniness and incandescence (all etymological developments of the idea of glowing, or being white), from which I associate an unexpected, all but paradoxical, connection between these nonobjective commitments and the power of photography and of nature's autonomy, or self-sufficiency. From here I derive the idea of this painting as facing us (an indebtedness to formative discussions with Fried), as if to perceive them is to turn to them, all at once. This line of thought extends a step further back into my *Senses of Walden* and its discussion of Thoreau's concept of our "nextness" to the world, or our neighboring of it, as the condition of ecstasy.[34] I add here that the idea of automatism in painting leads to the invoking of work that essentially exists in series, that is, necessarily in a collection. (What I referred to as philosophy's poor concept of animism, something that dogs, or should dog, a certain intensity in accounting for the work art does, can be taken, though not named, as a subtext of Heidegger's still formidable "The Origin of the Work of Art," as when he speaks of "let[ting] things encounter us" and claims that "all art is poetry," recalling—I take it—that, as we are forever told, *poesis* means making, but then goes on to ask what it is that art makes *happen*, and answers: "Art breaks open an open place . . . in such a way that only now, in the midst of beings, the Open brings beings to shine and ring out."[35] It does seem sometimes that we are destined to be told things unwelcome either because they are heard too often or because they are too unheard of, as though the world has become immeasurably tactless, inadequately traditional, insufficiently original.)

This line of thought was brought to mind when I attended a fine presentation at the recent meetings of the American Society for Aesthetics in Santa Fe by Stephen Melville. In taking up the ideas of a painting's candidness and its facing of the beholder, he cited among many other matters some of the material I have just alluded to. He startled me with the coup of projecting in this context an Andy Warhol multiple "portrait" of Marilyn Monroe—the image of her in ranks and files of differently tinted replications of the same frontal image. It thus, I suppose, not alone declares the issue of a painting's facing us but posits that the singularity of a face may be visible only in its repetition, achieving its aura precisely because of its existence as a collective property, as if the mark of the objective now, even of existence, is celebrity.

XIV

What has happened to the idea of the capacity of knowing as our fundamental relation to the world—the capacity so treasured by modern philosophy that it willingly exposed itself to its powers of skepticism? We have neglected here, and will mostly continue to neglect, the species of collection that may seem to have been made to inspire the response of, or motive to, knowledge, that of the natural history museum. If there is a decent justification for this neglect, it is that such collections are no longer readable as the work of individuals (e.g., as in the case of the painting and collecting activities of Charles Willson Peale, given so excellent an account by Stewart in "Death and Life, in That Order"), and the interest in collecting is apt to shift from the desire of the collector to the quality of the collection, and from the matter of our relation to objects to our relation to that of a theory of the relation of objects to one another, so that classification becomes more fundamental in presenting the collection than juxtaposition and progression.

In both arenas display is essential, but with the things dear to collectors, as is characteristically emphasized (most insistently, perhaps, by Pomian), the object is taken out of circulation (or, to respect Fisher's alliance of the making and the effacing of art, the object is put into a different circulation), whereas one could say that in a natural history collection the object (or part, or reconstruction) is put into circulation for the first time. Here the status, or life, of the work of art shifts again into view. If it is true, as stated previously, that objects of art are objects from their outset destined to be exhibited (unlike bones and stones), it might also be true that other objects share such a destiny without (quite) being known as objects of art. Was it before or after cultures collected that they also decorated and selected among options (shields, guards, garments), offering themselves grounds for a relation to an object of service not strictly required, or exhausted, by that service? From that moment, objects could exist within intersecting circles of circulation.

We should be cautious in saying that with natural objects we know where the next specimen or part fits, whereas with the artifact we have to find where it fits best—cautious because of what we learn from work made most famous in Foucault's texts, especially *The Order of Things*, that knowledge grounded in classification is not a discovery derived from a clear accumulation of facts, but itself required a set of intellectual/historical conditions in which a new conception of knowledge (or *episteme*) was possible, in which a new counting, or order, of facts was made visible. This is an insight marked as belonging to the same intellectual era in which Thomas Kuhn startled philosophers and historians with the suggestion that physical science, knowledge at its most prestigious, goes through periods of crisis in which accumulation is not driving research, and reconceptualization appears to wish to remake rather than to refine the picture of the world. And, of course, it was as if we had always known that.

In both arenas of display death is invoked, even death as present in life, but in collections of art, or artifacts, it is my death that is in question as I enter into the stopped time of the objects (Pomian remarks that their display is as on an altar), whereas the skeletons and parts of natural history speak of the death and the perpetuation of species, of their coexistence and succession, measured within the earth's time. (One of Foucault's favorite expressions of the new *episteme* exemplified by the natural history museum is to say that it displays its items on, or in, a table.)

XV

At the time of his visit to Paris in 1833, Emerson declared in his journal that he had had something like a revelation in his experience of the great collections in the Jardin des Plantes. In *The Emerson Museum: Practical Romanticism and the Pursuit of the Whole*, Lee Rust Brown takes that experience, always remarked on by Emerson's biographers, as more decisively significant than has been recognized before. He proposes that we understand what floored Emerson by the Paris exhibitions to be their presentation of an image of what he wanted his writing to be. I might formulate the image Brown constructs as one in which Emerson sees that his words may become specimens of a totality of significance, arrived at otherwise than by a system (philosophical or scientific or narrative), of which Emerson felt incapable. *The Emerson Museum* casts a wide net of social, philosophical, and historical reference, and I do not imagine my formulation does justice to it. For example, the formulation leaves deliberately open whether Emerson's "words" refers to single words, to sentences, to paragraphs, or to essays, and to what the idea of system is to be credited if not to laws or argument. Here I wish simply to give credit for the insistence that Emerson's experience and vow in Paris ("I will be a naturalist") was some kind of revelation to him of his project and practice as a writer. I have myself been too long preoccupied with the sound of the Emersonian sentence not to welcome an addition to its understanding, but also too long accustomed to asking how each of Emerson's essays characterizes its own writing not to be wary of a proposal of any fixed model for them.

This is too important a matter to me not to be a little more specific about it. Having indicated a connection between the concept of collecting and that of thinking (as in the history of disappointment with universals), and with the concept of the self (as in contemporary play with Humean ideas of the subject), I would not have satisfied my sense of my assignment to think publicly about the philosophical interest of collecting without including some speculation about its comparable connection with the concept of philosophical writing, particularly in the cases of Emerson and Wittgenstein. An obvious cause for this inclusion here is to recall Emerson's and Wittgenstein's relation, in their fashionings of discontinuity, to the medium of philosophy as fragment, in counterpoise to its medium as system. Wittgenstein is explicit about this, but implicitly everything about Emerson's practice as a writer bespeaks this sense of aggregation and juxtaposition—from his culling from his journals for individual essays, to the sense of his sentences as desiring to stand apart from one another, each saying everything, each starting over.

XVI

The first impulse Emerson records, on July 13, 1833, upon noting that he went "to the Cabinet of Natural History in the Garden of Plants," is "how much finer things are in composition than alone. 'Tis wise in man to make Cabinets." Here is some of what he took away with him that day:

> The fancy-colored vests of these elegant beings [in the Ornithological Chambers] make me as pensive as the hues & forms of a cabinet of shells, formerly. It is a beautiful collection & makes the visiter as calm & genial as a bridegroom. The limits of the possible are enlarged, & the real is stranger than the imaginary. . . .
>
> Ah said I this is philanthropy, wisdom, taste. . . . The Universe is a more amazing puzzle than ever as you glance along this bewildering series of animated forms . . . the hazy butterflies, the carved shells, the birds, beasts, fishes, insects, snakes,—& the upheaving principle of life everywhere incipient in the very rock aping organized forms. Not a form so grotesque, so sane, nor so beautiful but is an expression of some property

inherent in man the observer,—an occult relation between the very scorpions and man.
I feel the centipede in me—cayman, carp, eagle, & fox. I am moved by strange sympathies, I say continually "I will be a naturalist." . . .

Walk down the alleys of this flower garden & you come to the enclosures of the
animals where almost all that Adam named or Noah preserved are represented. . . . It is
very pleasant to walk in this garden.[36]

He does seem at the end of his visit to be well recovered from signs of revelation.
The scrupulous editor of this volume of Emerson's *Journals* notes that beneath the
ink entry "this is philanthropy, wisdom, taste" is written in faint pencil: "*Le moment
ou je parleestdeja loin de moi*"—a quotation from Boileau, presumably to mark that
Emerson is unsure what he has learned.

I think I can see that Emerson's sequence of descriptions of his condition at the
Jardin des Plantes—being pensive; calm and genial as a bridegroom; inspired as by
a perception of philanthropy, wisdom, and taste; moved by strange sympathies—
produces an outburst of dedication to qualities he wants for his writing. But I am
not so far able to see how Lee Rust Brown makes the leap from, for example, Emerson's description of "a beautiful collection" (of elegant birds) to the way we are to
see his sentences hang or perch together. An elegant bird, I should imagine, is, as
Emerson says of a squirrel running over a lawn and up into a tree, not made to go
unobserved; linking his writing with a display of bright feathers or a casual virtuosity
suggests that Emerson has his own uses for attractiveness. ("You are attracted to the
standard of the true man," from the first printing of "Self-Reliance."[37]) I think I can
see, more specifically, Emerson's "Self-Reliance" as describing its own writing when it
speaks of thinking as an aversion to conformity; "The American Scholar" of its own
writing when it speaks of thinking as a process of conversion going forward at every
hour; "Fate," similarly, when it describes freedom as resistance or counterstroke; the
"Divinity School Address" when it speaks of communion; "Circles" when it speaks of
circular forms and seems to imply a circle as an intimate audience; and "Experience"
when it speaks of "glancing blows" as opposed to direct grasps as the direction of
knowing. (Do we not have an internal gag when "Experience" speaks of originating
from three points—as when Emerson says Sir Everard Home has discovered that the
embryo originates "coactively"— because three points define a circle, three gathered
together in an arc.) But I do not know that I have in any case made clear or concrete
enough the transfer to Emerson's actual words or that the process is clear enough as
it stands. Enough for what?

Perhaps I am too attached to Thoreau's more explicit interest in literal classification and listing as the basis for self-allegory, such as when his series or tables of measurements or soundings in *Walden* show as emblems of the accuracy and systematic-
ity he claims for his words. Or when his tabulation of his expenditures on food, in
his first chapter, "Economy," shows as "thus publishing his guilt," thus assigning to
his writing the power to assess the guilt in acquiring, at who knows what expense to
others, the sustenance of his existence; and the writing is the sustenance, declaring
that its will is to make itself cost something to read.[38] The Emersonian sound seems

different, otherwise, as in the passage cited previously, in which Emerson expresses his shame about what we know and accept as History. "What does Rome know of rat or lizard?"—these neighboring systems of existence. There is an urgency here of the incessant bearing of unseen processes, to be registered in each sentence, that Thoreau can allow to be suspended across sentences, or chapters, or years. The idea broached earlier of every Emersonian sentence as a self-standing topic sentence of the essay in which it appears, hence of his paragraphs as bundles or collections that may be moved, is linked, in my mind, with Friedrich Schlegel's remark that in good prose it is as if every word is stressed.

XVII

Emerson's visit to the Jardin des Plantes collects (or is collected by) a pair of visits there by Chris Marker, first as recorded in his film *La Jetée* (made in 1962 and released in 1964) and then quoted in his film *Sans Soleil* (1982), that endlessly instructive autobiographical/anthropological meditation on art and technology, culture and memory, past and future, space and time, words and images, desire and death, nearness and distance. In the original scene in *La Jetée*, two people are looking and gesturing at a cut from a giant sequoia, the rings of which are inscribed with various historical dates; in *Sans Soleil*, which quotes this scene, Marker continues by quoting the passage from Hitchcock's *Vertigo* (1958) (on which his shot is based), in which Madeleine (Kim Novak) takes Scottie (James Stewart) to the Muir Woods near San Francisco, where she shows him a sequoia cut covered with historical dates and, pointing to one of the rings, says, "There I was born, and there I died." The memory of a memory of a Hitchcock film about the fatality of memory is preserved in the collections of inscriptions on the trunks of trees that were born before either French and English was formed, surviving all they have had to forget.

Taking the Emerson/Marker/Hitchcock/California intersection with me to Paris the summer I was preparing this text, as I went to visit again, for instance, the Centre Georges Pompidou and the Jardin des Plantes (the Paris sequoia cut is still, or again, on display, but moved inside, into an entrance hall of one of the museum buildings), you may imagine my momentary vertigo on being informed that Marker had accepted an invitation to make a piece to mark the very occasion of the exhibition that is the cause of these words. Upon returning to the Pompidou, I inquired of Bernard Blistène whether there were documents recording the ideas behind the Marker commission. He replied, "There is something better. Marker is downstairs shooting." What I found him shooting, or having just ceased shooting, was a sequence in which a visitor to the museum interactively views a provisional CD-ROM that Marker had installed on a monitor. The monitor, which was mounted on a stand with two chairs before it, stood in an otherwise empty space. Marker held up the small camera he had been using and said, "I've wanted this all my life. No more waiting for developing, adding tracks. . . . Things like *Sans Soleil* are past. It is why I tore up the poster of *Sans Soleil* before putting it up." I had noticed the collage-like shape on the wall as I entered the installation space, and looking at it again I saw that the poster appeared to have been torn, once lengthwise, once across, and then reassembled; the title was still quite legible, and the new form was no doubt more attractive than the original rectangle of the poster would have been. I felt encouraged that this master of his art, or arts, had found elation both in breaking with an old practice (that of the movie camera) and in calling upon an old practice (that of collage) to announce the fact.

The CD-ROM turned out to be an elaboration of material pertaining to *Sans Soleil*. On one of my routes interacting with it I came upon a voiceover reference to *Vertigo*, in which Marker says that he has seen the Hitchcock film—he calls it the best film ever made about time—nineteen times, and that his remarks about the film are for others who also have seen it nineteen times. And, I imagined, for those who will see *Sans Soleil* with that attention. This invitation to obsession—must I decide whether it is fetishistic attachment or honest labor?—is something I have sometimes felt I must ward off. The temptation is, I think, a reason I was struck early by Wittgenstein's self-reflection in the *Investigations*: "It is not our aim to refine or complete the system of rules for the use of our words in unheard of ways. For the clarity that we are aiming at is indeed complete clarity. But this simply means that the philosophical problems should completely disappear. The real discovery is the one that makes me capable of breaking off philosophizing when I want to.—The one that gives philosophy peace."[39]

The issue of completeness can haunt discussions of collecting, some writers (e.g., Stewart) taking it as essential to the desire in collecting, others (e.g., Forrester) taking it that a collection that is no longer growing is dead. Regarding Wittgenstein's *Investigations* (part I especially) as a collection, I have described the 693 sections of this work as showing the willingness to come to an end 693 times. Since I have understood the current overinsistence (so I judge it) on the idea of meaning as the deferral of significance to be an expression of the fear of death, I find Wittgenstein's practice here a memorable realization of Montaigne's assignment of philosophy as learning how to die. Since Wittgenstein also describes his philosophical practice as "[leading] back words from their metaphysical to their everyday use,"[40] in which, or at which, philosophy brings itself to an end (momentarily?—but how can we know that there will be a further call upon it, a 694th call?), the ordinary, in Wittgenstein's philosophy of the ordinary, is the realm of death, of the life of mortality, subjection to the universal collector.

Does the passion for collecting have something to say about such matters as coming to an end?

XVIII

A number of collections are depicted in the Tokyo sequences of *Sans Soleil*. One toward the beginning is of cat figurines lodged in a temple consecrated to cats; one near the middle is of dolls in a ceremony for the repose of the souls of broken dolls; and one toward the end is of the debris collected together from the accessories and decorations of the communal New Year ceremonies. The ceremonies for the broken dolls and for the debris both conclude with the burning of the collections. The film does not make explicit the significance of the burnings, but the suggestion is that debris, whose burning seems fairly natural, has as much right to immortality as do the souls of broken dolls. The burning of the dolls, however, is shocking. Perhaps one thinks of Kurt Schwitters's collages incorporating debris, tracing a fitful immortality of beauty upon what others have abandoned. There is also to ponder Robert Opie's self-described near-mania for collecting and displaying wrappings or packagings, enacting the mad wittiness of retaining and reorganizing precisely what is meant—is it not?—to be discarded. Many collections convey the wish to make the world immortal by, so to speak, forming a reconstruction or impression or shadowy duplicate of it (What is new about film?), but Opie's idea, in description, projects a sort of defiance of the world's availability or deliverability.

Thoreau, the philosopher of noncollection, of the way of responsible life as one of disencumbering oneself from false necessity (enacting and extending teachings from Plato and Rousseau), is struck by a ceremony of burning what he regards as debris, late in the opening chapter of *Walden*:

> Not long since I was present at the auction of a deacon's effects, for his life had not been ineffectual: "The evil that men do lives after them." As usual, a great proportion was trumpery which had begun to accumulate in his father's day. Among the rest was a dried tapeworm. And now, after lying half a century in his garret and other dust holes, these things were not burned; instead of a *bonfire*, or purifying destruction of them, there was an *auction*, or increasing of them. The neighbors eagerly collected to view them, bought them all, and carefully transported them to their garrets and dust holes, to lie there till their estates are settled, when they will start again. When a man dies he kicks the dust.[41]

Thoreau contrasts this ceremony, to its disfavor, with a certain celebration of a "busk" or "feast of first fruits," which the naturalist William Bartram describes as having been the custom of the Mucclasse Indians. Thoreau quotes Bartram: "When a town celebrates the busk, having previously provided themselves with new clothes, new pots, pans, and other household utensils and furniture, they collect all their worn out clothes and other despicable things, sweep and cleanse their houses, squares, and the whole town of their filth, which with all the remaining grain and other old provisions they cast together into one common heap, and consume it with fire." After adding several further critical details, Thoreau concludes the section by remarking: "I have scarcely heard of a truer sacrament, that is, as the dictionary defines it, 'outward and visible sign of an inward and spiritual grace.'"[42]

This is not quite allowing the debris of life its own right to remembrance, or abandonment. That idea of right is announced by *Sans Soleil* in connection with Sei Shonagon's *Pillow Book* and her passion for lists: of elegant things, of distressing things, among them a list of things not worth doing, and one—an enviable mode of composition—of things "to quicken the heart." In *Sans Soleil*, this passion has its own, to my taste, beautiful consequences, inspiring, for example, ideas of visits to post office boxes without expecting letters but just to honor letters unsent or unwritten, and of pauses at an empty intersection to leave space for the spirits of cars broken there. When the voice-over adds to the list of things to be honored in farewell, "All that I'd cut to tidy up" (i.e., in completing *Sans Soleil*), I found myself attaching a small prayer for thoughts that have never come or never been given sufficient appreciation. Priceless uncollecteds.

Thoreau joins in recognizing the air of abandonment, or farewell, in the character of what he calls an event of sacrament (as allowing divorce to the character of marriage). But Thoreau's main emphasis falls still farther, to make his leaving even of Walden unceremonious, a step on a way. As if he has so burned himself into every event of Walden's days, the aroma of which is *Walden*, that he can trust both his and their existences, entrust them to one another.

If collections can teach this, they may not exempt themselves from the knowledge they impart, that they are to be left. Some people need, or have, as luck would have it, a bequest to leave. Thoreau quite explicitly makes a bequest or deed of each form and depth and nameable object of Walden to whomever wants them properly. Thus he exhibits his obedience to St. Matthew's injunction: "Lay not up for yourself treasures upon earth where moth and rust doth corrupt." And he can say, evidently, in a worldly register, "A man is rich in proportion to the number of things he can leave alone,"[43] thus humoring the labor theory of possession that runs in Locke's formulation in his "Second Treatise of Government": "Whatsoever [any man] removes out of the State that Nature hath provided, and left it in, he hath mixed his Labour with, and joyned to it something that is his own, and thereby makes it his Property."[44] Locke wants something of the kind metaphysically to define ownership, and Marx wants the denial of something of the kind to reveal itself to us in the phantasmagoria of the exchange of commodities, so it is bracing that Thoreau isolates and makes explicit the religious, or animated, bearing of the features of nature left to us, as when he characterizes a lake (in the "Ponds" chapter of *Walden*) as "earth's eye."

But when Benjamin, in "Theses on the Philosophy of History," declares, "There is no document of civilization which is not at the same time a document of barbarism,"[45] the very power of the perception disguises the fact that it is as much phantasm as insight, an illumination of things indiscriminately in their aspect as spoils or booty. It can be done; in some moods it is irresistible. But in lashing together, say, the Elgin marbles with, perhaps, a collection of old jazz records that preserve treasures of a harsh time, and these, perhaps, with a collection of silver objects of observance that Jews carried from a disguised into an undisguised exile, or with their steamer trunks desperately packed with evening gowns and court slippers for which no future life will call—here is a frenzied invitation to a madness of misanthropy as much as it is to an enlightened liberation of conduct. For what is writing responsible? Not to hearten pointlessly, but not to dishearten expansively.

I said previously that we should encounter again the bearing of Wittgenstein's and Heidegger's work on the task of leaving or abandonment. In our relation to the things of the world, Heidegger proposes in *What Is Called Thinking?* (as he translates a phrase from Parmenides) "letting-lie-before-us" as the mode of thinking to be sought in stepping back from our fantasies of thinking as grasping the world in fixed concepts. Wittgenstein explicitly mentions just once the pertinent idea of leaving, as befits his discontinuous moments of philosophizing about philosophy: "[Philosophy] leaves everything as it is."[46] Perhaps he means to attract the interpretation this has largely received, a confession of philosophy's conservatism. Then one is left with having to put this together with the radical destruction of philosophical tradition that his writing undertakes. The immediate import of the claim is that modes of thought and practice other than the philosophical—for example, the political or the economic, as we know them—do *not* leave things as they are, but subject them to violence, the state in which they are given to us. "Our investigation must be turned around the fixed point of our real need."[47] Our thinking is faithless to our desire, oblivious to what it set out to express. Whatever instructs us here is to the good.

"Don't take it as a matter of course, but as a remarkable fact, that pictures and fictitious narratives give us pleasure, occupy our minds."[48] I know of no better initial tip in matters of aesthetics. We are advised to consult ourselves about whether a thing we have taken into our minds, have consented for that time to bear upon our lives, gives us pleasure or perhaps otherwise disturbs us, and if not, to demand of ourselves the cause, whether the thing that solicits us is unremarkable, or whether we are coarsened in what we can remark and can allow to matter to us. Why do we put things together as we do? Why do we put ourselves together with just these things to make a world? What choices have we said farewell to? To put things together differently, so that they quicken the heart, would demand their recollecting.

NOTES

1. Ludwig Wittgenstein, *Philosophical Investigations*, 3rd ed. (Oxford: Blackwell, 1958), §1.

2. Wittgenstein, *Philosophical Investigations*, §1.

3. Ludwig Wittgenstein, *Tractatus Logico-Philosophicus*, 2nd ed. (London: Routledge and Kegan Paul, 1961), 149.

4. Jean Baudrillard, "The System of Collecting," in *The Cultures of Collecting*, ed. John Elsner and Roger Cardinal (Cambridge, MA: Harvard University Press, 1994), p. 12.

5. Wittgenstein, *Philosophical Investigations*, §§65, 66, 67.

6. Martin Heidegger, "The Thing," in *Poetry, Language, Thought* (New York: Harper & Row, 1975), 165–166.

7. Heidegger, "The Thing," 174.

8. Heidegger, "The Thing," 171.

9. Wittgenstein, *Philosophical Investigations*, §371.

10. Wittgenstein, *Philosophical Investigations*, §373.

11. Martin Heidegger, "Building Dwelling Thinking," in *Poetry, Language, Thought* (New York: Harper & Row, 1975), 146.

12. Walter Benjamin, *Charles Baudelaire: A Lyric Poet in the Era of High Capitalism* (London: Verso, 1983), 168–169.

13. Benjamin, *Charles Baudelaire*, 172.

14. David Hume, *A Treatise of Human Nature* (Oxford: Oxford University Press, 1951), 152.

15. Hume, *A Treatise of Human Nature*, 269.

16. Hume, *A Treatise of Human Nature*, 265.

17. Hume, *A Treatise of Human Nature*, 252.

18. Hume, *A Treatise of Human Nature*, 253.

19. Hume, *A Treatise of Human Nature*, 251.

20. Hume, *A Treatise of Human Nature*, xx.

21. Georg Simmel, "The Metropolis and Mental Life," in *On Individuality and Social Forms* (Chicago: University of Chicago Press, 1971), 329–330.

22. Simmel, "The Metropolis and Mental Life," 324.

23. Walter Benjamin, "Eduard Fuchs, Collector and Historian," in *One-Way Street and Other Writings* (London: Verso, 1997), 361.

24. Ralph Waldo Emerson, "History," in *Essays; Essays: Second Series*. Facsimile of first editions (Columbus, OH: Charles E. Merrill, 1969).

25. Sigmund Freud, *Civilization and Its Discontents*. Standard Edition, vol. 21 (London: Hogarth Press, 1961), 142–143, 113.

26. Baudrillard, "The System of Collecting," 24.

27. John Rawls, *A Theory of Justice* (Cambridge, MA: Harvard University Press, 1971), 442.

28. Dave Hickey, *Air Guitar: Essays on Art and Democracy* (Los Angeles: Art Issues Press, 1997), 16.

29. Hickey, *Air Guitar*, 23.

30. Stanley Cavell, *Must We Mean What We Say? A Book of Essays* (New York: Scribner, 1969; reprint, Cambridge, MA: Cambridge University Press, 1976), 52.

31. Heidegger, "The Thing," 166.

32. Heidegger, "The Thing," 168ff.

33. Heidegger, "The Thing," 181.

34. Stanley Cavell, *The Senses of Walden* (Chicago: University of Chicago Press, 1972/1992), 100–104.

35. Martin Heidegger, "The Origin of the Work of Art," in *Poetry, Language, Thought* (New York: Harper & Row, 1975), 25, 72.

36. Ralph Waldo Emerson, *The Journals and Miscellaneous Notebooks of Ralph Waldo Emerson*, Volume IV (Cambridge, MA: Harvard University Press, 1964).

37. Ralph Waldo Emerson, "Self-Reliance," in *Essays; Essays: Second Series*, Facsimile of first editions (Columbus, OH: Charles E. Merrill, 1969), 50.

38. Henry David Thoreau, *Walden* (New York: Washington Square Press, 1970), 43.

39. Wittgenstein, *Philosophical Investigations*, §133.

40. Wittgenstein, *Philosophical Investigations*, §116.

41. Thoreau, *Walden*, 49.

42. Thoreau, *Walden*, 50.

43. Thoreau, *Walden*, 60.

44. John Locke, "The Second Treatise of Government," in *Locke's Two Treatises of Government*, 2nd ed. (Cambridge, UK: Cambridge University Press, 1967), ch. 5, sec. 27.

45. Walter Benjamin, "Theses on the Philosophy of History," in *Illuminations: Essays and Reflections* (New York: Schocken, 1969), 256.

46. Wittgenstein, *Philosophical Investigations*, §124.

47. Wittgenstein, *Philosophical Investigations*, §108.

48. Wittgenstein, *Philosophical Investigations*, §524.

III

COLLECTING AND IDENTITY, PERSONAL AND POLITICAL

8

From the Attic to the Mallpark: A Collection's Transition from Private to Public in a New Professional Baseball Stadium

Stephen P. Andon

A number of elements make baseball the American pastime, from its pastoral beginnings that underscore a nationalistic mythos to its perpetually nostalgic appeals that connect generations of fans with baseball icons like Babe Ruth and Jackie Robinson. For collectors of sports memorabilia, baseball stands out from other sports because of the game's relationship with a variety of material objects that are available for acquisition. Consider the overwhelming number of objects needed just to stage a professional game: bats, balls, jerseys, pants, caps, socks, bases, gloves, lineup cards, and score sheets, as well as protective equipment, home plate, the rosin bag, and pitching rubber.

Baseball also celebrates an ancillary materiality presented through a bevy of mass-produced items that have evolved as a result of the rise in consumer culture. Because of baseball's popularity in America, professional teams quickly realized the commercial potential of producing memorabilia and creating copromotional advertising materials. This approach meant that fans, already purchasers of game tickets, could be further enticed to purchase baseball cards, pennants, posters, programs, magazines, souvenir cups, soda bottles, cereals, pins, buttons, statuettes, bobble-head dolls, stuffed animals, and numerous other items.

These materials have reached prominence as sport collectibles, evidenced by the National Baseball Hall of Fame's collection of more than 38,000 items as well as by the hundreds of baseball memorabilia shows staged for private collectors across the country, hawking everything from cards to game-used cleats. Outside of these two avenues, one clearly institutional and promotional and the other designed for private collecting, Major League Baseball franchises have developed their own complex relationships with collectibles. Primarily, while the number of mass-produced commodities has continued to expand, teams have now made game-used items, such as jerseys, bats, and even stadium dirt, widely available for purchase. At the same time, teams are also looking to displays of unique collectibles in their stadiums to help foment nostalgia and solidify their team narrative. In recent years, especially as teams move from older stadiums into commercialized "mallparks," the use of these objects is meant to deliver a historical context to these grand, yet sanitized, stadium spaces. After opening a new stadium in 2009, the New York Yankees exemplified this new trend by dedicating stadium space to displaying a collection of artifacts and memorabilia in a specifically built team museum. The space featured game-used objects, documents, plaques and trophies, and team memorabilia, telling the story of America's most historic and successful baseball franchise. A year later, when the Minnesota Twins opened its new open-air stadium in downtown Minneapolis, the team was eager to deploy the same technique to help reestablish the outdoor baseball identity of the Twins, a team that had played inside a domed football stadium for decades. Unlike the Yankees, however, the Twins eschewed the idea of a centrally located museum and instead placed thousands of artifacts in displays spread throughout the stadium.

In the case of both the Yankees and the Twins, almost all of the items proudly displayed in their new stadiums are not the property of the respective franchises. In New York, many of the items are on loan from a group of renowned collectors, but the Minnesota case is unique, because the team has relied on a sole collector, former college baseball pitcher, local history teacher, and lifelong Twins fan Clyde Doepner. By offering him a full-time job as team curator and leasing his collection of more than 7,000 items, the Twins may have furnished Target Field for the team's own commercial ends, but in the process it also fundamentally altered the meaning of what Doepner spent a half-century collecting. Furthermore, the Twins' reliance on Doepner's collection has revealed its own failure to preserve the thousands of material artifacts that players have used and that the team produced since its first game in Minnesota in 1961. The team's failure to appreciate these items as anything more than profitable commodities is completely contradictory to Doepner's deep, personal relationship with a collection that is imbued with his own memories of various games, teams, players, and even stadiums. The result of Doepner's collaboration brings these two contrasting approaches to collecting together, as the team selects from a private collection in order to tell its own, very public, historical narrative. My purpose is to understand how differences between the private collection and the public collection, along with the role of capital, all inform the meaning of these collected objects.

CLYDE, THE COLLECTOR, AND
THE COLLECTION IN THE ATTIC

On the afternoon of 21 April 1961, sixteen-year-old Clyde Doepner, an outstanding baseball pitcher in his own right, attended the first-ever Minnesota Twins game. Then-owner Cal Griffith had moved the team from Washington, D.C., after the

1960 season, bringing professional Major League Baseball to Minnesota for the first time. That afternoon, after attending the game with his father, Doepner returned home with a program, a bobble-head doll, and a ticket stub; true to an accumulating nature he had possessed since early childhood, he never lost sight of any of these items. Unfortunately, after winning a Minnesota state high school baseball championship, Doepner's own pitching career was cut short in college due to injury. No longer able to aspire to the highest levels of baseball playing, his devotion to the game gradually manifested itself in the form of the most impressive Twins collection ever assembled.

Occupying the entire attic of his Victorian-era home, Doepner's collection is centrally located, and, as collecting scholar Susan Pearce notes of most male-gendered collections, "away from the family living spaces."[1] The more than 7,000 items in the collection include tickets from that first game in 1961; baseball cards and trophies from an untold number of players; dozens of game-used jerseys, bats, gloves, and team parkas; plus yearbooks, programs, buttons, bobble-head dolls, placards, silverware, cereal boxes, mugs, team schedules, pennants, signs, stadium bricks, and an indeterminable number of miscellaneous objects. It is a collection so publicly renowned that every major news outlet in the Twin Cities has visited the attic space; however, notably, few other members of the public have seen Doepner's collection in his home.

Conversations with Doepner as a collector of Twins memorabilia reveal a variety of motivations for gathering this material history of the Minnesota franchise. As have many collectors, Doepner has been lured by the powerful draw of "aura" as a means of connecting with great moments and great players. However, even as many collectors strive to reap the monetary benefits of these auratic objects, Doepner insists that he has never collected for financial gain. Instead, his drive to collect the Twins is fueled by a baseball nostalgia, one that is widespread in our society but especially relevant for him, given his unfulfilled dream to play professional baseball. The Twins collection thereby allows Doepner to stay connected with his youth as both a tremendous pitcher and burgeoning fan. Finally, implementing his talent for telling stories as well as his career as a high school history teacher, Doepner's collection grants him the agency to tell the story of Minnesota baseball and revel in local pride.

Collecting Twins Aura

Passionate collectors throughout history, and the scholars who study them, have taken multiple approaches in their quest to explain this often-addictive behavior. Philosopher Walter Benjamin outlined the powerful concept of "aura" as a means of suggesting the attractive power of original and authentic objects. For him, these kinds of objects (he mentions an ancient statue of Venus) may mean different things to different people over time, but they each possess a confronting and enveloping "uniqueness, that is, its aura."[2] In the game of baseball, game-used objects warrant categorization as auratic objects, especially because they are more than merely tools of the trade. Many players care for their equipment with special affection, naming their bats and relishing these wooden instruments during hitting streaks.

Often, these auratic objects become prized for their value. In 2001, for example, the "Black Betsy," a uniquely curved bat used by "Shoeless" Joe Jackson, sold for more than $577,000. Besides merely belonging to a famous player, items that take part in a historic event, whether a triple play, a no-hitter, a record stolen base, or any other significant moment or achievement, become imbued with that act and are prized. The uniform that Yogi Berra wore when he caught pitcher Don Larsen's perfect game in the 1956 World Series was recently purchased for $600,000; Mark McGwire's 70th home run ball was sold in 1999 for $3 million. Aside from game-used items caught up in the aura of the players and historic moments, mass-produced items that have been preserved throughout history have become equally valuable, though in different ways. Notably, baseball cards from the early 20th century, packaged in cigarette and tobacco products and prized for their scarcity as well as the number of early Hall of Fame players featured, have sold for millions of dollars.

Although the objects Doepner collected in his attic certainly have financial value, he professes his collection "was never about the money," and as a result he "has never sold anything."[3] Still, he has never been short of opportunities to sell, especially the many items he has received directly from Twins players throughout the years. Doepner matter-of-factly believes, "you don't sell gifts."[4] These personal connections underscore his specific admiration for a quartet of Twins Hall of Famers: Rod Carew, Tony Oliva, Harmon Killebrew, and Kirby Puckett. Each player has a dedicated space of collected items in the attic, serving as evidence of Doepner's appreciation for greatness imbued in their objects: "The thing I think is so special about the artifacts is that they were in the games."[5] These possessions include the bat that Twins slugger Harmon Killebrew used to hit his final home run, the 573rd of his career, and a pair of the third baseman's sunglasses from 1965, the season the Twins won its first American League pennant. Items from the other displays include game-used bats, game-used cleats and gloves, as well as socks and even jock straps.

Collecting Nostalgia as a Player, as a Fan

In addition to the appeal of auratic objects, Benjamin notes that the collector's "thrill of acquisition" acts as a rationale for the impassioned and chaotic exercise of collecting, "to renew the old world."[6] This old world is represented in baseball's nostalgic stranglehold on its fans, a position celebrated quite literally in the baseball film *Field of Dreams*, the 1989 commercial success that Michael Butterworth describes as a "uniquely nostalgic testament to an imagined past."[7] This aspect of baseball is prized as unique, epitomized by a recent article in *Sports Illustrated* that painted the sport as "a game out of time. This is the sport's defining quality, its badge of honor. The people who love the game . . . love baseball for its timelessness."[8] This timelessness suggests that the past and present are in constant contact or, as the article states, "In baseball, history is a living and breathing character."[9] Collecting and baseball are a perfect mix because, according to Kevin Moist, "many collecting scholars pick up on Benjamin's discussion of collecting as a kind of struggle with time."[10]

The struggle, for baseball and baseball collectors, seems grounded in the contrast between youth and age, cemented in the nostalgic appeal of childhood. Legendary Los Angeles Dodgers broadcaster Vin Scully eloquently explains, "Children love this game. And when we grow older, the game provides our escape from the troubles of day-to-day life."[11] But given the exclusivity of little league baseball as a predominantly all-male activity, Scully's assessment cannot be framed as universal to both genders. It is, strictly speaking, a sport that has special meaning for men because it elicits nostalgic memories of boyhood. Allen Guttman asserts that the game, played by American boys in little leagues throughout the country, is "most closely bound up with youth," and as a result, "middle-aged and elderly men continue to be faithful to the game they once played because it brings back their own youth."[12] Eldon Snyder posits that it is this nostalgic quality that draws fans to the collections in baseball's Hall of Fame, where the objects gathered trigger "positive feelings about the irretrievable past that they miss in sport today."[13] As Snyder dichotomizes nostalgia into two overlapping categories, collective and private, his focus on the latter kind of nostalgia allows for individuals to cultivate private, personal, and interpretive meanings from collected sports objects by "relat[ing] them to some segment of their own life."[14]

This theme is a central focus of John Bloom's work on baseball cards, in which he asserts that card collecting is a way for older men to retrieve their own youth by recalling their beginnings as players and young collectors: "The popular affinity for baseball cards demonstrated by adult men suggests that nostalgic fantasies surrounding boyhood are in fact an important way in which male spectators identify with the sports they watch."[15] His thorough investigations of card collectors suggest that their intent resides in a specific desire to connect with an innocent and preadolescent past as a means of dealing with a speculative crisis in masculinity.

Yet the constant buying and selling in Bloom's studies of baseball card collectors is not characteristic of Doepner's collecting motivations. Because he was physically unable to compete in the game he loved so dearly, the baseball collection helped Doepner to keep in touch with his youth and his dream of playing for the Twins. After his pitching career ended, a career as an educator blossomed. In 1966, as part of his teaching job, he took a position as a high school baseball coach. That same year, just five years removed from the Minnesota Twins' first game, team owner Cal Griffith sent out free season passes to all of the high school coaches in the Minneapolis area. When Doepner attended his first game that season, he took special care to visit Griffith's office to personally thank him. The result of that simple gesture was a lifelong friendship between the two men, and their bond opened a crucial lifeline for Doepner's collecting pursuits, even after Griffith sold the team in 1984 to banking entrepreneur Carl Pohlad.

When the team moved from the Metropolitan Stadium to the Herbert H. Humphrey Metrodome in 1981, Doepner's relationship with the Twins gave him the opportunity to peruse what the franchise was too frugal to send into storage. Over the course of one month, Doepner stood patiently by as Twins officials rummaged through the Metropolitan Stadium storage room; as he describes it, "whatever they were going to throw away on that day, I got to have a look at it."[16] The anecdote reveals Doepner's ability to appreciate the significance of these items as well as the team's failure to recognize its own history. Combined with a dedication to trolling yard sales and flea markets throughout Minnesota, Doepner implemented an intense drive to complete and catalog his quasi-encyclopedic Twins set. Such determination included peculiar methods, such as sending letters blind; in 2006, Doepner wrote letters to former Twins batboys from the 1960s and 1970s, which yielded a champagne bottle from the Twins' 1965 World Series trip and some game-used player pants.

Doepner's interest and drive speak to the power of these nostalgic objects to connect him to his own ball-playing past and the unfulfilled dream of a professional baseball career. "One of my goals in life," Doepner states, "was to never grow up and so far, so good."[17] Notably, the memories of his career as a Minnesota state champion and a collegiate player on scholarship still resonate with him: "I would have given my eye teeth to have a chance [to play professionally] before my arm blew out . . . what I would have given for one step, a guy could have hit a 500-foot home run off me, just one pitch."[18] Collecting, for Doepner, became the next best means of retaining contact with his potential as a pitcher. Attending college on a baseball scholarship, Doepner sees his pre-injury form on a path to make it to the big leagues, and the injury still nags at him. It is, as Bloom might assert, his crisis.[19] Thus, although he could never step on the professional mound, Doepner's dedication to collecting was a means of regaining some control over his life, his dreams, and the game of baseball, echoing collecting scholar Russel Belk's notion that "private collections help us to gain a sense of mastery and control over 'the little world' of objects we collect as individuals."[20]

Besides connecting with his own past as a baseball player, Doepner's collection provides a means for connecting with the sport as a Twins fan. The process of collecting as a fan, as Pearce attests, "helps in the construction of a personal narrative of selfhood and recognizable, individual identity."[21] Therefore, it is not surprising that Doepner's attic collection features special sections for 1961, the year the Twins arrived in the Twin Cities, and for 1965, the year of the team's first pennant. In the 1961 collection, Doepner holds a bevy of game-used artifacts as well as mass-produced objects like the team's first cereal boxes and baseball cards, plus a Minneapolis Chamber of Commerce welcome pamphlet and a number of welcome flags and pennants. "It's a hit," one sign reads, "for Major League baseball in the upper Midwest." These objects remind Doepner of his own fandom when professional baseball arrived in his hometown, triggering a kind of Minnesota pride that he not only relishes himself but seeks to spread in select public appearances. As his collection grew, Doepner soon realized that he could use his objects in public settings to help others retain their own memories of baseball: "I hope I can keep that youthful love of baseball alive in everyone so the seventy-year old remembers when he was a kid and who his heroes were and to bring that with you to the next generation and the next and the next."[22] During the 1980s and 1990s, therefore, Doepner became a de facto Twins historian, a position he held unofficially for over three decades. Frequently during that tenure, Doepner would neatly collect his Twins memorabilia from a given year or from a given player; place them into a sizable Rubbermaid container or two; and visit schools, banquets, or any number of functions throughout Minnesota to, as he puts it, "give a talk."[23]

Many of these speaking opportunities arose from the notoriety that Doepner received from public displays at an annual winter Twins fan celebration called Twins-Fest. The event, which began in the Metrodome in 1989 and is hosted by the team to raise funds for charity, has featured a Doepner collection display every year. Along with a number of other exhibits and booths sprawled out across the Metrodome outfield, Doepner's nine display cases, four feet wide by eight feet high, often feature thematic presentations. The annual event has become a wildly popular three-day celebration of the Twins, and as a permanent staple, Clyde the Collector has had a forum to display his museum-quality collection.

As a whole, the collection not only preserves history through great artifacts, but tells a story about Clyde Doepner as well. From a burgeoning professional career cut short, to a dedication to cherishing the moments of his childhood and retaining the legacy of his heroes, the collection serves a number of private purposes, none of them financial, from its home in that Victorian attic. Furthermore, Doepner's decision to display his collection outside of his home, on his own terms, reflects his desire to play the role of a storyteller and keep history alive for later generations. Those public appearances not only celebrate the Twins, but a Minnesota history that provides a kind of status for the upper Midwest.

THE TWINS' DISREGARD FOR ITS OWN HISTORY

Given the ways that history and baseball are intertwined, it is surprising that most MLB teams have done very little to maintain their own collections. Instead, the teams rely heavily on private collectors who have the sensibility to collect the massive number of baseball materials produced each year, as well as the baseball Hall of Fame, the game's official preservation entity.

The Twins' decision to throw away much of its material from Metropolitan Stadium in 1981 appears consistent with how other teams have treated their artifacts. As a result, according to Doepner, the Twins "had virtually nothing from before 1995."[24] Specifically, the Twins' lack of commitment to its own history is roughly equivalent to how the New York Yankees treated its stadium and its artifacts before beginning renovations at the end of the 1973 season. While season ticket holders were able to take seats straight out of the stadium after the final game, a fortunate few with connections to the Yankees were allowed to rummage the stadium and purchase what they found at incredibly low prices. According to the *New York Times*, the Yankees exhibited a general "apathy" toward the artifacts that had been stored in the stadium for decades, allowing sports historian Bert Sugar to make off with enough items to fill "a fleet of U-Haul trucks."[25] Those items (including a pair of Babe Ruth's underwear), buried "in rooms that hadn't been opened in years," proved to Sugar that the team simply did not care about its own treasures: "I don't think [Yankees owner] George Steinbrenner knew what he had."[26] Consequently, as noted previously, the Yankees' museum in its new stadium relies mostly on loaned artifacts from private collectors. A similar situation characterizes the artifacts in the New York Mets' museum in its new stadium, Citi Field. The franchise's most famous artifact—the baseball that Mookie Wilson hit between the legs of Red Sox first baseman Bill Buckner in game six of the 1986 World Series—was loaned to the museum by a prominent baseball collector.

The apparent zeal of private collectors to track and salvage historical items has been critical for teams that have suddenly realized the value of celebrating their organizations' narratives materially. Although it may have been seen as too difficult or too expensive to keep track of the full range of items, it is especially surprising that teams have failed to preserve the great number of mass-produced items sold and promoted throughout the decades. These items include baseball cards, team pennants, team and player posters, player-related soda cans, stamps, team programs and scorecards, pins, bobble-head dolls, Wheaties boxes, and magazine covers. Many of these items, which span nearly a century of baseball history, have inspired masses of fans to collect them.

Besides relying on private collectors, teams like the Yankees and Mets have descended upon the baseball Hall of Fame to fill out their museum installations. The displays in both Citi Field and Yankee Stadium, which borrowed dozens of artifacts from the Hall, underscore the great importance of the oldest sports hall of fame. Much of the burden of collecting seems to have fallen to the museum, which houses thousands of items but can only display about 15 percent of its collection at any given time.[27]

In the case of the Twins, the principle of profit-maximization and apathy toward material artifacts stands in direct contrast with Doepner's desire to preserve team history for future generations. This contrast became apparent after an incident during the 2008 season. During a road series against the Los Angeles Angels, Twins infielder Adam Everett played the first four innings of a game with a jersey that incorrectly spelled the team's home state as "Minnestoa." The misspelling was eventually spotted and corrected during the middle of the game. Given the extreme rarity with which baseball jerseys feature incorrect state spellings, Doepner called the Twins and asked to preserve and catalog the jersey. His request denied, Doepner was assured that the team would take responsibility for maintaining this unique piece of Twins history. A few months later, Doepner spotted the game-used jersey for sale with the Twins' other game-used jerseys in the stadium shop and felt compelled to purchase it himself. This oversight highlights both the team's unabashed profit motive and a general apathy toward its history, not to mention incompetence in determining what should be collected and preserved.

CLYDE THE CURATOR AND
THE COLLECTION IN TARGET FIELD

After nearly two decades of privately pining and publicly lobbying for a new stadium, the Twins opened a brand new, open-air baseball stadium, Target Field, in the spring of 2010. As with other recently built stadiums, the purpose for the new facility—siphoning off the public relations spin—aligned with the profit-maximization principles of late capitalist sport by adding new revenue streams via luxury boxes, club seats, team stores, and restaurants spread throughout the building's multiple concourses.[28] Although the overwhelming number of amenities seems purely beneficial for the franchise, a new facility is inevitably short on history and memory, devoid of the historical moments that become intertwined with older stadiums.[29] The Twins' former home, the Metrodome, may not have been well-suited for baseball, but it was the site of the team's only two World Series victories. In addition, most new stadiums are modern, standardized corporate structures that are primarily designed for consumption. Michael Kimmelman refers to these new stadiums as "mallparks," describing them as "packaged, Disney-like palaces of entertainment and commerce . . . [that] cater to our restless consumerism."[30] They could also be considered, using Marc Augé's term, "non-places," devoid of lived cultural meanings.[31]

Thus, furnishing a stadium with historical artifacts can more readily put fans at ease, since "without some proof of our history, we don't know who we are and we cannot forecast or plan where we're going."[32] This seems especially true for baseball, given its crucial relationship with cultural history. Moreover, the Twins realized that the team narrative was being revitalized by a return to outdoor baseball. This was a rhetorical situation, or opportunity, to assert a new identity and message.[33] After three decades inside the cavernous and vapid Metrodome, built for the primary purpose of increasing seating capacity for the NFL's Minnesota Vikings, the move to Target Field celebrated an open-air space designed to create a specifically baseball experience, complete with real grass and other elements of nature. Because, in Doepner's words, the Metrodome was "a football stadium where a baseball game broke out,"[34] the new stadium offered the opportunity for the team to reconnect with the pastoral nostalgia lodged in the memories of the Twins' previous outdoor stadium and the players who had made those pre-Metrodome years memorable.

Yet, as noted previously, the team had virtually no artifacts from that era to showcase. Thus, in 2009, after decades of informal relations, Twins president Dave St. Peter not only created a job that would make Doepner the team's official historian and curator, but included the lease—importantly, not purchase—of his 7,000-piece collection. The position was a dream job for Doepner, and certainly a relief for a franchise desperate to regain its history. At first the team thought that a museum, similar to ones installed in the new stadiums in New York, would be the best way to historicize its new space. The museum concept, furthermore, would make for a smooth transition out of Doepner's already meticulously organized attic. But as Target Field was slowly unveiled, Doepner and the Twins both realized how impressive and relevant his collection could become if it was spread out in smaller display cases distributed throughout the stadium. From that point in late 2009, several months before the opening game at Target Field, Doepner set about making the stadium a living and breathing museum by arranging his collection in a variety of locales.

With the stadium itself as his new display case, however, the tension between the private collector and the public institution became more pronounced. On a private level, Benjamin insists that "collecting loses its meaning as it loses its personal owner. Even though public collections may be less objectionable socially and more useful academically than private collections, the objects get their due only in the latter."[35] Jean Baudrillard privileged this concept via the collector's "secret seraglio," a place where the collection is kept for individual pleasure, or an emotional investiture for owners that Pearce states "is impossible for anybody else to score."[36] This tension is apparent for Doepner, whose insistence on leasing his collection, and thus maintaining possession and control, retains a connection between the individual items and his once-complete and organized attic. The partnership also meant that Doepner could continue to have tactile interaction with and control over his collection, a critical component of access and ownership.[37]

THE COMMERCIAL IMPACT ON COLLECTIONS

Still, even though Doepner and the Twins have, in his words, fused amicably, the collection's existence in the stadium reveals the tension between personal collecting and the commercial motivation of an institution like the Twins. If the franchise had not been so narrowly focused on profit, it might have found ways to keep the artifacts it created, used, and sold in a collection of its own. Instead, its reliance on Doepner as collector and curator highlights its primary function as a baseball *franchise*, underscoring the fact that professional baseball, despite its various meanings and cultural significance, has always been a business.

By moving pieces from Doepner's attic into Target Field, the Twins cannot help but attempt to corporatize and commercialize the collection, a trend that became central for museums throughout the 1980s and 1990s. At an institutional level, the move toward commercialized collections and corporate sponsorship to increase revenue initially seems tied to a shortage of funds.[38] However, though decreases in government funding and private donations have contributed to the trend, the development of a more commercialized museum appears to be a more complex mix of corporate influence at the executive level and the drive to create a more appealing museum experience to lure consumers. In relation to the corporate influence, which Rosalind Krauss notes has created a "profound shift in the very context in which the museum operates,"[39] Burton Weisbrod clarifies that "with the traditional balance of power between curators and administrators gradually shifting in favor of the latter, vital decisions are increasingly made in view of economic viability rather than based on artistic merit and quality."[40]

As a consequence, many contemporary museums have altered their aims from curatorial research and historical cataloging to "emphasiz[ing] education and visitors," acknowledging the commercial pressure to increase attendance and revenue that drives museums to become "products" that can create an "experience" for "consumers."[41] For Belk, this means that museums have moved toward "a marketing orientation" that positions "the customer [as] the potential museum-goer, [and] the product [as] the museum experience derived from exhibitions, facilities, brochures, restaurants, and shops within the museum."[42] The focus here accentuates the Twins as a corporate institution that views Doepner's collection, with much of it placed in its most exclusive and expensive stadium locales, as a means of attracting consumers to a high-priced stadium experience.

Ultimately, there are consequences for the makeup of collections when corporations get involved. Belk states that corporations that sponsor displays expect them to "perform the public-relations work of enhancing their image," as well as connect with consumption activities, as in 1990s exhibitions sponsored by Ferragamo and Polo Ralph Lauren.[43] Taking it a step further, he asserts, when corporations embark on displaying their own collections, a number of ulterior motives are at play: "[When these collections are] housed in a corporate gallery that is open to the public, the firm enhances corporate morale, builds public and community prestige and support, and maintains a good financial investment at the same time."[44] Rather than presenting a challenge to corporate history or highlighting injustices, these corporate displays are dominated by nostalgia and celebratory tones. Consequently, these museums—such as the Coca-Cola and Ford museums—have become "fantasyland[s] geared to corporate myth building."[45]

Encouraging Consumption

The transfer of Doepner's collection into this capitalist theater means that, whatever the items have meant to Doepner personally, they become fundamentally changed once they enter the Target Field mallpark. Although they may remain irrevocably personal for him, situated in the mallpark space, the items function rhetorically on behalf of the franchise. Since the displays are a manifestation of the Twins' decisions about what materials should be deployed and where, there is an inherent power in what is placed in the stadium. Lawrence Prelli notes this potential power, in that "whatever is revealed through display simultaneously conceals alternative possibilities; therein is display's rhetorical dimension.[46] In relation to sports halls of fame, this rhetorical capacity of collections means that "the halls of fame and museums . . . 'express and authenticate the established or official values and images of a society in several ways, *directly*, by promoting and affirming the dominant values and, *indirectly*, by subordinating or rejecting alternate values.'"[47]

Primarily, this public display of Doepner's private collection works to situate fans within the narrative of Twins history, and in doing so, to create a sense of materialized familiarity within a historical and commercialized nonplace. On the one hand, the display of historical items attempts to conceal the overtly commercialized spaces in the new stadium, specifically the numerous restaurants and bars that are scattered throughout Target Field. By placing famous items from Killebrew in the club-level dining area and bar that bears his name, for example, the team attracts and familiarizes consumers with a commercial space. A similar process takes place on the stadium's first level, where a game-used jersey timeline of Kent Hrbek, former Twins first baseman and native Minnesotan, covers the walls of Hrbek's bar. The jersey display provides a materialized career arc of a beloved hometown figure, thus instantly calling forth a sense of Minnesota pride. Critically, however, the collected items are used to invite fans into what is essentially a glorified concession stand. Even though Hrbek lent nothing to the project except his name and image, Twins president Dave St. Peter calls the bar a "kind of hometown spot," a depiction upheld by signature items of the bar's menu, including Bloomington onion rings and walleye, a Minnesota fish staple.[48] This local, and even heroic, cultural focus in both eateries ends up working on behalf of the commercial underpinnings of the restaurants, which like every restaurant in Target Field are operated by one of the largest privately owned companies in the world, Delaware North. A hospitality and food service giant based in Buffalo, New York, Delaware North is the primary food provider for almost fifty professional sports fields, arenas, and complexes across North America.[49] In all, Delaware North runs the six team stores and ten merchandise carts in place throughout the stadium, including a 4,800-square-foot flagship store that is open year-round, an upgrade from just one kiosk in the old Metrodome.

Furthermore, there is a rhetorical dimension to the mass-produced memorabilia items that are on display alongside the historical objects. These products, which trigger a context for audiences to recall their own experiences, include notable items like a Killebrew soda can, a Rod Carew batting trainer, and a Kirby Puckett Wheaties box. As a consequence, Doepner's original meanings surrounding the objects fade and give way to fans' own interpretations. While the memories surrounding these objects seem, once again, to orient the commercialized spaces as historical, the actual displays, which appear akin to department store displays, are more in line with the principles of the late capitalist spectacularization of sport, in which "intensive theming and merchandizing . . . seek to control and direct consumer emotions in a manner that enhances the aura of the sport event, and thereby further stimulates desires for its myriad commodified forms."[50] As a result, the display of mass-produced items throughout the stadium encourages fans to consume the current spate of mass-produced Twins offerings and begin their own collections, evidence of Garry Crawford's assertion that "being a fan is primarily a consumer act and hence fans can be seen first and foremost as consumers."[51] With particular focus on the ordinary objects associated with some of the Twins' best players, the displays advise fans that an opportunity awaits in cultivating the future aura—and, perhaps, future value—of the mass-produced objects available for purchase in the team gift shops. In addition, as Butterworth observed in the gift shop attached to a traveling baseball Hall of Fame exhibit, the displays indicate that the best means of preserving a memory for the future is to buy something today,[52] a sentiment that is echoed in the growing number, size, and profitability of gift shops in art and corporate museums.[53]

Using the Collection for Public Relations

Because fans are consumers, the Twins' exhibition of Doepner's collection is also carefully constructed so as not to offend or disrupt their positive emotions toward the franchise. One example of this positive approach to history is Target Field's Metropolitan Club, a swanky restaurant open to season ticket holders, encased in two stories of glass and perched adjacent to Target Field's right field foul pole. The club is an homage to outdoor baseball in Minnesota that relies heavily on the nostalgia evoked by images and objects from the city's previous open-air stadiums. The entrance to the club is lined with a mural photograph of Metropolitan Stadium, replete with plastic-colored panels that mimic the façade pattern of "The Old Met," the Twins' first stadium in Minnesota. Just beyond the entrance to the club, the walls are covered with black and white photos of older stadiums in Minneapolis and a handful of portraits of baseball greats who briefly played there, including Ted Williams and Willie Mays. Once inside the club, a series of glass display cases presents the Old Met through a broad array of memorabilia: game-used bats, jerseys, pants, caps, stadium seats, stadium bricks, popcorn containers, pennants, pictures, and programs from the era as well as the stadium's pitching rubber, home plate, and centerfield outfield sign. With all of the focus on the outdoor stadiums in Minnesota, it is interesting that the Metrodome, the Twins' home from 1982 to 2009, is not memorialized in the Metropolitan Club. Furthermore, outside of a small note on a stadium timeline in the plaza entrance to Target Field, mention of the Metrodome is completely absent from Target Field.

Given the purpose of the collection to offer a sanitized history by avoiding controversial topics, the Twins' omission indicates a conscious attempt to convince fans that the inherent goodness and nostalgia of outdoor baseball legitimates the expenditure of $387 million in public funds to build the privately owned Target Field for the Twins' billionaire owners, the Pohlad family. For more than two decades, although public opposition remained strong even among multiple relocation threats from the Pohlads, political lobbying efforts worked to push legislation through the Minnesota state legislature. The result squeezed Minneapolis residents into paying the lion's share for the Twins to occupy Target Field rent-free while maintaining control of all revenues from the sales of naming rights, merchandise, concessions, luxury boxes, club seating, and advertising.

Avoiding the material representation of this divisive political battle meant that the Twins had to ignore the Metrodome in Target Field, instead presenting a sanitized history of the team that overtly promotes the city's former outdoor stadiums as blurred symbols of memory. Specifically, the black-and-white photos, old signs, programs, and pieces of Metropolitan Stadium best serve the Twins franchise not as actual historical artifacts, but as conflated signs that feed into nostalgic sentiments of baseball pastoralism, such as innocence, simpler times, and a slower pace of life. This nostalgia is furthered because the Old Met, bulldozed in the 1980s to make way for the Mall of America, no longer stands. Belk compares these kinds of shallow symbolic displays to "that of Disneyland and Disney World where the presentation is sterilized and romanticized in order to make it more visually appealing; more appealing than reality; a hyped reality."[54] Without question, the Metropolitan Club is more appealing than the Metrodome, which has been described as "antiseptically modern" and "positively archaic,"[55] and the new field may also provide a more aesthetic visual outdoor baseball experience than the original Old Met Stadium. At the same time, the Metrodome still exists as a perfectly suitable stadium for baseball, though apparently not a financially acceptable locale for the capitalist business of the game. For over a decade, Twins' executives had called the Metrodome "economically obsolete,"[56] so perhaps only when the stadium is eventually demolished will its memory be celebrated and its reality be constructed and presented.

Because of his position as official team curator, Doepner's identity as a collector has also been sanitized, brought into the fold of the corporate goals of the team franchise. Beyond that, in some ways, his life as a private collector has also been abrogated: "Now that I'm with the Twins, once I signed the contract, anything that someone sends to me, I am honest, I send the Twins."[57] He is now fully under the jurisdiction of a commercial institution, whose primary aims for collecting and display are financial and thereby rhetorical. As a private collector in his attic, Doepner did not focus on any overt commercial or political messages that might be contained in the collection. Inside the stadium, however, both Doepner and his collection are part of an official public relations machine that is controlled by team executives and driven by the fans/consumers who attend games, eat food, and purchase merchandise. Doepner, the team curator, thus becomes complicit in this process as well. Whereas his motivations as a private collector might allow for antiestablishment memorabilia, his aim as the official team curator must always be guided toward creating a positive team image. Consequently, as Belk asserts, the Twins' displays in Target Field "may be 'safe' rather than provocative or adventurous."[58] This principle leaves no room in Target Field for Doepner's "Minnestoa" jersey, for example, or his game-used Kirby Puckett jock strap, and it reduces the likelihood that he will be encouraged to display these kinds of objects in the future. His job, therefore, while granting him unprecedented access to the Twins and Target Field, is also restrictive, because he no longer collects and displays for himself but always "for the benefit of others."[59] Although he does believe that, "Clyde the curator can get it all,"[60] the process of becoming the Twins curator has transformed a boundless private collector into a team official whose collecting pursuits are shaped by the franchise's promotional goals to maintain a positive image and a consumer-friendly environment.

NOTES

1. Susan M. Pearce, *Collecting in Contemporary Practice* (London: Sage Publications, 1998), 174.

2. Walter Benjamin, "The Work of Art in the Age of Mechanical Reproduction," in *Illuminations: Essays and Reflections*, ed. Hannah Arendt (New York: Shocken Books, 1968), 223.

3. Clyde Doepner, interview with author, 10 May 2010.

4. Doepner interview.

5. Doepner interview.

6. Walter Benjamin, "Unpacking My Library," in *Illuminations: Essays and Reflections*, ed. Hannah Arendt (New York: Shocken Books, 1968), 61.

7. Michael L. Butterworth, *Baseball and Rhetorics of Purity: The National Pastime and American Identity during the War on Terror* (Tuscaloosa: University of Alabama Press, 2010), 56.

8. Joe Posnanski, "Loving Baseball," *Sports Illustrated*, 25 July 2011, 1.

9. Posnanski, "Loving Baseball," 21.

10. Kevin Moist, "'To Renew the Old World': Record Collecting as Cultural Production," *Studies in Popular Culture* 31, no. 1 (2008): 102.

11. Posnanski, "Loving Baseball," 10.

12. Allen Guttmann, *From Ritual to Record: The Nature of Modern Sports* (New York: Columbia Free Press), 99.

13. Eldon E. Snyder, "Sociology of Nostalgia: Sport Halls of Fame and Museums in America," *Sociology of Sport Journal* 8 (1991): 230.

14. Snyder, "Sociology of Nostalgia," 235.

15. John Bloom, *A House of Cards: Baseball Card Collecting and Popular Culture* (Minneapolis: University of Minnesota Press, 1997) 12.

16. Doepner interview.

17. Doepner interview.

18. Doepner interview.

19. John Bloom, "Cardboard Patriarchy: Adult Baseball Card Collecting and the Nostalgia for a Presexual Past," in *Hop on Pop*, ed. Henry Jenkins, Tara McPherson, and Jane Shattuc (Durham, NC: Duke University Press, 2002), 116.

20. Russel W. Belk, *Collecting in a Consumer Society* (New York: Routledge, 1995) 110.

21. Pearce, *Collecting in Contemporary Practice*, 174.

22. Doepner interview.

23. Doepner interview.

24. Doepner interview.

25. Richard Sandomir, "Beneath the Hall, a Baseball Vault Full of Treasures," *New York Times*, 29 July 2008, 17.

26. Sandomir, "Beneath the Hall," 20–21.

27. Paul Lukas, "Cooperstown Field Trip Report," *UniWatch Blog*, 10 November 2009, http://www.uni-watch.com/2009/11/10/if-you-damage-this-i-will-beat-your-skull-in-with-it-cooperstown-field-trip-report/ (accessed 10 November 2009).

28. Neil deMause and Joanna Cagan, *Field of Schemes: How the Great Stadium Swindle Turns Public Money into Private Profit* (Lincoln: University of Nebraska Press, 2008).

29. Josh Boyd, "Selling Home: Corporate Stadium Names and the Destruction of Commemoration," *Journal of Applied Communication Research* 28, no. 4 (2000): 330–346.

30. Michael Kimmelman, "At the Bad New Ballparks" (review of *The Last Days of Shea: Delight and Despair in the Life of a Mets Fan*, by Dana Brand), *New York Review of Books*, 5 November 2010, http://www.nybooks.com/articles/archives/2009/nov/19/at-the-bad-new-ballparks.

31. Marc Augé, *Non-places: Introduction to an Anthropology of Supermodernity*, trans. John Howe (London: Verso, 1995), 78.

32. Russel W. Belk, "Possessions and the Sense of Past," in *Highways and Byways: Natural-istic Research from the Consumer Behavior Odyssey*, ed. Russel W. Belk (Provo, UT: Association for Consumer Research, 1991) 124.

33. Lloyd Bitzer, "The Rhetorical Situation," *Philosophy & Rhetoric* 1, no. 1 (1968): 1–14.

34. Doepner interview.

35. Benjamin, "Unpacking My Library," 67.

36. Jean Buadrillard, "The System of Collecting," in *The Cultures of Collecting*, ed. John Elsner and Roger Cardinal (Cambridge, MA: Harvard University Press, 1994), 10; Susan M. Pearce, *On Collecting: An Investigation into Collecting in the European Tradition* (New York: Routledge, 1995), 355.

37. Brenda Danet and Tamar Katriel, "No Two Alike: Play and Aesthetics in Collecting," *Play and Culture* 2 (1989): 253–277.

38. Burton A. Weisbrod, *To Profit or Not to Profit: The Commercial Transformation of the Nonprofit Sector* (Cambridge, UK: Cambridge University Press, 2000).

39. Rosalind Krauss, "The Cultural Logic of the Late Capitalist Museum," *October* 54, no. 3 (1990): 5.

40. Weisbrod, *To Profit or Not to Profit*, 248.

41. Barbara Kirshenblatt-Gimblett, *Destination Culture: Tourism, Museums, and Heritage* (Berkeley: University of California Press, 1998), 138–139.

42. Belk, *Collecting in a Consumer Society*, 133.

43. Belk, *Collecting in a Consumer Society*, 115.

44. Belk, *Collecting in a Consumer Society*, 116

45. Belk, *Collecting in a Consumer Society*, 118.

46. Lawrence J. Prelli, *Rhetorics of Display* (Columbia: University of South Carolina Press, 2006), 2.

47. Michael M. Ames, *Museums, the Public, and Anthropology: A Study in the Anthropology of Anthropology* (Vancouver: University of British Columbia Press, 1986), 9, quoted in Snyder, "Sociology of Nostalgia," 237.

48. Tyler Mason, "Hrbek's Adds Local Flavor to Target Field: Restaurant and Bar Named After Former Twins First Baseman," *MLB.com*, 9 September 2009, http://mlb.mlb.com/news/article.jsp?ymd=20090909&content_id=6874050&fext=.jsp&c_id=min (accessed 12 September 2009).

49. Delaware North Companies, "Delaware North Opens Baseball Season with Local Favorites," *Delaware North Press Release*, http://www.prnewswire.com/news-releases/delaware -north-opens-baseball-season-with-local-favorites-118941724.html (accessed 30 March 2011).

50. David L. Andrews, "Sport, Culture, and Late Capitalism," in *Marxism, Cultural Studies, and Sport*, ed. Ben Carrington and Ian McDonald (New York: Routledge, 2009), 226–227.

51. Garry Crawford, *Consuming Sport: Fans, Sport, and Culture* (New York: Routledge, 2004), 4.

52. Butterworth, *Baseball and Rhetorics of Purity*, 51.

53. Belk, *Collecting in a Consumer Society*, 135.

54. Belk, *Collecting in a Consumer Society*, 123.

55. deMause and Cagan, *Field of Schemes*, 66.

56. Jay Weiner, "Target Field: Some Impressions at the First of Many Openings," *MinnPost.com*, 29 March 2010, http://www.minnpost.com/jayweiner/2010/03/29/16975/target_field_some_impressions_at_the_first_of_many_openings (accessed 4 April 2010).

57. Doepner interview.

58. Belk, *Collecting in a Consumer Society*, 115.

59. Belk, *Collecting in a Consumer Society*, 125.

60. Doepner interview.

9

Collecting "History in the Making": The Privatization of Propaganda in National Socialist Cigarette Cards

Mechtild Widrich

> *The picture cards I so eagerly collected in my boyhood and youth were obtained with coupons that came in the packs out of which my mother tapped her cigarettes after closing the shop. . . . I see myself at the living-room table, pasting in the pictures. . . . [I]t is almost a ritual, the squirting out of the yellow Uhu tube.*[1]
>
> —Günther Grass, *Peeling the Onion*

In his memoir of a childhood lived in the shadow of World War II in Danzig on the Baltic coast (now Poland), German Nobel Prize winner Günther Grass writes at length about his passion for collecting cigarette cards.[2] His interest in art and eventual career as a writer are, according to Grass, traceable to the cheap color reproductions of masterpieces—Botticelli, Giorgione, Dürer—produced by the German cigarette company Reemtsma. "I lived in pictures," he affirms, bartering a Raphael for a Caravaggio, or begging for cards from adult smokers.[3] Collecting the cards and his increasing expertise in their distant referents is presented by Grass as an idyllic counter-reality amid the disasters of war.

Whatever we make of Grass's retrospective account, he did become an art student after the war, before committing himself decisively to writing. But even in Grass's narrative, the war encroaches on this idyllic pastime: one of his "most reliable providers" of cards dies on the front, and new series replaced the ones Grass liked: "animals, flowers, highlights of German history, and the powdered faces of popular film stars."[4] Did these *other* cards, particularly the highlights from German history, provoke in their collectors the same passionate conviction that the art cards provoked in Grass? After all, just like the new series, Grass's own desperate wartime activity—he briefly enlisted in the Waffen-SS in 1945, at sixteen years of age—interposed itself between Grass the card collector and Grass the artist.[5]

This essay discusses the collecting of cigarette cards, in its political and affective dimension, in Germany and Austria on the eve of World War II, a time when the subjects on the cards may have been less innocent than Grass's list would lead one to suppose. With the dual goal of making money and promoting National Socialism, cigarette cards were manufactured in Germany and the occupied territories as a form of propaganda. These cards fused youth culture and propaganda photography with the forceful means of dissemination that was cigarette packaging (even though, as is well known, Hitler himself was a fervent nonsmoker). Some of the issues Grass introduces in his memories of cigarette card collecting are important here: Can the process of collecting be seen as a refuge from reality, and in the spirit of fascist propaganda, as a mechanism of manipulation? What is at stake in this discussion is not just the political efficacy of collections, but the actual concrete mechanisms by which collecting and trading can elicit conviction. Grass claims that he was sufficiently captivated by the cheap cards to go to art school—could a contemporary of his have been sufficiently captivated to join the Waffen SS?

My case study is a series of cigarette cards edited by Hitler's personal photographer, Heinrich Hoffmann. Issued in the early 1940s, their subject is the then-recent annexation of Austria into the German Reich (March 1938), narrated with the help of diminutive black and white images that could be organized, according to their numbering, in a corresponding album (see figure 9.1). This series, titled *Hitler's Path to Great Germany* (*Großdeutschland*), was part of the endeavor to rewrite Austrian history into that of "Great-Germany." This operation was deemed necessary in Austria after years of anti-German propaganda during which National Socialism had been banned. The images were distributed solely on the Austrian market, in packs of the popular Austrian cigarette brand Korso. In contrast to the coupons Grass mentioned, which had to be sent in, in our case the cards were stuck inside the packs; hence they came into the households whether one wanted them or not.[6] They were mass products, mere ephemera riding a popular product, but they were also collectibles and thus to some extent the site of a private engagement. The resulting collections aimed not at being unique, but at being complete, at being identical. The strategy that I see at work here might be called the privatization of propaganda. The hypothesis is that the aim of the process of collecting, in this case, is the formation not of a collection, but of a collective.[7]

PHOTOGRAPHS AND PROPAGANDA

Let us begin with the photograph (see figure 9.2) in which an impressive baroque convent serves as background for girls in traditional Austrian dress (dirndl), cheering a male figure visible from behind in an open car. The atmosphere is that of a monarch ceremonially touring his country.[8] The man in the car is Adolf Hitler. It is 14 March 1938, and Hitler is on his way to Vienna. The resignation of the Austro-Fascist government in Vienna had formally taken place the day before, after months

Figure 9.1.   Trading cards from the series Hitler's Path to Great-Germany. Image courtesy of Mechtild Widrich.

of political pressure and infiltration; the situation was far from stable. The peaceful scene occludes the fact that we are made the witnesses of a military maneuver, wherein Austria became part of Germany in the famous Anschluss, an annexation certainly welcomed by many, but publicized as an entirely voluntary union. The seemingly neutral documentary photograph of the alleged spontaneous encounter with the Austrian populace is thus perfectly geared to the production of its correct "image" in history. Of course, this is what propaganda does, but it is difficult to understand how such imagery could function at all, let alone effectively, in a medium more notable for irreverent handling and exchange (Grass's extra Raphael traded for a Correggio) than for edification.

The fact that we are dealing primarily with photographs, posing as neutral documents, is the obvious first step in understanding their effectiveness. In the 1970s, Susan Sontag emphasized the power of photography to miniaturize and appropriate the world, not only by taking a photograph, but, and more important for her, by a similar if curious process through which the viewer of a mass-produced photograph imagines "being there," "taking the picture," and, in a sense, taking the place of that which is photographed. Sontag proposes that we can appropriate experience with the

Figure 9.2. Card nr. 196 "Begrüssung des Führersbei der Einfahrt in Melk an der Donau (März 1938)" [The greeting of the Führer as he enters Melk on the Danube, March 1938]. Image courtesy of Mechtild Widrich.

help of the camera.[9] Experience is a concept that might help us understand how and why propaganda joined card collecting so successfully. Collecting is an experience, and it binds together a whole series of coordinated experiences—both internal and subjective, and to some extent external and objective public experiences—because the acts of collecting, trading, and display are seen and appreciated as such by others.[10]

The manufacture of experience is no theoretical invention of mine, but was frankly acknowledged by Nazi propaganda minister Joseph Goebbels as central to propaganda. "History in the Making" (*Werdende Geschichte*) was the title of a speech he gave in 1928 demanding the professionalization of National Socialist agitation and leadership: "From now on, we no longer speak and write just for ourselves, but for Germany. . . . What we are doing today is real politics and as such, history in the making."[11] The awareness of a historical process taking place in the present strikes us by its almost postmodern vision of a play between distance and closeness that breaks down the patient making of history through linear time. For National Socialist aims, and in particular in the case of Austria, which—even though its politics after 1934 were authoritarian and essentially fascist—had positioned its Catholic nationalism against Germany (at least officially), history needed to be remade even faster and more efficiently.[12] And Hoffmann knew how to do it. The motorcade image is constructed to make us part of the road trip: the recession of the winding road and the cropped back figure of Hitler are, of course, classical methods for visually drawing the viewer into the picture. The arms of the girls performing the Hitler-Gruss and Hitler's gesture of acceptance form a gateway for the viewer. The pickets on the road take the movement up and carry us forward, toward the monastery, into Austria, in a natural flow. We appropriate the visual cliché and its content, we see where the road is going, and we can follow it ourselves.

But the mention of cliché already raises the major difficulty in using experience as a model of collecting, because the familiar threatens to turn banal. Indeed, Sontag's account of the possessive function of photography discussed above is to a great extent a moralizing discourse: through collecting photographs of the world, we trivialize and reduce it to a series of disconnected commodities. In her argument, the photographs of atrocities produced by the Vietnam War result in a desensitization to suffering.[13] But if something like this is the case—or if it can even be feared to be the case—for photographs as collectibles, then we must inquire why Hitler and his propagandists pursued it while being hostile to political kitsch in general.

To what extent are these cards part of a well-functioning, ideological apparatus of fascist propaganda? In some ways, Nazi propaganda was as well-organized as the party: as early as 13 March 1933, less than two months after Hitler became chancellor of Germany, part of the operations of the Ministry of the Interior was transferred to the newly founded "ministry for people's enlightenment and propaganda."[14] Under this new administrative unit, run by Joseph Goebbels, the propaganda machine he had built in the preceding years switched gears from being run by a party to being run by a state. Soon it controlled all cultural expression, from literature, theater, and art to the public mass media of radio, newspapers, and journals. On the edge of this ambitious propaganda machine, individual producers began to flood the German market with a variety of Nazi knick-knacks, from swastika-shaped lamps to kitchen utensils and ashtrays decorated with Hitler's portrait. Candles, hairpins, ties, brushes, transfer pictures, and even thimbles bore the faces of the new political celebrities or the symbols of the new regime. These items are not only telling about popular enthusiasm, and about the endless applicability of originally photographic images (remade in wax, embossed, embroidered), but also about how business needs could take precedence over the high rhetoric of Nazism. This ephemera was not to the liking of the Party, and so in May 1933, Goebbels enacted a "law for the protection of National symbols," which called a halt to the use of "National" (meaning National Socialist) symbols for advertisement or any other means that might "infract their sense of dignity," a law that was enforced by threat of confiscation.[15]

The familiarization of propaganda, its penetration of the private sphere—be it in the form of household goods, everyday objects, or cigarette cards—had an effect on personal investment in Nazism. With Nazi-kitsch, the political statement transferred into the decoration of the household. The knick-knacks charged the interior with the symbolic presence of political interaction; they became part of the surroundings, while at the same time remaining useful tools, almost casually carrying their political message. This collapse of the political into the commercial, as well as its ubiquity even in the heart of the private sphere, must have been difficult to control. Was there room for the subversive use of a swastika toilet brush? For my argument, the fact that photos could turn into kitsch is relevant, and it makes our inquiry even more pressing. Were the cigarette cards kitsch, and, could they collapse the heroic images of National Socialist endeavors into banal miniatures? Hoffmann, although he was close to Hitler, had to go through official censorship channels, perhaps because of Goebbels's dislike for the photographer. In any case, his merchandise was passed, partially because the documentary look of the images set them apart from more flagrant kitsch, but probably also because they had a precedent in the so-called *Reservisten-bilder* (army reservist images) popular in the nineteenth and early twentieth centuries. These images were mass-produced patriotic posters or ornamental frames, often leaving space for the photographic portrait of the individual soldier to be glued in.[16] This particular genre of photographic representation, combined with the manipulative neglect of context, was precisely what Goebbels prescribed. And yet Hoffmann's products were more than just well-placed propaganda; they were devotional objects, serving private desires and political goals at the same time. Collecting, in short, could become a political end in itself.

THE POLITICS OF CIGARETTE CARD COLLECTING

The question of kitsch aside, we must ask whether propaganda is that simple: Can private desires and political goals be reconciled so seamlessly by the products of what Sontag calls "fascinating fascism?" I think the compatibility of a collector's allegiance to his or her objects with allegiance to a political cause that the objects are supposed to serve cannot simply be read off the cards, nor reconstructed simply on the basis of an imaginative encounter with them. We need to know the habits of collecting through which they entered the private sphere, and what channels collecting kept open to the public world.

Although the production of cigarette cards devoted to Nazi propaganda began in 1933, the year Hitler came to power in Germany, as a collaboration between Hoffmann and Reemtsma, the concept was much older. Hoffmann had invented neither cigarette cards nor cigarette card albums, which were first introduced in 1895. Indeed, albums were particularly popular in Germany, a fact that led historian Erich Wasem to describe the psychology of collecting trading cards in terms of the "diligence of good pupils being rewarded for consumer achievement."[17]

Indeed, the album is crucial, and I attend to it now, because it is not just part of achieving a specific goal; rather it "dignifies" the content. Reemtsma had produced "Little Pictures" (*Kleine Bildchen*) for marketing cigarettes since 1923, and these were themselves a continuation of the trading cards introduced in Europe and the United States in the 1870s, at a time when color lithography became an affordable and qualitatively satisfactory method for the mass production of images. Although trading cards with various formats of distribution (by the salesperson, inside the box, or by mail through coupons) were thus a familiar device for fostering customer loyalty, they had by the 1930s become a popular mass product in their own right.[18] A particular series was usually in circulation for several months, after which missing cards—now mostly with photographic reproductions—could only be obtained by trading. Propagandistic cards proved highly successful in Germany; the editions numbered several millions.[19] In part this is because collecting trading cards simply was a mass phenomenon, but also in part because many Germans—particularly the young—were enthusiastic about the supposed Nazi renewal of their country after years of unemployment and depression.

Hoffmann was the biggest image contributor to the press of the Third Reich. Today we know that he helped shape Hitler's official appearance in hundreds of photographic sessions, rehearsing the gestures and mannerisms used in official speeches. Those pictures were not intended for circulation and became known only when Hoffmann proudly reproduced them in the memoirs he published after the war.[20] Germans of the time could encounter his photographs from various official commissions in journals and magazines. Hoffmann also knew how to use his connections to the party elite to produce various image-based devotional goods on his own account. Since the 1920s, he had provided the German market with postcards and photographic albums of various kinds, all with a broad political rhetoric that both established and fed off the Hitler cult, incorporating his own photographs as well as material he acquired from other sources (copyright was not yet an issue).[21] The fact that he always remained a private businessman, connected to the party and its leaders personally and financially, but without an official position in the propaganda ministry, shows his skill at mixing private and state interests; even his official-sounding title, *Reichsbildberichterstatter* ("Reich Picture Correspondent"), was Hoffmann's own invention.[22]

To understand the particularity of Hoffmann's operation, we need to examine the very interface of public and private interests that drove the cigarette card phenomenon: the collector's album that advertisements described as of "lasting value" to the collector. Available at tobacconists for one Reichsmark, it was in fact an elaborate book with a multicolored cardboard cover composed of almost 100 pages of text, with blank spaces marking where the cards should be glued in (see figure 9.3). Although no publication date is given, the inside of the cover tells us that the album passed censorship on February 1, 1940, several months after the outbreak of World War II. The length of the text and the number of images is beyond the conventions of the medium: with its 312 missing pieces and 96 pages of text, the enterprise is excessive by card-album standards. Cigarettes were the ideal product for such a large set, as an adult would buy up to one or more packs a day—in contrast to, let us say, the package of meat extract that the Liebig company (another company famous for trading cards) produced. The collector had to do a fair amount of work before everything was neatly put in order. The individual cards are 1.9 by 2.5 inches; on the verso is printed the subject, a number indicating where to place it in the album,

Gleich machtvolle Kundgebungen gab es im Jahre 1937 anläßlich des Besuches des Reichsaußenministers von Neurath in Wien am 22. Februar. Durch die Bewaffnung der Wiener Unterwelt mit Stahlruten suchte man diese Demonstration niederzuknüppeln, aber trotzdem wirkte der Empfang, den das deutsche Wien dem Abgesandten des Führers bereitete, überwältigend.

Jede der großen Taten Adolf Hitlers auf dem Wege der Befreiung von Versailles wurde in Österreich mit jubelndem Herzen aufgenommen; selbst der einfachste Volksgenosse fühlte es instinktiv, daß auch für seine Heimat, die ja auch die Heimat des Führers war, die Stunde der Befreiung kommen müsse. Darum weiter die Zähne zusammengebissen und gewartet, gewartet! Am Geburtstag des Führers trugen unzählige eine Blume im Knopfloch. Ein Oberstleutnant, der im Kriege ein Auge verloren hatte und auch eine Blume trug, wurde deshalb polizeilich bestraft, verlor auf Grund dieser Strafe sein Amt und seine Pension und stand mit seiner Familie vor dem Nichts. Das war die österreichische Wirklichkeit aller dieser harten Jahre!

Abfahrt des Führers von Mühldorf am Inn an dem denkwürdigen 12. März 1938

Einfahrt in Schärding bei der Befreiung Österreichs

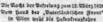

Zertrümmert liegt das Krukenkreuz, das Symbol der Knechtschaft, am Boden. Nacht zum 12. März 1938 in Wien

Die Nacht der Befreiung zum 12. März 1938. Vom Haus der „Vaterländischen Front" in Wien weht die Hakenkreuzfahne

177

Im Sommer 1937 begann die Regierung eine gewisse Verhandlungsbereitschaft mit der „nationalen Opposition" (das Wort Nationalsozialismus gab es offiziell nicht im Regierungslexikon) zu heucheln; Dr. Seyß-Inquart wurde in den Staatsrat berufen und beauftragt, die abseits stehenden nationalen Kreise zur Mitarbeit heranzuziehen. Aber diese ganze Angelegenheit war mehr ein Manöver der jesuitisch geschulten Regierungsmänner, um eine Spaltung innerhalb der Partei herbeizuführen zwischen jenen, die mit Schuschnigg unterhandeln wollten, und jenen, die da sagten, daß man sich mit Henkersknechten nicht an einen Tisch setzen könne. Durch das „Ordnungsschutzgesetz" vom 18. August blieb auch das Verbot der Partei und aller ihrer Abzeichen weiter in Kraft.

Erst der 12. Februar 1938, der Tag des Besuches Schuschniggs auf dem Obersalzberg beim Führer, brachte den Stein ins Rollen. Eine Erlösung war dieses „Berchtesgadener Abkommen" für das deutsche Volk Österreichs! Jeder mußte es mit absoluter Sicherheit, daß es jetzt, nachdem der Bewegung einige Freiheiten gegeben werden mußten, nachdem es sogar Seyß-Inquart als nationalsozialistischen Innen- und Sicherheitsminister im Kabinett gab und die Gleichberechtigung der österreichischen Nationalsozialisten wutschnaubend anerkannt werden mußte, für

Der Führer überschreitet die alte Grenze Österreichs auf der Braunauer Innbrücke am 12. März 1938

71

the logo of the issuing tobacco company (Austria Tabakwerke), and the title of the series. Individually, the cards were to some extent self-contained, the caption providing minimal information, and sometimes outrageous: the card showing the "Jewish dictator of Munich in 1919" reads, "This is how our men of power [*Machthaber*] looked then!"). Once glued into the album, the back was invisible, but the caption was reproduced in the album and supplemented by the continuous text in Gothic type. The arrangement of the cards seems less coherent, narrative continuity being due to the text. Because of the design, it sometimes seems that the story turns into stories; in many cases, the individual pages contain their own subplots. Text-only and image-only pages alternate with all possible variations, and we even find some drawings printed in the album. These variations notwithstanding, there is a master narrative culminating with the Anschluss, but the often-confusing image–text relationship impairs the clarity of any plot. The resulting sketchiness of the narrative does not necessarily reduce its force as propaganda. On the contrary, it leaves room for free associations and makes the album more individual, even if this individuality is an impression simulated by the mass-produced item. I return to this tension between individual and "corporate" identity at the end of this text.

Most striking is the title on the olive green cover: *Wie die Ostmark ihre Befreiung Erlebte*: "How the Eastmark [Austria's name after the Anschluss] experienced its liberation" (see figure 9.4).[23] This celebratory slogan, with its reference to lived experience—*erleben* literally means to live through something—points to the significance of personal experience in the use of cigarette cards as propaganda. It also points to its difficulties, because according to the title, it is not individual collectors or even Austrians, but Austria itself that experiences its liberation. The coming together of collectors as Austrians, as liberated Austrians, as Nazi citizens of the Eastmark, is a task that the cigarette cards cannot presuppose, but one to which they must in their modest way contribute.

MATERIALIZING HISTORY

Unlike propaganda in public space, such as photographs of the Führer on banners, organized marches, and film, the cigarette cards entered consciousness through the backdoor. The recipient's desire to actually enter the process of collecting could be activated even without an explicit decision to collect. The act of putting the photographs in the order suggested by their numbering, the need to complete the set, and the painstaking slowness of mounting one image after the other made the receiver into the orchestrator of an involved and coherent history that had not been common knowledge in Austria prior to annexation. Thus we must consider this act both as a means of letting history enter the private sphere and as a personalized "opportunity" to come to terms with this history via, very literally, taking possession of it. History becomes a game of individualized appropriation. The owner of the cards, in making the decision about which card to keep and which to exchange, in receiving new

Figure 9.4.   Cover of the album. Image courtesy of Mechtild Widrich.

pieces of the story over time, becomes involved in this official German history. The accompanying album was essential to stabilizing the fugitive cards. In the moment when the cards were transferred into the album, the incompleteness of the series became visible as blank spaces, yet another motivation to keep going. As we recall from Grass's description, the cards were often given to children by adults, thus involving more persons in the process than just those retaining the cards. Jean Baudrillard has pointed out that for children, "collecting represents the most rudimentary way to exercise control over the outer world: by laying things out, grouping them, handling them."[24] In this case, the metaphorical taking possession of the world through photography is turned into literal possession of the cards. This possession and play with the cards imparts a mass of historical detail that most of the children's parents did not have, having been educated in a different political system. The cards thus gave the child an advantage over the parental generation, an "I can tell you how it really was."

What exactly is the story that is being told? The unknown author of the text (Hoffmann, the publisher, did not usually write the texts himself) organized the cigarette cards into fourteen chapters based loosely on Hitler's biography and rise to power.[25] We start with Adolf's youth in the "land of his ancestors," Austria, with the first pictures showing—what could reveal so much about the Führer?—the landscape and rock formations of the place of his birth. The text exclaims: "Inexhaustible is the power of German peasantry. With a love in which the unity between man and earth manifests itself like a natural strength, with a force that resembles love in its will to sacrifice and its unscrupulous devotion, the peasant clings to his land."[26] This is the opening sentence of the text, which then launches into an account of the geographical specificities of Upper Austria, all prototypically "German," of course. The initial photos are not of exceptional quality; they are stock tourist shots of landscapes and buildings the Führer inhabited as a child, such as one might find in a tourist shop on the spot: a rather weak visual opening after the thunderous type and the hulking photographed figure of the mature Hitler on the cover. The text is much more exuberant, and its excesses make clear that we are not merely reading reportage, but rather attending to the voice of History itself, the official fascist version of history, aiming at an unbroken and unbreakable teleology of the events.

The peculiarity of the cigarette cards, and of the way they were distributed and collected, is that they threaten to disrupt rather than support the coherence of this narrative. Between chapter 1 ("About the ancestors and the land of his ancestors") and chapter 14 ("Defenders of the Reich"),[27] we are told the story of Hitler's youth in Austria, his service in World War I, the postwar crises, the foundation of the National Socialist Party, and its rise in Germany. This tale of steady success amid the ruinous politics of the Weimar Republic is balanced by disasters in Austrian politics since the dissolution of the monarchy in 1918: civil war, unemployment, suppression of National Socialism, and the subjugation of Austria's populace by communists and Jews. Surprising in retrospect is the number of cards devoted to the communist government in Bavaria (called by the Nazis the *Rätediktatur,* "council" or "soviet" dictatorship), its alleged crimes, and its eventual overthrow by conservative Freikorps—a set of circumstances that Hoffmann had already exploited in his first book, which resulted in Hoffmann's acquaintance with Hitler. The climax is reached in the union with Austria in 1938, on page 70. The text presents the event as the homecoming of Hitler as the son of the country, now grown into a powerful and fatherly leader. The Austrians' wishful longing for their Führer is the obvious subtext, most likely reflecting the actual sentiments of about half of the population at that time. The making visible of this implicit emotional and political content can be seen for instance in the cards illustrating Hitler's youth: the locations shown in the photographs carry swastikas, as if they had always been there (see figure 9.5, cards 10, 26). There might not have been "historical" images available, but presenting the region of Hitler's youth through the looking glass of the Anschluss has the advantage of showing the course of history as immanent in the very landscape. It was merely a matter of time, the cards seem to say, before the inevitable would come true.

Hitler's coming to power in Germany and the subsequent success of the German nation finally serve as an argument for history in the present, legitimating the whole story of Nazi struggle. Thus there are several demonstrations of military power (card 299), and the high quality of most of those images suggests that we are looking at professional press material, most of it from Hoffmann and his studio. They follow the aesthetic conventions of National Socialist propaganda photography, which skillfully emptied the *neu-sachlich* style of its critical potential, while the emphasis on shapes, sharp black and white contrasts, shadows, and dynamic composition evokes the avant-garde of the 1920s. Particularly suggestive is the shot of Hitler

Figure 9.5.   Card nr. 26 "Leonding. Zum 'Elternhaus des Führers'" [Leonding. The Führer's parents' house] and nr. 10 "Geburtshaus in Braunau" [birth house in Braunau]. Image courtesy of Mechtild Widrich.

breaking ground on the Autobahn connecting Salzburg and Munich: here, an event of symbolic precedence (the joining of Austria and Germany) is celebrated in a self-conscious image of media frenzy, with cameramen crowding around the Führer to capture the historic performance.

The quality of the images differs throughout the series and is seldom as high as in these last photographs. Many of the anonymous civil war pictures are from unknown sources, and some are clearly reproductions from journals or other published material; lithographs of unphotographed events, such as assassination attempts, seem to sit uneasily in the same frame as mug shots of the aggressors.[28] On the one hand, the cards' equal sizes and framing, as well as their physical identity as trading cards, make the recipient naturalize the incoherence in their formal presentation; on the other hand, the unevenness in quality actually works as an advantage in convincing the recipient about their truth value. Their character as documents, as sources, is foregrounded, concealing the obvious tendentiousness of the narrative, which is presented as coming together from various sources rather than as manufactured whole cloth. The album therefore does not give the impression of a simple vessel for archiving the images, a tool merely for putting them in order, but it has all the highs and lows of wordless affirmation and speechifying that a fully articulate propaganda product (e.g., a Riefenstahl film) would need.

Ultimately, this orchestral inconsistency of the finished card album probably did not have the force to mesmerize the collector so much as it facilitated more personal connection to the history one had pieced together oneself—an affiliation with the photos predicated on finding one's own place in the history of the movement. This insight answers, to some extent, the question about the kitsch status of the cigarette cards and its effect on their propaganda value. If there is an intrinsic potential for ridiculousness in handling and trading diminutive versions of Hitler, his friends, and his enemies (my "Führer at 21" for your "Jewish dictator of Munich"), this heterogeneity of the cards is only partially neutralized by the printed album with its sermon-like Gothic type. There is of course a kitsch element to this continuous text as well, but since in some ways the images tend toward the fragmentary and the text toward monumentalization, the two effectively balance each other, giving the finished product something of the roughness of the historical process, but also the artificial comfort of a fairy tale with a happy ending. Yet this narrative coherence imparted by the album ought not to be overestimated. Mieke Bal has pointed out the reducibility of some forms of collecting to "story-telling," but of course the collector-archivist is in our example always limited to putting "things in order."[29] What is interesting about this particular set of cards, in contradistinction to Grass's art masterpieces, for example, is that the potentially indifferent process of collecting here commits one to some extent to telling a particular kind of history. This history emerges the further one goes with the album, making, or aiming at making, the individual collectors members of a movement.

The external activation of seemingly private desires through more purchases and exchanges is a connection between propaganda and advertisement, and the participatory aspect granted to the collector, as well as the one-to-one experience in assembling the series, operates—ideally at least—as a slow approximation of the Anschluss narrative, enabling a budding identification with the new history. To this end, what is imperfect about the cigarette cards as propaganda, their apparent modesty, only serves to ingratiate them into a private life that may go untouched by more massive means of disinformation.

COLLECTING AS RECOLLECTING: THE CIGARETTE CARD COLLECTOR'S WORLDVIEW

Having acquainted ourselves with the model of propagandistic cigarette cards, with the content of one collection of National Socialist cards, and with their political and affective dimensions, we now inquire about the intellectual dimension of this collection and mode of collecting. What, if any, is the worldview of a collector of such cards? How we can arrive at a reconstruction of worldview from the facts of propaganda is pointed out on some of the cards themselves. History is very literally in the making on card number 90 of the series, titled *Fackelzug durch das Brandenburger Tor anlässlich der Ernennung Adolf Hitlers zum Reichskanzler, Berlin, 30. Januar 1933*: the torchlight procession through the Brandenburg gate on the occasion of Hitler's appointment as *Reichskanzler*, Berlin, 30 January 1933. The photograph was widely distributed after Hitler's takeover, in journals, posters, and postcards (see figure 9.6). Although this seems to prove that Hitler's propaganda machine was already at work in January 1933, both in staging as well as in documenting the "mass ornament," recent scholarship has revealed that the image was actually produced a few months later on the occasion of the shooting of a film about Hitler's coming to power in 1933.[30] The album text—insisting that the event was "not an arranged demonstration,"[31] but rather the unplanned celebration by hundreds of thousands of German citizens, with their "overfull hearts," on the day Hitler was named chancellor by President Hindenburg—is not simply untrue; the self-conscious use of simulation is part and parcel of a flexible view of history as essentially waiting to be made in the present.

Historian Rudolf Herz has unearthed an anonymous photographic document from the actual event that gives us a glimpse into the aesthetic strategy of Hitler's propaganda apparatus (see figure 9.7). The comparison of the two photographs shows the advantage of the photograph of the staged event over the real one. It is not only the weak technical quality of the latter, the blurring of the marching people with their torches into one smeared streak of light due to the exposure time of the camera, that must have led to the decision. The main difference lies in the overall impression of the "masses," the people on the street, who appear as perfectly choreographed patterns in the staged version. The rationale must have been to show the supporters of Hitler's regime in control, of their own representation if not of the political process, which is in the hands of the Führer. The individual is thus

Figure 9.6. Card nr. 90 "Der Fackelzugdurch das Brandenburger Tor am 30. Januar 1933" [Torchlight procession through the Brandenburger Tor on January 30, 1933]. Image courtesy of Mechtild Widrich.

Figure 9.7. Anonymous photograph showing the torchlight procession on January 30, 1933. Image courtesy of Mechtild Widrich.

shown willingly submerging into the pattern, and this formal synthesis as well as the Brandenburger Tor in the background thematize the idea of politics as theatrical performance. With the exchange of the image of the actual event for the one from the film, the restaging of history is taken for the historical fact. Almost ironically, the photographer of the staged event remains unknown, as if taking a picture with a camera was still considered only a mechanical procedure for capturing reality.[32]

Many of the cards show the individuals as a collective, either as iconic patterns of bodily discipline or in sentimentalized devotion to the Führer. If we look at the album for a moment without a single card put in, we become aware that it came equipped with several full-sized images, starting with the stern Hitler-as-father-figure on the cover. The photograph appears again as card number 179, titled "The unforgettable evening of March 12, 1938. The Führer on the balcony of the city hall in Linz," restating Hitler's abilities as statesman in the meeting with Mussolini, displaying his authority. This is countered by the compassionate father with his "suffering" boys, ultimately leading to the bird's-eye view of human bodies turned into military patterns. These images—the figures gendered along lines of National Socialist ideology—alone suffice to stage the range of emotional identification that is typical of fascist propaganda.[33] Sentiment and courage, homeboundness and the mass ornament, create a complex psychological construct that allows for a certain private involvement while at the same time staging authoritative power.[34] Nazism made the natural right of ownership one of its main sources of mythology: phrases such as "our race," "our history," and lands that "used to be ours" or were at least at some point in time populated by "our people" brought Germany into a war justified by the right of the Aryan race to possess the world. The idea of Hitler's birthright in the takeover of Austria is correspondingly a recurring theme in the narrative; in fact, the one that sets the stage from beginning to end, when, in the last image in the series, he is depicted revisiting the primary school of his youth after the annexation. Braunau, the little village in the countryside, has become the center now, and every boy in every village could make himself the center of this history as well.

The cigarette cards and the book are intimate items, both in their role as collectibles and in the way reception is built into them. An awareness of this informs the album text, which introduces the subject matter thus:

> How a World-War soldier without a name succeeded in initiating the most powerful renewal movement of all times, by transferring the pressing dynamics of our times to political life, how he made the battle and always again the battle the major issue of his confession to the German people, should become the content of this book, which purposely emphasizes the conquest of Austria as the idea of the Führer and, at the same time, complements the word with the image that has the same significance.[35]

The use of the German conditional *soll werden*, "should become," leaves no doubt that the book's content is not there yet. Does the phrase serve a merely rhetorical purpose to emphasize the dynamic of historical processes? In any case, the phrase does very literally point to the need to insert the photographs into the book in order for it to become Hitler's confession.

The author appeals here to the reader—who is by necessity a card collector, because only a card collector would buy the album—to become a maker of history. In a strange sense, the album and its images must first impart the lesson that history is not a real, ready-made, objective fact about the world; only then will the invitation to construct history together have the requisite meaning, that of putting together text and cigarette cards. The unstated final consequence, that the collector will "make history" by joining in National Socialist political activity, is only strengthened by making the act of collecting and pasting seem like committed National Socialist activities.

That, at least, is the ideological world that the cards and album, that Hoffmann, strives to create. The reality of Nazi Austria, with its militarization, elimination of undesirables, and shift to a war economy, made the cigarette cards one of the subtler means of indoctrination then available. From the individual's perspective, the tension between imaginative rejection (the impossibility of becoming part of the official history) and approval (the invitation to participate) might as well lead to a mechanism of fearful admiration. Historians have described Hitler's public image under Max Weber's formula of "charismatic leadership."[36] From the cover image, on which Hitler looks unreal, sculptured out of pure contrast, to the "old neighbor," visiting the place of his youth, Hitler stands for a historical fate that is at the same time—and almost contradictorily—intertwined with a personal life story. Theodor Adorno has phrased this ambivalence by describing Hitler's poses as ranging from "King-Kong" to "suburban hair dresser."[37] This range of identifications was designed as broadly as possible. Whether or not the collector was committed to the National Socialist cause, the handling of the cards tied each and every individual into propaganda without the need of direct authoritative action from above. The cards could be thrown away, and yet they would return with the next cigarette pack bought by the smoker. Considering the length and the tone of the album text, it is very possible that the target audience was not clearly thought out by Hoffmann and the cigarette company executives, as the text seems unsuited to attracting children. The main point, whether it is deliberate or not, is the process of reception and the little pieces of power that are inherent in the process of collecting. One might speculate about how the cards were in fact used. Were they "flipped" like coins, to decide who wins them?[38] In such at times irreverent acts of identification through collecting, the private sphere is seemingly left intact—while politics have already saturated it.

The complex status of the private sphere under fascism remains difficult to understand. The intimate politics of the cigarette cards seems to retain, or even sharpen, the discrepancy of the ideal of the sacrosanct Aryan family versus the need to place the nation before everything else. Even if we cannot account definitively for the cards' effect on individual recipients, the central point remains the offer to participate, a strategy that might ultimately work better than any top-down propaganda mechanism. It is obvious that the Party wanted to permeate not only the public, but also the private sphere. Assuming a forceful and straightforward seduction process not only carries the danger of negating the responsibility of the "masses"; it misses the point of propaganda. Without trying to downplay the enormous force of Goebbels's propaganda project, we have to assume players on more than just one side of the equation, the pattern of which, whether preplanned or not, needs active participation or at least the acceptance of the temptation to participate.

While I pointed toward the conflation of the private and the public as a typical Nazi strategy, Hoffmann the individual is a perfect example of the intersection of private interests with public ideology. The circumstances for an expansion into the Austrian market after the Anschluss proved ideal, as the state-run Austrian tobacco industries were remodeled into a stock company after Hitler's takeover. This "privatization" shows yet another fusion of market and politics under fascism: the German Reich held 39,996 of the 40,000 shares—the remaining four needed to be in different hands in order to comply with the law concerning the structure of stock companies. Simply put, the tobacco industries were private property in the hands of the German state.[39] Hoffmann's endeavor was itself, first and foremost, a profitable business venture, and perfectly in line with Walter Benjamin's observation that fascism "attempts to organize the newly created proletarian masses without affecting the property structure which the masses strive to eliminate."[40] In his memoirs, Hoffmann brags about the money he made from his celebratory albums, and that despite "taxes and expenses . . . we first had a small Opel, and then later a big Mercedes, and our household contained a cook, a maid and a chauffeur."[41] In short, Hoffmann the master propagandist is himself just the kind of "little man" whom he strove to reach. How the content of the cigarette cards would have changed as the war dragged on to defeat, we do not know. On 1 May 1942, the production of cigarette cards was discontinued due to paper shortages. In the 1950s, a law was enacted in Germany that regulated the content of cigarette cards.[42] They were to have no political imagery, but could function only as advertisements of their brand. This law is a testament to the power to bring propaganda into the home through the desire to collect. In comparison with the monumental light spectacles of Albert Speer, the torchlight marches, the films of Leni Riefenstahl, and the broadcasts of Joseph Goebbels, these cigarette cards might seem to be a humble means of indoctrination. And yet their minuteness allowed them to enter the daily lives of millions of people in ways that the monumental propaganda of the regime could not.

NOTES

1. Günther Grass, *Peeling the Onion*, trans. Michael Henry Heim (New York: Harcourt, 2007), 6–7. See also the German edition, Günther Grass, *Beim Häuten der Zwiebel* (Göttingen: Steidl, 2006), 10–11. All further translations from German are my own.
2. A version of this paper was first presented as "Hitler's Path to Great Germany. A Collection of Cigarette Cards" at the National Conference of the Popular Culture Association in

Atlanta, April 2006. I received helpful comments from Alice Friedman, Andrei Pop, Winnie Wong, and the editors of this book.

3. Grass, *Beim Häuten der Zwiebel*, 12. The English translation, "I lived through pictures," (*Peeling the Onion*, 6) does not do justice to the categorical literalness of Grass's word choice: "Ich lebte in Bildern."

4. Grass, *Beim Häuten der Zwiebel*, 12. *Glanzbilder* can mean shiny images or highlights (in a figurative sense). It is translated as "glossies" in the English version, presumably glossy photographs. This is linguistically eccentric and is also ruled out by the plain card stock used for the cards. See below.

5. Grass's public confession of having joined the SS shortly prior to the appearance of his memoir in 2006 led to very mixed reactions, from conservative historian Joachim Fest suggesting that Grass's pose as "conscience of the nation" was a sham to complaints by the president of the Central Council of Jews in Germany that Grass was engaging in a publicity stunt to promote his book. There was also disagreement between Grass and his biographer Michael Jürgs about whether Grass enlisted freely or was conscripted; Grass insists that he was conscripted, and successfully sued Random House to have the passage altered in 2008.

6. Georg Thiel from the Archive of the Austrian Tobacco Industries confirmed that the cards were in fact inside the packs. The advertisement for this series read: "The beautiful and historically important images are enclosed in all packs of Korso 3 1/3." E-mail to the author, 1 October 2010.

7. One of the few articles in English dealing directly with National Socialist cigarette cards reads them in terms of the formation of the Nazi male ideal; the card medium and the act of collecting are not discussed. See Geoffrey J. Giles, "Through Cigarette Cards to Manliness: Building German Character with an Informal Curriculum," in *Gender, Colonialism and Education. The Politics of Experience*, ed. Joyce Goodman and Jane Martin (London and Portland, OR: Woburn Press, 2002), 73–96.

8. Many Austrians were still mourning the loss of the great Austro-Hungarian Empire at that point.

9. Susan Sontag, *On Photography* (New York: Strauss & Giroux, 1977), especially chapter 1, "In Plato's Cave." This discourse on the possessive aspect of photography, and particularly on the role of scale in the process of appropriation, is developed further in Susan Stewart, *On Longing: Narratives of the Miniature, the Gigantic, the Souvenir, the Collection*, 2nd ed. (Durham, NC, and London: Duke University Press, 1993).

10. James Clifford argues that we collect objects in order to show them, on a bookshelf, to our friends and colleagues. "On Collecting Art and Culture," in *Out There. Marginalization and Contemporary Cultures*, ed. Russell Ferguson, Martha Gever, Trinh. T. Minh-ha, and Cornel West (Cambridge, MA: MIT Press, 1990), 143.

11. Speech given on 25 June 1928, printed as "Werdende Geschichte," in *Der Angriff: Aufsätze aus der Kampfzeit von Joseph Goebbels* (Munich: Zentralverlag der NSDAP, 1935), 178.

12. The question of Austria's annexation by Nazi Germany is complex. Hitler forestalled a referendum about the voluntary union of Austria with fascist Germany by marching into Austria; a manipulated plebiscite held by the Nazis on 10 April overwhelmingly "ratified" the union. See Hermann Hagspiel, *Die Ostmark. Österreich im Grossdeutschen Reich 1938–1945* (Vienna: Braumüller/Universitätsverlag, 1995), and *Betrifft Anschluss. Ein Almanach* (Vienna: Arbeitsgemeinschaft Österreichischer Privatverlage,1988).

13. In the wake of 9/11, Sontag famously rethought this thesis and concluded that images cannot destroy the horror of some catastrophes. But her early emphasis on the loss of a

Benjaminian "aura" in photography, even if one-sided, is crucial here, if only because cigarette cards are so easy to see as banal commodities. Sontag of course was very aware of the kitsch element in fascism, which she connected with aestheticism and sadomasochism in her essay on Leni Riefenstahl, "Fascinating Fascism," originally published in the *New York Review of Books* in 1975 and reprinted in *Under the Sign of Saturn* (New York: Picador, 1980).

14. Enactment from 13 March 1933. Excerpt reprinted in Joseph Wulf, *Kultur im Dritten Reich: Die Bildenden Künste* (Frankfurt am Main/Berlin: Ullstein, 1989), 99. In a catalog published by the Wolfsonian Institute, curator Marianne Lamonaca points out that it took Mussolini much longer to set up his control mechanism. Comparing Germany and Italy, she states: "Soon after Adolf Hitler seized power in 1933, he established the Ministry of Popular Enlightenment and Propaganda, headed by Joseph Goebbels. The ministry was charged with coordinating press, film, theatre, music, fine arts and other cultural expressions. The Italian Ministry for Popular Culture (1937) was based on the Nazi model, but it wasn't until the Ministry re-formed in 1943 . . . that it controlled broadcasting, film and press." Marianne Lamonaca, "Mobilizing for War," in *Weapons of Mass Dissemination: The Propaganda of War* (Miami Beach: The Wolfsonain/Florida International University, 2004), 16. Goebbels was not new to the job; he was appointed head of the Party's propaganda in April 1930.

15. Gesetz zum Schutz der nationalen Symbole, 19 May 1933. See Rolf Steinberg, ed., *Nazi-Kitsch* (Darmstadt: Melzer Verlag, 1975), 5 and 81–82.

16. I would like to thank David Banash for pointing me toward the *Reservistenbilder*.

17. Erich Wasem, *Sammeln von Serienbildchen* (Landshut: Trausnitz-Verlag, 1981), 10. It seems that at first the images were simply given to the costumer by the shop owner. The more regulated strategy of putting image cards inside the consumer goods, or having them be traded for coupons or certificates, marked the beginning of the professionalized marketing strategy of the advertising trading cards.

18. In Germany, the competition between two companies, Stollwerk (a sweets company) and Liebig (the inventor of meat extract), led to improvements in picture quality and even to design competitions. See Wasem, *Sammeln von Serienbildchen*; T. E. B. Clarke, "Cardio-Graphics," *Punch*, 25 February 1981, 320; and Martin Murray, *The Story of Cigarette Cards* (London: Murray Cards International Ltd., 1987). The parallel case of American baseball cards, disseminated in cigarette packs before they were put with candy and gum after World War I, is instructive. See John Bloom, *A House of Cards: Baseball Card Collecting and Popular Culture* (Minneapolis and London: University of Minnesota Press, 1997).

19. Mella Waldstein, "Adolf Hitler, vervielfältigt: Die Massenproduktion der Führerbildnisse," in *Kunst und Diktatur. Architektur, Bildhauerei und Malerei in Österreich, Deutschland, Italien und der Sowjetunion 1922–56*, ed. Jan Tabor (Baden, Austria: Verlag Grasl, 1994), 567. Although Hitler's studio photographs are unequivocally attributed to Hoffmann—he was the only photographer Hitler would allow in such an intimate setting—the authorship of other photographs signed by him or his studio is uncertain. Much of Hoffmann's archive was confiscated after the war and is held by the National Archives, Washington, DC.

20. Heinrich Hoffmann, *Hitler wie ich ihn sah. Aufzeichnungen seines Leibfotografen* (Munich: Herbig, 1974).

21. Hoffmann's first booklet, devoted to the Bavarian revolution, was published in 1919: *Ein Jahr bayerische Revolution im Bild*. Due to his experience as photojournalist and publisher, Hoffmann also became one of the cofounders of the official Party journal *Illustrierter Beobachter* in 1936.

22. In German, the title resembles the many newly invented official titles of the fascist regime, such as *Reichsministerium* (Reich Ministry). Hoffmann served in the Munich City

Council for the NSDAP before 1933 and became a member of the commission for "Verwertung der beschlagnahmten Werke entarteter Kunst" (Utilization of Confiscated Objects of Degenerate Art) in 1938.

23. "Hitler's Path to Great-Germany," the title given on the cards, is a subtitle on the album cover. Perhaps Hoffmann intended it as an umbrella designation for distinct regional versions of the series.

24. Jean Baudrillard, "The System of Collecting," in *The Cultures of Collecting*, ed. John Elsner and Roger Cardinal (Cambridge, MA: Harvard University Press, 1994), 9.

25. The fact that we can only speculate about the author of the text could of course be read as a sign of modest coherence; still, it seems more appropriate to speculate about a process of fast textual reproduction from sources that were already in circulation, maybe sampled, partly rewritten, and even collaboratively assembled. This is only speculation, of course, and sources suggest that Hoffmann's son-in-law, Baldur van Schirach—prominently shown in the album on card number 88 as the only image on the whole page—might have contributed as well. Schirach was the head of the Hitler Youth and would in 1940 become the *Gauleiter* and governor of Vienna. Before 1935, he copublished several albums with Hoffmann and was known as a dedicated writer, also of poetry. With Hoffmann, he copublished *Jugend um Hitler, Hitler wie ihn keiner kennt*. He also wrote his own book in 1938, entitled *Jugend und Erziehung*. Schirach started to study art history and German literature in the 1920s, but never finished university. After the war, he was sentenced to twenty years in prison at the Nuremberg trials. The website of the Deutsche Historische Museum (http://www.dhm.de) provides a good biography of Schirach and his activities. The fact that Schirach is referred to as head of the Hitler Youth in the image caption again supports a production date around 1938 or 1939, although the cataloging system of Harvard University dates the album (without the images) as 1940. There, as in other library entries in Austria and Germany, is no reference to the author of the text.

26. *Adolf Hitler und sein Weg zu Grossdeutschland*, 9.

27. "Von den Ahnen und dem Land seiner Ahnen," "Wehrer des Reiches."

28. Photo-historian Gerhard Jagschitz stresses the lack of clarity concerning patrons or authors of many of the photographs taken in the Anschluss era in "Photographie und 'Anschluss' im März 1938," in *Die Veruntreute Wahrheit: Hitlers Propagandisten in Österreichs Medien*, ed. Oliver Rathkolb, Wolfgang Duchkowitsch, and Fritz Hausjell (Salzburg: Otto Müller Verlag, 1988), 53.

29. Mieke Bal, "Telling Objects. A Narrative Perspective on Collecting," in *Cultures of Collecting*, ed. John Elsner and Roger Cardinal (Cambridge, MA: Harvard University Press, 1994), 97–115.

30. "The Mass Ornament" (Das Ornament der Masse) is of course the title of Siegfried Kracauer's famous essay from 1927. Rudolf Herz, *Hoffmann & Hitler: Fotografie als Medium des Führer-Mythos* (Munich: Klinkhardt and Biermann,1994), 204. Apart from the exact formation of the march, passersby are too lightly dressed for January in Berlin, even with the warmth of their "overfull hearts." The photograph was taken in summer 1933.

31. *Adolf Hitler und sein Weg zu Grossdeutschland*, 38.

32. Herz, *Hoffmann & Hitler*, 204.

33. See Giles, "Through Cigarette Cards to Manliness," 73–96.

34. See Siegfried Kracauer, "The Mass Ornament" [1927], in *The Mass Ornament: Weimar Essays* (Cambridge, MA: Harvard University Press, 1995).

35. *Adolf Hitler und sein Weg zu Grossdeutschland*, 7.

36. Weber's terminology and its application to Hitler as a public figure are discussed in depth in Ian Kershaw, *The "Hitler Myth": Images and Reality in the Third Reich* (Oxford: Oxford University Press, 1987).

37. Theodor W. Adorno, "Die Freudsche Theorie und die Struktur der faschistischen Propaganda," in *Kritik. Kleine Schriften zur Gesellschaft* (Frankfurt am Main: Suhrkamp, 1971), 50.

38. I would like to thank an auditor of my talk on this subject at the 2006 Popular Culture Association conference in Atlanta, who explained to me how children "flip cards" in the process of exchanging. Like flipping coins, one has to guess if the card will land on its front or back, and the winner receives the card.

39. See Ernst Trost, *Zur allgemeinen Erleicherung. Eine Kultur- und Wirtschaftsgeschichte des Tabaks in Österreich* (Wien: Brandstätter, 1984), 174. I would like to thank the archivists of the Archive of the Austrian Tobacco Industries for letting me go through their files and for pointing me in the direction of additional readings. Unfortunately, the files with internal correspondence are missing for the years 1939 to 1945. The scarce references to the cards are a result of the lack of paper during the war.

40. Walter Benjamin, "The Work of Art in the Age of Mechanical Reproduction," in *Illuminations*, ed. Hannah Arendt, trans. Harry Zorn (New York: Shocken, 1969), 241.

41. Heinrich Hoffmann, *Hitler Was My Friend*, trans. R. H. Stevens (London: Burke, 1955), 63. The passage is not included in the German version, the foreword to which was written by Hoffmann's daughter Henriette. Cf. Heinrich Hoffmann, *Hitler wie ich ihn sah. Aufzeichnungen seines Leibfotografen* (Munich: Herbig, 1974).

42. This information comes from the archive of the Austrian Tobacco Industries, Vienna.

10

"The Record of a Life": Nation and Narrative in Victorian Women's Collections

Terri Baker

Jean Baudrillard argues that collecting has "a strong whiff of the harem"[1] about it. Collectors, whom Baudrillard profiles as "men in their forties,"[2] search out objects of "absolute singularity"[3] to join or replace other objects in a paradigm that might focus on a certain period of art or a certain style, but are always exhibited for the collector with "an intimacy bounded by seriality."[4] There is no space in this definition for the female collector. Indeed, in her exploration of Isabella Stewart Gardner, Rosemary Matthews confirms that in the late Victorian era only men were perceived as serious collectors, whereas women were the purchasers of consumer objects, perceived as lacking the kind of vision and underlying philosophy with which men were engaged. Yet Gardner's legacy alone refutes this idea, through her creation of a museum at Fenway Court, which one contemporary critic called "a citadel of peace and dignity and beauty, not the result of a sudden desire for collection, which has become an American obsession."[5] Whereas Baudrillard, as one of the early theorists on collecting,[6] was a major contributor to the entrenchment of the idea of the collector as male, a close look at several new texts on the woman collector show[7] that women during the Victorian age were also engaged in collecting, sometimes as partners to male collectors and sometimes as collectors in their own right. British women such as Lady Dorothy Neville and Lady Charlotte Schreiber left important collections to the Kensington Museum; in the United States, collectors like Gardner and Catharine Lorillard Wolfe left enduring legacies to the cities of Boston and New York by virtue of a "long-sustained, slowly developed plan"[8] that these ladies demonstrated toward collecting.

Although the motivations of these women collectors are complex, it is possible to interpret these nineteenth-century collections as representations of women's participation in the development of a national narrative. In this chapter, I examine the collections of some prominent female collectors through the lens of Mieke Bal's theory of how collections can be read as narratives, focusing on rich women collectors because of their privileged position in society and their access to the means not only to make these purchases, but also to fund travel abroad in pursuit of them. By way of acknowledging that women collectors were not solely from this class, however, I would like to introduce the female collector from a novel by one of Gardner's friends, Henry James, as an exemplar of not only what was possible for the woman collector, but also how women collectors who struggled against the rules of propriety to create these collections were threatened with losing them by virtue of the laws of inheritance and the prejudice of a patriarchal hegemony.

A RECORD OF ADELA GARETH'S LIFE

In *The Spoils of Poynton*, a novel about a female collector who is called "the craftiest stalker who had ever tracked big game,"[9] Henry James creates Adela Gareth, a woman of intelligence and cunning. Whereas "[t]here wouldn't have been money enough for any fumbler"[10] to assemble the fine collection of antiques and rare objets d'art at her husband's estate, Poynton, according to Adela, "there had been money enough for her."[11] Here James employs the language usually reserved for the male pursuit of hunting as a metaphor for women collectors, a metaphor also employed by mid- to late-Victorian female collectors.[12] This metaphor is extended, as seen in the novel's title, when Adela[13] loses proprietorship of her collection due to the traditional British laws governing the property of married women[14] and exacerbated by primogeniture, the laws ensuring that a first-born son inherits his father's estate in its entirety. Thus, even though Adela herself carefully selected and artfully assembled objects, such as "the brasses that Louis Quinze might have thumbed . . . [and] Venetian velvets,"[15] those objects become the spoils in Adela's war against her own son over who—that is, the woman who would become his wife—would oversee the future of those objects. Through his close examination of how Adela strives to maintain control and access to a collection that is so critical to her subjectivity, James's turn-of-the-century novel can also be interpreted as an important representation of how real Victorian female collectors appropriated the male-dominated practice of collecting to claim historical space for a similar feminine practice in their society. Indeed, James's literary representation of the female collector makes a critical argument for the motivation of such a practice among Victorian women as the creation of "a record of a life . . . written in great syllables of colour and form, the tongues of other countries and the hands of rare artists."[16] As an Anglophile, James foregrounds Britain as a powerful, imperial force, for even though the collection is at Poynton, "[i]t was all France and Italy with their ages composed to rest. For England you looked out of old windows—it was England that was the wide embrace."[17] If a collection is a record, what other kinds of narrative might Victorian female collectors have constructed? How might these narratives influence not just the cultural capital of a nation, but its national narrative as well?

Susan M. Pearce tells us that the objects in all collections "come to us from the past; and they have been assembled with some degree of intention (however slight) by an owner or curator who believed that the whole was somehow more than the sum of its parts."[18] For Adela Gareth and her husband, this whole formed part of a house and estate within a British tradition. Acquired after their marriage, Poynton is described as an "exquisite old house . . . early Jacobean,"[19] as Adela describes it, "the matchless canvas for a picture."[20] This metaphor indicates the blankness of the canvas, hence an empty house, indicating that the Gareths created a pseudo-ancestral home, like those owned by the British aristocracy. This is confirmed by the absence of any allusion by James to past generations of Gareths that may or may not have inhabited Poynton, indicating that Mr. and Mrs. Gareth's "twenty-six years of planning and seeking"[21] to fill that house according to an English ideal represented a "wide embrace"[22] of all things found in an English country house. Like the rising middle class that would follow their example, the second sons of aristocracy or gentry often acquired country estates through wealth accrued from inheritance, industry, or colonial interests.[23] Traditionally, then, the acquisition of a country house necessitated hunting the British and European antique and art markets for those objects that might simulate the patina of the idealized British ancestral mansion. Therefore, while Adela had created a narrative for her own public reputation as "the craftiest stalker who had ever tracked big game,"[24] she was simultaneously creating at Poynton "the record of a life,"[25] one that formed part of the British narrative of English country life. It was this popular ambition to re-create an ancestral home that contributed to the success of the British magazine *Country Life*.[26] Established the same year that *Poynton* was serialized in *Atlantic Monthly, Country Life* magazine promoted, "more than other institutions of this period, [a] nostalgia for a preindustrial past."[27]

James's own experiences in Victorian country house culture formed the foundation for his representation of the Gareths' ambitions. After his arrival in England in 1869, the author lived with his friend, the art critic Charles Eliot Norton. It was at Norton's home in Mayfair that James met some of the men who greatly influenced trans-Atlantic male and female collectors: John Ruskin, William Morris, Leslie Stephen, Frederic Harrison, and Charles Darwin. Letters of introduction from Norton paved the way for James's role as "a participant observer in London society, dining out constantly and paying many country visits,"[28] during which he also met William Gladstone, Robert Browning, and Alfred Lord Tennyson. Indeed, Anne Higonnet argues that James was friends of collectors because "[i]n all his writing, James relied on descriptions of the domestic interior to cast the psychology of his characters."[29] His early novels—*The American* (1877), *Daisy Miller* (1879), and *The Portrait of a Lady* (1881)—represent American individuals colliding with European society, alluding to the late-Victorian trend among young American women of educating themselves in European culture, an experience that facilitated their engagement in collecting, thereby contributing to the maturation of American culture.

COLLECTIONS AS NARRATIVE: LADY DOROTHY NEVILLE

It is significant that romantic and Victorian artists often depicted women as readers, given the approval of such an activity for women at the time.[30] Collecting shares with literature its private practice: the enjoyment of the thing, a book or piece of art. A voracious reader, like an ardent collector, consumes a "series bounded by intimacy . . . and an intimacy bounded by seriality."[31] The acquisition of objets d'art, like literature, is often a result of private or public dialogue, acquired through a public transaction, and follows advice sought from expert sources. Narrative, however, can also be found in things collected; Mieke Bal argues that "verbal texts are not the only objects capable of conveying narrative."[32] Like narrative, collecting is not only "a process consisting of the confrontation between objects and subjective agency informed by an attitude"[33]; it also demonstrates a "mixed up"[34] chronology, either by the disparate provenances of the objects or by the objects' removal from their original context, usually altering their meaning as a result. In her examination of museum collections,[35] Pearce argues that "the whole of cultural expression, one way or another, falls within the realm of material culture."[36] Thus, collections can be considered part of a national cultural expression. How did women become part of this expression?

Before Queen Victoria ascended the throne in 1837, there was already a shift under way in which "businessmen were replacing aristocrats in the art market."[37] Art periodicals of the period were not only a resource for these collectors, but also a source of profiling the Victorian collector. In 1845, the *Art Union* observed that "by far the greatest number of recent productions of high value have their honoured places in the dwellings of our merchants and manufacturers."[38] Britain's landed aristocracy greeted this competition from below their ranks with condescension, as represented by the complaint made by Lady Elizabeth Rigby Eastlake (1809–1893) that "the note-book of the painter . . . exhibited *lowlier* names"[39] with higher prices. Perhaps it was this breakdown of class structure in Victorian art collecting circles that inspired women to also become collectors. Coming from the same class as Lady Elizabeth, Lady Dorothy Walpole (1826–1913) was the daughter of Horatio Walpole, third earl of Orford, and related to Lord Nelson, Sir Robert Walpole, and Horace Walpole. The earl, who had a passion for race horses, forced his family to economize by living in the country, yet inculcated an appreciation for culture in his children. As Lady Dorothy's memoirs reveal, "he was a kindly man . . . most anxious to cultivate [our] minds, frequently when in London taking us to museums and other places supposed to instruct the young."[40]

This early education in art would find a new outlet when, in 1847, Lady Dorothy married her cousin, Reginald Henry Nevill (1807–1878), son of George Nevill, first earl of Abergavenny, and his wife, Caroline Walpole, who had "inherited considerable wealth from a Walpole uncle."[41] The match provided Lady Dorothy with the financial backing she needed to enjoy "a heady experience—at Webb's in the Strand, or Christie's, or some other sale room—bidding for the eighteenth-century French furniture, pastels and porcelain that since the French Revolution and the Napoleonic wars could be bought for a song."[42] Lady Dorothy's penchant for collecting was strong: "She collected everything and everyone, turning them into possessions with which to festoon her houses."[43] Those houses included one in London and Dangstein, an estate purchased early in the Nevills' marriage, in west Sussex. Wherever Lady Dorothy went, she would find a memento, something that "had a story for them all"[44] when she brought it home. Perhaps Lady Dorothy, like Adela Gareth, sought to create her own ancestral home.

For Lady Dorothy, connections to the British past were important, as evidenced by the observations in her biography about the "good many interesting things"[45] at the estate belonging to her husband's family, including a model of the man-of-war that brought her own distant relative, Horatio Nelson, back from the Battle of Trafalgar, connecting the Nevills to that famous battle. There was also a Thomas Gainsborough portrait at the estate, as well as the robes of another relative who "was one of the judges at the trial of Mary Queen of Scots at Fothringay."[46] The impressions made on Lady Dorothy by these ancestral collections influenced her own collecting practices; among her collections could be found "a serious collec[tion] of eighteenth-century porcelain and pictures, particularly anything relating to her ancestor Horace Walpole, fourth earl of Orford."[47] But it is her collection of "Sussex iron-work,"[48] donated by Lady Dorothy to the Victoria and Albert Museum, that best exemplifies her passion for reclaiming narratives of British history:

> I formed this collection years ago when I used to live in Sussex, purchasing the different pieces for the most part in old cottages and farmhouses. Some of the old firebacks were extremely ornamental, but the fire-dogs[49] of which I collected a great number were my especial favourites. Most of the iron-work of my collection, such as rush-holders, fire-tongs, and the like necessities of old-world cottage life, has now become completely obsolete in the farmhouses and cottages, to which they formed a useful and artistic adornment.[50]

Lady Dorothy's reminiscences reveal not only a passion for her country's history, but also a "nostalgia for a preindustrial past."[51]

Lady Dorothy's narrative also demonstrates how subjectivity played an important role in the Victorian woman collector, because she had to deflect the criticism of her peers for valuing "old rubbish."[52] At a time when Coventry Patmore's 1854 poem came to define the married woman as "The Angel in the House," expecting a married woman to be "passive and powerless, meek, charming, graceful, sympathetic, self-sacrificing, pious,"[53] the kind of assertive behavior that Lady Dorothy demonstrates in her memoirs must have been met with condemnation and rejection by those who ascribed to Victorian ideals. Perhaps this is why Lady Dorothy cannot resist gloating over the earlier dismissal of her collection, confessing, "I am glad to say that my judgment has been completely vindicated, and today, instead of 'old rubbish,' I am told it is a 'valuable collection.'"[54] Eventually, that "valuable collection"—together with "a set of twelve wine-glasses made for Charles Edward, the Pretender"[55]—was donated by Lady Dorothy to the Victoria and Albert Museum.

I return to the implications of these donations later in this chapter, but here it is interesting to note the connection between women collectors and museums. Perhaps Lady Dorothy's connection was strengthened by the in-depth and broad knowledge of art and antiques that she demonstrates in her memoirs and by her temerity in rejecting a prevailing fashion among the early and mid-Victorians that she called a "cult of ugliness."[56] Her generosity toward museums was not limited to the Victoria and Albert. Indeed, she admitted to preferring the South Kensington museum[57] and to being "present at some of the early meetings when the first idea of the museum was mooted."[58] This early influence on the creation of museums can also be found among the American female collectors of the late Victorian era. So, how do these collections and connections help contribute to a national narrative?

As noted previously, Bal argues that collections, like verbal texts, can convey narrative. Collecting, according to Bal, "is an essential human feature that originates in the need to tell stories, but for which there are neither words nor other conventional narrative modes."[59]

Each consists of a "sequence of events, brought about and undergone by agents . . . the *fabula*, more commonly called plot; the agents, subjects of action on this level, are called *actors*."[60] Colliding in both collecting and narrative are the "[o]bjects and subjective agency informed by an attitude."[61] This collision then forms a "subjectivised plot . . . called *story*,"[62] presented by a *narrator* who is "[t]he semiotic subject producing or uttering."[63] Thus, in Lady Dorothy's case, the objects in one part of her narrative are the various pieces of Sussex ironworks that she, as *actor*, has removed from their place of origin to form a new kind of sign within the context of the collection. The *fabula* is represented by the individual purchases Lady Dorothy makes from Sussex farmhouses; the *story* is her recollection of those events, because she "had a story for them all."[64] Just as narrative is subject to interpretation, Lady Dorothy's collections are similarly subject, opening a space to interpret her objectives to preserve the past through collecting disappearing British artifacts (firebacks and fire-dogs) and artifacts that represent British history (Charles Stuart's wine glasses) as contributions to the national narrative. Because the collections of Sussex iron and Prince Charles Edward's glasses are synecdoches of domestic space, Lady Dorothy's donation also represents an important narrative within the sphere of Victorian women, elevating the value of that sphere.

Charles Saumarez Smith argues that "the original impulse behind the establishment of the South Kensington collections was essentially imperial. Nationally, economically, and industrially self-confident, Britain fervently desired to encompass within its reach the full spectrum of world cultures."[65] Whereas the ambition to expand upon the Great Exhibition of 1851 prevailed, Smith argues that "from the start, there was also a countervailing tendency—a wish to document and describe the specific characteristics of the British contribution to the cultures of the world and a desire to establish the legitimacy of British art and design, alongside British preeminence in industry and imperial conquest."[66] It was the arts and crafts movement, "[d]uring the 1880s and 1890s,"[67] that resulted in an aesthetic shift in which scholars and antiquarians moved "towards an appreciation of English domestic architecture of the sixteenth and seventeenth centuries and of the artifacts produced between the age of Queen Elizabeth and the age of Queen Anne. . . . Motivated by a sentimental appreciation of the relics of old English life, which were being swept away by urbanization."[68] Thus, the inclusion of Lady Dorothy's collection of Sussex iron in the Victoria and Albert Museum reflects this increased relevance of collecting things that belonged to a vanishing part of British history. Contrary to her confession that she had "always been fond of surrounding myself with such furniture and bibelots as I like, quite irrespective of their period, history, or style,"[69] Lady Dorothy assembled a vast array of objects that contributed to a British national narrative of the domestic sphere. Through her collections of "English art"[70]; silhouettes and mementoes of Lord Nelson, Sir Robert Walpole, and Horace Walpole; and English china, Lady Dorothy created *stories* in which she was the *actor*. Through her donation of those collections to museums, Lady Dorothy shared her *stories* with the nation, thereby situating herself and other women in a British national narrative.

THE *CHASSE*

If Lady Dorothy represents the aristocratic class of British collectors, Lady Charlotte Schreiber (1812–1895) bridged the gap between the aristocracy and the "businessmen [who] were replacing aristocrats in the art market."[71] The china mania that seized Victorian Britain from 1873 to 1876 drew Lady Charlotte Bertie Guest Schreiber into collecting china, forcing her to compete against both professional and amateur collectors. According to Lady Charlotte's grandson and biographer, it was during this period that, whenever she wrote in her journal,[72] it was to reference "hardly any other subject but the *chasse*."[73]

Lady Charlotte lost her father, the Earl of Lindsey, at a young age and eventually married a wealthy industrialist, John Guest, a widower twenty-seven years older than she. While actively contributing to her husband's ironworks in Wales, Lady Charlotte also gave birth to ten children in the space of thirteen years. Given the location of Guest's ironworks in Wales, Lady Charlotte took an interest in those who worked at his factories, learning Welsh, and collecting and translating twelve Welsh tales into three volumes, including three Arthurian romances. According to Angela V. John, Tennyson based his *Idylls of the King* on one of these Welsh tales. After Guest's death in 1853, Lady Charlotte's involvement in the ironworks increased, but her opposition to her competitors' suppression of the miners increased the awkwardness of her position in this patriarchal industry. Two years after her husband's death, Lady Charlotte withdrew from the ironworks when she married her son's tutor,[74] Charles Schreiber, fourteen years her junior. By 1873, she and her new husband had already embarked on a "married life on the continent as passionate, apparently indefatigable, collectors and connoisseurs of china, scouring Europe for bargains—which they usually found."[75] When Charles Schreiber died in Lisbon in 1884, Lady Charlotte decided to bequeath her collection of nearly two thousand pieces of English china to the Victoria and Albert Museum. To accompany that collection, she put together a "comprehensive catalogue."[76] Remarkably, it was only the English china that Lady Charlotte donated to the museum; the European china was either kept in the family or sold. Consequently, Lady Charlotte's donation is a significant contribution to the story of English china, one the nation can share through the museum.

As the editor of her multiple journals, the Earl of Bessborough[77] considered Lady Charlotte to be "the first private collector of English china,"[78] someone who "ransacked Europe from end to end"[79] while engaged in the *chasse*. Public testimony about Lady Charlotte's breadth of knowledge came from "the head of the great china emporium in Oxford Street,"[80] John Mortlock[81]: "He said that nearly all he knew about china he learnt from her, that Mr. Schreiber was a good judge, but that he was nowhere compared to his wife."[82] Lady Charlotte did not, however, limit herself to china; "[l]ater she turned her attention to fans and fan leaves, and afterwards to playing cards; of both she made exhaustive collections. These, too, she presented to the British Museum."[83]

If the Welsh tales offered a narrative promoting a diverse British heritage, the china collection is more what Walter Benjamin calls the "tide of memories which surges toward any collector as he contemplates his possessions."[84] For Lady Charlotte, her china collection represented the adventures she and her young husband would undertake in search of a treasure. For example, when on a trip to Madrid in the spring of 1871, the Schreibers discovered they could not travel through Paris because it was "impassable,"[85] and Amiens was occupied by the Prussians, as was Rouen, because of the end of the Franco–Prussian War only three months before. As Lady Charlotte recalled in her diary on 12 April 1871: "By the next train, we reached Le Mans in the afternoon. This was evidently a military centre, for here were French troops just returned from German and Swiss imprisonment. . . . The various cries of one of these military convoys were remarkable. Some shouted 'Vive la République!', others 'Vive Paris!' and some even 'Vive la Commune!'. . . The railway bridge at Le Mans had been blown up."[86] This entry demonstrates the same kind of subjectivity exhibited by Lady Dorothy: the record of a life taking risks not traditionally associated with Victorian women.

Like Lady Dorothy, Lady Charlotte sought, through her collections of Welsh manuscripts, to make a contribution to the national narrative. Like Lady Dorothy's shift from artifacts of imperialism to British domestic artifacts, Lady Charlotte shifted her collecting focus from claiming space for a Welsh literary tradition to privileging things associated with women or the domestic sphere. The story that emerges from her many journals situates objects manufactured in Britain as part of a larger "whole of what were regarded as the significant cultures of the world."[87] By donating her collection to a museum, Lady Charlotte also claimed space for her contribution to British heritage, not only through her participation in assembling such a large collection of china, but also by her contribution to establishing how "the specific characteristics of the British contribut[ed] to the cultures of the world"[88] and the legacy of "the legitimacy of British art and design."[89]

Other British women participated in collecting, and the objects they collected were as diverse as the women themselves. In the shadow of Charles Darwin's engagement with natural history, many women collected fossils; others collected botanical samples or historically specific memorabilia. Louisa Lawrence (1803/1804–1855) was a horticulturalist who collected rare plant species, Barbara Rawdon Hastings (1810–1858) collected fossils and wrote geological tracts, and Louisa Anne Meredith (1812–1895) collected and wrote about the natural world of Tasmania. The examples of these women resist the myth of the rich collector—male or female— exhibiting what could be called an "animal impulse." Charles Dickens's partner in philanthropy, Angela Georgina Burdett Coutts (1814–1906), was known as the "richest heiress in England,"[90] but was also "a keen collector of antiquarian books and paintings."[91] Elizabeth Barrett Browning's friend Ellen Heaton (1816–1894) was an art collector and philanthropist. The *Oxford Dictionary of National Biography* lists at least fourteen other women who acquired collections during the Victorian era. Their very presence in this national publication attests to these women's ability to claim space for their collecting practices and their participation in shaping Britain's national narrative. Could the same be said of the women across the Atlantic?[92]

THE DECORATION OF AMERICAN HOUSES

Whereas Henry James's social network in England took him to houses like those found in *Country Life*, his social network also extended into the United States and to women collectors like Isabella Stewart Gardner. His friend and protégée, Edith Wharton, was a bibliophile, but also a decorator of houses, like Adela Gareth. In fact, Wharton's book *The Decoration of Houses*, cowritten with Ogden Codman Jr. and published the same year that James's *Poynton* appeared in *Atlantic Monthly*, seeks to bridge the understanding of a word that could be the Americanization of the British "gimcrack"[93]: knick-knack. Without referring to collections, yet comparing the "inexpensive trifles"[94] produced in America at that time to a collection of Greek statues known as the Tanagra figurines,[95] Wharton and Codman despair of the American lack of definition, like the French, between "bric-a-brac, bibelots, *objets d'art*"[96]: "One of the first obligations of art is to make all useful things beautiful: were this neglected principle applied to the manufacture of household accessories, the modern room would have no need of knick-knacks."[97] So for Wharton, her collections were "household accessories" rather than a "series bounded by intimacy . . . and an intimacy bounded by seriality." There were, however, women in the United States who not only collected art, but also slave songs (Lucy McKim Garrison [1842–1877]) and literature (Anne Charlotte Botta [1815–1891]). Women collectors in America, however, differed because of their country's status as part of a larger "whole of what were regarded as the significant cultures of the world." Thus, American women collectors sought to raise cultural awareness in their society, one perceived to be in need of cultural refinement. Europe was seen, as mentioned previously, as the place to find taste and culture. At least three women were influential in not only bringing European culture to America, but also sharing that culture with the American public in a way that claimed space for them as contributing to their nation's national narrative as appreciators of culture.

When it was founded in New York City in 1870, the Metropolitan Museum of Art[98] declared as its purpose: "establishing and maintaining . . . a Museum and library of art, of encouraging and developing the study of the fine arts, and the application of arts to manufacture and practical life, of advancing the general knowledge of kindred subjects, and, to that end, of furnishing popular instruction."[99] One of the founders who agreed to this purpose was Catharine Lorillard Wolfe (1828–1887), who in 1866 inherited from her mother, Dorothea Ann Lorillard, a fortune based on tobacco holdings, and in 1872 from her father, John David Wolfe, a lucrative, New York–based income from rental properties and wholesale hardware. Catharine thus became known as "the richest single woman in America."[100] While Catharine emulated her father in her philanthropic endeavors, she is remembered nationally as an art collector, because of the large donation she made to the Met. According to Saul E. Zalesch, "The exact origin of her collection is not important; it is what she did with it that mattered."[101] Although there seems no indication of how or when Catharine began her art collection, Bal argues that one of the other similarities between narratives and collections is that "the beginning is exactly what is lacking. One object must have been the first to be acquired, but then, when it *was* first it was not being collected—merely purchased, given or found, and kept because it was especially gratifying."[102] Regardless of where she began, Catharine became an art collector of repute, transgressing on the patriarchal public domain to do so, despite all contemporary accounts of her being "a most quiet and unassuming person . . . [with] no eccentricities of habit or character."[103] In addition to the "adopt[ion] of traditionally masculine characteristics, such as aggressive bargaining and deal-making"[104] employed by the female collector, Catharine transgressed into another male practice: "creat[ing] art-filled country retreats where they could release tensions after expending energy on their business and philanthropic pursuits."[105] These retreats became Catharine's "inner sanctums."[106] In the section of *Enchanted Lives, Enchanted Objects* that Dianne Sachko Macleod devotes to Catharine, she argues that Catharine's displays of sensual paintings and sculptures in her home and in Vinland, her Newport retreat, represented a "rich woman's [exotic] fantasy,"[107] but it also exemplified how female collectors demonstrated the "principle of integrating art into everyday life."[108] This kind of integration was also supported by Wharton and Codman, who suggest that "a room should depend for its adornment on general harmony of parts, and on the artistic quality of such necessities as lamps, screens, bindings, and furniture."[109] Given Wharton's high social status in late nineteenth-century New York, she may have actually seen Catharine's uniquely feminine arrangement of art.

Perhaps it was the reputation of Catharine's Vinland that inspired the art historian Earl Shinn to visit and record his interpretation of Catharine's collection in his three-volume encyclopedia *The Art Treasures in America* (1879–1882). Mostly, his cataloging of the collections of American women was confined by what Tim Dolan argues is how the female collection "was virtually invisible as a cultural pursuit because it was considered meaningful only within the home."[110] Shinn himself considered the invasion of women into the collecting sphere distasteful, going so far as to label the popularity of the decorative arts a "destructive angel."[111] Shinn did, however, review twenty-two women's collections—visiting only eight—but most of these women were widows and had inherited their collections upon their husbands' deaths. Shinn passed over the collections of married women like Augusta Astor, Maria Vanderbilt, Caroline Belmont, and Frances Morgan, probably because he could not conceive that their contributions to their husband's collections were significant. In her examination of American women collectors, Macleod finds that, among women collectors in New York, Catharine was the only one to have substantial space devoted to her by Shinn. Quoting from Shinn's own work, Macleod draws our attention to how Catharine's collection, in Shinn's view, reflected the personality of its owner, more so than collections belonging to men: "Evidence of the most advanced 'collectorship' are everywhere visible, expressed in ivories, enamels and faience; their usefulness is to give a home character to the interior, and take away from the public-gallery or museum air which might otherwise be conferred by walls so completely covered with canvases."[112] By giving her collection physical space in his catalog of valuable art found in American collections, Shinn makes room for Catharine as a contributor to America's national narrative as a country intent on being accepted as one of the "significant cultures of the world."

THE GARDNER

From a public museum for the city of New York to a museum of their own, American women seemed more engaged with the creation and administration of museums than British women. Margaret Higgonet argues that because these American women lacked the class consciousness of their British counterparts, they doubted that their collections "deserved consecration as a museum."[113] The Isabella Stewart Gardner museum is an example of how one woman could create a national profile as a cultured American prepared to share with other Americans the wealth of her collection.[114]

Isabella Stewart Gardner met Henry James on that lady's visit to London in 1879. Although the two had grown up just blocks away from each other, they had never met until then and "became close friends and frequent correspondents for the remainder of James's life."[115] Isabella, who was married at the time of this meeting, had begun a modest art collection in 1873, and has been described as "unconventional, passionate and headstrong"[116] at a time when women were seen as "consumers of objects and only men were serious collectors."[117] Henry Adams, a mutual friend of James and Isabella's, wrote to Isabella during his later years: "I envy you, who always, even at your worst, loved the game, whatever it might be, and delighted in playing it. How we others must bore you—old mummies—Henry James and me—who can see nothing in the game and only lunacy in the players."[118] This demonstrates that, like Lady Charlotte, Isabella savored the competitive aspect of collecting. Unlike Lady Charlotte, Isabella wanted control over her collection even after her own death. She and her husband Jack "discussed at length where and how they would build"[119] a museum to house their treasures. Although Jack Gardner's death did not occur until three years after the publication of *The Spoils of Poynton*, Isabella may have spoken or written to James about her plans. Could this have been why James elaborates in his preface to this novel that he was "instantly . . . aware"[120] with a "sense for the subject"[121] when he refers to a newspaper article he had read about "a good lady in the north . . . at daggers drawn with her only son, ever hitherto exemplary, over the ownership of the valuable furniture of a fine old house just accruing to the young man by his father's death."[122] Could Isabella's collecting habits and arrogant pride in her own arrangement skills have been the spark that helped to create Adela Gareth? Like Adela's perception of Poynton as an entity—emphasized by James's reticence in describing those specific objects the Gareths had collected—Isabella's collection, when it opened to the public, was described in the Boston *Spectator* as "an unforgettable impression, not of five thousand beautiful things, but of one thing of beauty, one artistic whole."[123] In his survey of art collections in America, Shinn overlooked Isabella's collection in Boston in the 1870s, because it was still in its infancy. Yet Isabella is the most visible female collector among those mentioned in this chapter. Indeed, today the space Isabella occupies as an important contributor to America's narrative as a culturally sophisticated nation has received increased media attention because of a robbery in 1990 during which thirteen pieces were stolen from the collection. The blank spaces on the walls where these works of art used to hang form gaps in the narrative Isabella sought to create.

BUILDING A WORLD

No survey of American female collectors that makes connections between collectors and literature would be complete without recognizing the immense contribution of the Folger Shakespeare Library in Washington, D.C., a donation that came from Emily and Henry Clay Folger, who together had a passion for collecting Shakespeareana. When Henry C. Folger Jr. purchased Ralph Waldo Emerson's *Essays* (1880)[124] after his graduation from Amherst College, a line from one of these essays inspired him enough to inscribe it in the book: "Build therefore your own world."[125] By collecting such a diverse and critically important collection of Shakespearean and other Renaissance manuscripts, the Folgers indeed created a library that is its "own world" for academics, students, and lifelong learners.

Like other women collectors of the era, Emily shared a collecting passion with her husband "from the beginning."[126] She was his advisor and counselor, armed with the master's degree she earned from Vassar College in 1896 for her essay, "The True Text of Shakespeare." In 2002 the Folger Shakespeare Library, celebrating its seventieth anniversary, mounted an exhibition, *A Shared Passion: Henry Clay Folger, Jr., and Emily Jordan Folger as Collectors*, a testament to the historical space claimed by Emily. Among other things, this exhibit displayed Emily's thesis; her correspondence with her thesis advisor, Horace Howard Furness; and the "detailed notes made in Emily's hand, analyzing purchases."[127] One of those purchases, made in 1889, was their first: a "copy of the Fourth Folio (1685) of Shakespeare's plays."[128]

As president of her class at Vassar in 1879, Emily Jordan Folger's membership in "several literary clubs,"[129] and her position as an instructor at the Nassau Institute from her graduation until her marriage to Folger in 1885, showed her early passion for literature as well as her ability to participate in public space. Like Lady Charlotte, who began collecting with her second husband after her children had grown; Catharine, who remained unmarried; and Isabella, whose marriage was childless, Emily had no children to distract her, allowing her the freedom to pursue the passion she shared with her husband. After Folger's death in 1930, Emily's passion continued as his sole executor, in charge of conveying the bulk of his estate to Amherst College in trust for the Folger Shakespeare Memorial. When the disastrous effects of the stock market crash of 1929 wiped out Folger's endowment for a library for the couple's collection, Emily Folger contributed $3 million and "agreed to pay the salary of the library's director to ensure the library's opening."[130] The Folgers had already bought land in Washington, behind the Library of Congress, to build an institution to house their important collection, thus demonstrating how far-reaching and collaborative their vision was.

Whereas their shared passion for collecting rare manuscripts is well-documented, the Folgers' collecting of art is not. The archival information regarding the 2002 exhibit asserts that Folger, not being "content with the literary side,"[131] also sought out visual representations of famous performances of Shakespeare's plays: Henri Fuseli's painting *Macbeth Consulting the Vision of the Armed Head* (1793), Thomas Parr's *John Philip Kemble as "Hamlet,"* and Thomas Nast's *Immortal Light of Genius* (1908). Although these associated pursuits of visual art were overshadowed by the size and importance of the Folgers' manuscript collection, their inclusion in the Folgers' *chase* signifies an overarching narrative valuing the work and interpretation of authors from the distant past. The creation of the Folger Shakespeare Library not only makes that narrative available to educate all Americans about the important cultural value of Renaissance writing, it also reflects on America as a repository for some of the best examples of significant cultures of the world.

American Biography Online lists nine other female collectors; Macleod an additional twelve.[132] Like those collected by the women in Victorian England, the objects varied from art collections like Catharine's and Isabella's, from botany (Mexia, Ynes Enriquetta Julietta [1870–1938]), to an archaeologist who collected early Cretan pottery (Harriet Ann Boyd Hawes [1871–1945]), to a musician who collected slave songs (Lucy McKim Garrison [1842–1877]). Saul E. Zalesch argues that the art collection of Mary Jane Morgan (1830–1885) was very important, yet "Morgan's total obscurity remains the strongest documentation of historians' shameful neglect of women collectors."[133]

Despite Zalesch's condemnation of historians, recent studies of women as collectors in the Victorian period are emerging. Beginning with her earlier article on the Pre-Raphaelite collections of Ellen Heaton, Martha Combe, Alice Stevenson, Lady Pauline Trevelyan, and Maria Leathart, art historian Dianne Sachko Macleod has investigated women collectors of art on both sides of the Atlantic. Before her look at American art collectors,[134] Macleod surveyed the shift of Victorian art collectors from the aristocratic class to the rising merchant and industrialist class. Yet this study also discusses the women who may have influenced or participated in what appeared to be a male pursuit enjoyed outside of marital relations.

What British women like Lady Dorothy Nevill and Lady Charlotte Schreiber shared was their passion for the *chasse*, their determination to participate in public spaces, and their devotion to an idea of nationhood. Their collections reflect that devotion, contributing to a valorization of British industry and imperialism and standing as a tribute to their own female narratives within the country's history of collectors. Catharine Lorillard Wolfe, Isabella Stewart Gardner, and Emily Folger shared a passion for both collecting what they had learned were important works of art and sharing those works with the American public as a means of furthering a more elevated cultural profile for their nation. To a lesser extent, Edith Wharton also achieved this through the publication of her book with Codman, in which the authors sought to persuade their predominantly upper-class audience away from knick-knacks and toward the "inexpensive trifles"[135] of which they approved.

ENDINGS

If Lady Dorothy's donation of her Sussex iron to the Victoria and Albert Museum is indicative of the end of that collecting narrative, how do we interpret those female collectors, like Emily Folger, or Isabella Stewart Gardener, whose collecting only ended with their deaths? Bal argues that whereas there is an absence, as in narrative, of beginnings in collections, endings are more ambiguous. In the case of Lady Dorothy's donation, for example, she may have decided her Sussex iron collection was complete. So, like the ending of a short story within a collection of short stories, Lady Dorothy could begin a new collection with a new narrative. Emily, on the other hand, sought perfection: "the equivalent of death in the sense that it can only be closely approximated, not achieved 'during the life time' of the subject."[136] Thus, it is only in death that the collector who seeks perfection comes to the end of her collecting narrative.

The collection of female collectors that I have presented here is far from complete. Given that the institutions that benefited from the women discussed in this essay occupy the cornerstones of British and American culture, the examination of the collecting narratives created by these women deserves more attention. A feminist approach is required to study the space occupied by these Victorian women within public space and among previously perceived male-dominated practices. Such research would offer a new understanding of the participation of Victorian women in their nation's cultural identity. Further examinations of married male collectors in other countries might reveal other collecting partners like Lady Charlotte and Emily Folger, necessitating an adjustment to how we understand the formation of the rich cultural history not just of Britain and the United States, but of countries such as Canada and Australia as well. Like the dearth of female historical contributions to literature that Virginia Woolf famously found in the library at the British Museum when writing *A Room of One's Own*, evidence of those women whose intellectual contributions to the field of collecting contributed to their nation's narrative must be searched out in order for those narratives to reflect the true diversity of their contributors.

NOTES

1. Jean Baudrillard, "The System of Collecting," in *The Cultures of Collecting: From Elvis to Antiques—Why Do We Collect Things?*, ed. John Elsner and Roger Cardinal (Melbourne, Australia: Melbourne University Press, 1992), 10.
2. Baudrillard, "The System of Collecting," 9.
3. Baudrillard, "The System of Collecting," 10.
4. Baudrillard, "The System of Collecting," 10.
5. Rosemary Matthews, "Collectors and Why They Collect: Isabella Stewart Gardner and Her Museum of Art," *Journal of the History of Collections* 21, no. 2 (2009): 187.
6. Baudrillard's *The System of Objects* was first published in France in 1968.
7. These include, but are not limited to, Anne Higonnet, *A Museum of One's Own* (Pittsburgh, PA: Periscope Publishing, 2009); and Dianne Sachko Macleod, *Enchanted Lives, Enchanted Objects: American Women Collectors and the Making of Culture, 1800–1940* (Berkeley, Los Angeles, London: University of California Press, 2008).
8. Rosemary Matthews, "Collectors and Why They Collect," 187.
9. Henry James, *The Spoils of Poynton* (Oxford: Oxford University Press, 2008), 8.
10. Henry James, *The Spoils of Poynton*, 8.
11. Henry James, *The Spoils of Poynton*, 8.
12. There is a similarity of language between Adela and the female collectors I discuss that further strengthens James's connection with that culture. Adela uses the word "gimcrack" (20) disparagingly in describing her reaction of disgust at the interior decoration of the Brigstocks' home, Waterbath, not once but three times. Lady Dorothy uses the word to describe Strawberry Hill, the former home of Horace Walpole: "The whole place, no doubt, was very gimcrack, but still charmed the imagination, much as does the soft tinkling note of an old spinet" (275). Whereas the *Oxford English Dictionary* defines this quaint word as an adjective meaning "showy but insubstantial," in Lady Dorothy's memoirs the context seems to imply nostalgia, an attraction to old, sentimental things.

13. Although I refer to the men historically connected to these women and the scholars influencing this essay by their last names, I use these lady collectors' first names.

14. Whereas widows, like Adela, were not constrained from dealing with property in a public business transaction and were often appointed as executors or guardians in a will, the legal institution of marriage rendered a woman's legal rights void by merging her legal identity with her husband's. It wasn't until Britain's Married Women's Property Act of 1882 that "any property owned by a wife before marriage or acquired thereafter would be her separate property." See Rebecca Probert, "Women's Property Rights Before 1900," in *The New Oxford Companion to Law*, ed. Peter Cane and Joanne Conaghan (Oxford: Oxford University Press, 2008) *Oxford References Online*, http://www.oxfordreference.com/views/ENTRY.html?subview=Main&entry=t287.e2352 (accessed 24 November 2009).

15. Henry James, *The Spoils of Poynton*, 14.

16. Henry James, *The Spoils of Poynton*, 14.

17. Henry James, *The Spoils of Poynton*, 14.

18. Susan M. Pearce, *Museum, Objects and Collections* (Washington, DC: Smithsonian Institute Press, 1992), 7.

19. Henry James, *The Spoils of Poynton*, 7.

20. Henry James, *The Spoils of Poynton*, 7.

21. Henry James, *The Spoils of Poynton*, 7–8.

22. Henry James, *The Spoils of Poynton*, 14.

23. A good literary example of this practice can be seen in Jane Austen's *Mansfield Park*, in which Sir Bertram must visit his West Indian estate, indicating that it is the source of his wealth. See Brian Southam, "The Silence of the Bertrams: Slavery and the Chronology of *Mansfield Park*," *Times Literary Supplement*, 17 February 1995, 13–14.

24. Henry James, *The Spoils of Poynton*, 8.

25. Henry James, *The Spoils of Poynton*, 14.

26. It is perhaps significant that the British magazine *Country Life* began publishing the year *The Spoils of Poynton* appeared in *The Atlantic Monthly*, 1897. This magazine presented an idealistic view of country life in Britain and often followed those levels of society that could afford that lifestyle. See Roy C. Strong, *Country Life, 1897–1997: The English Arcadia* (London: Boxtree, 1997). For the influence on nationalistic sentiment through the images and ideals promoted inside the covers of this magazine, see also Patricia Rae, "Double Sorrow: Proleptic Elegy and the End of Arcadianism in 1930s Britain," *Twentieth Century Literature* 49, no. 2 (Summer 2003): 246–276.

27. Charles Saumarez Smith, "A Grand Design: A History of the Victoria & Albert Museum" and "National Consciousness," *The Victoria and Albert Museum Online*, http://www.vam.ac.uk/vastatic/microsites/1159_grand_design/ (accessed 31 October 2012).

28. Philip Horne, "James, Henry (1843–1916)," in *Oxford Dictionary of National Biography Online* (2004), http://www.oxforddnb.com.ezproxy.lib.ucalgary.ca/view/article/34150?docPos=3 (accessed 31 October 2012).

29. Anne Higonnet, *A Museum of One's Own* (Pittsburgh, PA: Periscope Publishing, 2009), 86.

30. See Pierre Auguste Renoir's *The Reader* (1872), Private Collection of Paul G. Allen; Vincent Van Gogh's *The Novel Reader* (1888), London, Private Collection.

31. Baudrillard, "The System of Collecting," 100.

32. Mieke Bal, "Telling Objects: A Narrative Perspective on Collecting," in *The Cultures of Collecting: From Elvis to Antiques—Why Do We Collect Things?*, ed. John Elsner and Roger Cardinal (Melbourne, Australia: Melbourne University Press, 1992), 98.

33. Bal, "Telling Objects," 100.

34. Bal, "Telling Objects," 101.

35. The source of many museum collections is the collector, for example, American Catharine Lollilard Wolfe or Britain's Lady Charlotte Elizabeth Guest Schreiber.

36. Pearce, *Museum, Objects and Collections*, 5.

37. Dianne Sachko Macleod, *Art and the Victorian Middle Class: Money and the Making of Cultural Identity* (Cambridge, New York, Melbourne: Cambridge University Press, 1996), 4.

38. Macleod, *Enchanted Lives*, 4.

39. Macleod, *Enchanted Lives* (emphasis added), 5. Eastlake refers to painters still living because the "lowlier" investors concentrated on modern art.

40. Dorothy Nevill, *The Reminiscences of Lady Dorothy Nevill*, ed. Ralph Nevill (London: T. Nelson, 1906), 18.

41. W. R. Trotter, and K. D. Reynolds, "Nevill [nee Walpole], Lady Dorothy Fanny," in *Oxford Dictionary of National Biography Online*, http://www.oxforddnb.com.ezproxy.lib.ucalgary.ca/view/article/37805?docPos=1 (accessed 15 October 2010).

42. Guy Nevill, *Exotic Groves: A Portrait of Lady Dorothy Nevill* (Salisbury, Wiltshire, UK: Michael Russell, 1984), 69.

43. Nevill, *Exotic Groves*, 83.

44. Nevill, *Exotic Groves*, 82.

45. Nevill, *Reminiscences of Lady Dorothy Nevill*, 84.

46. Nevill, *Reminiscences of Lady Dorothy Nevill*, 88.

47. Trotter and Reynolds, "Nevill, Lady Dorothy."

48. Nevill, *Reminiscences of Lady Dorothy Nevill*, 256.

49. A pair of iron or brass utensils placed one on each side of a fireplace to support burning wood. See "fire-dog," in *Oxford English Dictionary Online*, www.oed.com (accessed 31 October 2012).

50. Nevill, *Reminiscences of Lady Dorothy Nevill*, 256.

51. Smith, "A Grand Design."

52. Smith, "National Consciousness."

53. Lillian Melani, "William Makepeace Thackeray: The Angel in the House," CUNY Brooklyn College, 2 March 2011, http://academic.brooklyn.cuny.edu/english/melani/novel_19c/thackeray/angel.html (accessed 31 October 2012).

54. Nevill, *Reminiscences of Lady Dorothy Nevill*, 257.

55. Nevill, *Reminiscences of Lady Dorothy Nevill*, 274. Also known as Bonnie Prince Charlie, the figurehead of the bloody rebellion of the Scots against the English in 1745.

56. Nevill, *Reminiscences of Lady Dorothy Nevill*, 263.

57. Today the South Kensington museums are the Victoria and Albert Museum, the Natural History Museum, and the Science Museum. See Smith, "A Grand Design."

58. Nevill, *Reminiscences of Lady Dorothy Nevill*, 255.

59. Bal, "Telling Objects," 103.

60. Bal, "Telling Objects" (emphasis added), 100.

61. Bal, "Telling Objects," 100.

62. Bal, "Telling Objects" (emphasis added), 101.

63. Bal, "Telling Objects," 101.

64. Nevill, *Exotic Groves*, 82.

65. Smith, "National Consciousness."

66. Smith, "National Consciousness."

67. Smith, "National Consciousness."

68. Smith, "National Consciousness."

69. Nevill, *Reminiscences of Lady Dorothy Nevill*, 259.

70. Nevill, *Reminiscences of Lady Dorothy Nevill*, 259. "English art" is Lady Dorothy's euphemism for English furniture.

71. Macleod, *Art and the Victorian Middle Class*, 4.

72. Lady Charlotte was committed to writing in her journal, "devoting up to an hour daily," from her childhood until a few years before her death. See Angela V. John, "Schreiber [nee Bertie; other married name Guest], Lady Charlotte Elizabeth (1812–1895)," in *Oxford Dictionary of National Biography Online*, http://www.oxforddnb.com/public/index-content .html (accessed 31 October 2012).

73. Earl of Bessborough, introduction to *Lady Charlotte Schreiber: Extracts from Her Journal, 1853–1891*, by Lady Charlotte Elizabeth (Bertie) Guest Schreiber (London: John Murray, 1952), 127.

74. John, "Schreiber . . . Lady Charlotte Elizabeth."

75. John, "Schreiber . . . Lady Charlotte Elizabeth."

76. Vere Brabazon Ponsonby, also a grandson of Lady Charlotte.

77. Bessborough, introduction, xii.

78. Bessborough, introduction, xiii.

79. Bessborough, introduction, xiii.

80. Robert Griffiths, *Mortlock China*, May 2002, http://www.mortlock.info (accessed 24 October 2010).

81. Bessborough, introduction, xiii–xiv.

82. Bessborough, introduction, xiv.

83. Bessborough, introduction, xiv.

84. Walter Benjamin, "Unpacking My Library," in *Illuminations*, ed. Hannah Arendt, trans. Harry Zohn, (New York: Schocken Books, 1969), 60.

85. Lady Charlotte Schreiber, *Lady Charlotte Schreiber's Journals* (London: John Lane, 1911), 121.

86. Schreiber, *Journals*, 121–122.

87. Smith, "National Consciousness."

88. Smith, "National Consciousness."

89. Smith, "National Consciousness."

90. Edna Healey, "Coutts, Angela Georgina Burdett," in *Oxford Dictionary of National Biography*, http://www.oxforddnb.com.ezproxy.lib.ucalgary.ca/view/article/32175 (accessed 1 October 2010).

91. Healey, "Coutts, Angela Georgina Burdett."

92. New York's Married Women's Property Act was passed in 1848 and served as a model for other states to follow, seemingly establishing American women's right to property earlier than British women's. In her examination of American female collectors, Dianne Sachko Macleod argues that this did provide an advantage and contributed to the number of American women who collected (*Enchanted Lives*, xi). In practice however, "it was the effectiveness rather than the language of the law that diminished the rights of females" (xi).

93. James, *The Spoils of Poynton*, 20.

94. Edith Wharton and Ogden Codman Jr., *The Decoration of Houses* (New York: Charles Scribner's Sons, 1914), 186.

95. These figures form part of the collections of Greek statues in several museums.

96. Wharton and Codman, *The Decoration of Houses*, 184.

97. Wharton and Codman, *The Decoration of Houses*, 186.

98. Hereafter referred to as the "Met."

99. "About the Met," *The Metropolitan Museum of Art* (2010), http://www.metmuseum.org/about-the-museum (accessed 29 October 2010).

100. Macleod, *Enchanted Lives*, 64.

101. Saul E. Zalesch, "Wolfe, Catharine Lorillard," in *American National Biography Online*, http://www.anb.org.ezproxy.lib.ucalgary.ca/articles/17/17-00942.html?a=1&n=catharine%20%20wolfe&ia=-at&ib=-bib&d=10&ss=0&q=1 (accessed 20 October 2010).

102. Bal, "Telling Objects," 101.

103. Zalesch, "Wolfe, Catharine Lorillard."

104. Macleod, *Enchanted Lives*, 5.

105. Macleod, *Enchanted Lives*, 5.

106. Macleod, *Enchanted Lives*, 62.

107. Macleod, *Enchanted Lives*, 68.

108. Macleod, *Enchanted Lives*, 69.

109. Wharton and Codman, *The Decoration of Houses*, 195.

110. Quoted in Macleod, *Enchanted Lives*, 54.

111. Macleod, *Enchanted Lives*, 54.

112. Macleod, *Enchanted Lives*, 63.

113. Higonnet, *A Museum of One's Own*, 187.

114. Isabella directed her executors that her collection must remain intact and in the exact manner in which she had arranged it, "for the education and enrichment of the public forever." See "The Museum," in *Isabella Stewart Gardner Museum Online*, http://www.gardnermuseum.org/the_museum/introduction.asp (accessed 29 October 2010).

115. Martin R. Kalfatovic, "Gardner, Isabella Stewart," in *American National Biography Online*, http://www.anb.org.ezproxy.lib.ucalgary.ca/articles/17/17-00315.html (accessed 21 October 2010).

116. Matthews, "Collectors and Why They Collect," 183–189.

117. Matthews, "Collectors and Why They Collect," 187.

118. Matthews, "Collectors and Why They Collect," 189.

119. Matthews, "Collectors and Why They Collect," 187.

120. James, "Preface," *The Spoils of Poynton*, xli.

121. James, "Preface," *The Spoils of Poynton*, xli.

122. James, "Preface," *The Spoils of Poynton*, xli.

123. Quoted in "The Museum," in *The Isabella Stewart Gardner Museum Online*.

124. It is significant that this collection of Emerson's was an exploration of the American national character, linking the Folger collection to ideas of educating Americans.

125. "A Shared Passion," *The Folger Library* (11 October 2002), http://www.folger.edu/html/exhibitions/shared_passion/passionintro.htm (accessed 25 October. 2010).

126. "A Shared Passion."

127. "A Shared Passion."

128. "A Shared Passion."

129. Kathleen Lynch, "Emily Jordan Folger," in *American National Biography Online* (2000), http://www.anb.org.ezproxy.lib.ucalgary.ca/articles/20/20-01300.html (accessed 21 October 2010).

130. Lynch, "Emily Jordan Folger."

131. Lynch, "Emily Jordan Folger."

132. See Macleod, *Enchanted Lives*, in which the author examines women art collectors from the antebellum era through the modernist era.

133. Saul E. Zalesch, "Morgan, Mary Jane," in *American National Biography Online*, http://www.anb.org.ezproxy.lib.ucalgary.ca/articles/17/17-01531.html (accessed 21 October 2010).

134. Zalesch, "Morgan, Mary Jane."

135. Wharton and Codman, *The Decoration of Houses*, 184.

136. Bal, "Telling Objects," 113.

IV

COLLECTING PRACTICES AND CULTURAL HIERARCHIES

11

Distraction and Display: The Curiosity Cabinet and the Romantic Museum

Sophie Thomas

This chapter takes as its starting point a model for collecting that the modern museum is generally thought to have rendered obsolete: the curiosity cabinet. The curiosity cabinets (or *Wunderkammer*) of the early modern period, often characterized as haphazard assemblages of curious, wondrous, or singular things, were generally the private productions of princes and scholars. By contrast, the modern museum, as it took recognizable shape in the nineteenth century, was public in orientation and founded on principles that emphasized very different paradigms for the systematic, collective, and rational ordering of knowledge. Thus, the curiosity cabinets of the pre-romantic era, in which things were often randomly juxtaposed and radically decontextualized, were eventually superseded by more "disciplined" models. This narrative of the historical evolution of the museum, however, has had the effect of deflecting our attention from some of the persistently fascinating features of curiosity cabinets as modes of collection and display—not least the "wonder" of the *Wunderkammer*—and also, as I have argued elsewhere, of leaving the collections and museums of the romantic period in an undifferentiated middle zone, as expressions of a dying or merely transitional model that would be firmly left behind.[1]

The romantic period, in fact, offers particularly rich territory for reconsidering the lingering attractions of the curiosity cabinet, and perhaps especially the imaginative visual engagement it encouraged. Prominent collectors, such as Sir Ashton Lever, William Bullock, and Sir John Soane, created museums to house their extensive personal collections that were frequently understood as large-scale curiosity cabinets; moreover, visitors to their collections were stimulated as much by the careful visual effects that were created as by the specific contents. The success of Bullock's museum, particularly, derived from his canny deployment of display strategies drawn from the visual culture industry of contemporary London. In each case, the nature of the collection was conveyed by the structural language of exhibition, expressed both through the spaces in which the collection was accumulated and articulated and through the visual experiences they gave rise to. Although this attention to the visual was often directed toward producing novel effects, I argue that the excitement surrounding these museums derived from qualities proper to the curiosity or wonder cabinet, specifically its evocative power, which is largely unlocked by the activity of (active) looking.

The imaginative possibilities, and indeed demands, of curiosity cabinets have been attended to more closely in recent scholarship. Barbara Maria Stafford has noted that the multiply material nature of the cabinet invited viewers to supply points of contact between objects as well as to navigate between them. She thus characterizes wonder or curiosity cabinets as springboards for imaginative activity, as "monumental poetic *armoires*," in which the artifacts are "less physical phenomena and more material links permitting the beholder to retrieve complicated personal and cultural associations."[2] She has also suggestively argued that such cabinets may be understood as early modern forms of interdisciplinarity, offering "a parallel to the interlocking dynamics of the contemporary universe," particularly in the digital age.[3] A similar position had been advanced by Horst Bredekamp in *The Lure of Antiquity and the Cult of the Machine*, in which he related the conceptual problems negotiated by baroque *Kunstkammer*, "with their lessons of visual association and thought processes," to the breakdown of boundaries between science, technology, and art characteristic of the modern world.[4] It is precisely these qualities that have made the curiosity cabinet a suggestive point of reference in art practice. In some cases this has taken the form of reconstituting historical cabinets, such as Rosamond Purcell's re-creation of the Museum Wormianum for the Santa Monica Museum of Art in 2003.[5] In others, the cabinet's key attraction is as a "pre-programmable personal environment," one that sanctions creative accumulation and activity in ways that are intimately bound up with memory and the imagination, as we see in Kurt Schwitters's use of his house as part of his *Merzbau* project, or Joseph Cornell's magical boxes, with their poetic assemblages of found objects.[6] James Putnam, in *The Museum as Medium*, suggests that there are two dominant ways in which artists have engaged the model of the *Wunderkammer*: first, as collectors who create assemblages by arranging and juxtaposing diverse objects, and second, by manipulating and transforming natural and artificial materials in ways that interrogate the distinction between them.[7] Although the precise place of curiosity cabinets in the genealogy of the modern museum has been the subject of considerable debate, they remain inspirational because of the questions their eclectic and unruly qualities allow us to ask. This means they can still be functional systems for gathering and ordering what, as Francis Bacon put it, "singularity, chance, and the shuffle of things hath produced."[8] They also permit us to better appreciate the collecting and exhibition practices that stood behind the "new" museums of the romantic period.

OPENING THE CABINET

The "cabinet" was, in its earliest form, simply a cupboard with various compartments that contained a collection of small objects, both natural and man-made.[9] By the seventeenth century, the term had come to designate the room or chamber in which the cabinet was located (hence a variety of other terms come into use: the closet, *gabinetto*, *Kammer*, *Kabinett*). This room was designed to display rare or unusual objects—a chamber of treasures or *Wunderkammer*—in which the collection itself was a constitutive element of the look of the room. Michael McKeon, in *The Secret History of Domesticity*, comments that as "a private space within a private space, the cabinet encapsulated the great world within its odd and wondrous confines, and it announced its owner to be a gentleman of polite and cosmopolitan understanding." The most distinguished examples were located in "the estates and palaces of the Renaissance patriciate," where the aim was to "amass objects that amaze not only in their odd singularity but also in the way this singularity is reinforced by the arbitrariness of their arrangement."[10]

Early modern cabinets were thus as notable for their distinctive display practices as for their exotic contents. Similar objects were not likely to be placed near each other, but rather according to the requirements of the space, or for maximum visual appeal, as is clear in Ferrante Imperato's cabinet in sixteenth-century Naples, the first such museum for which an illustration exists (see figure 11.1).[11] Although it is common to think about such displays as a form of promiscuous assemblage, it is also the case that sought-after effects of "harmonious symmetry" were created through clear and deliberate principles. In her discussion of Antonio Giganti's *studi* from sixteenth-century Bologna, Laura Laurencich-Minelli observes that larger visual rhythms were created by not displaying similar-looking items alongside each other, but by interspersing or alternating them with dissimilar ones and by arranging groups of objects thematically.[12] The desired result, as with other such cabinets, was "a harmonious evocation, or *arsmemoriae*, of the whole of art and nature."[13] Katie Whitaker points out that this very juxtaposition of things crammed together was what created the desired effect: objects were arranged precisely to emphasize their diverse and contrasting nature, and the models of classification that followed in the eighteenth-century natural history museum, for example, would have had no place in a sixteenth- or seventeenth-century collection, "since an object surrounded by similar but slightly different species would have seemed unsurprising and ordinary."[14]

In the cabinet of curiosities, as in the *Wunderkammer*, the scarce—the singular—object was meant to be perceived and appreciated in comparative isolation. However, the rationalization of objects in the modern museum, as McKeon points out, "emphasizes collectivity over singularity."[15] Moreover, the emphasis on rarity and variety in the baroque cabinet was replaced by a widespread enthusiasm for natural history that conformed to new ideals of linearity, all of which made the curiosity cabinet look increasingly disorderly.[16] The museum as it emerged over the course of the eighteenth century has been seen as increasingly informed by the principles of

Figure 11.1. The Natural History Museum of Emperor Ferdinand III from *Historia Naturale* by Ferrante Imperato (1550–1631) pub. in 1672 (engraving). © The British Library Board.

the encyclopedia, or the library, rather than animated by the spirit of adventure that was present in the curiosity cabinet. This is clear in Louis Marin's suggestion that the museum is the "rationalized illustration of the encyclopaedia."[17] Indeed, he views the museum as, ideologically speaking, rationalist and nationalist (while universalist in destination), in contrast with the cabinet of curiosities, with its devotion to a "hedonism of knowledge, a *jouissance* of information born of surprise, of wonder, or from a fascination that is nearly always *ponctuel*, nearly always singular."[18]

The spirit of adventure that animated the curiosity cabinet, however, by no means vanished. In addition to the way cabinets have inspired artists, as noted previously, we find the model of the curiosity cabinet to be widely taken up as "a valuable conceptual asset in the reordering and restructuring of museum collections today."[19] David Martin considers this reinvestment in the cabinet collection and its powers of enchantment as "something of a contemporary museological trope," evident in a number of recent examples, from the "Microcosms: Objects and Knowledge (a University Collects)" project at the University of California in 1995, to the New York Public Library's 2002 exhibition *The Public's Treasures: A Cabinet of Curiosities.*[20] This phenomenon expanded, moreover, to the very structure of the contemporary museum: Daniel Libeskind's extension to the Royal Ontario Museum in Toronto contains a central "Stair of Wonders" intended to showcase some of the museum's more extraordinary holdings in an interstitial exhibition space unconnected to a programmed or themed gallery. More than a thousand items, both scientific and historical, are displayed in sections of the stairwell that are explicitly modeled on the curiosity cabinet.

The *Wunderkammer*'s power as a "spectacle-enclosing" box was also suggestively used by Barbara Maria Stafford and Frances Terpak as an analogy for their exhibition and accompanying catalog, *Devices of Wonder: From the World in a Box to Images on a Screen,* mounted at the Getty in 2001. The exhibition, they suggest, "emulates the curiosity cabinet's epistemic organization by juxtaposition and superimposition of heterogeneous elements."[21] When such a cabinet is opened, its contents, now freed, are fragments that spill "into adjacent spaces," allowing new connections to form.[22] Certainly the cosmos, as displayed in a *Kunst-* or *Wunderkammer*, was "not so much a static tableau to be contemplated as it was a drama of possible relationships to be explored."[23] Yet the "sensory heightening" that results from the forced compression of the object by virtue of its containment in a cabinet display is likened to the "spatial compression" performed by optical instruments. As Stafford and Terpak elaborate, the "prisms, mirrors, microscopes, telescopes, magic lanterns, and camera obscuras of the time also produced perceptual, imaginative, and intellectual intensification"; indeed, the way these instruments brought together and abstracted, enlarged, or multiplied objects, made *them* "collecting apparatuses," analogous to the curiosity cabinet in their capacity to concentrate, conjoin, and transform "the universe's unruly singularities."[24] Like the cabinet, they allow us to focus and refocus different features of the object, along with aspects of its (dis)orderly conduct.

Stafford and Terpak's suggestion that the curiosity cabinet can function as an analogy for an exhibition, for the ordering (or disordering) of objects on a larger scale, and for how we approach them, resonates with the collections of a number of romantic era figures, several of whom, at least initially, used their homes as a space for both collection and display. Questions of spatial setting, arrangement, and the effects created by the proximity of other objects were at least one reason why these collections were frequently characterized in terms of the curiosity cabinet. Turning now to a few specific examples, I suggest that as the cabinet increased in scale and scope with the emergence of the more publicly oriented museum, the imaginative potentialities of the traditional cabinet or *Wunderkammer* were neither overcome nor suppressed, but rather harnessed in fresh ways.

LEVER'S *HOLOPHUSIKON*

Sir Ashton Lever was the avid collector behind one of the most important natural history collections in late eighteenth-century England. He spent over a million pounds in the process of building his collections, which were first displayed in his home near Manchester, Alkrington Hall; as Lever later reflected, "it was a passion of mine to possess all nature's wonders, no expense was spared."[25] By the early 1780s, the result of all this single-minded activity was a collection of close to 28,000 items, many of which were rare natural specimens, but Lever's collections also included British and foreign antiquities, as well as ethnographic materials, principally from Cook's voyages of exploration to the South Pacific, North America, and Asia. A description of Lever's museum at Alkrington Hall can be found in *The Gentleman's Magazine* for May 1773, wherein the writer comments on being "most agreeably entertained and surprised to find one of the grandest collections of the most perfect specimens of Natural History that are to be seen in any private gentleman's possession in Europe."[26] The collection was estimated to consist of "upwards of 1300 glass cases, containing curious subjects, placed in three rooms, besides four sides of rooms shelved from top to bottom, with glass doors before them."[27]

Lever opened his collections to the public in 1771, and as many as a 1,000 people on a single day visited them. The collections also grew rapidly, expanded by donations as well as by purchases. Here one observes the social network surrounding collecting in practice: Lever corresponded actively with other collectors, appealed to friends to help secure items, advertised opening times in the local papers, and invited neighbours and friends to witness the uncrating of new acquisitions.[28] He also gave generously to other collectors. So successful was all this that he decided in 1774 to move his collection to London, where he intended "to pursue Natural History and carry the exhibition of it to such a height as no one can imagine; and to make it the most wonderful sight in the world."[29] He moved into Leicester House in Leicester Square (at that time, the largest private residence in London) and renamed it the "Holophusikon," which means "whole-nature," or nature in its entirety. The public opening was advertised in *The Morning Post* in February 1775: "Mr Lever's Museum of Natural and other curiosities, consisting of beasts, birds, fishes, corals, shells, fossils extraneous and native, as well as many miscellaneous articles in high preservation, will be opened on Monday the 13th of February for the inspection of the public."[30] Lever's new museum rapidly became a fashionable venue for informed amusement: the royal family visited in 1778, and George III conferred a knighthood upon Ashton Lever in that same year.[31]

In its new location, seventeen rooms and adjoining corridors were used for the museum, the majority on the upper floor. A watercolor of the interior, painted by Sarah Stone in 1786, captures the view down the length of this principal part of the museum (see figure 11.2). As the illustration makes clear, the collection was arranged to achieve striking visual effects, to provoke surprise and wonder in the viewer. At the same time, the dramatic nature of the display advertised the wealth of the collector and his virtuoso power to identify and amass the wonders of nature and of man.[32] Visitors to the museum would first ascend a staircase, the top of which is visible in the right foreground. In the entrance hall below, weapons such as spears and pistols were hung, while knives, longbows, and arrows were displayed in cases.[33] On the staircase itself, Lever displayed an array of animal parts (such as horns, teeth,

Figure 11.2. *Interior of Leverian Museum;* view as it appeared in the 1780s, ca. 1835 watercolor, after Sarah Stone. © The Trustees of the British Museum.

and tusks) as well as whole animals, such as stuffed crocodiles, and displayed the elephant on the landing. This area at the top of the stairs contained a selection of odd and unique things as well as others, such as birds, shells, and plant specimens, that indexed what would be found in the collection as a whole. It has been argued that the thousand or so objects on show here "seemed to be operating, through diversity and profusion, on the model of a cabinet of curiosity: it was a room for wonder."[34] The astonished visitor would then proceed through the curtained archway into the individual rooms beyond.

The presence of the curtain, pulled aside as though dramatically to reveal the wonders of nature, suggests a change in register as one passes through it. The exhibits in the twelve rooms on the other side of the curtain (there were a further five on the ground floor) were more concentrated and specialized. The first rooms, for example, were devoted to birds, which were displayed alongside other kinds of objects, such as shells, fossils, and geological specimens. In fact, most rooms juxtaposed two kinds of objects, such as the fifth room, which contained some large quadrupeds and was also lined with glass cases displaying insects and crabs; hence it was referred to variously as the "Insect Room" or the "Hippopotamus Room."[35] Clearly, as Haynes has suggested, a certain kind of visual pleasure could be experienced by such juxtapositions, for example in the texture and color of the bird specimens, in relation to those of fossils and shells.[36] In other rooms, the contrasts were at work within one broader category, such as in the "Wardrobe" which contained clothes from a variety of nations (items of British costume, footwear from China and Persia, and a suit of armour said to have belonged to Cromwell). A further contrast could be experienced by moving from this room, through the "Club Room" with its extensive displays of weaponry, to the two devoted to objects and artifacts—from hunting and fishing equipment to clothing and religious idols—collected on Cook's voyages.[37]

Stone's illustration, which conveys both a sense of the particular as well as the whole, captures the crucial balance in Lever's museum, between inviting the eye to move freely and even randomly, and offering the opportunity for concentrated looking. Knowledgeable visitors interested in particular specimens could gratify their curiosity, while those stimulated by the imaginative possibilities generated by the overall spectacle would be equally satisfied. Lever's emphasis on visual delight in the arrangement of his exhibits, through sheer quantity and careful juxtapositions, was intended to create a sense of wonder that would resonate with the diversity and complexity of nature *outside* the museum. For the eighteenth-century visitor and collector alike, this wonder had a theological component, which the study of nature could lead us to understand. Yet it is also the case that the scale and intensity of Lever's collecting, and the fact that he charged entry fees to his museum, led to him being described by one contemporary as "having 'more the swelling strut of a common showman, than the *dignified* exhibitioner'" about him.[38]

This last charge was perhaps also related to the fact that Lever, in his unceasing efforts to expand the collection, had sold off a great deal of his own personal capital, and even though the museum remained popular with the public, he found himself in a desperate financial position. He disposed of the museum in 1786, by lottery, at which time it passed to James Parkinson, who moved it across the river at Blackfriars Bridge (where it nevertheless retained the name Leverian Museum). Parkinson later closed the museum and sold off the collections in 1806. Despite its demise, Lever's Holophusikon speaks to a number of issues central to the evolution of the modern museum as a distinct entity. Yet some accounts of the Leverian make it sound like a museological dinosaur. Christine Cheater describes it as the last of the large "premodern" museums and suggests that it was "out of step with developing views on how to improve the morals and manners of the lower classes."[39] It failed to promote an "orderly" approach to viewing and was too reminiscent of the old cabinets of curiosities, in which the principles governing the collection were not foregrounded or readily intelligible. By the nineteenth century, of course, items would be grouped by function, origin, genus, and species, in keeping with Nicholas Thomas's definition of museum exhibits, by contrast with those of a collection, as expressing a distant mastery over an array of objects "abstracted from the circuits of exchange," rather than reflecting "the personal preoccupations of its owner."[40] This view, however, is not entirely fair to Lever's approach and his achievement. His collections, though eccentric in certain ways, and arranged to emphasize their spectacular possibilities, tend to complicate claims about the museum as a medium of scientific rationality or (conversely) as a place of entertainment, where distraction tended to prevail. The Holosphusikon was, in its historical moment, surprisingly successful on both counts. His exhibits were celebrated by the public, but also taken up by fellows of the Royal Society and the Society of Antiquaries, both "scientific" organizations of which he was himself a member.[41] Although difficult now to reconstruct, museums such as Lever's, in which elements of the curiosity cabinet remain in play, are part of an important episode in the history of collecting.

BULLOCK'S LONDON MUSEUM

William Bullock's prominence as a collector and museum entrepreneur dates from the first decades of the nineteenth century. Not long after the Leverian closed its doors permanently in 1806, Bullock was moving his principal exhibition rooms from Liverpool to London; according to the seventh edition of his *Companion*, published in 1809, his "London Museum" had recently opened, and his collections were growing quickly. The tenth edition (1811) of the *Companion* announced itself as "*Containing a brief Description of upward of Seven Thousand Natural and Foreign Curiosities, Antiquities, and productions of the fine arts.*"[42]

At this stage, natural history specimens occupied a large place in the collection, and one of the museum's chief attractions was an immense "artificial forest," which, though simulating a tropical forest, contained a remarkably diverse array of "larger Quadrupeds, Birds and Reptiles," all attractively (and where feasible "naturally") arranged in a landscape of artificial trees. The aquatint published in Ackermann's *Repository of Arts* for 1810 (see figure 11.3) shows clearly the general disposition not just of this central display, but of the exhibition room it occupied, which also contained (in addition to visitors displaying varying degrees of interest) an array of glass cases and display objects along the perimeter walls. Bullock's collections also included a significant quantity of arms and armor (derived at least partly from Dr. Richard Greene's Lichfield museum and later sold to Sir Samuel Meyrick at Goodrich Court), and ethnographic items, some from Cook's Pacific voyages, and of those, some purchased from the sale of Lever's collections. The *Companion* also contains details of objects from North Africa, North America (Bullock displayed, for example, Inuit clothing and equipment, including a kayak), and Egypt (a mummy).[43]

In 1812 Bullock unveiled what would become the famous "Egyptian Hall," his own purpose-built museum on the south side of Piccadilly, so named because its façade was designed to resemble an ancient Egyptian temple. Still billed as "An

Figure 11.3.   Bullock's Museum. Aquatint in Ackermann's *Repository of the Arts*, 1810.
© **The British Library Board.**

Establishment for the advancement of the Science of Natural History," one of its key attractions was the "Pantherion," which, like the artificial forest, contained mainly large animal specimens displayed in careful reconstructions of their natural habitats. In the fourteenth edition of his *Companion*, Bullock promoted this innovation, "completed with much labour and great expence," as presenting a dramatic and engaging exhibition of animals—such as "the lofty Giraffe, the Lion, the Elephant, the Rhinoceros, &c."—roaming in a landscape that gives "all the appearance of reality" through the careful replication of "the rarest and most luxurient plants from every clime."[44] The whole effect was completed by a panoramic background painting that supplied appropriate scenery and the illusion of distance. Using a broadly Linnaean arrangement throughout his collections, Bullock attempted to merge the demands of classification with convincingly simulated natural habitats.[45]

Like the Holophusikon, Bullock's Museum was an enormously popular success: by early 1810, in its first London location, it was declared by *Bell's Weekly Messenger* to be "the most fashionable place of amusement in London."[46] Unlike Lever, however, Bullock appears not to have been a single-minded collector; that is, he was willing to sell his material when its popularity waned and took an inventive approach to the use of his rooms at the Egyptian Hall, hiring them out for sales and the exhibition of paintings (often new and noteworthy ones, such as Haydon's *Christ's Triumphal Entry into Jerusalem* and Géricault's *Raft of the Medusa*, in 1820), and using them to mount increasingly complex exhibitions. These included the wildly popular Napoleon's carriage in 1816, the Roman Gallery (a themed exhibition of antiquities, sculptures, mosaics, and paintings), Belzoni's dramatic reconstruction of an ancient Egyptian tomb from the Valley of the Kings in 1821, a family of Laplanders (1822), and ancient and modern Mexican artifacts (1824). For his exhibition of the Laplanders (modern-day Sami), Bullock juxtaposed diverse elements from their material culture, prepared detailed and realistic visual backdrops of icy northern landscapes, and even included living human examples, in the form of a whole Lapland family and their reindeer, complete with their huts, enclosures, and sleds.

In preparation for his Mexican exhibit, Bullock and his son spent six months traveling in Mexico (his published account of their travels coincided neatly with the exhibition). In addition to collecting animal and mineral specimens and archaeological objects, he made plaster casts of significant antiquities such as an Aztec calendar stone, an immense "serpent-idol," and statues such as the "War Goddess," to whom the hearts of sacrificial victims were brought.[47] The exhibitions, mounted in the spring of 1824, included pictures of Aztec life, fragments of historic maps, manuscripts, drawings, models and copies of buildings and antiquities, ancient statues and idols, and many domestic objects and implements, from vessels to weapons. Two initially distinctive exhibitions, one of ancient and one of modern Mexico, appear to have been merged into one in 1825; accompanying "modern" Mexico was a large panorama of Mexico City, which provided a key visual and experiential element, capitalizing on the popularity of the panorama as a form of visual spectacle in its own right. Bullock's Mexican panorama was produced by John Burford, who was an important figure from 1816 onward at the Panorama in Leicester Square; indeed, it subsequently went on show there in 1826.

These last exhibits in particular reveal Bullock's innovative approach. Because he was (like Lever) a clever showman as well as a committed collector and natural historian, his intellectual credentials were also regarded with some suspicion by contemporaries, yet it has been argued that he "invented a new visual language of objects," one that had a lasting impact on museums internationally.[48] Although he was not the first to mount his displays in naturalistic settings (Charles Willson Peale had done this more than ten years earlier), he was, Pearce argues, "the first to marry a natural-style setting with a Linnean-based arrangement of the animals, which drew attention to their interrelationships."[49] He also, as in the "Pantherion," cleverly integrated additional elements of visual illusion by incorporating painted panoramas in the background of his displays. Arguably, in the exhibitions he mounted after 1819 (the year in which he probably wisely auctioned off his natural history collections), his deployment of diverse media and material, particularly in bringing the techniques associated with visual spectacle to the display of objects, was at its height. Implicit in his approach is a complex set of assumptions about how objects and people interact: visual elements situate or contextualize objects and offer viewers an experience that is both emotional and intellectual.[50]

THE ROMANTIC MUSEUM OF SIR JOHN SOANE

My final example from this transitional period in the history of the romantic museum is the Sir John Soane Museum in London's Lincoln's Inn Fields, which has been thought of as a halfway house between the Renaissance cabinet and the modern museum: "one of the final historical examples," as Donald Preziosi has called it, "of the *Kunst- und Wunderkammern* of the sixteenth and seventeenth centuries."[51] Although Soane's collections were extensive and eclectic, they were also largely classical and antiquarian in focus and reflected his interests, professional and personal, in art and architecture. Soane thought of them as a resource as well as an inspiration for his own (and for future) students. They featured models and plaster casts, fragments of statuary and buildings, drawings and paintings, approximately 7,000 books, an array of oddities and curios, as well as some singular and quite spectacular items such as the alabaster sarcophagus of the Egyptian king Seti I. Like the collections of Lever and Bullock, they were constantly growing and changing, such that the house itself required frequent renovation and expansion, necessitating new editions of Soane's published descriptions. Unlike them, however, the collections have been preserved in something very close to the form they were in at the time of their collector's death: at first the objects of an active process of accumulation and rearrangement, they are now fixed in the form of a museum.[52] As John Elsner suggests, Soane's museum "embodies and freezes for posterity the moment at which collecting (and redeploying a collection) ceases, the moment when the museum begins."[53]

What was once the dynamic production of a creative imagination thus has become a monument to the man and his achievement. But it nevertheless captures very effectively the extent to which Soane's house-museum was a carefully staged production in which a variety of interests and pursuits coalesced, and in which the architecture and the collections worked together to create complex visual and psychological effects in their framing and dramatization of the objects of the past. Like other collector's houses (related examples are Horace Walpole's faux gothic villa at Strawberry Hill or Walter Scott's Abbotsford), Soane created a fully realized "theater of display" in which he mobilized "a whole range of scenographic and aesthetic tropes—from a *lumière mystérieuse* formed from light, shadow and colour, to the fragment and the mirror—to produce a spectacular space in the service of memorialization and display."[54] These "tropes" were in conversation with contemporary aesthetic discourses such as the picturesque and the sublime and with developments in visual culture—such as the Eidophusikon, dioramas and panoramas, and Phantasmagoria—that aimed to disturb and enchant through their manipulation of the visual field and their illusion-creating capacities.

Gustav Friedrich Waagen, in his 1838 account of the most noteworthy English collections, *Treasures of Art in Great Britain*, expressed some ambivalence about the total effect Soane created and described it as "a splendid example of English eccentricity": "I observe that the whole, notwithstanding the picturesque, fantastic charm, which cannot be denied, has, in consequence of this arbitrary mixture of heterogeneous objects, something of the unpleasant effect of a feverish dream."[55] The problems and qualities of arbitrariness and heterogeneity are generally used unfavorably to describe curiosity cabinets, and as with the Leverian, it was common in contemporary descriptions of Soane's house to compare it to a large-scale cabinet of curiosities. Yet the "architectures of sensation and affect,"[56] as Helene Furján aptly calls it, that Soane's efforts point toward, arguably signaled a fresh view of the culture of the cabinet, and they did so by heightening the visual experience of the visitor.

John Britton, in his commentary on the house written in 1827, also registered a sense of confusion that features of the house, such as its profusion of objects, its potentially unruly particulars, might create: "From the multiplicity of objects with which it is stored, and from the intricacy of its plan, a stranger must view the scene with astonishment, and can hardly know where first to direct his attention."[57] However, Britton's account described in some detail the unique visual arrangements of the space. He noted how in the main dome and museum of the house (see figure 11.4), the viewer took in two floors at once, since the lower level—where the Monk's Parlour and the Egyptian crypt, with its famous sarcophagus, were located—was visible through a central opening in the floor. As one moved around the parapet surrounding the opening, "various views of unusual combination and effect are obtained, both of the subterranean recesses below, the gallery and dome above, and of vistas eastward towards the picture cabinet."[58] Britton's account is full of observations of this kind, in which the viewer encountered features of the physical space that appeared to exceed their material bounds. Some of these effects were created by the use of mirrors and windows as well as visual passages from one room into the contents of another: as visitors moved through the rooms of the house, they encountered fresh and constantly shifting views "that unexpectedly burst upon the spectator, so as to fascinate him with delight"; these produced "that species of complexity which destroys all monotony."[59]

A museum such as Soane's elicits an imaginative response, in a way that recalls the optical dimensions of curiosity cabinets mobilized by Stafford and Terpak. It also involves the viewer in what could be called acts of "imaging": acts of visualization that Stafford argues have come to inform our cognitive habits at least since the eighteenth century, when the "creation of galleries, museums, libraries and natural history cabinets was grounded in a visual encyclopedism" that encouraged mental wandering amid the "fluid this's and that's of a rising phenomenal tide."[60] Stafford draws upon the logic of the "discontinuous *Wunderkammer*" as a structure of "ill-assorted assemblages" that, by exposing uncertainty to sight and disclosing the interruptions that inevitably exist in systems of classification, demonstrate "how we learn painstakingly by gathering and arranging bits and pieces in the dark."[61] The house-museum of Sir John Soane remains a vivid demonstration of this, long after the death of its creator.

Svetlana Alpers has usefully reminded us of the extent to which the objects gathered together in cabinet collections, "those encyclopaedic collections of Renaissance princes," were valued for their visual power: "Much has been said of the ideology of power, political and intellectual, engaged in both the collecting of objects and the

Figure 11.4. View of the interior, the dome (photo). © Courtesy of Trustees of Sir John Soane's Museum, London/The Bridgeman Art Library.

taxonomic manner of ordering them. But I want to stress that what was collected was judged to be of visual interest."[62] To this extent, the museum is, she argues, first and foremost, and then as now, "a way of seeing." This features prominently, as we have seen, in discussions of early collections, which have been thought of as places to view nature "at play," places to minimize the boundaries between objects and the classes to which they belong, to let the eye and the "associative powers of sight" build "visual bridges" across different elements of collections.[63] In this view, the *Wunderkammer* did not just offer the opportunity to make links between artifacts from different cultures (different historically, ethnically, or geographically), but also "provided an opportunity for experimentation in merging form and meaning."[64] It was, precisely, "visual exchange" between objects in a collection that enabled these "metamorphoric" potentialities to emerge.

Although the *Wunderkammer* has been often treated as a "curious" stage in the prehistory of the modern museum, it is also clear that its powerful potential was unlocked in collections such as those of Lever, Bullock, and Soane, where the mobility of the eye fostered a fruitful interplay between architecture and object, between the conditions of exhibition and the forms of understanding they fostered. It is arguably one of the great strengths of late eighteenth-century and romantic museums that this dynamic still animated the activities of collectors and museum entrepreneurs alike, even at a time when increasingly "orderly" models were in the ascendancy. It is easy to dismiss attention to visual effects as responding to the commercial side of the public's appetite for visual spectacle, but this mobilization of the eye has much more far-reaching sources and effects and is closely tied not only to a way of seeing, but also to a fundamental way of thinking that we are still learning to comprehend.

NOTES

1. Sophie Thomas, "'Things on Holiday': Collections, Museums, and the Poetics of Unruliness," *European Romantic Review* 20, no 2 (April 2009): 167–175.

2. Barbara Maria Stafford, *Good Looking: Essays on the Virtue of Images* (Cambridge, MA, and London: MIT Press, 1997), 75.

3. Barbara Maria Stafford and Frances Terpak, *Devices of Wonder: From the World in a Box to Images on a Screen* (Los Angeles: Getty Research Institute, 2001), 5.

4. Horst Bredekamp, *The Lure of Antiquity and the Cult of the Machine: The Kunstkammer and the Evolution of Nature, Art and Technology* (Princeton, NJ: Markus Wiener, 1995), 113.

5. See Paul Grinke, *From Wunderkammer to Museum* (London: Quaritch, 2006), 10.

6. James Putnam, *The Museum as Medium*, 2nd ed. (London: Thames and Hudson, 2009), 11. On the engagement of artists with the museum (the "artist's museum"), see also Jean-Hubert Martin, "The 'Musée Sentimental' of Daniel Spoerri," in *Visual Display: Culture Beyond Appearances*, ed. Lynne Cooke and Peter Wollen (Seattle: Bay Press/DiaCenter for the Arts, 1995), 54–67.

7. Putnam uses the work of the surrealists as an example of this second tendency (8–10).

8. Francis Bacon, *GestaGrayorum* (1594), cited in Oliver Impey and Arthur MacGregor, eds., *The Origin of Museums: The Cabinet of Curiosities in Sixteenth-Century Europe* (Oxford: Clarendon Press, 1985), 1.

9. Michael McKeon, *The Secret History of Domesticity: Public, Private, and the Division of Knowledge* (Baltimore, MD: Johns Hopkins University Press, 2005), 218.

10. McKeon, *Secret History*, 218.

11. See Carla Yanni, *Nature's Museums: Victorian Science and the Architecture of Display* (London: The Athlone Press, 1999), 18.

12. Laura Laurencich-Minelli, "Museography and Ethnographical Collections in Bologna During the Sixteenth and Seventeenth Centuries," in *The Origin of Museums*, ed. Impey and MacGregor, 19.

13. Laurencich-Minelli, "Museography and Ethnographical Collections," 19.

14. Katie Whitaker, "The Culture of Curiosity," in *Cultures of Natural History*, ed. N. Jardine, J. A. Secord, and E. C. Spary (Cambridge, UK: Cambridge University Press, 1996), 87.

15. McKeon, *Secret History of Domesticity*, 218.

16. Paul Holdengräber, "'A Visible History of Art': The Forms and Preoccupations of the Early Museum," *Studies in Eighteenth Century Culture* 17 (1987): 110.

17. Louis Marin, "Fragments d'histoires de musées," *Cahiers du Musée national d'art moderne* 17–18 (March 1986), 16.

18. Marin, "Fragments d'histoires de musées," 14.

19. David L. Martin, *Curious Visions of Modernity: Enchantment, Magic, and the Sacred* (Cambridge, MA, and London: MIT Press, 2011), 10.

20. Martin, *Curious Visions of Modernity*, 10–11. Although Martin understands modernity as haunted by its post-Enlightenment repression of wonder and curiosity, he is keen to emphasize the historical specificity of the culture of the *Wunderkammer* in relation to this modern revival.

21. Stafford and Terpak, *Devices of Wonder*, 2.

22. The cabinet is also, then, "a tantalizing emblem of the endless struggle to incorporate infinite variables into our lives," and its contents offer an analogy for the "open-endedness" of information in contemporary global networks (Stafford and Terpak, *Devices of Wonder*, 3). Stafford has also suggested that the new optical technologies of our own historical moment could be deployed to frame a theory of "imaging" (a hybrid form of art-science visualization) that intersects with old historical arts—such as the *Kunstkammer*. "True interdisciplinarity," she argues, "would be grounded in the acknowledgement that perception (*aisthesis*) is a significant form of knowledge (*episteme*), perhaps even the constitutive form." *Good Looking*, 39.

23. Stafford and Terpak, *Devices of Wonder*, 6.

24. Stafford and Terpak, *Devices of Wonder*, 6–7.

25. Reported by Sophie von la Roche in *Sophie in London, 1786: Being the Diary of Sophie von la Roche*, trans. Clare Williams (London: Jonathan Cape, 1933), 1. Historical accounts of Lever's life and collecting activities include W. J. Smith, "Sir Ashton Lever of Alkrington and his Museum 1729–1788," *Transactions of the Lancashire and Cheshire Antiquarian Society* 72 (1962): 61–92; W. H. Mullens, "Some Museums of Old London. I.—The Leverian Museum," *The Museums Journal* 15, no. 4 (October 1915): 123–128 and (November 1915): 162–171; and most recently, Adrienne Kaeppler's long-awaited book, *Holophusicon: The Leverian Museum; An Eighteenth-Century English Institution of Science, Curiosity, and Art* (Altenstadt, Germany: ZKF Publishers, 2011).

26. Anonymous, *The Gentleman's Magazine* 43 (May 1773): 219.

27. *The Gentleman's Magazine*, 221.

28. Clare Haynes, "A 'Natural' Exhibitioner: Sir Ashton Lever and his Holosphusikon," *Journal for Eighteenth-Century Studies* 24, no. 1 (2001): 3. Haynes further comments that Lever's collecting was "on a scale and of such energy [as was] likely to breach the standards of gentlemanly decorum" (3).

29. Reported in a letter from John to Gilbert White. See Mullens, "Some Museums of Old London. I.—The Leverian Museum," 125.

30. Christine E. Jackson, *Sarah Stone: Natural Curiosities from the New World* (London: Merrell Holberton and the Natural History Museum, 1998), 37.

31. Kaeppler, *Holophusicon*, 9.

32. Christine Cheater, "Collectors of Nature's Curiosities: Science, Popular Culture and the Rise of Natural History Museums," in *Frankenstein's Science: Experimentation and Discovery in Romantic Culture, 1780–1830*, ed. Christa Knellwolf and Jane Goodall (Aldershot, UK: Ashgate, 2008), 172.

33. For these details, I am indebted to the description of the museum provided by Clare Haynes in "A 'Natural' Exhibitioner," 4–7. Kaeppler's *Holophusicon* also provides detailed information about its layout and contents (8–9), which were well documented in *The European Magazine* (January 1782): 17–21.

34. Haynes, "A 'Natural' Exhibitioner," 4.

35. Haynes, "A 'Natural' Exhibitioner," 6.

36. Haynes, "A 'Natural' Exhibitioner," 7.

37. On Lever's collections of Cook voyage objects, see my essay "Feather Cloaks and English Collectors: Cook's Voyages and the Objects of the Museum," in *Objects of Inquiry and Exchange: Eighteenth-Century Thing Theory in a Global Context*, ed. Ileana Baird and Christina Ionescu (Aldershot, UK: Ashgate, forthcoming).

38. Haynes, "A 'Natural' Exhibitioner," 4.

39. Cheater, "Collectors of Nature's Curiosities," 174.

40. Cheater, "Collectors of Nature's Curiosities," 174.

41. Haynes, "A 'Natural' Exhibitioner," 1.

42. *A Companion to Mr. Bullock's Museum*, 10th ed. (London: Henry Reynell and Son, 1811). Bullock's companions went through seventeen editions between 1801, when the collection was open to the public in Liverpool, and 1816. The collection expanded to include some thirty-two thousand items valued at "considerably exceeding £30,000." W. H. Mullens, "Some Museums of Old London: William Bullock's London Museum," *Museums Journal* 17 (1917–1918): 133.

43. For general information about Bullock, I am drawing from Mullens and from Susan Pearce, "William Bullock: Collections and Exhibitions at the Egyptian Hall, London, 1816–1825," *Journal of the History of Collections* 20, no. 1 (2008): 17–35.

44. Bullock, *Companion to Mr. Bullock's Museum* (1813), iv.

45. For further description, including illustrations from the 1812 *Companion*, see Susan Pearce, "William Bullock: Inventing a Visual Language of Objects," in *Museum Revolutions: How Museums Change and Are Changed*, ed. Simon J. Knell, Suzanne MacLeod, and Sheila Watson (London and New York: Routledge, 2007).

46. The report remarks that "more than 22,000 have already visited it during the month it has been opened." See Pearce, "William Bullock: Inventing a Visual Language of Objects," 18.

47. Mullens, "Some Museums of Old London: William Bullock's London Museum," 55; Pearce, "William Bullock: Collections and Exhibitions at the Egyptian Hall," 26.

48. Pearce, "William Bullock: Inventing a Visual Language of Objects," 15.

49. Pearce, "William Bullock: Inventing a Visual Language of Objects," 26–27.

50. Pearce, "William Bullock: Collections and Exhibitions at the Egyptian Hall," 30. More negatively, however, as Pearce asserts, these factors "helped to create the culture of passive entertainment, which relies on spectacle seen rather than active participation, and which was to be so marked a feature of the nineteenth and twentieth centuries" (30).

51. Donald Preziosi, "Modernity Again: The Museum as *Trompe l'oeil*," in *Deconstruction and the Visual Arts: Art, Media, Architecture*, ed. Peter Brunette and David Wills (Cambridge, UK: Cambridge University Press, 1994), 148.

52. Soane arranged through an Act of Parliament in 1833 for the house and its collections to be donated to the nation upon his death, on condition that they remain unaltered.

53. John Elsner, "The House and Museum of Sir John Soane" in *The Cultures of Collecting*, ed. John Elsner and Roger Cardinal (London: Reaktion Books, 1994),156.

54. Helene Furján, *Glorious Visions: John Soane's Spectacular Theater* (London and New York: Routledge, 2011), 4. For discussions of Walpole and Scott, see Clive Wainwright, *The Romantic Interior: The British Collector at Home 1750–1850* (New Haven, CT, and London: Yale University Press, 1989).

55. Jonah Siegel, ed., *The Emergence of the Modern Museum: An Anthology of Nineteenth-Century Sources* (Oxford and New York: Oxford University Press, 2008), 33.

56. Furján, *Glorious Visions*, 8.

57. John Britton, *Union of Architecture, Sculpture and Painting; Exemplified by a Series of Illustrations, with Descriptive Accounts of the House and Galleries of John Soane* (London, 1827), 27.

58. Britton, *Union of Architecture*, 37.

59. Britton, *Union of Architecture*, 13.

60. Barbara Maria Stafford, "Presuming Images and Consuming Words: the Visualization of Knowledge from the Enlightenment to Post-modernism," in *Consumption and the World of Goods*, ed. John Brewer and Roy Porter (London and New York: Routledge, 1993), 469.

61. Stafford, "Presuming Images and Consuming Words," 469.

62. Svetlana Alpers, "The Museum as a Way of Seeing," in *Exhibiting Cultures: the Poetics and Politics of Museum Display*, ed. Ivan Karp and Steven D. Lavine (Washington and London: Smithsonian Institution Press, 1991), 26.

63. Bredekamp, *Lure of Antiquity and the Cult of the Machine*, 73.

64. Bredekamp, *Lure of Antiquity and the Cult of the Machine*, 110.

12

Collection and Parody:
Taliesin and House on the Rock

Mary Titus

Almost every account of the origins of Wisconsin's notorious tourist attraction, House on the Rock, begins with an anecdote. Tellers describe Frank Lloyd Wright's arrogant response to a set of building plans presented to him for approval by Madison, Wisconsin, entrepreneur Alex Jordan Sr. After glancing at the plans, Wright supposedly told Jordan, "I wouldn't hire you to design a cheese case for me, or a chicken coop."[1] Alex Jordan's response ostensibly came through the next generation. On a high rock just down the valley from Wright's Taliesin, Jordan's son, Alex Jordan Jr., built a wildly imaginative structure that he eventually stuffed with vast collections whose contents—carousels, sea creatures, doll houses—trumpet a lowbrow raspberry at Wright's high-minded design. Visitors to House on the Rock sometimes revel in, but are more often exhausted by, the enormity of its contents, room after room of illuminated, revolving, labeled and mislabeled, gigantic, grotesque, and miniature stuff, accompanied by the sounds of thousands of mechanical musical devices. To quote from a few astounded, post-visit bloggers, the place looks like a "manic mishmash of mechanical mayhem"; "an LSD-splattered version of Disneyland"; or—astutely—"Frank Lloyd Wright on drugs."[2] In part the House exhausts because it seems to have no narrative, no frame of reference; visitors can no more easily encapsulate its exuberance than (to cite a common complaint) they can find an exit during a tour. Perhaps because Jordan's response to Wright took the form of a tourist attraction, the relationship between Taliesin and House on the Rock has received little attention beyond brochure gossip.[3] However, critical analysis of these two architectural installations reveals an especially rich and decidedly American example of the relationship between elite modernism and a carnivalesque popular culture in the early twentieth century. Not only does House on the Rock reveal the role that collection and display can play in cultural debates about hierarchy and value, but contemporary responses to Jordan's massive collection also illuminate an increasing anxiety in American culture about "stuff."

The primary mode of the initial House on the Rock, particularly evident in its earliest architectural forms and contents, is parody—a mode primary as well to the postmodern architecture that emerged as a rejoinder to the severities of modernism. Parody is also a central genre for carnival, from the irreverent liturgies of medieval festival, explored in the work of Michael Bakhtin, to the comic energies of the Simpsons in contemporary television. In her influential study *A Theory of Parody: The Teachings of Twentieth-Century Art Forms*, Linda Hutcheon defines parody as "ironic playing with multiple conventions" and "extended repetition with critical distance."[4] She joins other theorists in seeing parody as not only characteristic of twentieth-century art, but also central to the postmodernist endeavor. Through reference and repetition, especially if skewed—made grotesque, gigantic, miniature—postmodern parody can mock and even deflate the truth and status claims of high modernism. Employing both architectural reference and exuberant collection, Alex Jordan Jr. created in his House on the Rock a carnivalesque parody of Frank Lloyd Wright's Taliesin that in innumerable ways repeats, with critical distance, the high modernist ideals Wright articulated in the design, objects, and rituals of his Wisconsin country home.

When Wright created Taliesin, he was at a low point in his career and sought personal refuge. Like Thoreau just over a half century earlier, Wright wanted to build a house that in every way expressed his vision and values. In his autobiography, he described Taliesin's origins in words that echo *Walden*: "I meant to live if I could an unconventional life. I turned to this hill in the Valley as my grandfather before me had turned to America—as a hope and a haven."[5] Choosing the site in south central Wisconsin, Frank Lloyd Wright sought to build an ancestral home rooted in family history, fulfilling the act that less than a decade later in his Irish tower an equally embittered modernist poet imagined, "some powerful man / Called architect and artist in, that they . . . might rear in stone / The sweetness that all longed for night and day."[6] As Wright scholars point out, Taliesin is much more than a house; "it signifies a domain, an estate in the country that Wright established on land his Welsh forefathers had settled . . . in the previous century."[7] Wright's design connected the house with the landscape in the manner "of a full-fledged country estate, not unlike the typical European or Colonial American estate of the pre-industrial period."[8] Fittingly, Wright named Taliesin after an ancient Welsh bard; the house is his poem in stone.[9]

In architectural terms, Taliesin belongs to the genre of the country house, or villa, and represents Wright's most personal expression of his own ideal relation to the world, human and natural. It is a conservative vision, one that presents class privilege as a natural part of a hierarchical, organic order. In this the house is true to precedents: The villa inevitably expresses the mythology that causes it to be built: the attraction to nature . . . the dialectic [between] nature and culture or artifice; the prerogatives of privilege and power; and national, regional or class pride.[10]

In his autobiography, Wright exulted in Taliesin's mythical power. By building the house, he continued his family's American saga: "I turned to this hill in the Valley as my Grandfather before me had turned to America." Solidly bound to "my beloved southern Wisconsin," the house would wed the family to the land so fully that it "would belong to that hill as trees and the ledges of rock did; as Grandfather and Mother had belonged to it."[11] Wright's description of Taliesin drew deeply on the imagery of the ancestral house poem. He envisioned children, laden with baskets of flowers, "gentle Holsteins and a monarch of a bull," "swans floating upon the water," life fecund and peaceful rising up on "My Grandfather's ground," and built for posterity, "recreation ground for my children and their children perhaps for many generations more."[12]

True to its architectural genre, Taliesin as villa was "supremely conservative socially." In its barns and workshops, Wright installed an apprentice program that he named the Fellowship. It was, as Robert McCarter argues, near-feudal in its rituals and hierarchy: the "Fellowship at Taliesin was from the start set up as 'the Master' and his much younger apprentices . . . the Taliesin apprentices remained at a distance . . . and their relationship to Wright inevitably became a kind of worship, which the ritualized lifestyle of the Taliesin compound did little to deter."[13] By the 1940s, Wright and his family's exaltation received daily physical confirmation: Wright ate all meals seated on a "raised dais," his family around him, his apprentices at tables below.[14] Like royalty and court, these stagey meals were, as one recent biographer notes, one "sign of the ever-more undemocratic nature of Taliesin."

Thoroughly hierarchical, Taliesin was in Wright's terms also "supremely natural."[15] He sought to build as nature did; as he declared in his autobiography: "Everything found round about was naturally managed except when man did something. When he added his mite he became imitative and ugly. Why? . . . I wanted a *natural* house to live in myself" (emphasis in original).[16] What Wright "found round" were the materials and forms of the Wisconsin landscape: "[T]he lines of the hills were the lines of the roofs, the slopes of the hills their slopes, the plastered surfaces of the light wood-walls, set back into shade beneath broad eaves, were like the flat stretches of sand in the river below and the same in color, for that is where the material that covered them came from."[17] These natural materials integral to their environment opposed the "imitative and ugly," the "mite" of money or the market. Wright envisioned a settlement as free as possible of economic exchange, unsullied by commercialism. Taliesin was to be "a complete living unit . . . from pig to proprietor. The place was to be self-sustaining if not self-sufficient, and with its domain of two hundred acres was to be shelter, food, clothes and even entertainment within itself."[18] Central to this unsullied order was an overall simplicity, not only in food and daily ritual, but in materials, lines, and design. In Taliesin nothing would be "imitative" and hence unnatural, ostentatious and hence ugly. Three years before he began building his Wisconsin home, Wright published one of his central statements of architectural design principles, "In the Cause of Architecture." Here he placed simplicity and natural or organic forms and materials against contemporary popular culture, the façades of theater, the cheap amusements of commerce. To quote from this statement's third principle or proposition: "An excessive love of detail has ruined more fine things from the standpoint of fine art or fine living than any one human shortcoming—it is hopelessly vulgar. Too many houses, when they are not little stage settings or scene paintings, are mere notion stores, bazaars, or junk shops. Decoration is dangerous."[19]

Vulgarity—a word bound to social class—endangers the present. On the other hand, architecture that adheres to natural or organic forms is at once entirely new and deeply traditional. Such architecture in Wright's own home confirmed the stature of its inhabitants; in the buildings he imagined for public habitation, these organic forms would inspire and elevate their inhabitants. As he proclaimed in a 1908 essay, "This work shall prophesy and idealize the character of the individual it is fashioned to serve. . . . It shall become in its atmosphere as pure and elevating in its humble way as the trees and flowers are in their perfectly appointed way."[20] Linda Hutcheon sums up this stance: "The Modernist elitist rejection of all but pure form was presumed to have good social effects. . . . Modernism saw itself as 'prophetic, severe, and prescriptive' . . . utopian in its belief that architecture could shape the social behavior of the masses."[21]

Taliesin (and Taliesin West) now houses the Frank Lloyd Wright School of Architecture and attracts admiring scholars and Wright enthusiasts to Spring Green, Wisconsin, every year. The buildings are carefully preserved, the tours intelligent and expensive, the gift shop elegant. Visitors, if they have any money left over (and perhaps restive children, barred from Taliesin's tours and now clamoring for entertainment) may subsequently make their way down the valley for a bit of lowbrow fun at House on the Rock. There, for a far more modest sum, they can enjoy the "Ultimate Experience" of a full tour, from the Gate House through the Doll Carousel Room.[22] Although it has never received scholarly attention or high culture acclaim, House on the Rock does enjoy financial success. According to Midwest writer Jane Smiley, "Though most people outside of the Midwest have never heard of it, the House on the Rock is said to draw more visitors every year than any other spot in Wisconsin."[23]

Alex Jordan Jr., a generation younger than Wright, began his country house in 1945; the architectural installation that evolved over the next forty years revealing "the spirit of its builder . . . to be as single-minded and eccentric as Wright's, but in substance almost absurdly opposed."[24] Although nowhere near as recorded as Wright's, Jordan's life has resulted in two biographies. One portrays him as a scoundrel: *House of Alex: A True Story of Architecture and Art; Greed, Deception and Blackmail*; the other portrays a visionary: *Alex Jordan: Architect of His Own Dream*.[25] Like Frank Lloyd Wright's, Jordan's life invites oxymoron. Before this adventure, Jordan had achieved some athletic stardom in college and worked at a variety of entrepreneurial enterprises, continuing the energies of his father, who had brought the Jordans out of the poor immigrant neighborhoods of Madison, Wisconsin, achieving moderate financial success as a developer. Wright, with his baronial estate, velvet jackets, and diased dining, no doubt dealt a class blow to the family, as well as a professional one, when he scorned the elder Jordan's attempt at architecture. Choosing a pinnacle of rock just a few miles down the valley from Taliesin, not bothering to ask permission of the farmers who owned the land, Alex Jordan Jr. responded to Wright by building a parody of the famous architect's "shining brow on a hill." The young Jordan's initial labors have mythic dimensions: a large man, he supposedly labored alone, legends tell us, heroically climbing up his pinnacle carrying building materials on his back. The first small structure, aptly described as a "low-slung, precariously perched, Japanese-style shanty," ostensibly served as Jordan's love pad, where Wisconsin's larger than life folk hero played out his shag carpet version of Wright's notorious affairs.[26] (Despite Wright's fame and the aura of Taliesin, "local preachers and newspapers constantly referred" to his country home as "Wright's sinful 'lovenest.'"[27])

Jordan's house grew without a blueprint, its forms reproducing freehand the famous house up the valley. According to the curator of Chicago's Atheneum Museum:

> Stylistically, the earliest phases of House on the Rock are a homage and a mockery of his famous and citified neighbor to the north. Jordan caricatures all of Wright's architectural signatures. Ceilings are impractically lower, and cantilevers are more extreme. There is more stained glass, there is more orientalism, there are more and larger hearths and more of the natural environment is literally brought indoors.[28]

Here the key terms "homage" and "mockery" invoke the complex stance of parody, Hutcheon's "repetition with critical distance."[29] According to Hutcheon, postmodern architecture is the "archetypal manifestation" of this formal gesture: "an integrated structural modeling process of revising, replaying, inverting, and 'trans-contextualizing' previous works of art."[30] At every step, Jordan's playful project inverts Taliesin's lofty designs. If Wright built his villa just below the hilltop, describing it as a "shining brow" on the body of family land, down the valley Jordan placed "The House" smack dab on Deer Shelter Rock, "a column of rock approximately 60 feet tall, 70 feet by 200 feet on the top."[31] Both locations were former childhood haunts. On Taliesin's hill, a Wordsworthian Wright had wandered, "looking for pasque flowers"; at Deer Shelter, a James Deanish Jordan had enjoyed picnics in his teen years, "A little steak, a small hibachi . . . a whole gallon of Tom Collins."[32] In detail after detail, House replicates Taliesin with a twist. Both buildings were quarried from local stone; both contain massive fireplaces, though the Rock's could easily engulf its neighbor's (one at the Rock is, in fact, touted as "the world's largest fireplace"). Both celebrate the cantilever. Wright saw it as an important "new structural resource" for modern architecture, a form based in nature that expresses continuity "as in the branch of the tree." Jordan's dream of his own cantilevered creation finally manifested in "The Infinity Room." As described by one visitor:

> [A]pproximately 300 feet long and constructed progressively smaller over its length. At one end the Infinity Room is 30 feet wide. At the other end the Infinity Room is one inch wide. The resulting effect as seen from the large end is looking into infinity. Most

people would consider this enough for one room. Not Alex. In addition, 218 feet of the infinity room is cantilevered over the adjacent valley with no vertical support over the entire distance. Still not resting, Alex added 3,264 windows allowing visitors to look in every direction.

In room after room, detail after detail, House on the Rock offers "a parody of Wright's fancy-pants architecture" that "spits in the eye of Mr. Big Deal Dead Architect."[33] As charismatic as Wright in his own way, Jordan gathered around him a team of craftspeople who realized his visions as they grew: room on tumbling room, "a claustrophobic shamble through darkened dens and hallways," each space spawning another: the Doll Room, the Cannon Room, the Carousel Room, the Heritage of the Sea, the gift shop.[34] Fueled more by a collector's exuberance than nature's harmonies, the House expanded for decades, growing, in the words of one visitor, like a "riot" of "architectural kudzu."[35]

As parody, House on the Rock provides an energetically lowbrow response to Wright's revered work up the valley. Where modernist Wright aspired to create architecture that would elevate its inhabitants—invoke tradition, eschew decoration, and echo natural forms—Jordan sought to entertain. The house he built clearly "clowns around" with Taliesin's dignities, but it is in its enclosed collections that Jordan's parody takes on its most carnivalesque forms. Collection offered Jordan a way to continue his irreverent and playful installation free of the formal bonds that necessarily connect a parody to its original, for a "parody cannot free itself from the text it internalizes."[36] Staying with parody, Jordan's vision remained caught in Wright's formal net. But moving to collection, Jordan embraced a form that offered endless flexibility and room for play. Viewed from a distance, it is clear that much of what House on the Rock contains is Taliesin inspired; on the other hand, much is not—at times Jordan simply accumulated. In doing so, he aptly followed Robert Venturi's critique of modernist forms; the carnivalesque collection that Alex Jordan Jr. amassed trumpets "More is not less," and even more loudly, "Less is a bore."[37]

Between 1960 and 1989, enormous sheds full of stuff sprang up around the original House—together housing a collection that blogging tourists describe as enormous, incredible, extraordinary, amazing, mind-blowing. Eventually, like its up-valley neighbor, House on the Rock became a tourist attraction, and Alex Jordan Jr. became rich. According to his biographer, Jordan began charging an entrance fee in 1960: "Word got out that there was something to see out here, and people began coming around," Jordan said. "They'd holler up, 'Can we see your place?' One day we were picnicking and I said, 'By golly, I'm going to charge those folks 50 cents a piece.' And you know, they paid gladly. Thanked me even more when they left. We drank real Scotch that night!"[38] A year later, the House earned Jordan $31,000 in entrance fees, and he began adding on. Today, visitors can choose among three tours, the first of the Original House, the second including a selection of additions to the original—the Mill House, Streets of Yesterday, The Heritage of the Sea, Tribute to Nostalgia, Atrium Restaurant, Music of Yesterday, Spirit of Aviation, The Carousel—and the third including yet more.

Throughout his life Alex Jordan Jr. accumulated stuff. Archaeologist Peter Young, who describes Jordan as a "pathological collector," lists some of the objects that first filled House on the Rock: "Tiffany-esque lamps, bronze sculptures, a 30-piece bell set, shrubbery and watery grottoes, pools with recirculating water, and a startling collection of self-playing instruments—harp, drums, piano, and cello."[39] These mechanical instruments became a consistent theme, eventually expanding far beyond the original House to include innumerable mechanical performers.[40] From music boxes to player pianos, calliopes to carousels, these mechanical sound devices parody the highbrow concerts Wright enjoyed at Taliesin, where each performance was a unique work of art, enjoyed by a select few, including Wright enthroned on his dais. In his 1943 autobiography, Wright nostalgically recalled the centrality of music to Taliesin: "Good music is essential to our life at Taliesin. A grand piano stands by the living room fireplace, a cello resting against its hollow side, a violin on the ledge beside it. . . . Olgiviana plays Bach, Beethoven, old Russian music. I let the piano play itself a few moments sometimes while the feeling lasts, knowing nothing. Something comes out. And I can never play any of the things, such as they are, a second time."[41] Impossible to duplicate, the music Wright enjoyed represents pure inspiration and singular experience. A music box, on the other hand, moves gears around a set track and so ensures duplication. Like any "work of art in the age of mechanical reproduction"—to invoke Benjamin's classic title—music on calliope or carousel is never unique, has no genius, no "aura." Benjamin's observations highlight the popular culture impulses underlying House on the Rock's collections. According to Benjamin, mechanical reproduction takes away "the authority of the object"—its aura—moving it from sacred to secular, from "cult value" to "exhibition value," from elite singularity to an experience endlessly replicable for mass consumption. This transition, he writes, replaces elitism with equalization, is "the mark of a perception whose 'sense of the universal equality of things' has increased to such a degree that it extracts it even from a unique object by means of reproduction."[42] If Wright saw decoration as dangerous, and excess as vulgar—belonging to "notion stores, bazaars, or junk shops"—Jordan wallows in the pleasures of excess and celebrates the joys of the market. Visitors to the House are encouraged to purchase tokens to activate the countless music boxes; one room contains a collection of one hundred cash registers.

Not just through mechanization, but in many other ways, Alex Jordan's collections respond in carnivalesque forms to Taliesin's strictures. Bakhtin's identification of parody as one of the ancient genres employed in carnival provides a way to connect Jordan's collections to the same impulses that shaped his architecture. Carnival embraces parody because of its ability to relocate high culture in low. As Bakhtin says of a noted carnival figure, the clown, "One of the main attributes of the medieval clown was precisely the transfer of every high ceremonial gesture or ritual to the material sphere."[43] Carnival brings everything to the marketplace and invites all to join in the irreverent festivities. It celebrates the physical, the fun, and notably, the grotesque. In *Rabelais and His World*, Bakhtin traces the etymology of "grotesque," finding at the word's origins forms that intermingle natural categories and rupture defining boundaries, "no longer the movement of finished forms, vegetable or animal, in a finished and stable world; instead the inner movement of being itself . . . expressed in the passing of one form into the other, in the ever incompleted character of being."[44] Inarguably, House on the Rock's carnivalesque spirit finds its ultimate expression in its famous carousel, which Jordan began installing in 1977: "in all probability the largest Carousel in history." Covered with flashing lights, incessantly blaring music, and rotating against a mirrored background in an immense room that also holds three steam engines, hundreds of suspended mannequin angels, and an additional stampede of carousel animals mounted on its walls, House on the Rock's carousel epitomizes carnival. It is a gigantic music box, endlessly circling to the same tunes. Rising and falling in endless repetition, the carousel's mounts include walruses, centaurs, and dragons: "269 handcrafted carousel animals (and not one of them a horse)" according to the official website.[45] Body parts interchange; human heads are grafted to animal bodies; the sacred—mannequin angels—mingles with the secular, and the carousel promises all of the egalitarian delights of the marketplace: for the cost of a ticket, anyone can ride and, if lucky, grab the golden ring.

Although the carousel epitomizes Jordan's carnivalesque installation, other collections housed at House on the Rock participate in the same spirit. One interesting quality of Jordan's collection is how much of it works with extremes. In place of the natural, Jordan amassed the unnatural, artificial, and mechanical—as one might expect in a parody of Wright's "supremely natural" aesthetic. But the collections are equally obsessed with size—tiny furnished dollhouses and a two-hundred-foot sea monster—the miniature and the gigantic. Both the too too little and the too too big heighten the collection's function as parody. Like Swift's Lilliputians and Brobding-nagians, they destabilize the relations of significance and scale. As Susan Stewart argues in her well-known study, *On Longing: Narratives of the Miniature, the Gigantic, the Souvenir, the Collection*: "We cannot have a *mammoth* petite and graceful ballerina unless we want a parody, for the history of the depiction of ballerinas has fixed their relation to scale."[46] Stewart connects distortions in scale—especially gigantism—to the postmodern energies of pop art: "Pop art's primary qualities of gigantification and novelty, its obsession with the mechanical possibilities of exaggeration, and its anti-classicism, are the modern expression of the qualities of gigantification we find in previous uses of the spectacle—the articulation of quantity over quality, of 'facade' over content, of materiality and movement over mediation and transcendence."[47] For Wright, a sense of scale belongs to the great architect by nature, as he argues in "the Logic of the Plan": "Scale is really proportion. Who can teach proportion? Without a sense of proportion no one should attempt to build. This gift of sense must be the diploma Nature gave to the architect." Buildings, he believed, should be "related to human proportions," so that house and habitant repeat the harmonies of natural scale. "Human beings should look as well in the building or of it as flowers do."[48] But for Alex Jordan Jr., scale supported spectacle, another tool for producing amazement. Representative of the gigantic at House on the Rock is a two-hundred-foot-long sea monster fighting a giant squid, their frozen four-story-high battle an apt representation of Stewart's definition of the gigantic as "a physical world of dis-order and disproportion."[49] The gigantism at House on the Rock is evident not just in the enormous, grotesque objects it contains, but in the story of Jordan himself, an American folk hero; larger than life, hauling rocks on his back, he laughs a jolly "Ho Ho Ho" down the Wisconsin valley.

Antipodal to four-story sea monsters is the dollhouse. If Taliesin demonstrates the organic design principle of utility over decoration, the dollhouse collection at House on the Rock exhibits just the opposite. In the dollhouse miniature, as Susan Stewart observes, "use value is transformed into display value."[50] Viewed frontally, frozen in time, purely material spectacle, the dollhouse mimics architecture; build-ing, decorating, and inhabiting all become part of play, the patrons (ostensibly) children. It is possible to push this relation further yet and to see Jordan's collection of miniature homes, housewares, and tiny inhabitants as an even more complex re-sponse to Taliesin. According to Stewart, the well-kept dollhouse bears a heavy ideo-logical burden. She links these big houses in miniature form to the commemorative house poem, arguing that both constructs "functioned to display and hypostatize the status of the interior world of the ascending and upper classes." As noted previ-ously, Wright's visions for Taliesin also draw on the imagery and traditions invoked by the house poem. Each idealized construct—villa, poem, miniature—speaks a message of "wealth and nostalgia."[51] However, Jordan, a committed collector, displays not one well-furnished dollhouse but 250, repeating the signifying gesture again and again. From colonial manor to curlicued cottage to doll-sized carousel, his collection aptly meets Hutcheon's definition of modern parody; it is indeed "repetition with difference."

Alex Jordan Jr.'s exuberant collection juxtaposed to Wright's sober craft recalls an earlier American pair: Charles Wilson Peale and P. T. Barnum, respectively museum maker and circus man. With his exhibited world wonders, Barnum "blurred the boundaries between museum and carnival side shows, between the theatre and the circus, between the real and the contrived."[52] Like many other acts of category confu-sion, such blurring was irremediably lowbrow and faintly disreputable. To retain its claims to transcendent truth and its aura of permanence, the memorialization of cul-ture staged in a museum collection must remain untainted by the marketplace and popular entertainment. As museum historian Elaine Gurian notes, "Somewhere in the history of exhibitions, certain nonrational strategies were deemed theatrical. Be-ing in the theater is still not wholly respectable. Museum professionals do not want to be in show business."[53] But Alex Jordan—the Barnum of Wisconsin—certainly did. Like Barnum's American Museum, House on the Rock mingles and manipulates the tropes of museum and carnival. Both men created entertainment for the masses and invoked "folk laughter" rather than reverence. Both invited the marketplace into the museum. But Jordan goes beyond generic confusion to parody—"ironic playing with multiple conventions"—to recall again a phrase from Hutcheon's definition. Carefully curated and elaborately if not painstakingly displayed for a viewer, the collection at House on the Rock presents many of the formal characteristics of a museum exhibit. But it lacks all pretension to hushed significance. Instead, Jordan's exhibit destabilizes the narratives of authority and permanence that not only give Taliesin its aura, but are also historically central to museum collection.

Traditionally, museums place their collections in frameworks that affirm and shape significance: "These frameworks are embodied in the exhibition apparatus, which consists of accompanying texts (captions, brochures, wall texts, catalogues). . . . to produce a 'narrative' that unfolds within a broader social and material context. In short, through their ordered display, objects make arguments."[54] But the displays at House on the Rock destabilize this scaffolding. Overall Jordan's collection refuses any solid ideological footing; viewers do not know what or how to value the spectacle they confront. As one visitor recounts with horror, "Jordan began mixing the authentic with the inauthentic, antiques beside re-creations from the workshop with no signage to assist visitors in distinguishing between the two."[55] Even more disturbingly, Jordan enjoyed inventing authenticating stories—inventing provenance—for items he either purchased or produced himself. When once reprimanded for misleading visitors, he tellingly replied that perhaps he had "a little too much showbiz."[56] The result is a disorienting spectacle—a "fun house"—that in some visitors evokes delight. Following is a 1989 account of the Organ Room from the *Milwaukee Journal*:

> The room is crammed with huge copper vats and bronze fittings that seem like they should join somewhere, pieces of old and unidentifiable electrical equipment, curved iron walkways and spiral staircases, many inaccessible; that lead nowhere. . . . And, of course, there are the organs for which the room is named. Organ pipes are everywhere. . . . There are three organ consoles in the room. One is a genuine antique theater organ. One was made for the House on the Rock. One is just a joke. You figure it out.[57]

However, for those accustomed to and reliant on the authenticating power of the museum to dictate and affirm their aesthetic or intellectual judgments, Jordan's carnivalesque museum/fun house horrifies. As one such visitor lamented: "In the almost total absence of signage, there is virtually no way to tell if an item is old or new or just where it came from—if it came from anywhere at all."[58] Real is indistinguishable from fake, high from low; that worthy of admiration and that worthy of disdain cannot be differentiated. And clearly Jordan felt no remorse. As a spokesperson for the House once remarked, "The fun of it is not knowing what is authentic and what isn't. . . . Even if I knew I wouldn't tell you. It's not our policy."[59] For one archaeologist who toured Jordan's gaudy accumulation, nothing could be more appalling. House on the Rock, he announced, is "an exhibition from hell."[60] Like pop art's postmodern parodies, Alex Jordan's collections as displayed embrace an "anti-classicism," exuberantly choosing the side of "quantity over quality, of 'facade' over 'content,' of materiality and movement over mediation and transcendence."[61] House on the Rock opened to the public in 1959, and Jordan kept up active collection and curating for at least two decades, the same decades that witnessed Warhol's enormous soup cans and his Raid the Ice Box exhibit, an exhibit that also utilized excess and parody to call into question the conventions of museum collection and valuation.

Half a century later, Alex Jordan's parodically curated accumulations continue to disturb visitors. In his recent book, *In Praise of Copying*, Marcus Boon claims that "*everybody*" now knows that the cheesiest mass-media image or mass-market commodity and the most rigorous abstraction by Barnett Newman or Jackson Pollock contains exactly the same degrees of emptiness," but in fact this is a belief held by only some in the intellectual elite, and as a stance rarely informs cultural practices, especially if one steps outside of academic circles.[62] (Even there it can still evoke a frisson.)

With its winding ways, obscure signage, unreliable exhibit labels, and strange curatorial aesthetic, House on the Rock retains significance as an early expression of current impulses in museum practice to call into question or expose the discourses guiding collection. As one scholar summarizes, "all critics agree that museums should do more to expose the interests and assumptions governing their mediation of objects to visitors. As visitors become aware of the constructed nature of museum exhibits, they argue, they can more actively use the museum's interpretation to fashion their own."[63] Indeed, museums can and often now do call into question how the apparatus of exhibition mediates between object and visitor. However, ongoing responses to House on the Rock suggest that some form of narrative must be retained, some cultural codes by which a viewer may know boundaries and gauge relevance, perhaps assign purpose, such as authenticity or value. In *Distinction: A Social Critique of the Judgment of Taste*, Pierre Bourdieu describes how a viewer who lacks a narrative or, in his words, "a cultural competence, that is, the code, into which [a work of art] is encoded . . . feels lost in a chaos of sounds and rhythms, colours and lines, without rhyme or reason,"[64] feels—to quote again the words of visitors to House on the Rock—as if the displayed objects are a "manic mishmash of mechanical mayhem"; "an LSD-splattered version of Disneyland"; even—perhaps—"Frank Lloyd Wright on drugs."[65] Read as a postmodern museum, Alex Jordan Jr.'s House on the Rock points to the risks of such an enterprise: that destabilizing authenticity makes all value insecure, that blurring the demarcating lines of display and frame allows a collection to sprawl endlessly—until what is inside cannot be distinguished from what is out; that puncturing the aura of transcendence leaves only hot air. All and anything can be in this parodic museum: art and kitsch, originals and copies, objects singular and endlessly reproduced—the replication, mechanization, transgression, and exhaustion of a carnival with no closing time. Certainly in its expanse, exuberance, and rejection of any significance except—in Jordan's words, "fun"—House on the Rock raises interesting questions about the museum's democratization, transformation, and (dare we say?) potential demise.

Although some visitors to House on the Rock do recognize that Jordan's installation destabilizes cultural assumptions about the relations between provenance, authenticity, and value, this is not what most find either exhilarating or disturbing when touring his collection. Rather, what most visitors respond to is the sheer experience of excess, or, to stay with Marcus Boon, "copia": "an infinity of things."[66] Boon, in *In Praise of Copying*, deftly ties copia/abundance to copying, "the copy as an object that is inherently multiple, that is more than one, that is a copy of some-thing, and thus part of an excess or abundance, of a *more*."[67] House on the Rock as a parody of Wright's Taliesin is itself also a copy, albeit distorted; its contents, as has been made clear, embrace replication. It is the copia of the collections in House on the Rock that—positively or negatively—most engages visitors. In their responses to this copia, they add their voices to an increasingly audible debate in American culture: the debate about stuff.

In his autobiography, *Made in America*, Sam Walton recounts several early market-ing triumphs. Whether it be heaped bins of women's underpants, rows of Murray 8 horsepower riding mowers, or "the world's largest display of Tide," all of these triumphs involved merchandising displays that have two qualities in common: excess and replication. As Walton tells his readers, "I really love to pick an item—maybe the most basic merchandise—and then call attention to it. . . . So we would buy huge quantities of something and dramatize it." Stacking, he quickly learned, works eco-nomic wonders. "Man, in the early days of Wal-Mart it really got crazy sometimes," Walton exults. "We would blow it out of there when everybody knew we would have sold only a few had we just left it in the normal store position."[68] But for every Wal-Mart-embracing American stimulated by a mountain of objects, another simplicity movement disciple is equally repelled. For every happy visitor to House on the Rock who finds "the collections . . . amazing," another—like novelist Jane Smiley—feels overwhelmed, "almost from the beginning, it is too much. . . . Everything is simply massed together, and Alex Jordan comes to seem like the manifestation of pure American acquisitiveness."[69]

Since the first commodity slid off an automated assembly line, both fascina-tion with and anxiety about replication without limitation have attended mass production. Walt Disney's 1940 *Sorcerer's Apprentice* delightfully encapsulates these twinned responses: when one bucket becomes one million through the "magic" of continuous compounding, poor Mickey first triumphs over and then drowns in the products of his labor. As Marcus Boon suggests, "Above and against all the avowed utilitarian goals that . . . mass production is said to enable—from the satisfaction of economic wants at a lower cost to the equitable distribution of needed items—lies a fascination with the magic by which things, including money, can be multiplied, a still-mysterious power."[70] "Things are in the saddle, / And ride mankind," Emerson lamented well over a century ago, and since then American ambivalence about mass-produced goods has itself compounded.[71] Multiplication can evoke amazement—the visual wow of an enormous PEZ dispenser collection—or anxiety. "The fear of being inundated, submerged in a crowd, or trapped in an unending repetition," Marcus Boon notes, "is a basic human fear, although it has taken particular forms in modern societies."[72]

Reading tourist accounts of Alex Jordan Jr.'s House on the Rock, it is impossible to avoid the anxiety and even hostility Jordan's sprawling installation evokes in many visitors. Not only the archaeologist quoted previously experiences House as "an exhibition from hell." Other tourists record exhaustion, feeling overwhelmed and disoriented, unable to process their surroundings, desperate to find ways out into the open air. For many, House on the Rock is not the collection to end all collections but—and terrifyingly—a collection without end. A few quotes from tripadvisor. com say it all:

"Couldn't find are (sic) way out."
"Trapped in a dark, dank maze."
"There is so very, very much of it, you become overwhelmed within a short time."
"By the end I was running to try to find the exit—I just wanted it to stop."
"It just goes on forever."

Like Mickey bobbing in a torrent of endlessly replicating buckets and brooms, Americans increasingly fear being overwhelmed by stuff. We're starting to worry that there may be too much of it, and perhaps even worse, that all of it is, in Boon's terms, equally empty. Here two responses to Jordan's collection are particularly relevant, because both employ the terminology of contemporary debates about stuff. Says one visitor: "It's like a tour of the brain of someone who suffers from a bad case of obsessive compulsive disorder. This is where garage sale junk goes to die." Another points to a currently popular television show: "It is definitely a piece of Americana. With today's building codes, a house like that will probably never be built today. And if he had not had enough money to build the buildings that house his 'collection,' he would probably be featured on *Hoarders*."

Knee deep in stuff and going deeper, Americans are increasingly anxious about accumulation. Perhaps this explains the current popularity of the simple, even stark photographs of carefully curated objects popular on the Internet at such sites as "A Collection a Day" or "Things Organized Neatly."[73] As a recent commentator on these digitally displayed collections observes: "After too many years when stuff seemed to rule many lives, these things have been culled, sorted, mastered. Best of all, we don't have to deal with these collections as physical things; we can simply enjoy them as digital presentations. . . . [W]e can consume these lovely objects and not-have them, too."[74] From the elegant modernism of Frank Lloyd Wright's Taliesin, to the carnival carousels of House on the Rock, from the carefully arranged objects recorded on "Things Organized Neatly," to the tangled heaps and bursting trash bags of "Hoarders"—collection in all of its forms continues to be a central language in American culture.

NOTES

1. Doug Moe, *Alex Jordan: Architect of His Own Dream* (Spring Green, WI: House of Wyoming Valley, n.d.), 21.

2. Angie, "House on the Rock: Manic Mishmash of Mechanical Mayhem," http://weburbanist.com/2010/06/09/house-on-the-rock-manic-mishmash-of-mechanical-mayhem

(accessed 15 September 2012); Angela Strassheim, "Bad Trip: The Scariest Museum on Earth," http://www.vice.com/read/pictures-v11n11 (accessed 15 September 2012); Jim L., "The House on the Rock," http://www.yelp.com/biz/the-house-on-the-rock-spring-green (accessed 15 September 2012).

3. I have found two essays on House on the Rock that undertake scholarly analysis: Julie Reichert-Marton, "Visionary Architecture: Frank Lloyd Wright vs. House on the Rock," *U-Turn: An Art E-Zine*, http://www.uturn.org/ Marton/marton.htm (accessed 15 September 2012); and Peter A. Young "Nightmare on Memory Lane," *Archaeology* 54, no. 1 (2001): 80.

4. Linda Hutcheon, *A Theory of Parody: The Teachings of Twentieth-Century Art Forms* (New York: Methuen, 1985), 7.

5. Frank Lloyd Wright, *An Autobiography* (New York: Duell, Sloan and Pearce, 1943), 167–168.

6. William Butler Yeats, "Meditations in Time of Civil War" (1928), reprinted in *Selected Poems and Two Plays* (New York: Collier, 1962), 103.

7. Neil Levine, "The Story of Taliesin: Wright's First Natural House," in *Taliesin 1911–1914*, ed. Narciso G. Menocal (Carbondale: Southern Illinois University Press, 1992), 2–3.

8. Levine, "Story of Taliesin," 8.

9. Wright, *An Autobiography*, 167, 169.

10. James Ackerman, "The Villa as Paradigm," *Perspecta* 22 (1986): 29.

11. Wright, *An Autobiography*, 168.

12. Wright, *An Autobiography*, 170–171. It is delightful to compare Wright's description of Taliesin to the close of Ben Jonson's "To Penshurst":

> Wright: "There must be a natural house, not natural as caves and log-cabins were natural, but native in spirit and the making, having itself all that architecture had meant whenever it was alive in times past. Nothing at all I had ever seen would do. The country had changed all that old building into something inappropriate. Grandfather and Grandmother were something splendid in themselves that I couldn't imagine living in any period-houses I had ever seen or the ugly ones around there. Yes, there was a house that hill might marry and live happily with ever after. I fully intended to find it. I even saw for myself what it might be like. And I began to build it as the brow of that hill" (168–169).
>
> Jonson:
> Now, Penshurst, they that will proportion thee
> With other edifices, when they see
> Those proud, ambitious heaps, and nothing else,
> May say, their lords have built, but thy lord dwells.

13. Robert McCarter, "Abstract Essence: Drawing Wright from the Obvious," in *On and by Frank Lloyd Wright: A Primer of Architectural Principles*, ed. Robert McCarter (New York: Phaidon Press, 2005), 8.

14. Robert McCarter, *Frank Lloyd Wright*, Critical Lives Series (London: Reaktion, 2006), 192.

15. Wright, *An Autobiography*, 173.

16. Wright, *An Autobiography*, 168.

17. Wright, *An Autobiography*, 171.

18. Wright, *An Autobiography*, 171.

19. Frank Lloyd Wright, "In the Cause of Architecture" (1908), reprinted in *On and by Frank Lloyd Wright*, 339.

20. Wright, "In the Cause of Architecture," 344.

21. Hutcheon, *A Theory of Parody*, 113.

22. "The House on the Rock," http://www.thehouseontherock.com/HOTR_Attraction_TicsAndTours.htm (accessed 15 September 2012).

23. Jane Smiley, "Wisconsin: Three Visions Attained," *New York Times*, 19 March 1993, http://www.nytimes.com/1993/03/07/magazine/wisconsin-three-visions-attained.html (accessed 15 September 2012).

24. Smiley, "Wisconsin: Three Visions."

25. Marc Balousek, *House of Alex: A True Story of Architecture and Art: Greed, Deception and Blackmail* (Oregon, WI: Waubesa Press, 1990); Doug Moe, *Alex Jordan: Architect of His Own Dream* (Spring Green, WI: House of Wyoming Valley, 1991).

26. Young, "Nightmare on Memory Lane," 80.

27. Levine, "The Story of Taliesin," 21.

28. Reichert-Marton, "Visionary Architecture."

29. Hutcheon, *A Theory of Parody*, 18.

30. Hutcheon, *A Theory of Parody*, 11.

31. "House on the Rock," in *Wikipedia*, http://en.wikipedia.org/wiki/House_on_the_Rock (accessed 15 September 2012).

32. Wright, *An Autobiography*, 167; Jordan, quoted in Moe, *Alex Jordan*, 25.

33. The Field Review Team of Roadside America, "House on the Rock," http://www.roadsideamerica.com/story/2254 (accessed 2 February 2011).

34. Field Review Team, "House on the Rock."

35. Reichert-Marton, "Visionary Architecture."

36. Joao Ferreira Duarte, "'A Dangerous Stroke of Art': Parody as Transgression," *European Journal of English Studies* 3, no. 1 (1999): 74.

37. Robert Venturi, *Complexity and Contradiction in Architecture* (New York: Museum of Modern Art, 1966), 23, 25.

38. Moe, *Alex Jordan*, 49–50.

39. Young, "Nightmare on Memory Lane," 80.

40. Douglas Henkle has attempted to list "all the animated, automated Music Machines that can be seen and/or heard" at House on the Rock on his website, http://www.folklib.net/index/discog/labels/house_rock_tour.shtml (accessed 15 September 2012).

41. Wright, *An Autobiography*, 371.

42. Walter Benjamin, "The Work of Art in the Age of Mechanical Reproduction," in *Aesthetics: Classic Readings from the Western Tradition*, ed. Dabney Townsend (Belmont, CA: Wadsworth, 2001), 286–289.

43. Mikhail Bakhtin, *Rabelais and His World*, trans. Helene Iswolsky (Cambridge, MA: MIT Press, 1968), 20.

44. Bakhtin, *Rabelais and His World*, 32.

45. "The House on the Rock," http://houseontherock.com/HOTR_Attraction_TicsAndTours_Reg_Tour2_Carousel.htm (accessed 15 September 2012).

46. Susan Stewart, *On Longing: Narratives of the Miniature, the Gigantic, the Souvenir, the Collection* (Durham, NC: Duke University Press, 1993), 94.

47. Stewart, *On Longing*, 92–93.

48. Wright, "The Logic of the Plan" (1928), reprinted in *On and by Frank Lloyd Wright*, 345.

49. Stewart, *On Longing*, 74.

50. Stewart, *On Longing*, 62.

51. Stewart, *On Longing*, 62.

52. Gary Kulik, "Designing the Past: History-Museum Exhibitions from Peale to the Present," in *History Museums in the United States: A Critical Assessment*, ed. Warren Leon and Roy Rozensweig (Urbana: University of Illinois Press, 1989), 5.

53. Elaine Gurian, "Noodling Around with Exhibition Opportunities," in *Exhibiting Cultures: The Poetics and Politics of Museum Display*, ed. Ivan Karp and Steven Lavine (Washington, DC: Smithsonian Institution Press, 1991) 182.

54. John Pedro Schwartz, "Object Lessons: Teaching Multiliteracies through the Museum," *College English* 71, no. 1 (2008): 28.

55. Young, "Nightmare on Memory Lane," 80.

56. Moe, *Alex Jordan*, 107.

57. Dave Hendrickson, "Is All That Stuff for Real? No But That's Show Biz," *Milwaukee Journal*, 18 June 1989, http://news.google.com/newspapers?nid=1499&dat=19890618&id=4GYaAAAAIBAJ&sjid=7CsEAAAAIBAJ&pg=2205,1765209 (accessed 15 Septemebr 2012). Quoted in Moe, *Alex Jordan*, 116.

58. Young, "Nightmare on Memory Lane," 80.

59. Quoted in Young, "Nightmare on Memory Lane," 80.

60. Young, "Nightmare on Memory Lane," 80.

61. Stewart, *On Longing*, 92–93.

62. Marcus Boon, *In Praise of Copying* (Cambridge, MA: Harvard University Press, 2010), 30 (emphasis added).

63. Schwartz, "Object Lessons," 37.

64. Pierre Bourdieu, *Distinction: A Social Critique of the Judgement of Taste*, trans. Richard Nice (Cambridge, MA: Harvard University Press, 1984) 2.

65. See note 2.

66. Boon, *In Praise of Copying*, 44.

67. Boon, *In Praise of Copying*, 45.

68. Sam Walton and John Huey, *Made in America: My Story* (New York: Bantam Books, 1993), 73–75. I want to thank David Banash for reminding me of Sam Walton's displays.

69. Jane Smiley, "Wisconsin: Three Visions."

70. Boon, *In Praise of Copying*, 181.

71. Ralph Waldo Emerson, "Ode, Inscribed to William H. Channing," in *Poems* (Boston: James Munroe and Company, 1847), http://www.internal.org/Ralph_Waldo_Emerson (accessed 15 September 2012).

72. Boon, *In Praise of Copying*, 181.

73. Lisa Congdon, "A Collection a Day, 2010," http://collectionaday2010.blogspot.com/ (accessed 15 September 2012); Austin Radcliffe, curator, "Things Organized Neatly, " http://thingsorganizedneatly.tumblr.com/ (accessed 15 September 2012).

74. Rob Walker, "Fun Stuff: Why Pictures of Object Collections Are Popular Now," *New York Times Magazine*, 13 February 2011, 26.

13

Record Collecting
as Cultural Anthropology

Kevin M. Moist

From a few decades down the line, I can more or less pinpoint when I began collecting records. I was about ten or eleven years old, growing up in rural, small-town Pennsylvania. Beautiful countryside, good people, hearty food, somewhat limited in cultural options. I was a musically inclined kid; I had played the piano for a few years by then and was starting on saxophone when my teacher, Mr. Ressler, passed me some big band jazz charts (second alto) to fool around with and some recommendations for listening.

It required a family trip to a nearby college town before I found the opportunity to plunk down my hardly earned allowance in exchange for long-playing records by two of the names on that list, walking out of the record store with a Duke Ellington collection under one arm and a Count Basie record called *Blues by Basie* under the other. (An LP by Thelonious Monk also looked intriguing, but I only had enough money for two, and it seemed wise to start with the royal recommendations first.)

Music was always around the house; in addition to the classical music I was trying to learn on the piano, my mother was (still is, in fact) the organist at a country Methodist church, and country and pop hits were always playing on the radio. But those LPs from the college town, they were something else. My music teachers had prepared me well: I could immediately appreciate the creativity of the compositions, the skill of the playing. That much was obvious. *What* they were playing, though—their musical language and what they did with it—that was a different thing; it certainly didn't sound like the music in my immediate environment (although I had probably heard occasional echoes of it on television via old movies).

I played those records over and over, fascinated. It wasn't a matter of just liking them; I felt compelled to try to understand them, to get a handle on where the musicians were coming from, because they clearly had something for me to learn. Some of those lessons were musical: how effortlessly tight Basie's bands could play, and the richness of Ellington's compositions and arrangements. But beyond that, I wanted to know more, about the people who made that music, and about the music itself—*Why* were they doing those things musically? In those pre-Internet days, that meant some visits to the local library, which did indeed have books on the subject—more than a few. (Apparently this "jazz" thing was pretty significant.) And as I found out more about the musicians, I also learned about their world, and how jazz and blues developed, and what the music meant to the people who played it.

That, I think, is what I started to collect—not just the LPs as objects, but the experiences they generated, the wider view of the world they provided. The records did more than just play music; they expanded how I thought about where things came from and what they meant, about history and culture. Because of those records, my own world changed—I understood certain things differently as a result of listening to the sounds in the grooves. With that awareness came the inevitable follow-up question: What other musical worlds, separated from me by time or geography or circumstance, were out there to be found? And might there be even more recordings that could bring those worlds to me?

RECORD COLLECTING

Why Collect Records

I would not want to suggest that what I have just described is a primary motivation for all record collectors.[1] There are many reasons for collecting recorded music, both by individuals and institutions, and various situations in which that collecting takes place. Sociologist Roy Shuker described a wide range of them in *Wax Trash and Vinyl Treasures: Record Collecting as a Social Practice*, and I won't try to list them all here. He noted one thing they mostly have in common: Whereas collecting many types of objects involves setting them aside and removing them from regular use, records by necessity "retain a strong element of use value—people will play them," because that is the only way to experience their contents.[2]

I have heard tales of extreme record collectors whose new acquisitions are immediately sealed hermetically and hidden away in light- and temperature-controlled vaults; however, no one I know seems to have actually met such a character. Collectors, in my experience, generally love to share what they find, with friends via listening sessions or by swapping mixes, or more publicly as DJs or music writers. They would agree with rock musician Jeff Connolly that the whole point is "using the music": "There is no joy in ownership," he said. "The joy comes when you play the record."[3] Music critic Simon Reynolds described his record collection as "material with use value, whether that was pleasure or research."[4]

In his insightful book *The Recording Angel: Music, Records and Culture from Aristotle to Zappa*, Evan Eisenberg wrote about the unique motivations that lie behind the collecting of "cultural objects" such as records, noting five motives as particularly significant. The first relates to time: "the need to make beauty and pleasure permanent," based in a fear of its possible/likely disappearance, a motive common to cultural preservation efforts of all kinds. His second reason is related to the first: "the need to comprehend beauty" in that which is collected, which can become "more beautiful the better it's understood . . . [and] certainly owning a book or record permits one to study the work repeatedly and at one's convenience." Third, he discussed the "need to distinguish oneself as a consumer," to become "heroic consumers" who "spend on an heroic scale, perhaps, or with heroic discrimination," acquiring the rarest items or the most complete set, or going to the greatest lengths for a purchase. The fourth motive has to do with nostalgia, a sense of belonging felt through collecting bits of the past; the collection itself serves as a bridge, and "each object connects its owner with two eras, that of its creation and that of its acquisition." The final reason is about the quest for social capital in all its forms, "the need to impress others, or oneself."[5]

As suggested by his book's subtitle, Eisenberg is interested in record collecting from a philosophical point of view, in the existential, ontological, or aesthetic significance of recorded music. Such an enlightened perspective obviously contrasts a bit with most popular images of record collecting. Depictions of record collectors in such stories as the comic book/movie *Ghost World* and the novel/movie *High Fidelity* tend toward the unbalanced and antisocial, portraying record collecting as a symptom of some form of psychological disorder. Music writer Simon Reynolds suggested that music collecting can wander off track into destructive behavior—obsessiveness, completism, and consumer fetishism—often combined with an "idiot savant" level of data accumulation. He thinks of it as a "particularly 'masculine' sickness . . . related to the impulse to control, contain, master what actually masters, ravishes, disorganizes you." Or, he says, perhaps record collecting should be seen as a "perverse consumerism" that literally "eats up your life."[6]

Of course, human beings have proven capable of all kinds of extreme behavior, and critics can always find an example that fits a loaded stereotype. But collecting scholar Russell Belk believes that such negative images of collectors serve as a kind of social defense mechanism for all consumers, an "unwitting metaphor for our own fears of unbridled materialism in the marketplace." The stereotypes play a scapegoat role: "We escape blame ourselves by caricaturing the collector as being the silly non-rational consumer in comparison to our own equally obsessive but less focused consumption behavior."[7] In fact, Belk's research indicates that collectors are often more careful about their consumer activities than are noncollectors, adjusting to limitations in time, money, and effort by being self-aware and conscious in their purchasing decisions.

Shuker concludes that the stereotype "is just that; there is no 'typical' record collector."[8] The interviews and portraits displayed on photographer Eilon Paz's *Dust & Grooves* website—part of an ongoing project "documenting vinyl collectors in their most natural and intimate environment: the record room"—seem to illustrate that diversity. Paz has collected collectors on his travels to France, Ghana, Turkey, and Israel, as well as across the United States, and as displayed in the "Archives" section of his website, they certainly resist easy generalization. From Markey Funk, a music producer in Jerusalem who collects experimental music from Europe and Israel; to Margaret Barton Fumo, a Brooklyn, New York, graduate student and psychedelic rock DJ; to Mustafa, a former truck driver in Istanbul who maintains a detailed collection of Turkish popular music from the 1960s and 1970s; to Frederick, Maryland's legendary "King of 78s," Joe Bussard—the main things those collectors seem to have in common are a curiosity about the world around them, a passion for the music they love, and a willingness to open their homes and share their collections.[9]

Connoisseurship, Canons, and Culture

They are also clearly connoisseurs of that which interests them, with a high level of knowledge about the music and a developed critical sense of evaluation in terms of musical quality, rarity, background, context, and so forth. As Eisenberg says, the presence of music in recorded form provides the collector with the ability to study the beauty, in multiple senses of both "study" and "beauty." Renowned cartoonist and record collector Robert Crumb said that "a true collector is more of a connoisseur, and that's the good thing about collecting. It creates a connoisseurship to sort out what's worthwhile in the culture and what isn't. . . . If you're collecting a lot of objects of one particular kind, you develop a very acute sense of discrimination."[10]

There are definitely canons of collectible records, just as there are in the musics they document. Some of those canonical items may be based on simple material scarcity or rarity, but for the most part they are directly connected to the broader cultural processes that establish and maintain consensus views of musical history. Shuker points out that lists of the most popularly collected musical artists "have clear similarities to the recurring presentation of a 'mainstream' canon of rock and pop recordings,"[11] citing a 2000 poll that unsurprisingly found The Beatles, The Rolling Stones, Elvis Presley, and Bob Dylan at the top of the collected-record rankings. Collectors are, Shuker said, not simply the recipients of popular culture canons; "they also play an important role in canon creation through their vernacular scholarship and their involvement in (re-) releasing selected recordings and compilations."[12] The role of collectors has also been significant in relation to specific musical genres, such as blues, by selecting and defining what recordings become established as the essence of the tradition.[13]

On the other hand, Shuker said, some types of collectors may have a more "oppositional" attitude toward their collecting, interested not in canon maintenance but in pursuing the obscure, exotic, or outsider. Rock musician and record collector Thurston Moore said that collecting mainstream material is "more like collecting toys, more object-oriented. I'm more interested in defending the cultural value of music that's not allowed into the mainstream." Echoing Walter Benjamin, Moore said, "When you're a collector, you're creating order out of this chaotic information. That's necessary in a way, and it caters to creative impulses." But for that kind of "renegade practice" collecting, the most important thing is that "you're gathering information that falls below the radar, so it becomes less ignored."[14]

In his writings about collecting art and culture, anthropologist James Clifford is interested in the role collecting plays in relation to those formalized canons. His own goal is a critical history of collecting processes themselves, an inquiry into "what from the material world specific groups and individuals choose to preserve, value, and exchange," to understand how and why people collect particular "categories of meaningful objects," and how those collected objects "function within a ramified system of symbols and values" that gives them significance.[15] Those systems of meaning develop canons, conferring authenticity and value on certain examples—considered important or worthy of keeping, for whatever reasons—even as they lay out the boundaries of the consensus framework by which we understand those examples.

At the same time, Clifford is also interested in how collecting can transgress those boundaries and undermine those very canons. That might be done, for example, by gathering items that do not fit within the framework of some dominant system, or by presenting and displaying the collected objects in ways that directly challenge the existing consensus. Such an approach, according to Clifford, can call forth a sense of wonder regarding the collected objects, by assembling and displaying them in ways that rearrange the established rules, that produce "intimate encounters with inexplicably fascinating objects"[16] and "make their self-evident orders seem strange."[17]

Harry Smith and His *Anthology*

A classic example of the latter is the work of artist, filmmaker, collector, and general trickster Harry Smith, in compiling his famous *Anthology of American Folk Music* in the early 1950s. Although he was not the first music collector to compile and release older recordings—that distinction seems to go to German ethnomusicologist Erich von Hornbostel, for his 1931 *Music of the Orient*[18]—Smith was one of the most influential.

During the 1940s, Smith gradually acquired approximately 20,000 records, focused particularly on a wide range of regional styles that would collectively come to be known as "folk music" (e.g., blues, hillbilly, Cajun). Old 78-rpm records were getting ever more scarce at that time; many were melted down for reuse during the Second World War, and there were few if any organized efforts at preservation. At the same time, the music and culture they documented were in danger of slipping away in the modern rush toward progress. In the early 1950s, Smith convinced Folkways Records to release a series of three double-LP compilations drawn from his collection, assembled and annotated from his own unique perspective.

The compilations were notable both for the diversity and interest of the music itself—a major influence on the burgeoning folk revival of the 1950s, as songs from the *Anthology* became cornerstones of the collective repertoire—and for their presentation, which combined discographic detail with vintage imagery, arranged the music thematically, and filtered it all through Smith's own esoteric, mystical philosophy.[19] The *Anthology* didn't just dump a bunch of songs in a bucket; it transformed the music from quaint, dusty period pieces into pressing but cryptic messages from other times and places. Music writer Greil Marcus said the *Anthology* "made the familiar strange, the never known into the forgotten, and the forgotten into a collective memory," a place he referred to as the "Old, Weird America."[20] Folk music historian Robert Cantwell noted that, with its diverse contents and unique packaging logic, the *Anthology* "confuses the classifying impulse" and suggests "the complete breakdown of the old cultural geography."[21]

Smith received a Grammy award in 1991 for his work on the *Anthology*, shortly before he died, and the *Anthology* itself became a sensation a second time when it was reissued on CD in the late 1990s. In its wake came an increasing flow of reissues to feed a steady listener interest in "lost" music of all sorts. Established reissue labels such as Yazoo stepped up their activities, while new labels went further in depth with specific types of music: American roots and outsider music from guitarist John Fahey's Revenant records, reggae from Blood and Fire, the self-explanatory Soul Jazz, and many more besides.

Reissues remain a significant portion of music releases every year, and industry statistics show that "catalog" sales are especially strong, particularly physical recordings (vinyl LPs have in fact reestablished themselves in the age of digital downloads as a significant niche market for fans and collectors). The most popular of those tend to be "canonical" reissues, repackaging established artists' back catalogs and related items (unreleased outtakes, side projects) in the form of "deluxe" re-releases of classic albums (which are usually already in print, often in multiple versions).[22] At the same time, and at the other end of the canonical spectrum, some of the more interesting and revelatory music reissues of recent years have been produced by smaller, independent labels with motivations seemingly closer to those of Harry Smith: to make some older musical world new again through its collection and creative display. A number of them are in fact run by record collectors, whose own musical and collecting interests shape the labels' philosophy and releases. I discuss here four of these labels: Dust-to-Digital, Numero Group, Soundway, and Analog Africa. All were started by record collectors as extensions of their collecting, as ways to share the great lost music they discovered by re-releasing it into the world. All have built considerable critical and listener followings for their reissues of music from times and places well off the beaten track of consensus musical history.

FOUR LABELS

Dust-to-Digital

Lance Ledbetter was working as a radio DJ at Georgia State University in the late 1990s, and he took over the roots music show, having already fallen under the spell of Smith's *Anthology*. Ledbetter became especially interested in early twentieth-century gospel music, about which very little seemed to be known, and he felt compelled to dig further, sensing that such stuff had to be out there somewhere. One of his first contacts was Joe Bussard, who was known in collecting circles for sharing rare records from his massive collection by recording them onto cassette for a nominal fee; from there Ledbetter was off down the rabbit hole of record archaeology.

Those digs resulted in the Dust-to-Digital label's first release in 2003, a six-CD compilation of American gospel music from the early twentieth century titled *Good-bye, Babylon*. The music was arranged thematically on five CDs ("salvation," "judgment," etc.), plus one disc of vintage recordings of sermons, all of it opening directly onto a century-old sacred world that had largely disappeared from contemporary life. The package looked like an artifact from that era: the CDs fit into a cedar box, with handpicked cotton for padding, and were accompanied by an expansive book designed like an old hymnal. The six discs themselves were housed in cardboard sleeves bearing printed designs that could be assembled, puzzle-like, into a cross-shaped image of a cotton plant. For an inaugural release by a small, independent label, the packaging alone made quite a splash; together with the expertly organized music, the release was acclaimed by both reviewers and historians and was nominated for two Grammy awards.[23]

The label's subsequent releases continued that high conceptual standard, including further box sets featuring subjects such as Joe Bussard's own Fonotone label (which continued to release rural American music on 78s well into the 1960s) and the remarkable four-disc set *Opika Pende: Africa at 78 RPM*; compilations covering everything from sacred harp singing in the United States to throat singing and folk songs from Tuva; deluxe book-and-music packages on themes such as *Take Me to the Water: Immersion Baptism in Vintage Music and Photography*; plus several DVDs, including a documentary film about Bussard. Many of Dust-to-Digital's releases are practically museum pieces in their own right, elaborately designed to provide a rich informational and visual context for the unearthed musical artifacts. Ledbetter explained, "We want to include texts to educate people about the recordings, and we want to include photographs and create design in such a way as to recreate the era in which the recordings were made," with the goal of "putting essential recordings from the past in people's record collections today."[24]

Numero Group

Record collector Ken Shipley, along with partners Rob Sevier and Tom Lunt, started the Chicago-based Numero Group in 2003, initially to work on reissue projects that were too adventurous for Shipley's day job at the independent Rykodisc label. Shipley says the goal was to "try to go out there and go deeper than anyone else has ever gone" in documenting music recorded outside the major thoroughfares of popular culture.[25] There is apparently quite a lot of that still to be (re)discovered, as proven by the label's extensive catalog, which has covered a wide array of rock, soul, pop, and folk music. Numero Group's most elaborate single release to date is probably the six-LP/four-CD collection of early independent-label releases by under-heralded Chicago soul singer Syl Johnson, though the label has become especially known for several ongoing series of compilations that focus in depth on local and regional recording scenes, particularly the Eccentric Soul series, each volume of which documents local soul record labels with unique sounds from highways and byways across America.

The owners' collecting interests shape the label's releases, which have mined rich seams of locally and privately released American music from the 1960s to the 1980s, a period when creativity was "unleashed but limited," said Sevier. "That is a magical time frame when widespread recording technology became available, but there was still a barrier of entry. You had to invest money and time. You had to get other people involved. Those obstacles filtered out a lot of garbage."[26] Numero Group's archivalist sensibility is reflected in its packaging, which usually features vintage candid/amateur cover photographs of the artists involved, as well as in the prominence of the label's numbering system. Simon Reynolds described the label's mission as "a grand sonic-reclamation project that blends aspects of archaeology and anthropology,"[27] an extended effort to redress and expand the historical record by celebrating the independent, the unique, and the off-the-beaten path.

Soundway

Miles Cleret of London-based Soundway began DJing while in his teens, having already picked up record collecting from his father. "I was immersed in vinyl from a very young age and was always fascinated by the format, the cover art, the story behind the recording," Cleret recalled.[28] Searching for records during a late 1990s vacation in Ghana, he was turned on to the west African music of the 1970s, a musically productive and exciting time when highlife and juju were combining with rock and soul; much of this music, he found, was being neglected and becoming more difficult to track down. "By immersing myself in these areas and researching and examining the small recording industries that existed and used to thrive there," he said, "it was apparent that this music might not have ever left the areas it was recorded in so this was just more of a reason for us to try and reissue the music."[29]

Soundway's mission was to present the cream of Cleret's African excursions via his own sensibilities as a jazz and hip-hop DJ, rather than in a standard "world music" presentation. Starting in 2002, the label's initial releases of classic music from Nigeria and Ghana struck a chord with both DJs and listeners and coincided with other reissues, including the back catalog of the legendary Fela Kuti, to bring much wider international attention to Nigerian music. Although the label's reissues have come from as far afield as Thailand, many have focused on a transatlantic diaspora stretching from Nigeria and Ghana to the Caribbean, Panama, and Colombia. All are composed of choice cuts organized with a DJ's sense of flow, accompanied by liner notes that trace the background of musicians, releases, and the context of the time, as well as reproductions of original record covers and labels. Soundway's releases have received as much acclaim from independent rock and dance music circles as from conventional "world music" audiences and have been sampled in hip-hop and dance tracks. Cleret said Soundway's mission is a straightforward one: "To keep the music from dying so as many people as possible can hear it."[30]

Analog Africa

The Analog Africa label had its origins in Samy Ben Redjeb's 1990s hunt for rare records throughout western Africa; he went so far as to take a job as an airline flight attendant to facilitate travel around the region. Currently based in Frankfurt, Germany, Redjeb still goes on "records safaris" to out-of-the-way locales in search of sounds and people. "I travel to Africa to meet the artists, to ask for permission to use their music, pay for the rights and to ask them to share their story—that to me is fundamental." He is also on the lookout for documentation from the time period—everything from vintage photos to original documents, objects, and other ephemera. "I also spend a huge amount of time searching for pictures, old posters, documents, and obviously for original vinyl, reel tapes, matrices, acetates, and so on." His search for objects is combined with a search for the people behind them: "To get a better picture of the general music scene during the '70s, I try to locate the people who worked in the music industry at the time—sound engineers, sales managers, club owners, label founders."[31]

Both the search and the results are documented in audio and visual form on Analog Africa's dozen or so releases through mid-2012, which bring to light recording scenes from even further off the established map of popular music reissues and general knowledge—places such as Benin, Togo, Burkina Faso, and Algeria—and the unique music produced there during the 1960s and 1970s. Each release includes an elaborate booklet filled with photos, memorabilia, reminiscences from musicians and producers, as well as Redjeb's own colorful accounts of his safaris. As in much travel writing, there is a sense of sharing the journey as well as learning what was found there. "I realise more and more that the essence of my music label is travelling and searching in dusty warehouses and personal collections for forgotten music which otherwise would get thrown away or burned," Redjeb said. "But some people are trying to limit the damage and that's what I hope I can contribute to, too."[32]

RECORD LABELS AND RECORD COLLECTING

History, Significance, and Meaning

Each of those labels explores its own musical and cultural territory, and each exhibits a unique attitude toward both the collecting process and the display or presentation of what it collects. That makes sense: as Russell Belk pointed out, collectors don't simply accumulate things; in the process of collecting, they produce some new larger unity, in the form of the collection itself. "Collectors create, combine, classify, and curate the objects they acquire in such a way that a new product, the collection, emerges," Belk wrote. "More precisely, they participate in the process of socially reconstructing shared meanings for the objects they collect."[33]

The meanings being reconstructed play a central role for each of the labels. All provide information-rich packages, the music accompanied by text and imagery that tells the story of and provides a context for the music. Ledbetter said that the contextualizing step is especially important for music that exists outside the established record. "Everyone knows old gospel music is out there and if you look hard enough you can find it," he said. "But where does one start? That's why I thought it was so important to include lengthy annotations and introductory essays by some of the most knowledgeable researchers and writers from each subgenre."[34]

Although history and context are essential, Numero Group's Shipley likes to avoid "dry research": "When I read something, I want to get a sense for the world that was out there, that this person was either surviving in or not surviving in," he said. "There's all these bits and pieces of minutiae that are important to some people, like who played on what session, but it's the human element of these records that ultimately make them interesting."[35] His partner Sevier adds that the goal is not simply to amass historical detail. "We try to breathe new life into old music," he said. "We're repositioning it as a piece of history that a different generation wants to find out about and take on as their own."[36] Shipley described the label's releases as "stuff for the library of the future."[37]

James Clifford believes that sort of enhanced historical self-consciousness in collecting can call attention to the limitations of existing canons, by putting forward previously unknown information or by suggesting other ways of making sense of things. It can, he said, "at least jostle and set in motion the ways in which anthropologists, artists, and their publics collect themselves and the world" and illustrate the ways in which "the categories of the beautiful, the cultural, and the authentic have changed and are changing."[38]

Musical Objects in a Virtual World

I have heard it argued of late that, in our new virtual digital world, such a sense of authenticity has had to be sacrificed on the altar of ease and portability. Music in particular, it is said, has finally become truly "free" (in multiple senses of that word). Lost are all its former limitations of being in and belonging to a particular time or place, and by transmuting into pure information it has become loosed from the tyranny of chronology and geography—and in many cases any sort of payment for the artist. Certainly Marcus Boon's chapter in this volume suggests that music in digital data form has a very different existential status than it would in material form—that the loss of his MP3 collection raises a different level of concern than would, say, the destruction of Joe Bussard's collection of irreplaceable 78s. Simon Reynolds describes the post-file-sharing music world as one in which "history and geography are transcended, the linear flow of pop time is suspended, and there's a free-for-all" of disembodied accumulation and consumption.[39] However, all of the labels discussed here seem to work against that tendency, instead reasserting the importance of context, of history and geography and culture, both for the original music and for the labels' own re-presentations of it.

None of the four could be described as even mildly Luddite in its approach to new online media. As with most labels today, these labels' releases are available in digital downloadable formats, and all of them have online presences through label websites, catalogs, and social media. Although obviously some of that is commercial or promotional in nature, at the same time they all use the expanded options of online content as an extension of the collecting process, adding to the experience of their releases. For example, the Soundway website includes features such as special stream-only Miles Cleret "DJ mixes," composed of rare and unreissued material, and an interactive musical map of Colombia with audio and video tracing the origins of artists and songs on the label's Colombian compilations. Numero Group features an expanded section on its website called "Digital Dig," which allows the downloading of individual 45 tracks as well as entire albums; the label's record-finding excursions have also featured on its blog. Dust-to-Digital and Soundway make extensive use of the online Bandcamp platform for sharing radio shows and DJ mixes as well as individual tracks. Analog Africa's Redjeb posts photos and updates to his Facebook page about his collecting activities. All of them make extensive use of social media.

Although they all embrace new technology as an enhancement to the overall experience, the main focus for those labels remains the production of music in object form—and as noted previously, very distinctive ones, creatively designed and full of evocative period imagery and extensive information. Numero Group, Analog Africa, and Soundway releases all come out on LP as well as CD and downloadable formats; Dust-to-Digital's elaborate projects do not move between formats as easily, but they have started an offshoot, Parlortone, for unique vinyl-only releases.

Numero Group's Sevier sees the packaging and presentation as an essential part of the experience. Without that, he said, "What would contextualize the albums in a way that is key to the appreciation? What would anybody get out of it?"[40] Soundway's Cleret said the goal for its releases is not just to put some songs on an album, but to construct "a slice of culture from a certain time" in a compelling and accessible way.[41] Ledbetter feels that the object status of Dust-to-Digital's releases generates a sense of presence that is difficult to translate into a digital form. Although ease of access and sharing is definitely a strength of digital media, he said, in the process "the music becomes more disposable. . . . Also, the 200 page book could be downloadable, but I've yet to see a downloadable cedar box."[42]

The labels' focus on object status for their releases seems in part to grow from their mindset as collectors, which also shapes their creative sense of how best to display and present the collected examples. Their reissues have an aesthetic and cultural weight of their own, and the fact of their embodiment guarantees at the very least that in some future era those objects could be rediscovered in the same way as were the original records; their existence as elaborate, collectible objects in their own right serves as a hedge against the disembodiment of virtual existence. In the same way that the labels insist on the history and context of the objects they collect, they also insist on a similar status for their own releases.

Objects and Ethics

There is also an ethical component at work here that grows out of the labels' commitment to producing formal releases. All of them place a priority on tracking down the music's original creators or owners, both to share credit where it is due and to arrange licensing deals to ensure remuneration. In some cases, the archives of the labels that originally released the music may be housed somewhere: Soundway has worked with some of Colombia's classic record labels, and Numero Group's *Eccentric Soul* and *Local Customs* series are sourced directly from the original local studios and labels. In other cases, that work involves finding the artists themselves, who might have copyrights and master tapes.

The labels could just go ahead and re-release their long-forgotten finds without obtaining permission; unofficial and often poor-quality pirated reissues have long been produced surreptitiously at the margins of the record business. The Internet complicates the situation even further, as unlicensed digital copies of both popular musical items and total obscurities run free across the interwebs, set loose by blogs and torrents in downloadable form to be fruitful and multiply. Simon Reynolds referred to that online ethos as "sharity" and described it as a "grand giveaway bonanza" in which everything is available for download, for free, anytime.[43] Record collector and blogger Uchenna Ikonne said that the justification given is generally that in the digital age everything is "fair game," that "since the records I was posting were very rare and long out of print I might as well just share them online." The Nigerian American Ikonne started out sharing his rare African music finds via his Comb & Razor blog, including audio files of rare records; however, he said he increasingly felt "a certain sense of uneasiness with the kind of music blogging I was doing. I felt like it was little more than new wave bootlegging." Eventually he decided, "maybe I should just get them back in print myself so that they can generate some much-deserved income for the artists?"[44] Ikonne has begun releasing compilations on his own label, as well as working with the Soundway label on the collection *The World Ends: Afro-Rock & Psychedelia in 1970s Nigeria.*

Record collecting is often described, even by record collectors, as a particularly competitive and cutthroat business. However, the labels profiled here regularly collaborate with other collectors in finding and compiling the rare music they reissue, and with music experts of various kinds on research, information, and liner notes for their projects. They seem to see the work itself as part of the sharing process. Numero Group's Shipley said, "We spend the time and money to go through this and give you the best listening experience. . . . We want to find what makes something so special that you want to put it on over and over again."[45] An underlying ethic of sharing seems to drive the enterprise. In spring 2012, Redjeb posted a series of photos to the Analog Africa Facebook page humorously documenting his ongoing (perhaps futile) efforts to organize his record collection in his small apartment. When a reader commented in joking envy on the stacks of vintage African 45s in the pictures, Redjeb replied, "No need to be jealous Juergen. I'll boil this down to the best and then its yours :)"[46]

CONCLUSION

Clearly some part of both the motivation for and the significance of what these labels are doing is preservationist: adding to the world's musical library, broadening the documentation of musical history in both recorded and written form. In 2012, Dust-to-Digital even started a nonprofit organization, Music Memory, to digitize and document rare 78-rpm records, in many cases traveling to collectors' homes to make digital transfers of fragile recordings. The organization's goal is to create an expanding database, also including discographies, biographies, and related information, that could "serve as a musical Rosetta Stone for future generations."[47] Evan Eisenberg wrote, "the collector wishes to preserve history while escaping it—to save history from itself. And the man who makes records may have a similar motive."[48] All of the labels discussed here, and others like them, are helping to fill in large gaps in the history of popular music, many of which were not necessarily even known to *be* gaps prior to their compilations and reissues.

Miles Cleret says that information about 1970s popular music from western Africa seemed almost nonexistent when Soundway began. Publicly available recordings, even those by once-famous artists, had become lost or simply neglected, lying "un-listened-to amongst piles of records kept under beds, in cupboards and suitcases and in lock-ups all over Nigeria." But more recently, in the wake of reissues by his own and other labels, a larger and clearer picture has been developing, via "the amount of information that people have started to collate on the assorted blogs and websites dedicated to Nigerian and African music, which seem to be springing up almost daily across the world," many fueled by the findings of other collectors.[49]

At some point this goes beyond simply adding to the historical record, more than a refinement of the level of detail about known territory; rather, it is the terrain itself—what is there to be known—that changes. A 2012 magazine profile of Numero Group described the label as "[sketching] an alternate historical narrative,"[50] similar perhaps to the redrawing of cultural maps with which the Harry Smith *Anthology* was credited. Many of these labels' releases, by their very existence, but also through their creative and detailed presentation, call attention to various (mostly unstated) assumptions that underlie consensus musical history. They suggest the limitations of what we (think we) know about that history, and, as James Clifford discussed, "make their self-evident orders seem strange." It's not only a preservation effort, but also a re-presentation of the music that brings it to life in a new time or place.

According to Clifford, in Europe in the 16th and 17th centuries, collected objects from other "wheres" and "whens" were not necessarily viewed as primitive antiquities from dead times, but were seen in terms of a "category of the marvelous" right there in the present.[51] They stood as evidence of something beyond the ordinary; they generated a sense of wonder about the world. To some extent, he argued, that kind of "more intimate" sense of the objects has to do with the individual's attitude toward the collection. But he also points out how certain types of collections can generate or catalyze an experience that returns their lost status as fetish objects—in this case our own fetishes—by allowing them the "power to fixate rather than just the capacity to edify or inform." Clifford wanted those artifacts to once again become *"objets sauvages*, sources of fascination with the power to disconcert." By challenging what we think we know, and the ways we make sense of it, such collections end up reminding us of "our lack of self-possession, of the artifices we employ to gather a world around us."[52]

That original copy of *Blues by Basie* still lives in my collection; I dug it out and gave it a spin while writing this essay. It still sounds great, though I can't say it still triggers the sort of mind-expanding experience I had some thirty-odd years ago; at this point, both the music and what I learned from it have been pretty well absorbed. Lately, a good bit of my listening time has been fixated on some of those African music reissues discussed above; in the process, I have found myself reading up on west African history, delving into Nigerian fiction, digging around online for old BBC documentaries about the Biafran war, and trying to pick up electric guitar techniques from music recorded in Angola around the time I was born. I have also noticed a sense of wonder on at least a few occasions.

NOTES

1. For the sake of simplicity, I am following sociologist Roy Shuker in using the terms "record collecting" and "music collecting" generally in reference to the process of collecting sound recordings in a variety of formats, including "shellac 78s, vinyl LPs and 45s, audiotapes, CDs and as digital downloads," drawing distinctions among these when relevant. See Roy Shuker, *Wax Trash and Vinyl Treasures: Record Collecting as a Social Practice* (Burlington, VT: Ashgate Publishing Company, 2010), 3.
2. Shuker, *Wax Trash and Vinyl Treasures*, 6.
3. Brett Milano, *Vinyl Junkies: Adventures in Record Collecting* (New York: St. Martin's Griffin, 2003), 13.
4. Simon Reynolds, "Lost in Music: Obsessive Record Collecting," in *This Is Pop: In Search of the Elusive at Experience Music Project*, ed. Eric Weisbard (Cambridge, MA: Harvard University Press, 2004), 289.
5. Evan Eisenberg, *The Recording Angel: Music, Records and Culture from Aristotle to Zappa*, 2nd ed. (New Haven, CT, and London: York University Press, 2005), 14–16.
6. Reynolds, "Lost in Music," 294.
7. Russell W. Belk, *Collecting in a Consumer Society* (New York: Routledge, 2001), ix.
8. Shuker, *Wax Trash and Vinyl Treasures*, 56.
9. *Dust & Grooves: Vinyl, Music, Culture*, http://www.dustandgrooves.com (last modified 2 November 2012).

10. Milano, *Vinyl Junkies*, 70.

11. Shuker, *Wax Trash and Vinyl Treasures*, 92.

12. Shuker, *Wax Trash and Vinyl Treasures*, 90.

13. John Dougan, "Objects of Desire: Canon Formation and Blues Record Collecting," *Journal of Popular Music* 18, no. 1 (April 2006): 40–65.

14. Milano, *Vinyl Junkies*, 14.

15. James Clifford, "On Collecting Art and Culture," in *The Predicament of Culture: Twentieth-Century Ethnography, Literature, and Art* (Cambridge, MA: Harvard University Press, 1988), 221.

16. Clifford, "On Collecting Art and Culture," 216.

17. Clifford, "On Collecting Art and Culture," 217.

18. Jonathan Ward, liner notes to *Opika Pende: Africa at 78 RPM*, Dust-to-Digital 22, 2011, compact disc box set, 7–8.

19. I have previously written about Harry Smith's interest in the philosophy of alchemy and Western mysticism and their influence on the *Anthology*. Kevin M. Moist, "Collecting, Collage, and Alchemy: The Harry Smith *Anthology of American Folk Music* as Art and Cultural Intervention," *American Studies* 48, no. 4 (Winter 2007): 111–127.

20. Greil Marcus, "The Old, Weird America," liner notes to *Anthology of American Folk Music*, Smithsonian Folkways Recordings, 1997, compact disc box set, 7.

21. Robert Cantwell, *When We Were Good: The Folk Revival* (Cambridge, MA: Harvard University Press, 1996), 194.

22. Businesswire, "The Nielsen Company & Billboard's 2011 Music Industry Report," 25 January 2012, http://www.businesswire.com/news/home/20120105005547/en/Nielsen-Company-Billboard%E2%80%99s-2011-Music-Industry-Report (accessed 5 June 2012). For more on the rise of the deluxe box set reissue, see Alexis Petridis, "The Rise of the Super-Deluxe Box Set," *Guardian*, 22 December 2011, http://www.guardian.co.uk/music/2011/dec/22/rise-super-deluxe-box-set (accessed 6 June 2012).

23. For more on Dust-to-Digital, see James Calemine, "Lance Ledbetter Interview: The Divine Grace of Dust to Digital," *Swampland.com* (blog), January 2010, http://www.swampland.com/articles/view/title:lance_ledbetter_interview_the_divine_grace_of_dust_to_digital (accessed 10 May 2012); and Burkhard Bilger, "The Last Verse: Is There Any Folk Music Still Out There?" *New Yorker*, 28 April 2008, http://www.newyorker.com/reporting/2008/04/28/080428fa_fact_bilger (accessed 6 May 2012).

24. "Label of Love: Dust-to-Digital Bringing It All Back to Life: Q&A Founder Lance Ledbetter," *Record Collector*, April 2007, http://www.dust-digital.com/icn//RecordCollector4-2007.jpg (accessed 5 May 2012).

25. Gretta Cohn, "Numero Group," *Pitchfork*, 16 April 2006, http://pitchfork.com/features/interviews/6311-numero-group/ (accessed 15 May 2012).

26. David Peisner, "Diggin' Beyond the Crates," *SPIN*, 27 September 2012, http://www.spin.com/articles/numero-group-worlds-greatest-reissue-label?page=6 (accessed 30 September 2012).

27. Simon Reynolds, *Retromania: Pop Culture's Addiction to Its Own Past* (New York: Faber and Faber, 2011), 156.

28. "Soundway Interview," *Choice Cuts* (blog), 27 April 2010, http://www.choicecuts.com/blog/soundway-interview/ (accessed 16 June 2012). For more on Soundway, see Rhys James, "Vinyl Anthropology," *Vice* (blog), 20 October 2010, http://www.vice.com/read/vinyl-anthropology (accessed 14 May 2012).

29. "Soundway Interview."

30. David Dacks, "Miles Cleret," *Exclaim!*, March 2008, http://exclaim.ca/Interviews/WebExclusive/miles_cleret/Page/3 (accessed 10 May 2012).

31. "Waking the Muse," *Properganda Online* (blog), 31 March 2012, http://blog.propermusic.com/waking-the-muse-samy-ben-redjeb/ (accessed 30 May 2012). For more on Analog Africa, see Jace Clayton, "Search and Rescue," *Frieze*, September 2008, http://www.frieze.com/issue/article/search_and_rescue/ (accessed 9 May 2012).

32. "Waking the Muse."

33. Belk, *Collecting in a Consumer Society*, 55.

34. "Lance Ledbetter, Dust to Digital Interview," *Since1968* (blog), 9 June 2004, http://since1968.com/article/7/lance-ledbetter-dust-to-digital-interview (accessed 8 May 2012).

35. Cohn, "Numero Group."

36. Peisner, "Diggin' Beyond the Crates," http://www.spin.com/articles/numero-group-worlds-greatest-reissue-label?page=4.

37. Reynolds, *Retromania*, 156.

38. Clifford, "On Collecting Art and Culture," 229.

39. Reynolds, "Lost in Music," 306.

40. Peisner, "Diggin' Beyond the Crates," http://www.spin.com/articles/numero-group-worlds-greatest-reissue-label?page=7.

41. "Soundway Interview."

42. "Lance Ledbetter, Dust to Digital Interview."

43. Reynolds, *Retromania*, 105.

44. "Nigerian Boogie Down! Q&A with Uchenna Ikonne," Light in the Attic Records (blog), February 1, 2011, http://blog.lightintheattic.net/?p=3297 (accessed 5 June 2012).

45. Cohn, "Numero Group."

46. Analog Africa's Facebook Page, 29 April 2012, http://www.facebook.com/analogafrica (accessed 12 May 2012).

47. "Our Mission," Music Memory, http://www.musicmemory.org/mission (accessed 15 September 2012).

48. Eisenberg, *Recording Angel*, 37.

49. Miles Cleret, liner notes to *Nigeria Special Volume 2: Modern Highlife, Afro Sounds, & Nigerian Blues 1970–6*, Soundway Records 20 (2010), 3.

50. Peisner, "Diggin' Beyond the Crates," http://www.spin.com/articles/numero-group-worlds-greatest-reissue-label?page=1.

51. Clifford, "On Collecting Art and Culture," 222.

52. Clifford, "On Collecting Art and Culture," 229.

Bibliography

Ackerman, James. "The Villa as Paradigm." *Perspecta* 22, (1986): 10–31.

Adaptation. Directed by Spike Jonze. 2002. Los Angeles: Image Entertainment, 2010. DVD.

Adorno, Theodor W. "Freudian Theory and the Pattern of Fascist Propaganda." In *The Essential Frankfurt School Reader*, edited by Andrew Arato and EikeGebhardt, 118–137. London: Continuum, 1982.

———. *Kritik: Kleine Schriften zur Gesellschaft*. Frankfurt am Main, Germany: Suhrkamp, 1971.

Agamben, Giorgio. *The Coming Community*. Translated by Michael Hardt. Minneapolis: Minnesota University Press, 1993.

Alpers, Svetlana. "The Museum as a Way of Seeing." In *Exhibiting Cultures: The Poetics and Politics of Museum Display*, edited by Ivan Karp and Steven D. Lavine, 25–32. Washington and London: Smithsonian Institution Press, 1991.

Ames, Michael M. *Museums, the Public, and Anthropology*. Vancouver: University of British Columbia Press, 1986.

Analog Africa's Facebook Page. 29 April 2012. http://www.facebook.com/analogafrica (accessed 12 May 2012).

Andrews, David L. "Sport, Culture, and Late Capitalism." In *Marxism, Cultural Studies, and Sport*, edited by Ben Carrington and Ian McDonald, 213–231. New York: Routledge, 2009.

Angie. "House on the Rock: Manic Mishmash of Mechanical Mayhem." http://weburbanist.com/2010/06/09/house-on-the-rock-manic-mishmash-of-mechanical-mayhem (accessed 15 September 2012).

Apostolos-Cappadona, Diane. "Havemeyer, Louisine Waldron." In *American National Biography Online*. www.anb.org (accessed 30 October 2010).

Augé, Marc. *Non-places: Introduction to an Anthropology of Supermodernity*. Translated by John Howe. London: Verso, 1995.

Bakhtin, Mikhail. *Rabelais and His World*. Translated by Helene Iswolsky. Cambridge, MA: MIT Press, 1968.

Bal, Mieke. "Telling Objects: A Narrative Perspective on Collecting." In *The Cultures of Collecting*, edited by John Elsner and Roger Cardinal, 97–115. Cambridge, MA: Harvard University Press, 1994.

Batkin, Norton. "Conceptualizing the History of the Contemporary Museum: On Foucault and Benjamin." *Philosophical Topics* 25, no. 1 (Spring 1997): 1–10.

Baudrillard, Jean. "The System of Collecting." In *The Cultures of Collecting*, edited by John Elsner and Roger Cardinal, 7–24. Cambridge, MA: Harvard University Press, 1994.

Bayard, Pierre. *How to Talk About Books You Haven't Read*. Translated by Jeffrey Mehlman. New York: Bloomsbury, 2007.

Belk, Russell W. *Collecting in a Consumer Society*. The Collecting Cultures Series. London/New York: Routledge, 1995.

———. "Collectors and Collecting." In *Interpreting Objects and Collections*, edited by Susan M. Pearce, 317–326. London: Routledge, 1994.

———. Possessions and the Sense of Past. In *Highways and Byways: Naturalistic Research from the Consumer Behavior Odyssey*, edited by Russell W. Belk, 114–130. Provo, UT: Association for Consumer Research, 1991.

Benjamin, Walter. *The Arcades Project*. Translated by Howard Eiland and Kevin McLaughlin. Cambridge, MA: Harvard University Press, 1999.

———. *Charles Baudelaire: A Lyric Poet in the Era of High Capitalism*. London: Verso, 1983.

———. "Edouard Fuchs: Collector." 1937. Translated by Howard Eiland and Michael W. Jennings. In *Walter Benjamin, Selected Writings*, edited by Howard Eiland and Michael W. Jennings, vol. 3, 260–285. Cambridge, MA: Harvard University Press, 2002.

———. "From the Work of Art in the Age of Mechanical Reproduction." In *Aesthetics: Classic Readings from the Western Tradition*, edited by Dabney Townsend, 286–289. Belmont, CA: Wadsworth, 2001.

———. *Illuminations*. Edited by Hannah Arendt. Translated by Harry Zorn. New York: Shocken, 1969.

———. "On the Concept of History." 1940. Translated by Harry Zohn. In *Walter Benjamin, Selected Writings*, edited by Howard Eiland and Michael W. Jennings, vol. 4, 389–397. Cambridge, MA: Harvard University Press, 1999.

———. "Theses on the Philosophy of History." Translated by Harry Zorn. In *Illuminations*, edited by Hannah Arendt, 253–264. New York: Schocken, 1969.

———. "Unpacking My Library: A Talk About Collecting." 1931. Translated by Harry Zohn. In *Walter Benjamin: Selected Writings*, edited by Michael W. Jennings, Howard Eiland, and Gary Smith, vol. 2, 486–493. Cambridge, MA: Harvard University Press, 1999.

———. "The Work of Art in the Age of Its Technological Reproducibility." 1935–1936. Translated by by Edmund Jephcott and Harry Zohn. In *Walter Benjamin, Selected Writings*, edited by Howard Eiland and Michael W. Jennings, vol. 3, 101–122. Cambridge, MA: Harvard University Press, 2002.

Bessborough, The Earl of. Introduction to *Lady Charlotte Schreiber: Extracts From Her Journal, 1853–1891*, xi–xv. London: John Murray, 1952.

Bilger, Burkhard. "The Last Verse: Is There Any Folk Music Still Out There?" *New Yorker*, 28 April, 2008. http://www.newyorker.com/reporting/2008/04/28/080428fa_fact_bilger (accessed 6 May 2012).

Birley, Richard. E-mail message to author, 10 June 2007.

Bitzer, Lloyd. "The Rhetorical Situation." *Philosophy & Rhetoric* 1, no. 1 (1968): 1–14.

Bloom, John. "Cardboard Patriarchy: Adult Baseball Card Collecting and the Nostalgia for a Presexual Past." In *Hop on Pop*, edited by Henry Jenkins, Tara McPherson, and Jane Shattuc, 68–87. Durham, NC: Duke University Press, 2002.

———. *A House of Cards: Baseball Card Collecting and Popular Culture*. Minneapolis: University of Minnesota Press, 1997.

Boon, Marcus. *In Praise of Copying*. Cambridge, MA: Harvard University Press, 2010.

Bourdieu, Pierre. *Distinction: A Social Critique of the Judgement of Taste*. Translated by Richard Nice. Cambridge, MA: Harvard University Press, 1984.

Boyd, Josh. "Selling Home: Corporate Stadium Names and the Destruction of Commemoration." *Journal of Applied Communication Research* 28, no. 4 (2000): 330–346.

Bredekamp, Horst. *The Lure of Antiquity and the Cult of the Machine: The Kunstkammer and the Evolution of Nature, Art and Technology*. Princeton, NJ: Markus Wiener, 1995.

Britton, John. *Union of Architecture, Sculpture and Painting; Exemplified by a Series of Illustrations, with Descriptive Accounts of the House and Galleries of John Soane*. London, 1827.

Broadcast Pioneers of Philadelphia. http://www.broadcastpioneers.com (accessed 31 October 2012).

Brown, Lee Rust. *The Emerson Museum: Practical Romanticism and the Pursuit of the Whole*. Cambridge, MA: Harvard University Press, 1997.

Brunton, Finn. "Keyspace: WikiLeaks and the Assange Papers." *Radical Philosophy* 166 (2011): 8–20.

Bullock, William. *A Companion to Mr. Bullock's Museum*. 10th ed. London: Henry Reynell and Son, 1811.

Butterworth, Michael L. *Baseball and Rhetorics of Purity: The National Pastime and American Identity During the War on Terror*. Tuscaloosa: University of Alabama Press, 2010.

———. "Ritual in the 'Church of Baseball': Suppressing the Discourse of Democracy after 9/11." *Communication and Critical/Cultural Studies* 2, no. 2 (2005): 107–129.

Caillois, Roger. *Man, Play, and Games*. Translated by Meyer Barash. New York: Free Press, 1961.

Calemine, James. "Lance Ledbetter Interview: The Divine Grace of Dust to Digital." *Swampland.com* (blog), January 2010. http://www.swampland.com/articles/view/title:lance_ledbetter_interview_the_divine_grace_of_dust_to_digital (accessed 10 May 2012)

Cantwell, Robert. *When We Were Good: The Folk Revival*. Cambridge, MA: Harvard University Press, 1996.

Carey. James W. "A Cultural Approach to Communication." *Communication* 2 (1975): 1–22.

Carr, Nicholas. *The Shallows: What the Internet Is Doing to Our Brains*. New York: W. W. Norton, 2010.

Cavell, Stanley. "Finding as Founding." In *This New Yet Unapproachable America: Lectures after Emerson after Wittgenstein*. Albuquerque, NM: Living Batch Press, 1989.

———. *Must We Mean What We Say? A Book of Essays*. New York: Scribner, 1969. Reprint, Cambridge, UK: Cambridge University Press, 1976.

———. *The Senses of Walden*. Chicago: University of Chicago Press, 1972/1992.

———. *The World Viewed: Reflections on the Ontology of Film*. Cambridge, MA: Harvard University Press, 1979.

Cheater, Christine. "Collectors of Nature's Curiosities: Science, Popular Culture and the Rise of Natural History Museums." In *Frankenstein's Science: Experimentation and Discovery in Romantic Culture, 1780–1830*, edited by Christa Knellwolf and Jane Goodall, 167–182. Aldershot, UK: Ashgate, 2008.

Chow, Rey. "Fateful Attachments: On Collecting, Fidelity, and Lao She." In *Things*, edited by Bill Brown, 362–380. Chicago: University of Chicago Press, 2004.

Clarke, T. E. B. "Cardio-Graphics." *Punch*, 25 February 1981, 320.

Clayton, Jace. "Search and Rescue." *Frieze* (September 2008). http://www.frieze.com/issue/article/search_and_rescue/ (accessed 9 May 2012).

Cleret, Miles. Liner notes to *Nigeria Special Volume 2: Modern Highlife, Afro Sounds, & Nigerian Blues 1970–6*. Soundway Records 20, 2010.

Clifford, James. "On Collecting Art and Culture." In *The Predicament of Culture: Twentieth-Century Ethnography, Literature, and Art*, 215–251. Cambridge, MA: Harvard University Press, 1988.

———. *The Predicament of Culture*. Cambridge, MA: Harvard University Press, 1988.

Cohn, Gretta. "Numero Group." *Pitchfork*, 16 April 2006. http://pitchfork.com/features/interviews/6311–numero-group/ (accessed 15 May 2012).

Congdon, Lisa. "A Collection a Day, 2010." http://collectionaday2010.blogspot.com/ (accessed 15 September 2012).

Connerton, Paul. *How Societies Remember*. New York: Cambridge University Press, 1989.

Cooke, Lynne, and Peter Wollen, eds. *Visual Display: Culture Beyond Appearances*. Seattle, WA: Bay Press/Dia Center for the Arts, 1995.

Craig, Pamela B., Barbara O. Natanson, and Dominique Pickett. "American Women: Married Women's Property Laws." *Law Library of Congress*. 2003. http://memory.loc.gov/ammem/awhhtml/awlaw3/property_law.html (accessed 15 October 2010).

Crawford, Garry. *Consuming Sport: Fans, Sport, and Culture*. New York: Routledge, 2004.

Csikszentmihalyi, Mihaly, and Eugene Rochberg-Halton. *The Meaning of Things: Domestic Symbols and the Self*. Cambridge, UK: Cambridge University Press, 1981.

Dacks, David. "Miles Cleret." *Exclaim!* (March 2008). http://exclaim.ca/Interviews/WebExclusive/miles-cleret (accessed 10 May 2012).

Danet, Brenda, and T. Tamar Katriel. "No Two Alike: Play and Aesthetics in Collecting." *Play and Culture* 2, no. 3 (1989): 253–277.

Delaware North Companies. "Delaware North Opens Baseball Season with Local Favorites." *PR Newswire*. Delaware North Companies press release, 30 March 2011. http://www.prnewswire.com/news-releases/delaware-north-opens-baseball-season-with-local-favorites-118941724.html (accessed 5 April 2011).

deMause, Neil, and Joanna Cagan. *Field of Schemes: How the Great Stadium Swindle Turns Public Money into Private Profit*. Lincoln: University of Nebraska Press, 2008.

Dibbell, Julian. "Unpacking My Record Collection." http://www.juliandibbell.com/texts/feed_records.html (accessed 17 January 2011).

Doctorow, Cory. "The Coming Civil War over General Purpose Computing." *Boing Boing*, 23 August 2012. http://boingboing.net/2012/08/23/civilwar.html (accessed 31 October 2012).

Dougan, John. "Objects of Desire: Canon Formation and Blues Record Collecting." *Journal of Popular Music* 18, no. 1 (April 2006): 40–65.

Duarte, Joao Ferreira. "'A Dangerous Stroke of Art': Parody as Transgression." *European Journal of English Studies* 3, no. 1 (April 1999): 64–78.

Dust & Grooves: Vinyl, Music, Culture. http://www.dustandgrooves.com (modified 2 November 2012).

Eisenberg, Evan. *The Recording Angel: Music, Records and Culture from Aristotle to Zappa*. 2nd ed. New Haven, CT, and London: York University Press, 2005.

Elsner, John. "The House and Museum of Sir John Soane." In *The Cultures of Collecting*, edited by John Elsner and Roger Cardinal, 155–176. London: Reaktion Books, 1994.

Elsner, John, and Richard Cardinal, eds. *The Cultures of Collecting*. London: Reaktion, 1993.

Emerson, Ralph Waldo. *Essays; Essays: Second Series*. Facsimile of first editions. Columbus, OH: Charles E. Merrill, 1969.

———. *The Journals and Miscellaneous Notebooks of Ralph Waldo Emerson*. Volume IV. Edited by Alfred R. Ferguson. Cambridge, MA: Harvard University Press, 1964.

———. "Ode, Inscribed to William H. Channing." In *Poems*. Boston: James Munroe and Company, 1847. http://www.internal.org/Ralph_Waldo_Emerson (accessed 15 September 2012).

Epland, David. Telephone interview with author, 4 June 2006.

Esposito, Robert. *Communitas: The Origin and Destiny of Community.* Translated by Timothy Campbell. Stanford, CA: Stanford University Press, 2010.

The Field Review Team of Roadside America. "House on the Rock." http://www.road sideamerica.com/story/2254 (accessed 2 February 2011).

"Fire-dog." In *Oxford English Dictionary Online*, edited by John Simpson. 2nd ed. Oxford: Oxford University Press, 1989. http://dictionary.oed.com/view/Entry/70512?reirectedFrom=fire-dog (accessed 25 October 2010).

Fisher, Philip. *Making and Effacing Art.* Cambridge, MA: Harvard University Press, 1997.

Forrester, John. "Collector, Naturalist, Surrealist." In *Dispatches from the Freud Wars*, 107–137. Cambridge, MA: Harvard University Press, 1997.

Fosdick, Todd. E-mail message to John Whisler, 11 April 2005. http://www.house ofjitters.com/drjittersguestbook.htm.

Foucault, Michel. *The Order of Things: An Archaeology of the Human Sciences.* 1966. Reprint, New York: Vintage, 1994.

"Franco-Prussian War." In *World Encyclopedia. Oxford Reference Online.* http://www. oxfordreference.com/views/ENTRY.html?subview=Main&entry=t142.e4293 (accessed 28 October 2010).

Freud, Sigmund. *Civilization and Its Discontents.* Standard ed. Vol. 21. London: Hogarth Press, 1961.

Fried, Michael, "Art and Objecthood." 1967. In *Art and Objecthood*, 148–172. Chicago: University of Chicago Press, 1998.

Furján, Helene. *Glorious Visions: John Soane's Spectacular Theater.* London and New York: Routledge, 2011.

Geary, Richard. *PEZ Collectibles.* Atglen, PA: Schiffer, 1994.

Gibson, William. *Zero History.* New York: Berkley, 2010.

Giles, Geoffrey J. "Through Cigarette Cards to Manliness: Building German Character with an Informal Curriculum." In *Gender, Colonialism and Education. The Politics of Experience*, edited by Joyce Goodman and Jane Martin, 73–96. London/Portland, OR: Woburn Press, 2002.

Goebbels, Joseph. *Der Angriff: Aufsätzeaus der Kampfzeit von Joseph Goebbels.* Munich: Zentralverlagder NSDAP, 1935.

Goffman, Erving. *The Presentation of Self in Everyday Life.* Garden City, NY: Doubleday Anchor Books, 1959.

Golick, Ed. *Detroitkidshow.com.* http://www.detroitkidshow.com.

Gomery, Douglas. "Rethinking Television History." In *Television Histories: Shaping Collective Memory in the Media Age*, edited by Gary Edgerton and Peter Rollins, 282–308. Lexington: University Press of Kentucky, 2001.

Grainge, Paul. "Nostalgia and Style in Retro America: Moods, Modes, and Media Recycling." *Journal of American and Comparative Cultures* 23 (2000): 27–34.

Grass, Günther. *Peeling the Onion.* Translated by Michael Henry Heim. New York: Harcourt, 2007.

Greenberg, Clement. *Collected Essays and Criticism*. Vol. 4, *Modernism with a Vengeance*. Chicago: University of Chicago Press, 1993.

Greene, Jean A. E-mail to John Whisler, 23 July 2004. http://www.houseofjitters.com/drjittersguestbook.htm.

Grinke, Paul. *From Wunderkammer to Museum*. London: Quaritch, 2006.

Gross, Christopher. Sandy Becker's Page. http://www.christophergross.com/becker/becker.html.

Guest, Montague. Introduction to *Lady Charlotte Schreiber's Journals*. London: John Lane, 1911.

Guest, Revel, and Angela V. John. *Lady Charlotte: A Biography of the Nineteenth Century*. London: Weidenfeld and Nicolson, 1989.

Gurian, Elaine. "Noodling Around with Exhibition Opportunities." In *Exhibiting Cultures: The Poetics and Politics of Museum Display*, edited by Ivan Karp and Steven Lavine, 176–190. Washington, DC: Smithsonian Institution Press, 1991.

Guttman, Allen. *From Ritual to Record: The Nature of Modern Sports*. New York: Columbia University Press, 1978.

Hagspiel, Hermann. *Betrifft Anschluss: Ein Almanach*. Vienna: Arbeitsgemeinschaft Österreichischer Privatverlage, 1988.

———. *Die Ostmark: Österreich im Grossdeutschen Reich 1938–1945*. Vienna: Braumüller/Universitätsverlag, 1995.

Hanks, Tom. "Rock and Roll Hall of Fame Induction Remarks: The Dave Clark Five." Speech presented at the Twenty-third Annual Rock and Roll Hall of Fame Induction Ceremony, New York, 10 March 2008.

Hardt, Michael, and Antonio Negri. *Multitude: War and Democracy in the Age of Empire*. New York: Penguin, 2004.

Hayles, N. Katherine. *How We Became Posthuman: Virtual Bodies in Cybernetics, Literature, and Informatics*. Chicago: University of Chicago Press, 1999.

Haynes, Clare. "A 'Natural' Exhibitioner: Sir Ashton Lever and His Holosphusikon." *Journal for Eighteenth-Century Studies* 24, no. 1 (2001): 1–14.

Healey, Edna. 2012. "Coutts, Angela Georgina Burdett-, suo jure Baroness Burdett-Coutts (1814–1906)." In *Oxford Dictionary of National Biography Online*, edited by Lawrence Goldman. 2004. http://www.oxforddnb.com.ezproxy.lib.ucalgary.ca/view/article/32175 (accessed 1 October 2010).

Heidegger, Martin. "Building Dwelling Thinking." In *Poetry, Language, Thought*, 141–162. New York: Harper & Row, 1975.

———. "The Origin of the Work of Art." In *Poetry, Language, Thought*, 15–86. New York: Harper & Row, 1975.

———. "The Thing." In *Poetry, Language, Thought*, 161–184. New York: Harper & Row, 1975.

Heffernan, Virginia. "The Attention-Span Myth." *New York Times*, 19 November 2010. http://www.nytimes.com/2010/11/21/magazine/21FOB-medium-t.html (accessed 21 September 2012).

Henkle, Douglas. "House on the Rock Music Machines." http://www.folklib.net/index/discog/labels/house_rock_tour.shtml (accessed 15 September 2012).

Hendrickson, Dave. "Is All That Stuff for Real? No But That's Show Biz." *Milwaukee Journal*, 18 June 1989. http://news.google.com/newspapers?nid=1499&dat=19 890618&id=4GYaAAAAIBAJ&sjid=7CsEAAAAIBAJ&pg=2205,1765209 (accessed 15 September 2012).

Herz, Rudolf. *Hoffmann & Hitler: Fotografie als Medium des Führer—Mythos*. Munich: Klinkhardt and Biermann, 1994.

Hickey, Dave. *Air Guitar: Essays on Art and Democracy*. Los Angeles: Art Issues Press, 1997.

Hickey, Neil. "Skipper Chuck and Buckskin Bill Are Not Feeling Very Jolly." *TV Guide*, 2 June 1973, 9–15.

Higonnet, Anne. *A Museum of One's Own*. Pittsburgh, PA: Periscope, 2009.

Hoffmann, Heinrich. *Hitler Was My Friend: The Memoirs of Hitler's Photographer*. London: Burke, 1955.

———. *Hitler wie ich ihn sah: Aufzeichnungen seines Leibfotografen*. Munich: Herbig, 1974.

Holdengräber, Paul. "'A Visible History of Art': The Forms and Preoccupations of the Early Museum." *Studies in Eighteenth Century Culture* 17 (1987): 107–117.

Hollis, Tim. *Hi There, Boys and Girls! America's Local Children's TV Programs*. Jackson: University Press of Mississippi, 2001.

Homrighausen, Michael. E-mail message to Richard Birley, 16 August 2006. http://www.captainerniesshowboat.com/seabag.html.

Horne, Philip. "James, Henry (1843–1916)." In *Oxford Dictionary of National Biography Online*, edited by Lawrence Goldman. 2004. http://www.oxforddnb.com.ezproxy.lib.ucalgary.ca/view/article/34150 (accessed 21 October 2010).

"The House on the Rock." http://www.thehouseontherock.com/HOTR_Attraction_TicsAndTours.htm (accessed 15 September 2012).

"House on the Rock." *Wikipedia*. http://en.wikipedia.org/wiki/House_on_the_Rock (accessed 15 September 2012).

Huizinga, Johan. *Homo Ludens: A Study of the Play Element in Culture*. Boston: Beacon Press, 1950.

Hume, David. *A Treatise of Human Nature*. Oxford: Oxford University Press, 1951.

Hutcheon, Linda. *A Theory of Parody: The Teachings of Twentieth-Century Art Forms*. New York: Methuen, 1985.

Hutchison, Phillip J. "The Lost World of Marshal J: History, Memory, and Iowa's Forgotten Broadcast Legend." *Annals of Iowa* 68 (Spring 2009): 137–167.

———. "Magic Windows and the Serious Life: Rituals and Community in Early American Local Television." *The Journal of Broadcasting and Electronic Media* 56, no. 1 (March 2012): 21–37.

———. "Transmitters, Antennas, and Rituals: Constructing Television Communities in Illinois, 1949–1975." *The Journal of Illinois History* 14, no. 2 (Spring 2011): 21–40.

Impey, Oliver, and Arthur MacGregor, eds. *The Origin of Museums: The Cabinet of Curiosities in Sixteenth-Century Europe*. Oxford: Clarendon Press, 1985.

Interiano, Manny. E-mail message to author, 9 August 2005.

———. *KPIX Dance Party: The Dick Stewart Show*. http://www.kpixdanceparty.org.

Jackson, Brenda. E-mail message to Richard Birley, 1 April 2007. http://www.captainerniesshowboat.com/seabag.html.

Jackson, Christine E. *Sarah Stone: Natural Curiosities from the New World*. London: Merrell Holberton and the Natural History Museum, 1998.

James, Henry. 1897. *The Spoils of Poynton*. Edited by Bernard Richards. Oxford, New York: Oxford University Press, 2008.

James, Rhys. "Vinyl Anthropology." *Vice* (blog), 20 October 2010. http://www.vice.com/read/vinyl-anthropology (accessed 14 May 2012).

John, Angela V. "Schreiber, Lady Charlotte Elizabeth (1812–1895)." In *Oxford Dictionary of National Biography online*, edited by Lawrence Goldman. 2004. http://www.oxforddnb.com.ezproxy.lib.ucalgary.ca/view/article/24832 (accessed 21 October 2010).

Jonson, Ben. "To Penshurst." 1616. Reprint. http://www.poetryfoundation.org/poem/181031 (accessed 15 September 2012).

Kaeppler, Adrienne. *Holophusicon: The Leverian Museum. An Eighteenth-Century English Institution of Science, Curiosity, and Art*. Altenstadt, Germany: ZKF Publishers, 2011.

Kalfatovic, Martin R. "Gardner, Isabella Stewart." In *American National Biography Online*. 2000. http://www.anb.org.ezproxy.lib.ucalgary.ca/articles/17/17–00315.html (accessed 21 October 2010).

Karp, Marilynn Gelfman. *In Flagrante Collecto (Caught in the Act of Collecting)*. New York: Harry N. Abrahams, 2006.

Kennedy, Randy. "Cormac McCarthy's Typewriter Brings $254,500 at Auction." *The Arts Beat* (blog), *New York Times*, 13 December 2009. http://artsbeat.blogs.nytimes.com/2009/12/04/cormac-mccarthys-typewriter-brings-254500–at-auction/.

Kershaw, Ian. "The Hitler Myth." In *Images and Reality in the Third Reich*. Oxford: Oxford University Press, 1987.

Kimmelman, Michael. "At the Bad New Ballparks." Review of *The Last Days of Shea: Delight and Despair in the Life of a Mets Fan*, by Dana Brand. *New York Review of Books*, 19 November 2009. http://www.nybooks.com/articles/archives/2009/nov/19/at-the-bad-new-ballparks/ (accessed 31 October 2012).

King, William Davies. *Collections of Nothing*. Chicago: University of Chicago Press, 2008.

Kirshenblatt-Gimblett, Barbara. *Destination Culture: Tourism, Museums, and Heritage*. Berkeley: University of California Press, 1998.

Klein, Melanie. *Envy and Gratitude and Other Works, 1946–1963*. New York: Free Press, 1984.

Korsgaard, Christine. "The Reasons We Can Share: An Attack on the Distinction between Agent-relative and Agent-neutral Values." In *Creating the Kingdom of Ends*, 275–310. Cambridge, UK: Cambridge University Press, 1996.

Kracauer, Siegfried. *The Mass Ornament: Weimar Essays.* Cambridge, MA: Harvard University Press, 1995.

Kramer, Hilton. "Going Beyond the 'Edifice Complex.'" *New York Times*, 7 May 1978. http://proquest.umi.com.ezproxy.lib.ucalgary.ca/pqdweb?index=0&did=1 10945575&SrchMode=1&sid=1&Fmt=2&VInst=PROD&VType=PQD&RQT =309&VName=HNP&TS=1289838360&clientId=12303 (accessed 24 October 2010).

Krauss, Rosalind. "The Cultural Logic of the Late Capitalist Museum." *October* 54, no. 3 (1990): 3–17.

Kulik, Gary. "Designing the Past: History-Museum Exhibitions from Peale to the Present." In *History Museums in the United States: A Critical Assessment*, edited by Warren Leon and Roy Rozensweig, 3–37. Urbana: University of Illinois Press, 1989.

L., Jim. "The House on the Rock." http://www.yelp.com/biz/the-house-on-the-rock-spring-green. (accessed 15 September 2012).

"Label of Love: Dust-to-Digital Bringing It All Back to Life: Q&A Founder Lance Ledbetter." *Record Collector* (April 2007) (accessed 5 May 2012).

Labine, Lydia. E-mail message to Manny Interiano, 1 December 2005. http://www.kpixdanceparty.org/Memories.html.

Lacan, Jacques. *The Ethics of Psychoanalysis, Seminar VII (1959–1960).* New York: Norton, 1992.

Lamonaca, Marianne. "Mobilizing for War." In *Weapons of Mass Dissemination: The Propaganda of War,* 13–27. Miami Beach: The Wolfsonian/Florida International University, 2004.

"Lance Ledbetter, Dust to Digital Interview." *Since 1968* (blog), 9 June 2004. http://since1968.com/article/7/lance-ledbetter-dust-to-digital-interview (accessed 8 May 2012).

Lanier, Jaron. *You Are Not a Gadget.* New York: Knopf, 2010.

Laurencich-Minelli, Laura. "Museography and Ethnographical Collections in Bologna During the Sixteenth and Seventeenth Centuries." In *The Origin of Museums: the Cabinet of Curiosities in Sixteenth-Century Europe*, edited by Oliver Impey and Arthur MacGregor, 17–23. Oxford: Clarendon Press, 1985.

La Roche, Sophie von. *Sophie in London, 1786. Being the Diary of Sophie von la Roche.* Translated by Clare Williams. London: Jonathan Cape, 1933.

Levine, Neil. "The Story of Taliesin: Wright's First Natural House." In *Wright Studies, Volume One: Taliesin 1911–1914*, edited by Narciso G. Menocal, 2–27. Carbondale: Southern Illinois University Press, 1992.

Locke, John. "The Second Treatise of Government." In *Locke's Two Treatises of Government.* 2nd ed. Cambridge, UK: Cambridge University Press, 1967.

Lukas, Paul. "Cooperstown Field Trip Report." *UniWatch* (blog), 10 November 2009. http://www.uni-watch.com/2009/11/10/if-you-damage-this-i-will -beat-your-skull-in-with-it-cooperstown-field-trip-report/ (accessed 11 November 2009).

Lynch, Kathleen. "Folger, Emily Jordan." In *American National Biography Online.* 2000. http://www.anb.org.ezproxy.lib.ucalgary.ca/articles/20/20–01300.html (21 Oct. 2010).

Macleod, Dianne Sachko. *Art and the Victorian Middle Class: Money and the Making of Cultural Identity.* Cambridge, UK: Cambridge University Press, 1996.

———. *Enchanted Lives, Enchanted Objects: American Women Collectors and the Making of Culture, 1800–1940.* Berkeley: University of California Press, 2008.

———. "Heaton, Ellen (1816–1894)." In *Oxford Dictionary of National Biography Online,* edited by Lawrence Goldman. 2004. http://www.oxforddnb.com/index/62/101062814/

Malone, Sean. "No Ordinary Pencil: A Portrait of the Eberhard Faber Blackwing 602." *The Blackwing Pages.* http://blackwingpages.com/no-ordinary-pencil/ (accessed 13 October 2012).

Marcus, Greil. "The Old, Weird America." Liner notes to *Anthology of American Folk Music.* Smithsonian Folkways Recordings SFW 40090, 1997 reissue. 6 CD box set.

Marin, Louis. "Fragments d'histoires de musées," *Cahiers du Musée national d'art moderne* 17–18 (March 1986): 8–17.

Marr, Gerry. E-mail message to Richard Birley, 19 October 2005. http://www.captainerniesshowboat.com/seabag.html.

Martin, David L. *Curious Visions of Modernity: Enchantment, Magic, and the Sacred.* Cambridge, MA, and London: MIT Press, 2011.

Mason, Tyler. "Hrbek's Adds Local Flavor to Target Field: Restaurant and Bar Named After Former Twins First Baseman." *MLB.com,* 9 September 2009. http://mlb.mlb.com/news/article.jsp?ymd=20090909&content_id=6874050&fext=.jsp&c_id=min (accessed 12 September 2009).

Matthews, Rosemary. "Collectors and Why They Collect: Isabella Stewart Gardner and Her Museum of Art." *Journal of the History of Collections* 21, no. 2 (February 2009): 183–189. http://jhc.oxfordjournals.org.ezproxy.lib.ucalgary.ca/content/21/2/183.full (accessed 20 October. 2010).

McCarter, Robert. "Abstract Essence: Drawing Wright from the Obvious." In *On and By Frank Lloyd Wright: A Primer of Architectural Principles,* edited by Robert McCarter, 6–21. New York: Phaidon Press, 2005.

———. *Frank Lloyd Wright.* London: Reaktion, 2006.

McKeon, Michael. *The Secret History of Domesticity: Public, Private, and the Division of Knowledge.* Baltimore, MD: Johns Hopkins University Press, 2005.

Melani, Lillian. "The Nineteenth Century British Novel: William Makepeace Thackeray: The Angel in the House." *Department of English: Lillian Melani.* (2009) http://academic.brooklyn.cuny.edu/english/melani/novel_19c/thackeray/angel.html (accessed 9 December 2009).

Milano, Brett Milano. *Vinyl Junkies: Adventures in Record Collecting.* New York: St. Martin's Griffin, 2003.

Moe, Doug. *Alex Jordan, Architect of His Own Dream*. Spring Green, WI: House of Wyoming Valley Press, 1991.

Moist, Kevin M. "Collecting, Collage, and Alchemy: The Harry Smith Anthology of American Folk Music as Art and Cultural Intervention." *American Studies* 48, no. 4 (Winter 2007): 111–127.

———. "'To Renew the Old World': Record Collecting as Cultural Production. *Studies in Popular Culture* 31, no. 1 (2008): 99–119.

Mortlock China. 2002. http://www.mortlock.info/ (accessed 24 October 2010).

Mullens, W. H. "Some Museums of Old London. I.—The Leverian Museum." *Museums*

———. "Some Museums of Old London: William Bullock's London Museum." *Museums Journal* 17 (1917–1918): 51–56, 132–137, 180–187.

Murray, Martin. *The Story of Cigarette Cards*. London: Murray Cards International Ltd., 1987.

Murray, Michael D., and Donald G. Godfrey. *Television in America: Local Station History from Across the Nation*. Ames: Iowa State University Press, 1997.

"The Museum." Isabella Stewart Gardner Museum Online. http://www.gardnermuseum.org/the_museum/introduction.asp (accessed 29 October 2010).

Music Memory. "Our Mission." http://www.musicmemory.org/mission (accessed 15 September 2012).

Nebeker, Brent. *Wallace and Ladmo*. http://www.wallaceandladmo.com.

Nevill, Dorothy, and Ralph Nevill. *The Reminiscences of Lady Dorothy Nevill*. London: T. Nelson, 1906.

Nevill, Guy. *Exotic Groves: A Portrait of Lady Dorothy Nevill*. Salisbury, Wiltshire, UK: Michael Russell, 1984.

"The Nielsen Company & Billboard's 2011 Music Industry Report." *Businesswire*, 25 January 2012. http://www.businesswire.com/news/home/20120105005547/en/Nielsen-Company-Billboard%E2%80%99s-2011–Music-Industry-Report (accessed 5 June 2012).

Nievas, Patricia. Correspondence to author, 13 October 2005.

"Nigerian Boogie Down! Q&A with Uchenna Ikonne." *Light in the Attic Records* (blog), 1 February 2011. http://blog.lightintheattic.net/?p=3297 (accessed 5 June 2012).

Opie, Robert. "'Unless You Do These Crazy Things' . . . An Interview with Robert Opie." In *The Cultures of Collecting*, edited by John Elsner and Roger Cardinal, 25–48. Cambridge, MA: Harvard University Press, 1994.

Packard, Vance. *The Waste Makers*. New York: David McKay, 1960.

"Palomino Blackwing." Pencils.com. http://www.pencils.com/blackwing (accessed 12 October 2012).

Pearce, Susan M. *Collecting in Contemporary Practice*. London: Sage Publications, 1998.

———. "Collecting Reconsidered." In *Interpreting Objects and Collections*, edited by Susan M. Pearce, 193–204. London: Routledge, 1994.

————. *Museums, Objects and Collections: A Cultural Study*. Washington, DC: Smithsonian Institution Press, 1992.

————. *On Collecting: An Investigation into Collecting in the European Tradition*. New York: Routledge, 1995.

————. "William Bullock: Collections and Exhibitions at the Egyptian Hall, London, 1816–1825." *Journal of the History of Collections* 20, no. 1 (2008): 17–35.

————. "William Bullock: Inventing a Visual Language of Objects." In *Museum Revolutions: How Museums Change and Are Changed*, edited by Simon J. Knell, Suzanne MacLeod, and Sheila Watson, 15–27. London and New York: Routledge, 2007.

Peisner, David. "Diggin' Beyond the Crates." *SPIN*, 27 September 2012. http://www.spin.com/articles/numero-group-worlds-greatest-reissue-label (accesed 30 September 2012).

Petridis, Alexis. "The Rise of the Super-Deluxe Box Set." *The Guardian*, 22 December 2011. http://www.guardian.co.uk/music/2011/dec/22/rise-super-deluxe-box-set (accessed 6 June 2012).

Petroski, Henry. *The Pencil: A History of Design and Circumstance*. New York: Knopf, 2000.

Pomian, Krysztof, *Collectors and Curiosities: Paris and Venice, 1500–1800*. Cambridge, MA: Blackwell, 1990.

Posnanski, Joe. "Loving Baseball." *Sports Illustrated*, 25 July 2011. http://sportsillustrated.cnn.com/vault/article/magazine/MAG1188482/1/index.htm (accessed 30 July 2011)

Prelli, Lawrence J. *Rhetorics of Display*. Columbia: University of South Carolina Press, 2006.

Preziosi, Donald. "Modernity Again: The Museum as *Trompe l'oeil*." In *Deconstruction and the Visual Arts: Art, Media, Architecture*, edited by Peter Brunette and David Wills, 141–150. Cambridge, UK: Cambridge University Press, 1994.

Probert, Rebecca. "Women's Property Rights before 1900." In *The New Oxford Companion to Law*. 2010. http://www.oxfordreference.com.ezproxy.lib.ucalgary.ca/views/ENTRY.html?entry=t287.e2352&srn=1&ssid=31974085#FIRSTHIT (accessed 24 November 2009).

Putnam, James. *The Museum as Medium*. 2nd ed. London: Thames and Hudson, 2009.

Quine, W. V. *Pursuit of Truth*. Cambridge, MA: Harvard University Press, 1990.

Radcliffe, Austin. "Things Organized Neatly." http://thingsorganizedneatly.tumblr.com/ (accessed 15 September 2012).

Rae, Patricia. "Double Sorrow: Proleptic Elegy and the End of Arcadianism in 1930s Britain." *Twentieth Century Literature* 49, no. 2 (Summer 2003): 246–276. http://www.jstor.org.ezproxy.lib.ucalgary.ca/stable/3176003 (accessed 21 October 2010).

Ransom, Mike. *Tulsa TV Memories*. http://tulsatvmemories.com/mazmem.html.

Rathkolb, Oliver, Wolfgang Duchkowitsch, and Fritz Hausjell, eds. *Die veruntreute Wahrheit: Hitlers Propagandisten in Österreichs Medien*. Salzburg: Otto Müller Verlag, 1988.

Rawls, John. *A Theory of Justice.* Cambridge, MA: Harvard University Press, 1971.

Reichert-Marton, Julie. "Visionary Architecture: Frank Lloyd Wright vs. House on the Rock." *U-Turn: An Art E-Zine.* http://www.uturn.org/writings.htm (accessed 15 September 2012).

Reynolds, Simon. "Lost in Music: Obsessive Record Collecting." In *This Is Pop: In Search of the Elusive at Experience Music Project,* edited by Eric Weisbard, 289–307. Cambridge, MA: Harvard University Press, 2004.

———. *Retromania: Pop Culture's Addiction to Its Own Past.* New York: Faber and Faber, 2011.

Rheims, Maurice. *Art on the Market.* London: Weidenfeld and Nicolson, 1961.

Sandomir, Richard. "Beneath the Hall, a Baseball Vault Full of Treasures." *New York Times,* 29 July 2008. http://www.nytimes.com/2008/07/29/sports baseball/29sandomir.html (accessed 12 September 2009).

Schor, Naomi. "Collecting Paris." In *The Cultures of Collecting,* edited by John Elsner and Roger Cardinal, 252–274. Cambridge, MA: Harvard University Press, 1994.

Schreiber, Lady Charlotte. *Lady Charlotte Schreiber's Journals.* London: John Lane, 1911.

Schreiber, Lady Charlotte Elizabeth (Bertie) Guest. *Lady Charlotte Schreiber: Extracts from Her Journal, 1853–1891.* Edited by Earl of Bessborough. London: John Murray, 1952.

Schwartz, John Pedro. "Object Lessons: Teaching Multiliteracies Through the Museum." *College English* 71, no. 1 (September 2008): 27–47.

"A Shared Passion" *The Folger Library.* 2002. http://www.folger.edu/html/exhibi tions/shared_passion/passionintro.htm (accessed 25 October 2010).

Shuker, Roy. *Wax Trash and Vinyl Treasures: Record Collecting as a Social Practice.* Burlington, VT: Ashgate Publishing Company, 2010.

Siegel, Jonah, ed. *The Emergence of the Modern Museum: An Anthology of Nineteenth-Century Sources.* Oxford: Oxford University Press, 2008.

Simmel, Georg. "The Metropolis and Mental Life." In *On Individuality and Social Forms,* 324–339. Chicago: University of Chicago Press, 1971.

Smiley, Jane. "Wisconsin: Three Visions Attained." *New York Times,* 19 March 1993. http://www.nytimes.com/1993/03/07/magazine/wisconsin-three-visions-attained. html (accessed 15 September 2012).

Smith, Charles Saumarez. "Exhibition: A Grand Design, A History of the Victoria & Albert Museum: National Consciousness." *Victoria & Albert Museum.* 1999. http://www.vam.ac.uk/vastatic/microsites/1159_grand_design/essay-national-consciousness_new.html (accessed 21 October 2010).

Smith, W. J. "Sir Ashton Lever of Alkrington and his Museum 1729–1788." *Transactions of the Lancashire and Cheshire Antiquarian Society* 72 (1962): 61–92.

Sontag, Susan. "Fascinating Fascism." 1975. In *Under the Sign of Saturn.* New York: Picador, 1980.

———. *On Photography.* New York: Straus & Giroux, 1977.

Spariosu, Mihai I. *Dionysus Reborn: Play and the Aesthetic Dimension in Modern Philosophical and Scientific Discourse*. Ithaca, NY: Cornell University Press, 1989.

Stafford, Barbara Maria. *Good Looking: Essays on the Virtue of Images*. Cambridge, MA, and London: MIT Press, 1997.

———. "Presuming Images and Consuming Words: the Visualization of Knowledge from the Enlightenment to Post-modernism." In *Consumption and the World of Goods*, edited by John Brewer and Roy Porter, 462–477. London and New York: Routledge, 1993.

Stafford, Barbara Maria, and Frances Terpak. *Devices of Wonder: From the World in a Box to Images on a Screen*. Los Angeles: Getty Research Institute, 2001.

Starnes, Michael. E-mail to Richard Birley, 19 September 2007. http://www.captain erniesshowboat.com/seabag.html.

Steinberg, Rolf, ed. *Nazi-Kitsch*. Darmstadt: Melzer Verlag, 1975.

Stevens, Anne. E-mail message to Manny Interiano, 28 October 2007. http://www. kpixdanceparty.org/Memories.html.

Stewart, Susan. "Death and Life, in That Order, in the Works of Charles Willson Peale." In *The Cultures of Collecting*, edited by John Elsner and Roger Cardinal, 204–223. Cambridge, MA: Harvard University Press, 1994.

———. *Museums, Objects, and Collections*. Washington, DC: Smithsonian Institution Press, 1992.

———. *On Longing: Narratives of the Miniature, the Gigantic, the Souvenir, the Collection*. Durham, NC: Duke University Press, 1993.

Stone, Allucquère Rosanne. *The War of Desire and Technology at the Close of the Mechanical Age*. Cambridge, MA: MIT Press, 1995.

Strassheim, Angela. "Bad Trip: The Scariest Museum on Earth." http://www.vice. com/read/pictures-v11n11 (accessed 15 September 2012).

Streitfeld, David. "Dispenser of Instant Treasures." *Los Angeles Times*, 22 November 2001, sec. A.

Strong, Roy C. *Country Life, 1897–1997: The English Arcadia*. London: Boxtree, 1997.

"Soundway Interview." *Choice Cuts* (blog), 27 April 2010. http://www.choicecuts. com/blog/soundway-interview/ (accessed 16 June 2012).

Sweeney, Sandra. E-mail message to Manny Interiano, 9 June 2008. http://www. kpixdanceparty.org/Memories.html.

Taylor, Alex. "The Great Blackwing Pencil Brouhaha." *CNN Money*, 18 May 2011. http://money.cnn.com/2011/05/18/smallbusiness/blackwing_pencil_controversy. fortune/index.htm (accessed 13 October 2012).

Thomas, Sophie. "Feather Cloaks and English Collectors: Cook's Voyages and the Objects of the Museum." In *Objects of Inquiry and Exchange: Eighteenth-Century Thing Theory in a Global Context*, edited by Ileana Baird and Christina Ionescu. Aldershot, UK: Ashgate, forthcoming.

———. "'Things on Holiday': Collections, Museums, and the Poetics of Unruliness." *European Romantic Review* 20, no. 2 (April 2009): 167–175.

Thoreau, Henry David. *Walden*. New York: Washington Square Press, 1970.

Trost, Ernst. *Zur allgemeinen Erleichterung: Eine Kultur -und Wirtschaftsgeschichte des Tabaks in Österreich*. Wien: Brandstätter, 1984.

Trotter, W. R., and K. D. Reynolds. "Nevill, Lady Dorothy Fanny (1826–1913)." In *Oxford Dictionary of National Biography Online*, edited by Lawrence Goldman. 2004. http://www.oxforddnb.com.ezproxy.lib.ucalgary.ca/view/article/37805?docPos=1 (accessed 15 October 2010).

Turkle, Sherry. *Life on the Screen: Identity in the Age of the Internet*. New York: Simon & Schuster, 1995.

Turner, Victor. *From Ritual to Theatre: The Human Seriousness of Play*. New York: PAJ, 1982.

Vargas, Jose Antonio. "The Face of Facebook: Mark Zuckerberg Opens Up." *New Yorker*, 20 September 2010, 54–64.

Wainwright, Clive. *The Romantic Interior: The British Collector at Home 1750–1850*. New Haven, CT, and London: Yale University Press, 1989.

"Waking the Muse." *Properganda Online* (blog), 31 March 2012. http://blog.propermusic.com/waking-the-muse-samy-ben-redjeb/ (accessed 30 May 2012).

Waldstein, Mella. "Adolf Hitler, vervielfältigt: Die Massenproduktion der Führerbildnisse." In *Kunst und Diktatur: Architektur, Bildhauerei und Malerei in Österreich, Deutschland, Italien und der Sowjetunion 1922–1956*, edited by Jan Tabor. Baden, Austria: Verlag Grasl, 1994.

Walker, Rob. "Fun Stuff: Why Pictures of Object Collections are Popular Now." *New York Times Magazine*, 13 February 2011, 26.

Walton, Sam, and John Huey. *Made in America: My Story*. New York: Bantam Books, 1993.

Ward, Jonathan. *Opika Pende: Africa at 78 RPM*. Book accompanying Dust-to-Digital 22, 2011. 4 CD box set.

Warden, Kathy. Correspondence to author, 12 May 2005.

Wasem, Erich. *Sammeln von Serienbildchen*. Landshut: Trausnitz-Verlag, 1981.

Watson, Elena M. *Television Horror Movie Hosts—68 Vampires, Mad Scientists and Other Denizens of the Late-Night Airwaves Examined and Interviewed*. Jefferson, NC: McFarland, 2000.

Welch, David. 1994. *Collecting PEZ*. Murphysboro, IL: Bubba Scrubba, 1994.

Wells, Russell. *Birmingham Rewound*. http://www.birminghamrewound.com/about.html.

West, Julian. *Axel's Treehouse*. http://mnkidvid.com/twincities/wcco/axel/treehouse.html.

Wharton, Edith, and Ogden Codman Jr. *The Decoration of Houses*. New York: Charles Scribner's Sons, 1914.

Whisler, John. E-mail message to author, 13 April 2004.

Whitaker, Katie. "The Culture of Curiosity." In *Cultures of Natural History*, edited by N. Jardine, J. A. Secord, and E. C. Spary, 75–90. Cambridge, UK: Cambridge University Press, 1996.

Williams, Alex. "The Word 'Curate' No Longer Belongs to the Museum Crowd." *New York Times*, 2 October 2009. http://www.nytimes.com/2009/10/04/fashion/04curate.html (accessed 21 September 2012).

Wittgenstein, Ludwig. *Philosophical Investigations.* 3rd ed. Oxford: Blackwell, 1958.

———. *Tractatus Logico-Philosophicus.* 2nd ed. London: Routledge and Kegan Paul, 1961.

Wright, Frank Lloyd. *An Autobiography.* New York: Duell, Sloan and Pearce, 1943.

———. "In the Cause of Architecture." In *On and By Frank Lloyd Wright: A Primer of Architectural Principles*, edited by Robert McCarter, 338–344. New York: Phaidon Press, 2005.

———. "The Logic of the Plan." In *On and By Frank Lloyd Wright: A Primer of Architectural Principles*, edited by Robert McCarter, 345–347. New York: Phaidon Press, 2005.

Wulf, Joseph. *Kultur im Dritten Reich: Die Bildenden Künste.* Frankfurt am Main/Berlin: Ullstein, 1989.

Yanni, Carla. *Nature's Museums: Victorian Science and the Architecture of Display.* London: The Athlone Press, 1999.

Yeats, William Butler. "Meditations in Time of Civil War." In *Selected Poems and Two Plays*. New York: Collier Books, 1962.

Young, Peter A. "Nightmare on Memory Lane." *Archaeology* 54, no. 1 (January/February 2001): 80.

Zalesch, Saul E. 2000. "Morgan, Mary Jane." In *American National Biography Online.* 2000. http://www.anb.org.ezproxy.lib.ucalgary.ca/articles/17/17–01531.html (accessed 21 October 2010).

———. 2000. "Wolfe, Catharine Lorillard." In *American National Biography Online.* 2000. http://www.anb.org.ezproxy.lib.ucalgary.ca/articles/17/17–00942.html?a=1&n=catharine%20%20wolfe&ia=-at&ib=-bib&d=10&ss=0&q=1.

Index

About the Editors

David Banash is professor of English at Western Illinois University, where he teaches courses in contemporary literature, film, and popular culture. His essays and reviews have appeared in *Postmodern Culture, Reconstruction, Bad Subjects, American Book Review*, and *PopMatters*. His book *Collage Culture: Readymades, Meaning and the Age of Consumption*, is forthcoming from Rodopi in 2013.

Kevin M. Moist is associate professor of communications at Penn State Altoona, where he teaches a range of courses in mass media and popular culture. His research on collecting (particularly record collecting), alternative and independent media, and the music and popular culture of the 1960s has been published in a variety of scholarly journals, including *American Studies* and the *Journal of Popular Culture*. He serves as the collecting and collectibles area chair for the national Popular Culture Association and is a member of the editorial boards of the *Journal of Popular Culture* and *Reconstruction: Studies in Contemporary Culture*.

About the Contributors

Stephen P. Andon received his PhD from the College of Communication and Information at Florida State University in 2011, after writing a dissertation on the materiality of sport. Playing on the theoretical dynamic between political economy and cultural populism, his research interests involve a wide array of topics dealing with sport, including the commodification and the nostalgic influences of media sport and the development of sports fan cultures. He now teaches at Nova Southeastern University in Fort Lauderdale, Florida.

Terri Baker is a PhD candidate in the Department of English at the University of Calgary and specializes in contemporary British literature. Her research interest is how British historical fiction challenges national narratives. She has published reviews in the *Historical Novel Society* magazine and is the author of "Ian McEwan's *Saturday:* Nation, Media, and Being 'In the Club,'" forthcoming in *Writing Difference: Nationalism, Literature and Identity* (Atlantic Books). She has presented research on Hilary Mantel at the University of Leiden's international conference, Barbarism Revisited.

Marcus Boon is associate professor of English at York University, Toronto. He is the author of *In Praise of Copying* (Harvard University Press, 2010) and *The Road of Excess: A History of Writers on Drugs* (Harvard University Press, 2002). He writes about music for *Boing Boing* and *The Wire* and is currently working on a book on the politics of vibration.

Stanley Cavell is professor emeritus in the Department of Philosophy at Harvard University. He has published eighteen books, among them *Must We Mean What We*

Say? (1969); *The World Viewed: Reflections on the Ontology of Film* (1971); *The Senses of Walden* (1972); *The Claim of Reason* (1979); and *Philosophical Passages: Wittgenstein, Emerson, Austin, Derrida* (1995). Recently, he has published a memoir, *Little Did I Know: Excerpts from Memory* (2010).

D. Robert DeChaine has a PhD in cultural studies from Claremont Graduate University and is a professor in the Departments of Liberal Studies and Communication Studies at California State University, Los Angeles. His research explores rhetorical and cultural dimensions of social change through the lenses of globalization, human rights, social movements, popular culture, and critical pedagogy. He is the author of *Global Humanitarianism: NGOs and the Crafting of Community* (Lexington Books) and editor of *Border Rhetorics: Citizenship and Identity on the US–Mexico Frontier* (University of Alabama Press), as well as more than a dozen scholarly articles, book chapters, and reviews. His current research examines the affective dimension of rhetoric and its bearing on the construction of civic imaginaries.

Phillip J. Hutchison received his PhD in communication from The University of Utah. He is an assistant professor of integrated strategic communications with the University of Kentucky's School of Journalism and Telecommunications. His research interests emphasize cultural approaches to media history. His work has been published in scholarly journals, including *American Journalism*, the *Historical Journal of Film Radio and Television*, the *Journal of Broadcasting and Electronic Media*, and *Journalism History*. His research addresses the social impact of early local television; journalistic coverage of historical weather and environmental disasters; and the relationships among race, sports, and commercial media.

William Davies King is professor of theater at the University of California Santa Barbara. He is the author of *Collections of Nothing* (among Amazon's "best books" of 2008), as well as *Henry Irving's "Waterloo"* (winner of the 1993 Callaway Prize), *Writing Wrongs: The Work of Wallace Shawn*, and *Another Part of a Long Story: Literary Traces of Eugene O'Neill and Agnes Boulton*. He has edited several volumes of writings by Agnes Boulton and a forthcoming critical edition of *Long Day's Journey into Night*. He also edits the *Eugene O'Neill Review*. Many of his "ruined books" (bibliolages) can be seen at www.williamdaviesking.com.

Sophie Thomas is associate professor of English at Ryerson University in Toronto, where she teaches eighteenth- and nineteenth-century literature. She is the author of *Romanticism and Visuality: Fragments, History, Spectacle* (Routledge, 2008) and has contributed chapters to numerous books on romantic literature and visual culture. She has published articles in *Studies in Romanticism, European Romantic Review, Romantic Circles*, and the *Journal of Literature and Science*. She is currently working on a book about objects, collections, and museums in the romantic period.

Mary Titus is an English professor and director of American studies at St. Olaf College in Minnesota. She works on race, gender, and class in literature and material culture and regularly teaches courses on such topics as money and stuff. She is the author of *The Ambivalent Art of Katherine Anne Porter* (Georgia, 2005) and has published articles in journals and essays in collections on food, illness, sexuality, and other bodily matters in the work of American women writers. Most recently she enjoys thinking and writing about collecting.

Matthew James Vechinski received his doctorate in English and textual studies from the University of Washington. His scholarship explores the specific conditions of composition, publication, and reception of British and American fiction after 1900. He is also interested in changing modes of textual engagement in the digital age, especially how Web 2.0 technologies influence readers' attitudes to digital and print texts. Matthew is writing a book about the reception of modern American short story sequences, volumes of interconnected works of short fiction originally published in magazines.

Mechtild Widrich is a scholar of contemporary architecture and art. She earned her doctorate in the history and theory of art and architecture at MIT in 2009 and has taught at MIT; the University of Vienna; the Academy of Fine Arts, Vienna; and ETH Zurich, where she is a postdoctoral fellow in the Department of Architecture. She is the editor of *Ugliness: The Non-Beautiful in Art and Theory* (I. B. Tauris, 2013) and *Krzysztof Wodiczko, A 9/11 Memorial* (London: Black Dog, 2009), and has published on performance art, contemporary monuments, and the city in *Grey Room*, *PAJ—Performance Art Journal*, *TDR—The Drama Review*, *Art Journal*, *Thresholds*, and various anthologies. Her book *Performative Monuments* is forthcoming.